The Way of the Psychonaut

Encyclopedia for Inner Journeys

Volume One

Stanislav Grof, M.D., Ph.D.

The Way of the Psychonaut

Encyclopedia for Inner Journeys

Volume One

Multidisciplinary Association for Psychedelic Studies (MAPS)

100% of the profits from the sale of this book will be used to fund psychedelic and medical marijuana research and education. This MAPS-published book was made possible by the generous support of Dr. Bronner's.

The Way of the Psychonaut: Encyclopedia for Inner Journeys Volume One
ISBN-13: 978-0-9982765-9-5
ISBN-10: 0-9982765-9-6

Multidisciplinary Association for Psychedelic Studies (MAPS)
P.O. Box 8423, Santa Cruz, CA 95061
Phone: 831.429.6362, Fax 831.429.6370
Email: askmaps@maps.org

Book and cover design: Sarah Jordan
Cover image: Brigitte Grof
Printed in the United States of America by McNaughton & Gunn, Saline, MI

About the cover image: "Shiva Nataraja appeared in my most important psychedelic sessions and I consider it to be my own personal Archetype. I also had many extraordinary experiences with Swami Muktananda around Shiva, described in *When the Impossible Happens.* This special image of Shiva was taken in my house in Big Sur by Brigitte, at the time when I lived for fourteen years at Esalen, a very important period in my life."—Stanislav Grof

Dedication

For Brigitte,
love of my life and my other half, who has brought light,
shakti, inspiration, enthusiasm, and unconditional love into my world,
wonderful wife and ideal companion on inner and outer journeys—with
deep gratitude and admiration for who you are and what you stand for.

"The expression...*psychonaut* is well chosen, because the inner space is equally endless and mysterious as outer space; and just as astronauts are not able to remain in outer space, similarly in the inner world, people must return to everyday reality. Also, both journeys require good preparation in order to be carried out with minimum danger and become truly beneficial."

—Albert Hofmann, *Memories of a Psychonaut* (2003)

In celebration of the seventy-fifth anniversary of Albert Hofmann's discovery of LSD-25.

"The scientific revolution that started 500 years ago and led to our current civilization and modern technologies has made tremendous progress in the last 100 years. Today we take for granted exploration of outer space, digital technologies, virtual reality, artificial intelligence, and communication at the speed of light. Despite all this progress the nature of fundamental reality eludes us. If you do an internet search on the open questions in science you will discover that the two most important questions regarding the nature of reality remain unanswered—What is the universe made of? What is the biological basis of consciousness? It is obvious that these questions are related. To know existence we must be aware of existence!

More than any person I can think of Stan Grof has pioneered our understanding of inner reality and its relationship to the experience of so called outer reality over the last sixty years. These volumes systematically explore his journey from personal to transpersonal to transcendent domains of existence. If anyone wanted to delve into the mysteries of existence and experience then ignoring this monumental work would be reckless.

What is the meaning of life and death? How does birth trauma influence our experience of life? Do other realms of experience beyond our waking "dream" exist? Why do we need to know them in order to alleviate our personal and collective suffering? How does humanity heal itself from its self-inflicted trauma? How do we overcome our fear of death? What is our true nature beyond the experience of mind body and universe?

Stan Grof is a giant amongst us and we are fortunate to stand on his shoulders. To call him the Einstein of consciousness would be an understatement. I am deeply personally indebted to him for leading the way. Future generations will forever acknowledge him for helping us wake up from our collective hypnosis that we call everyday reality.

I stayed up all night to read Stan Grof's magnificent magnum opus."

—Deepak Chopra, M.D.

Contents

Foreword
by Richard Tarnas, Ph.D.

We all sense today that humanity and the Earth community have reached a tremendous crossroads, and the stakes can hardly be overstated—ecological, spiritual, psychological, social, political. Pervading our era is an atmosphere of crisis, of radical transformation, perhaps a moment for "the changing of the gods," as C. G. Jung put it near the end of his life. The fundamental principles and symbols that have governed our civilization are undergoing a profound revisioning.

In this process, humanity seems to be going through a dramatic deconstruction of its old identity and world view, a kind of symbolic dying and transformation that may be necessary to avoid more literal forms of dying and destruction. Because world views create worlds, and world views are shaped by our individual and collective psyches, our collective future depends on the willingness of enough individuals and communities to undergo that depth of transformation and awakening that can support our civilization's re-entry into the larger community of being from which modern Homo sapiens has imagined itself to be fundamentally separate.

There is probably no one alive today who possesses as broad and profound a practical knowledge of the processes of deep psychological transformation and non-ordinary states of consciousness as does Stanislav Grof.

For over sixty years, Grof has courageously worked with thousands of individuals as they explored their inner depths in the service of healing, spiritual awakening, liberating their minds and souls, and opening their doors of perception. The present work summarizes this extraordinary lifetime of experience and accumulated knowledge of a domain that most psychology and psychotherapy today has barely allowed itself to recognize, let alone explore and adequately understand.

Grof's expanded cartography of the psyche, based on six decades of clinical experience and thousands of session reports, brought forth a new and much deeper understanding of the etiology of emotional and psychosomatic disorders. By introducing such concepts as COEX systems, Basic Perinatal Matrices (BPMs), and the contents of the transpersonal domain of the unconscious, Grof was able to connect and integrate the ideas of Sigmund Freud, C. G. Jung, Otto Rank, Wilhelm Reich, as well as Karl Abraham, Sandor Ferenczi, and Melanie Klein, among others, into a comprehensive understanding of the human psyche.

On the one hand, Grof's careful analysis of different levels of the psyche and their role in the etiology of emotional disorders made it possible to see the correctness of Freud's basic intuition of the ways that unconscious memories of early life experiences and traumas shape the growing psyche. However, Grof's research also demonstrated that Freud's interpretations were compromised by his superficial model of the psyche limited to postnatal biography and the individual unconscious. By recognizing the psychotraumatic impact of physical injuries, diseases, biological birth, and a wide range of transpersonal influences (ancestral, collective, racial, karmic, phylogenetic, and archetypal), Grof was able to provide much more plausible, clinically grounded explanations for many pathological symptoms and syndromes.

Many of Freud's less convincing and problematic explanations—for phobias, suicidal behavior, Thanatos, vagina dentata, the castration complex, various sexual disorders, mysticism, and the "oceanic experience"—could be corrected and given a larger context once one had broken free of his reductionist conceptual constraints. This radical expansion of our understanding of the human psyche and the intricate matrix of factors at work is a liberating theoretical clarification in itself. But it also opens new perspectives for self-exploration and psychotherapy by identifying a range of therapeutic mechanisms that can be used for skillful experiential therapy and self-exploration.

While Grof has written numerous professional papers and books directed to the psychiatric and academic worlds, with the present work he is directly addressing those many readers who are deeply committed to inward self-exploration and a deepening of their ordinary consciousness—the "psychonauts" of the encyclopedia's title. These are individuals who recognize that such an exploration and deepening can not only serve their own healing and expansion of consciousness, but can contribute to the healing and transformation of the larger human and Earth community in which we are all embedded.

It has become clear to many that without such effective initiatory practices spread widely in our culture, too few people will have the opportunity to encounter those unconscious forces and deeper archetypal meanings and purposes that allow one entrance into a larger ensouled cosmos, and a trust in the powerful transformative energies that are already breaking through into the collective psyche whether or not our mainstream executive ego structures are ready to process them.

In the course of his long professional life, Grof has essentially managed to bring into the contemporary modern context the great initiatory practices of ancient and indigenous wisdom traditions, but, crucially, these have been rigorously integrated with precise psychiatric and psychoanalytic formulations based on decades of unparalleled clinical experience. Moreover, he has connected this research and experience with a wide range of revolutionary advances in other fields—quantum-relativistic physics, systems theory, religious studies, anthropology, mythology, thanatology, archetypal astrology, esoteric studies, new paradigm thought in many fields—working closely with many leading authorities at these frontiers. The result is a work of a master teacher and healer that can serve us all as an invaluable and enduring source book of personal transformation for many years to come.

Grof had no guidebooks or maps to begin with. He entered the depths of the underworld and the heights of the higher worlds and held the space for countless others to do so—day after day, year after year, decade after decade. This was brave work, compassionate, skillful in the Buddhist sense—and brilliant. It eventually came to have relevance for many fields beyond psychology—for history, cosmology, philosophy of science, ecology, politics, peace movements, feminism, sexuality, and birth practices, as well as the evolution of consciousness.

But it all began with Grof's quietly heroic work in the private crucible of psychotherapy with individual women and men, often suffering and deeply disturbed. To this task he brought a spiritual centeredness, patience, and wisdom forged through his own journeys of self-exploration. In time Grof's work affirmed not only the sacred depths of the human psyche, but of the *anima mundi* itself, the soul of the world, the sacredness of all being. He trusted that great loss and trauma can unfold into great healing and spiritual awakening, that dying leads to new life. And he transmitted that trust to thousands of others, who now carry on this crucial work throughout the world.

Richard Tarnas, Ph.D.
July 2018

Preface

My decision to write this encyclopedia was prompted by several circumstances. The first one was the realization that I was advancing far into the ninth decade of my life, the time when researchers tend to look back and try to review and sum up what they have discovered. I have dedicated six of these decades to the research of what I call holotropic states: a large and important subgroup of non-ordinary states of consciousness that have therapeutic, transformative, heuristic, and evolutionary potential. Since this has been a venture into new territories as yet undiscovered and unrecognized by mainstream psychiatry and psychology, it would be unrealistic to expect that I could present all the information that I have amassed throughout this quest into its final form before now.

As I was delving deeper into the new domains of the psyche and was describing my research in a series of books, my understanding was undergoing certain changes. Although the basic facts remained the same, the importance that I was attributing to my various findings was shifting. In the early years of my psychedelic research, I discovered, to my surprise, that we carry in our unconscious psyche a detailed record of all the stages of biological birth. This was a finding that contradicted what I had been taught during my medical studies. Once I became convinced that this was an authentic finding, I put great emphasis on the importance of the birth trauma in a variety of areas, including a new understanding of emotional and psychosomatic disorders, the ritual and spiritual life of humanity, human violence and greed, sexuality, death and dying, and the content of works of art.

In retrospect, the acceptance of the extraordinary psychological importance of biological birth was actually not a major intellectual feat. The brain of the newborn is certainly a sufficiently developed organ to carry the memory of hours of potentially life-threatening experience. Research also exists which shows the sensitivity of the fetus when it is still in the womb, and the capacity to form memories exists in organisms that are much lower on the evolutionary tree than a human infant. Once I accepted that birth is obviously a major psychotrauma, it was more difficult for me to understand that mainstream clinicians and academicians are not able to see it.

In my later years of psychedelic research, my interest shifted to phenomena whose existence was much more intellectually challenging to embrace, because it was not possible to find any material substrate for them. This included ancestral and phylogenetic memories, past life experiences, experiential identification with animals and plants, historical and archetypal domains of the collective unconscious, synchronicities, cosmic consciousness, and "higher creativity." In this new understanding, birth lost its dominant role and the primary emphasis shifted to archetypal dynamics. The basic perinatal matrices (BPMs), experiential patterns governing the reliving of the stages of biological birth, became themselves specific manifestations and expressions of these archetypal dynamics.

This conceptual shift also made it possible to connect my new conceptual framework to archetypal astrology as developed by Richard Tarnas and his colleagues. The alliance between these two disciplines brought clarity and refinement to the understanding of psychedelic and Holotropic Breathwork experiences, as well as episodes of spiritual emergency, which was previously impossible to achieve. In writing this encyclopedia, I thought it was important to describe all the phenomena I have studied the way I see them now.

The second catalyzing situation for this book was the rapidly approaching seventy-fifth anniversary of Albert Hofmann's epoch-making discovery of LSD. It is a good time to reflect on what LSD has brought to the world and how it changed the understanding of consciousness and the human psyche. No other substance has ever brought such great promise in so many different disciplines. However, drastic irrational legislation ended what was considered the golden era of psychopharmacology and turned Albert's "wonder child" into a "problem child." After several decades, during which legal research into psychedelics was virtually impossible, we are now experiencing an unexpected global renaissance of interest in these fascinating substances. It is becoming increasingly clear that LSD was a wonder child, but it was born into a dysfunctional family.

In the interim period, the common practice of passing experience and knowledge from generation to generation was interrupted for many decades, and the early pioneers of the 1950s and 1960s are rapidly disappearing from the stage due to age and death. At present, many new research projects with psychedelics and entheogens are being initiated, and new generations of young therapists are appearing on the scene. I felt that they could benefit from the information amassed by those of us who had the opportunity to conduct research during the time when psychedelics were legal and by those who found legal loopholes and continued their research underground. I hope that we are on the way to fulfill Albert's dream of a *New Eleusis,* a future when the legal use of psychedelics will be woven into the fabric of modern society for the benefit of humanity.

The third and most immediate impetus for my writing was the invitation from Stephen Dinan, Chief Executive Director of Shift Network, to create an eight-week telecourse, *Psychology of the Future.* The telecourse had a good turnout (more than six hundred viewers), which prompted Stephen to ask me for a follow up in an advanced twenty-four-week course that we decided to call *The Way of the Psychonaut.* I accepted his offer with some reluctance and deliberation. It was a tall order to follow an eight-week course with an additional twenty-four modules without many repetitions. But it was also an opportunity to take a look at my early writings and see where I would modify or refine my original formulations. I also had to explore some areas which I had not yet addressed in the past or which I had not yet given the attention they deserve. My wife Brigitte, who was watching the telecourses, strongly encouraged me to make the information in them available in book form. She also suggested that I conceive this work as an encyclopedia, in which people interested in inner journeys would find all the relevant information without having to look for it in various books or on the Internet.

When I decided to write the current work, I had several goals in mind. I wanted to provide, in a concise and comprehensive form, the information that the new therapists beginning to conduct psychedelic sessions, their clients, and people embarking on their own inner journeys would need or would find useful. I decided to include in this work the paradigm-breaking observations from the research of holotropic states of consciousness that make mainstream concepts of consciousness and the human psyche obsolete and indicate an urgent need for radical revision. I have also suggested the changes in psychiatric theory and practice that would be necessary to integrate these "anomalous phenomena" into the main body of psychological knowledge. This would provide psychiatrists with a better and deeper understanding of emotional and psychosomatic disorders and more effective methods of treating them.

The first section of this encyclopedia describes the history of psychonautics, defined as the "systematic pursuit and use of holotropic states of consciousness for healing, self-exploration, spiritual, philosophical, and scientific quest, ritual activity, and artistic inspiration." The craving for transcendental experiences, the motivating force behind psychonautics, is the strongest drive in the human psyche; its pursuit can be traced back to the dawn of human history, to shamans of the Paleolithic era. It continued throughout the centuries in the high cultures of antiquity, in the ancient mysteries of death and rebirth, in rites of passage, and in healing ceremonies and other tribal events of native cultures. Great religions of the world developed their own "technologies of the sacred," methods of inducing spiritual experiences, used in monasteries and their mystical branches.

The modern era of psychonautics started at the beginning of the twentieth century with Arthur Heffter's isolation of mescaline from peyote, followed by the isolation of ibogaine from the African bush *Tabernanthe iboga* and harmaline from the Syrian herb *Peganum harmala*. Clinical experiments with mescaline were carried out in the first three decades of the twentieth century. The golden era of psychonautics started in 1943 with Albert Hofmann's discovery of the psychedelic effects of LSD-25. His chemical tour de force then continued with the isolation of psilocybin and psilocin, the active alkaloids from the "magic mushrooms" of the Mazatec

Indians, and of monoamid of lysergic acid (LAE-32) from morning glory seeds *(ololiuqui)*. These new psychoactive substances inspired an avalanche of laboratory and clinical studies. When it seemed that a major consciousness revolution was underway, it was abruptly terminated by ignorant legal and administrative measures.

The four decades when virtually no legal research with psychedelics was possible actually became an important chapter in psychonautics, thanks to semi-legal and illegal research and experimentation that produced and explored a rich array of entheogens, derivatives of phenethylamine and tryptamine. In the atmosphere of the present renaissance of psychedelic research, the information generated by these informal studies might provide inspiration for legal controlled studies, as has already happened with MDMA. Hopefully, we are experiencing the dawn of another exciting era of psychonautics.

The following section of this encyclopedia focuses on the observations and experiences from the research of holotropic states that indicate an urgent need for a radical revision of some basic assumptions of mainstream psychiatry and psychology. It also suggests the areas in which these changes are needed and describes their nature. There is overwhelming evidence that consciousness is not the product of the human brain, but a basic aspect of existence; the brain mediates consciousness, but does not generate it. The human psyche is also not limited to postnatal biography and the Freudian individual unconscious. It contains two additional domains that are of critical importance—the *perinatal* layer, closely related to the trauma of biological birth, and the *transpersonal* layer, which is the source of experiences which transcend the limitations of space, time, and the range of our physical senses.

The next area that requires important revision is the origin and nature of emotional and psychosomatic disorders that are psychogenic in nature (have no biological basis). Many of these do not originate in infancy and childhood; they have additional deeper roots that reach to the perinatal and transpersonal levels. On the positive side, therapeutic interventions on the level of postnatal biography do not represent the only opportunity for improving the clinical condition. Powerful mechanisms for healing and positive personality transformation become available when the regression in holotropic states reaches the perinatal and the transpersonal levels.

Another suggestion for a radical change of perspective in psychiatry involves the attitude toward spirituality. In view of the observations from holotropic states, spirituality is not an indication of superstition, primitive magical thinking, lack of scientific knowledge, or mental illness, as it is viewed by materialistic science. It is a legitimate dimension of the human psyche and of the universal order. When age regression in holotropic states reaches the perinatal and transpersonal levels, the experiences assume a new quality, which C. G. Jung called numinosity. It is a direct apperception of the extraordinary, otherworldly nature of what is being experienced.

The most interesting insights from holotropic states are those concerning the strategy of therapy. There exists a large number of schools of psychotherapy, which disagree with each other in regard to some fundamental aspects of theory and therapy. As a result, representatives of different schools disagree about the relevance of various issues and interpret the same situations differently. The work with holotropic states resolves this dilemma by offering a radical alternative. Entering these states activates an inner self-healing intelligence, which automatically guides the process to unconscious material that has a strong emotional charge and is close to the threshold of consciousness. It then spontaneously brings this material to the surface for processing.

The third section of this volume presents a review of the most important maps of the psyche created by the founders of various schools of depth psychology—its father Sigmund Freud, the famous renegades Alfred Adler, Otto Rank, Wilhelm Reich, and Carl Gustav Jung, and Sandor Ferenczi. It examines the teachings of these schools, using the lens of observations from the research of holotropic states of consciousness, and determines which of these pioneers' ideas were confirmed, and which have to be modified, complemented, or discarded. This review showed that each of these pioneers focused on a certain limited band of the vast spectrum of experiences that the human psyche can manifest and then described, in an adequate way, its particular phenomenology and dynamics.

The problem was that each of them seemed to be blind to the bands of the spectrum studied and emphasized by the others, and reduced them to his own model and way of thinking. Thus Freud specialized in postnatal biography, and with one small and short exception ignored the perinatal domain, and reduced mythology and psychic phenomena to biology.

Rank recognized the paramount significance of the birth trauma, but reduced archetypal phenomena to derivatives of birth. Jung, who recognized and correctly described the vast domain of the collective unconscious, emphatically denied that biological birth had any psychological significance. This historical analysis made it clear that the safe navigation of alternate realities requires an extended cartography of the psyche, a model that includes and integrates the biographical, perinatal, and transpersonal levels.

The fourth section of this volume brings a radically new understanding of emotional and psychosomatic disorders, which becomes available as soon as we expand our understanding of the psyche by adding the perinatal and transpersonal dimensions. It becomes clear that Freud and his followers were on the right track when they were trying to trace the roots of emotional disorders to their origins in early childhood, but they did not look deep enough, and missed the perinatal and transpersonal roots of psychoneuroses, sexual problems, depression, suicide, and particularly, psychoses. The experiential patterns associated with reliving the consecutive stages of birth (Basic Perinatal Matrices, or BPMs) provide logical and natural templates for symptoms and the way that symptoms cluster into syndromes.

The fact that at the core of emotional disorders is the birth trauma, a process of life and death, explains the intensity and depth that otherwise would be incomprehensible. Extremes of human behavior—unbridled violence leading to brutal murder and violent suicide—have to have a source that is of comparable intensity and relevance. The Freudian approach to psychopathology, although going in the right direction, was unconvincing and at times even absurd and ludicrous. Mainstream psychiatrists responding to this situation threw out the baby with the bathwater. They responded by giving up looking for believable causes of emotional disorders in people's early history and replaced it with the "neo-Kraepelinian approach," which involves mere descriptions of symptoms without etiological considerations.

Introducing the perinatal domain into the cartography of the psyche also resolves the conflict between psychiatrists who prefer biological explanations for emotional problems and those who emphasize psychological influences. Birth is a powerful and complex process that involves emotions and physical sensations of extreme intensity in an inextricable amalgam.

Postnatal experiences can then accentuate one aspect or other of this hybrid, but on a deeper level, they represent two sides of the same coin. The participation of the transpersonal dimension in psychopathology and its interaction with the perinatal level can then explain phenomena that link spirituality and violence together, such as flagellantism, or a combination of murder and suicide with a religious goal.

The section on the architecture of emotional and psychosomatic disorders reviews a wide range of emotional disorders—Freud's classical psychoneuroses (phobias, conversion hysteria, and obsessive-compulsive neurosis), depression, suicidal behavior, sexual dysfunctions and deviations, psychosomatic diseases, and functional psychoses. My goal is to show how many aspects of their characteristic symptomatology can be explained from a combination of biographical, perinatal, and transpersonal elements. This new understanding also has important implications for the therapy for these conditions.

The fifth section of this encyclopedia discusses what is probably the most important implication of the work with holotropic states of consciousness, and of the extended cartography of the psyche: the concept of transpersonal crisis or "spiritual emergency." On the basis of our experiences with psychedelic therapy and Holotropic Breathwork, my late wife Christina and I became interested in a large and important group of spontaneous holotropic experiences that mainstream psychiatry diagnoses and treats as manifestations of serious mental diseases, or psychoses.

We discovered that if these conditions are correctly understood and properly supported, they have extraordinary therapeutic, transformative, heuristic, and even evolutionary potential. In this section, I describe the phenomenology, the triggers, the differential diagnosis, and the therapy for these conditions. I also briefly discuss the various forms that spiritual emergency takes, such as shamanic initiatory crisis, the activation of Kundalini, Abraham Maslow's "peak experience," John Perry's renewal process by descent to the Central Archetype, problems with past life memories, crisis of psychic opening, possession states, and more.

The sixth and last section of this book focuses on Holotropic Breathwork, an innovative experiential form of psychotherapy that my late wife Christina and I developed when we lived at the Esalen Institute in Big Sur, California. This approach induces powerful holotropic states of consciousness by very simple means—a combination of accelerated breathing, evocative music, and releasing bodywork in a special setting. Participants work in pairs, alternating in the roles of breathers and sitters. Following the sessions, participants paint mandalas, reflecting what they have experienced. They then meet in small groups, sharing and processing what transpired in the sessions.

Holotropic Breathwork combines the basic principles of depth psychology with elements from shamanism, rites of passage, the great spiritual philosophies of the East, and the mystical traditions of the world. Its theory is formulated in modern psychological language and is grounded in transpersonal psychology and in new paradigm science. After describing the healing power of breath, the therapeutic potential of music, and the use of releasing and supportive physical interventions, this section describes the setting and preparation for the sessions, the roles of the breathers and the sitters, the phenomenology of the experience, the painting of the mandalas, and the processing in the sharing groups. Special attention is given to the discussion of the therapeutic results and the follow-up periods after the sessions.

I wrote the first volume of this encyclopedia and the one that follows with the hope that they will become useful guides for psychonauts, bringing some useful retrospective insights into the experiences they have already had on their past journeys, or providing the basic information necessary for safe and productive journeys into alternate realities for those who are about to embark on the exciting adventures of discovery and self-discovery. Bon voyage!

Stanislav Grof, M.D., Ph.D.
Mill Valley, California, March 2018

Acknowledgments

The Way of the Psychonaut is an attempt to present, in a concise and comprehensive way, the results of more than sixty years of consciousness research, which I conducted at the Psychiatric Research Institute in Prague, the Maryland Psychiatric Research Institute in Baltimore, Maryland, the Esalen Institute in Big Sur, California, and in Holotropic Breathwork workshops and training programs worldwide. During these years, I have received generous intellectual, emotional, and material support from many individuals, institutions, and organizations. It is not possible for me to mention all of them by name. I have to limit my list to the most important ones and apologize to all of those whom I have left out.

My own initiation into the way of the psychonaut started in November 1956 when I had my first LSD session at the Prague Psychiatric Clinic, under the aegis of my preceptor Doc. MUDr. George Roubíček and under the personal supervision of my younger brother Paul, who was at the time a medical student. I feel very grateful to both of them for the role they played in that incredible life-changing experience. I started my own psychedelic research in the complex of research institutes in Prague-Krč under the guidance of and in cooperation with MUDr. Miloš Vojtěchovský. Although I moved after two years of this primarily laboratory work to clinical research, I very much value the experience that I obtained there.

In January 1960, I became the Founding Member of the newly established Psychiatric Research Institute in Prague-Bohnice. There I had the extraordinary fortune that Doc. MUDr. Lubomír Hanzlíček, the Director of the Institute, was a very liberal person who believed in intellectual freedom and allowed me to conduct research on the diagnostic and therapeutic potential of LSD-25 and psilocybin. Without his support, I would not have been able to conduct my basic research in this fascinating but controversial area. In 1967, thanks to a generous scholarship from the Foundations Fund for Psychiatric Research in New Haven, Connecticut, and a personal invitation from Prof. Joel Elkes, Chairman of Henry Phipps Clinic of The Johns Hopkins University in Baltimore, Maryland, I was able to come to the United States as a Clinical and Research Fellow. After the Soviet invasion of Czechoslovakia, I decided not to return. I will be forever grateful for the opportunities that opened up for me in my new homeland.

I also very much appreciate the warm welcome, support, and friendship that I received from Dr. Albert Kurland, Director of the Maryland Psychiatric Research Center at Spring Grove, and its staff, who opened their hearts and homes for me and became my new colleagues and family. We conducted the last surviving psychedelic research project in the United States together, working with alcoholics, narcotic drug addicts, neurotics, terminal cancer patients, and mental health professionals. In this context, I can only briefly mention the names of the members of our Spring Grove staff and thank them from my heart for all the wonderful memories that I carried with me when I moved from the East Coast to California in 1973. The people who participated in different stages of the Spring Grove project were: Sandy Unger, Walter Pahnke, Charles Savage, Sid Wolf, John Rhead, Bill and Ilse Richards, Bob and Karen Leihy, Franco di Leo, Richard Yensen, John Lobell, Helen Bonny, Robert Soskin, Mark Schiffman, Lock Rush, Thomas Cimonetti, and Nancy Jewell.

I would like to express my deep gratitude to my late friend Abraham Maslow, for inviting me to a small Palo Alto circle of colleagues to be at the cradle of transpersonal psychology, together with Tony Sutich, Miles Vich, Sonja Margulies, and Jim Fadiman. This gave me the opportunity to contribute my research findings to this fledgling discipline and later carry its message to the world as Founding President of the International

Transpersonal Association (ITA). Mentioning the ITA brings to my mind the Esalen Institute in Big Sur, California, where the ITA was born. My heartfelt thanks go to Michael Murphy, the owner and co-founder of Esalen, who in 1973 invited me to go there for my sabbatical as Scholar-in-Residence. I became enchanted by the natural beauty of Big Sur and the intellectually stimulating atmosphere of Esalen and stayed there for fourteen years, which were among the most professionally rewarding years of my life.

With the enthusiastic support of Dick Price, the other co-founder of Esalen, my late wife Christina and I conducted thirty month-long workshops at Esalen with a stellar cast of guest faculty, including Joseph Campbell, Jack Kornfield, Huston Smith, Fritjof Capra, Rupert Sheldrake, Karl Pribram, Michael and Sandra Harner, Frances Vaughan, Roger Walsh, John Lilly, Tim Leary, Ram Dass, Ralph Metzner, Richard Tarnas, Angeles Arrien, Humphrey Osmond, Gordon Wasson, psychics, parapsychologists, Tibetan teachers, Indian yogis, American and Mexican shamans, and many others. In the enchanting, informal, and intimate setting of Esalen, we developed deep friendships with these people, and most of them became ardent and loyal presenters at our ITA conferences. Michael Murphy and Dick Price became the founding members of the ITA with me.

I would like to express my gratitude to several of my friends and colleagues who have provided great intellectual inspiration and creatively expanded and complemented my work, introducing it to new areas. Fritjof Capra's criticism of monistic materialism and the Cartesian-Newtonian paradigm in his book *The Tao of Physics* provided inspiration on how to connect transpersonal psychology to the hard sciences. It became clear that the connection had to be made to quantum-relativistic physics and modern advances in science rather than to seventeenth-century materialistic philosophy and an outdated paradigm. Another major support for transpersonal psychology and the findings of modern consciousness research was Karl Pribram's holographic model of the brain and David Bohm's theory of holomovement.

Jack Kornfield, dear friend and extraordinary Buddhist teacher, helped us find spiritual grounding for our work. We have jointly conducted more than thirty very popular retreats in the United States and Europe, entitled *Insight and Opening,* in which we explored the common ground between

Vipassana Buddhism, transpersonal psychology, and Holotropic Breathwork. Rupert Sheldrake's revolutionary book *The New Science of Life* brought strong criticism of the monistic, materialistic philosophy which underlies the natural sciences. His concept of morphic resonance and morphogenetic fields was a welcome contribution to the understanding of transpersonal experiences by replacing the requirement of a material substrate for memory with immaterial fields that are carriers of memory.

The research of Rick Tarnas, close friend and brilliant historian, philosopher and astrologer, has connected my findings with archetypal astrology. This unlikely and controversial alliance brought a surprising breakthrough. After forty years of fascinating cooperation with Rick, exploring extraordinary correlations between planetary transits and timing and archetypal content of non-ordinary states of consciousness, I refer to archetypal astrology as the "Rosetta Stone of consciousness research." I believe that a combination of work with non-ordinary states of consciousness and archetypal astrology as a guide for this work is the most promising strategy for the psychiatry of the future.

Ervin Laszlo, the world's foremost systems theorist, provided in his connectivity hypothesis and his concept of the Akashic holofield a plausible explanation for a variety of anomalous phenomena, observations, and paradigmatic challenges occurring in psychedelic therapy, in sessions of Holotropic Breathwork, and during spontaneous episodes of non-ordinary states of consciousness ("spiritual emergencies"). Laszlo's brilliant map of reality based on theories and findings on the cutting edge of several scientific disciplines offers an elegant solution for these dilemmas and paradoxes. It makes the seemingly absurd findings believable and scientifically acceptable.

In honoring people who have helped me to take my work into new areas, I need to acknowledge my late wife Christina. Her motivation for these ventures was that she was looking for help with the problems she suffered from—spiritual emergency, addiction to alcohol, and post-traumatic syndrome, a residue of sexual abuse. As Roger Walsh said about Christina during her fiftieth birthday celebration, she managed like few others to "turn her personal problems into projects that help society at large." Her drinking problem inspired an Esalen month long workshop and two large International Transpersonal Conferences, entitled *Mystical Quest, Attach-*

ment and Addiction, creating an alliance between the Twelve Step programs and transpersonal psychology. In 1980, she started the Spiritual Emergency Network (SEN), which grew into a worldwide movement seeking new alternative treatment for these disorders, and her book *The Eggshell Landing* has brought solace and inspiration to many sexual abuse survivors.

I reserve very special thanks for the circle of close personal friends, pioneers of the transpersonal movement, who came regularly as guest faculty to our month long seminars, ITA conferences, and Holotropic Breathwork trainings, as well as participants in our various social events: Michael and Sandy Harner, Jack Kornfield, Wes Nisker, Frances Vaughan, Roger Walsh, Rick Tarnas, Ram Dass, Jack and Ricci Coddington, Ralph Metzner, and Angeles Arrien. Our books, papers, and lectures expressing various aspects of the vision that we all shared were mutually empowering and made the development of the transpersonal field an exciting collective project. Betsy Gordon with J. B. Merlin, and Bo Legendre, dear members of our circle, deserve kudos for hosting many of our parties over the years, which combined delicious food, great company, and exciting intellectual exchanges. Carmen Scheifele-Giger has been for many years a dear friend and supporter of my work; she provided for me inestimable help when I was writing a book on her late husband, the genius of fantastic realism H. R. Giger. She also hosted our training modules in the H. R. Giger Museum in Gruyères, and her translation of my book on the psychology of the future made it available to German-speaking audiences.

My deep admiration goes to the California Institute of Integral Studies (CIIS) in San Francisco, an unusually progressive and open-minded school, offering high quality programs and academic degrees in transpersonal psychology for students from all over the world. I would like to thank presidents Robert McDermott and Joseph Subbiondo for allowing Rick Tarnas and myself to teach the popular "Psyche and Cosmos" graduate seminars, combining research into two areas too controversial for mainstream institutions—holotropic states of consciousness and archetypal astrology.

I feel greatly honored by the moral support that I received from the Czech president Václav Havel and his wife Dagmar, who in 2007 granted me the highly prestigious Vision 97 Award for my role in founding transpersonal psychology and developing Holotropic Breathwork. I would also like to express my gratitude to my friends who have offered financial support for my work, some of them over many years, others more recently: John Buchanan, Betsy Gordon, Bokara Legendre, Oleg Gorelik, Bo Shao, Bill Melton, Meihong Xu, George Sarlo, Friederike Meckel-Fischer, Fischer Konrad, and Paul Grof. I would like to use this opportunity to thank Susan Logeais, Portland filmmaker and woman of many talents, for a different kind of support—for all the time, energy, and love that she has given to her work on a documentary about my life and work, as well as the healing potential of psychedelic substances. I also very much appreciate the great help of our assistant Jean Friendly, who has been taking care of the organization of our travels and life in California.

I feel blessed by the support I have received from the members of my immediate family. Brigitte, with whom I have been happily married since April 2016, brought light, joy, and unconditional love to my life. It was she who, after listening to the telecourse modules that I did for Shift Network, convinced me that I should make this material available for larger audiences in an encyclopedic book form. She has also provided an ideal setting for writing by taking on the majority of practical tasks. Brigitte is a psychologist and psychotherapist. We have known each other for more than thirty years; she has been practicing and teaching Holotropic Breathwork all these years and knows me and my work better than anyone else. This makes it possible to discuss with her in our free time the issues I am writing about and get very useful feedback.

I am equally fortunate to have a wonderful brother. Paul is four and a half years younger than I and is also a psychiatrist. His special area of interest is different than mine; he is highly respected in the academic world as an expert in the area of affective disorders, for which he received the prestigious NARSAD Award. However, he is also deeply interested in transpersonal psychology and has had personal experiences with psychedelics and with meditation. I can rely on getting honest judgment from him, whether it is a positive comment or a strict constructive criticism.

It is hard to find adequate words of appreciation for the amazing work that Rick Doblin and his enthusiastic and dedicated team at the Multidisciplinary Association of Psychedelic Studies (MAPS) have done in the last several decades. They achieved what seemed impossible—to lift the dark spell that ignorant and irrational legislation cast on psychedelic research and to initiate the current global renaissance of interest in research of these remarkable substances. I owe them special thanks for publishing several of my books on psychedelics. I would like to thank especially Sarah Jordan and Brad Burge for the expertise, time, and love that they have given to *The Way of the Psychonaut.* I am also very grateful to Renn Butler, who volunteered to edit both volumes of this encyclopedia. It would have been difficult to find another person with the necessary experience in both Holotropic Breathwork and psychedelic research. Renn is an archetypal astrologer in the lineage of Rick Tarnas, whose focus is on helping people understand and integrate their holotropic and psychedelic experiences.

Unfortunately, the thousands of people whose contributions to this book were essential will have to remain anonymous. I am talking about my patients in Europe, the United States, and Canada, the participants in our workshops, and the teachers, facilitators, and trainees in our breathwork modules. They had the courage to undertake journeys into hidden recesses of their psyches and shared their experiences with me. Their verbal reports about what they had encountered, and the art with which they illustrated their adventures in alternate realities, have been for me essential sources of information. My indebtedness and gratitude to these people from many countries around the world can hardly be adequately expressed in words. Without them, this book could not have been written.

Stanislav Grof, M.D., Ph.D.

The Way of the Psychonaut

Encyclopedia for Inner Journeys

Volume One

I

The History of Psychonautics: *Ancient, Aboriginal, and Modern Technologies of the Sacred*

Before we start exploring specific topics in this encyclopedia, I would like to clarify some terms that I will be using throughout this work. I will be drawing on sixty years of my observations and experiences in the research of a large and important subgroup of non-ordinary states of consciousness that have remarkable healing, transformative, evolutionary, and heuristic potential. Modern psychiatry has no specific name for these states and sees all of them as pathological distortions ("altered states").

Holotropic States of Consciousness

Early in my professional career, I realized the great positive potential of these states and the urgent need to correct this error. I decided to coin the term "holotropic," meaning moving toward wholeness (from the Greek *holos,* meaning whole and *trepo/trepein,* meaning moving toward or being attracted by something). The word holotropic is a neologism, but it is related to the commonly used term *heliotropism*—the property of plants to always move in the direction of the sun.

The term commonly used by mainstream clinicians and theoreticians, "altered states of consciousness," is not appropriate because of its one-sided emphasis on the distortion or impairment of the "correct way" of experiencing oneself and the world. (In colloquial English and veterinary jargon, the term "alter" is also used to signify castration of domestic animals). The somewhat better term "non-ordinary states of consciousness" is too broad and general, since it includes a wide range of conditions that do not have the beneficial properties of holotropic states. This includes trivial deliria caused by infectious diseases, the abuse of alcohol, or circulatory and degenerative diseases of the brain. These alterations of consciousness are associated with disorientation, impairment of intellectual functions, and subsequent amnesia; they are clinically important, but lack therapeutic and heuristic potential.

By comparison, the states which I call holotropic have great theoretical and practical importance. These are the states that novice shamans experience during their initiatory crises and later induce in their clients for therapeutic purposes. Ancient and native cultures have used these states in rites of passage and in their healing ceremonies. The experiences of initiates in the ancient mysteries of death and rebirth, as well as those described by mystics of all ages and from many countries, are also holotropic experiences.

Procedures inducing these states ("technologies of the sacred") were developed and used in the context of the great religions of the world—Hinduism, Buddhism, Jainism, Taoism, Islam, Judaism, and Christianity. They involve meditation, movement meditation, breathing exercises, prayers, fasting, sleep deprivation, and even the use of physical pain. The most powerful means for inducing holotropic experiences are psychedelic plants, the pure active alkaloids extracted from them, and synthetic entheogens. There are also powerful forms of experiential psychotherapy, such as rebirthing, Holotropic Breathwork, and others that can induce these states without the use of psychedelic medicines.

The name holotropic suggests something that might come as a surprise to the average Westerner—that in our everyday state of consciousness, we use only a small fraction of our perceptual and experiential potential and are not aware of the full extent of our being. Holotropic states of consciousness have the potential to help us—to use the terms of the British-American philosopher and writer Alan Watts—to break the "taboo against knowing who we are" and realize that we are not "skin-encapsulated egos" and that, in the last analysis, we are commensurate with the cosmic creative principle itself (Watts 1973). Pierre Teilhard de Chardin, the French paleontologist, Jesuit, and philosopher, expressed it differently: "We are not human beings having spiritual experiences, we are spiritual beings having a human experience" (Teilhard de Chardin 1975).

This astonishing idea is not new. In the ancient Indian Chandogya Upanishad, the answer to the question: "Who am I?" is "Tat tvam asi." This succinct Sanskrit sentence means literally: "Thou art That," or "You are Godhead." It suggests that we are not "namarupa"—name and form (body/ego), but that our deepest identity is that of a divine spark of cosmic creative energy that we carry in our innermost being *(Atman),* which is ultimately identical with the supreme universal principle that creates the universe *(Brahman).* For the Hindus, this is not a belief, or unsubstantiated conviction but something that can be experientially validated if we follow certain rigorous spiritual practices, and various forms of yoga.

Hinduism is not the only religion that has made this discovery. The revelation concerning the identity of the individual with the divine is the ultimate secret that lies at the mystical core of all great spiritual traditions. Therefore, the name for this principle could be the Tao, the Buddha, Shiva (of Kashmir Shaivism), Cosmic Christ, Pleroma, Allah, and many others. This can be seen in quotes from various religions.

We have already seen that the Hindus believe in the essential identity of Atman with Brahman and that the Upanishads reveal our divine nature in their "Tat tvam asi." Swami Muktananda, the head of the Siddha Yoga tradition, used to say, "God dwells in you as You." In the Buddhist scriptures, we can read: "Look inside, you are the Buddha." The intention during Buddhist practice is not to attain something or become something other than what we are, but realize who we are already.

In mystical Christianity, Jesus tells his followers: "Father, you, and I are one" and "the Divine Kingdom does not come by expectation; the Divine Kingdom is here and people do not see it." According to St. Gregory Palamas, "the Kingdom of Heaven, nay, the King of Heaven is within us." Kabbalist Avraham ben Shemu'el Abulafia proclaimed, "He and we are one." In the Confucian texts we read, "Heaven, earth, and humans are the same." According to Mohammed, "Whoever knows himself, knows his

Lord." And the Persian poet, Sufi Mansur Al-Hallaj, who had realized his own divinity and had the courage to declare it publicly, "Ana'l Haqq—I am God, the Absolute Truth," had to pay a great price—he was killed and his body was burned.

Holotropic experiences have the potential to help us discover our true identity and our cosmic status; they also provide deep insights into the nature of reality, far beyond what is available in the everyday state of consciousness (Grof 1998). Sometimes this happens in small increments, other times in the form of major breakthroughs. Psychonautics can be defined as the systematic pursuit and use of holotropic states of consciousness for healing, self-exploration, ritual activity, artistic inspiration, and as a spiritual, philosophical, and scientific quest. It is a response to a deep craving for transcendental experiences that Andrew Weil described in his book *The Natural Mind* as the deepest drive in the human psyche, more powerful than sex (Weil 1972).

Psychonauts of the Paleolithic Era

The practice of inducing holotropic states of consciousness can be traced back to the dawn of human history. It is the most important characteristic feature of shamanism, the oldest spiritual system and healing art of humanity. Shamanism is extremely ancient, probably at least thirty to forty thousand years old; its roots can be found as far back as the Paleolithic era. The walls of the famous caves in Southern France and northern Spain, such as Lascaux, Font de Gaume, Les Trois Frères, Altamira, and others, are decorated with beautiful images of animals. Most of them represent species that actually roamed the Stone Age landscape—bisons, aurochses, wild horses, stags, ibexes, mammoths, wolves, rhinos, and reindeer. However, others are mythical creatures that clearly have magical and ritual significance, such as the "Mythic Beast" from the Lascaux cave, with long parallel horns (a "double unicorn") protruding from his front that resemble the masks of the Australian Aborigines. Several of these caves have paintings and carvings of strange figures that combine human and animal features, which undoubtedly represent ancient shamans.

The best known of these images is the "Sorcerer of Les Trois Frères," a

"Mythic Beast" from the Lascaux cave with long parallel horns ("double unicorn") protruding from his front resembling the masks of the Australian Aborigines (top); ritual of the Australian Aborigines: the natives wearing masks with two parallel horns.

mysterious composite figure combining various male symbols. He has the antlers of a stag, eyes of an owl, tail of a wild horse or wolf, human beard, and paws of a lion. Another famous carving of a shaman in the same cave complex is the "Beast Master," presiding over the happy hunting grounds teeming with beautiful animals. Also well known is the hunting scene on the wall in Lascaux. It shows an eviscerated bison pierced with a spear, and a figure lying on the ground. It was originally interpreted as a hunting accident until it was noticed that the figure has an erect penis, an unlikely occurrence in a wounded or dying person, but a very common sign of a shamanic trance.

The grotto known as La Gabillou harbors a carving of a shamanic figure in dynamic movement whom the archaeologists call "The Dancer." On the clay floor of one of these caves, Tuc d'Audoubert, the discoverers found footprints in a circular arrangement around two clay bison effigies, suggesting that its inhabitants performed dances similar to those that are still being conducted by many aboriginal cultures for the induction of trance states. The origins of shamanism can be traced back to an even older group, a Neanderthal cult of the cave bear, as exemplified by the animal shrines from the interglacial period found in grottoes in the Swiss region of Engadin and southern Germany (Campbell 1984).

It must have been extremely hard to carve and paint these images in the inaccessible depths of these caves, using only primitive torches, and standing, in some instances, on smalls knolls high on the walls. It would have been much easier to portray animals, depict scenes of the hunt, or use images for hunting magic on the surface of the earth. There clearly had to be a special reason to undergo such challenges. Rock art scholar David Lewis-Williams suggested in his book *The Mind in the Cave* that the artists in these caves were ancient shamans who were experiencing trance states and portraying their visions (Lewis-Williams 2002). Mythologist Joseph Campbell proposed that these caves with long narrow passages leading into them were places for rituals celebrating the Great Mother Goddess, and that they represented her genitals and belly. He also thought that the ancient Venus figures and figurines celebrating female fertility, such as Venus of Willendorf, Venus of Dolní Věstonice, or Venus of Laussel, were related to the same cult of the Great Mother Goddess.

Shamanism is not only ancient, it is also global; it can be found in North,

"Sorcerer of Les Trois Frères." Cave painting of a mysterious composite figure combining various male symbols—antlers of a stag, eyes of an owl, tail of a wild horse or wolf, human beard, and paws of a lion (left); "The Dancer," an anthropomorphic figure, possibly a dancing shaman, from the Gabillou cave (carving, below left; line drawing, below right).

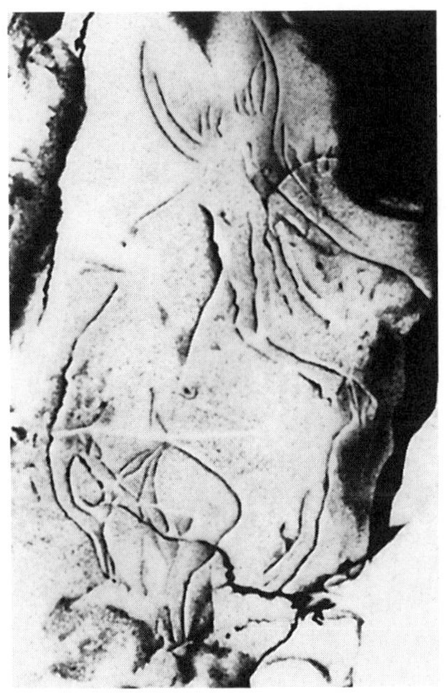

"The Beastmaster." Detail from a large wall painting in Les Trois Frères cave showing an anthropomorphic figure, most likely a Paleolithic shaman, surrounded by animals.

Bee shaman covered with mushrooms, a petroglyph in a cave in Tassili, Sahara Desert. Neolithic Period, 9,000 to 6,000 BC.

Central, and South America, in Europe, Africa, Asia, Australia, Micronesia, and Polynesia. The fact that so many different cultures throughout human history have found shamanic techniques useful and relevant suggests that the holotropic states engage what the anthropologists call the "primal mind," a basic and primordial aspect of the human psyche that transcends race, gender, culture, and historical period. In cultures that have escaped the disruptive influence of Western industrial civilization, shamanic techniques and procedures have survived to this day.

The career, for many shamans, begins with a spontaneous psychospiritual crisis ("shamanic illness"). It is a powerful visionary state during which the future shaman experiences a journey into the underworld, or the realm of the dead, where he or she is attacked by evil spirits, subjected to various ordeals, killed, and dismembered. This is followed by an experience of rebirth and an ascent into the celestial realms. Shamanism is also connected with holotropic states in that accomplished and experienced shamans are able to enter into a trance state at will, and in a controlled manner. They use it for diagnosing and healing when the client, the healer, or both of them are in a holotropic state at the same time. The shamans play the role of "psychopomps" for holotropic states of other members of their tribes; they provide the necessary support and guidance for traversing the complex territories of the Beyond.

Native Spirituality and Rites of Passage

Native tribes of many different countries and time periods have spent a lot of time and effort developing methods to induce holotropic experiences, or "technologies of the sacred." This often includes a combination of drumming, rattling, and other forms of percussion, music, chanting, rhythmic dancing, changes of breathing, and social and sensory isolation—such as staying in a cave, the desert, arctic ice, or in high mountains. The natives also frequently use extreme physiological interventions, including fasting, sleep deprivation, dehydration, circumcision, subincision, the use of powerful laxatives and purgatives, and even massive bloodletting and infliction of severe pain.

Native cultures use holotropic states for a variety of purposes: direct experiential contact with the archetypal dimensions of reality (deities, mythological realms, and numinous forces of nature); the healing of individuals and groups or even an entire tribe, as exemplified by the Bushmen in the African Kalahari Desert; artistic inspiration (ideas for rituals, paintings, sculptures, and songs); and the cultivation of intuition and extrasensory perception (finding lost persons and objects, obtaining information about people in remote locations, and following the movement of the game they hunt).

Another important reason for inducing holotropic states is to expand the consciousness of participants in the ritual events of native cultures, which the Dutch anthropologist Arnold van Gennep called rites of passage (van Gennep 1960). Ceremonies of this kind existed in all known native cultures and are still being performed in many preindustrial societies. Their main purpose is to redefine, transform, and consecrate individuals, groups, and even entire cultures. Rites of passage are conducted at times of important biological or social transitions, such as childbirth, circumcision, puberty, marriage, menopause, and before death. Similar rituals are also associated with initiation into warrior status, acceptance into secret societies, calendrical festivals of renewal, healing ceremonies, and geographical movement of human groups.

Rites of passage involve powerful consciousness-expanding procedures that induce psychologically disorganizing experiences, resulting in a higher level of integration. This episode of psychospiritual death and rebirth is then interpreted as dying in the old role and being born into the new one. For example, in the puberty rites, the initiates enter the procedure as boys or girls and emerge as adults with all the rights and duties that come with this status. In all these situations, the individual or social group leaves behind one mode of being and moves into totally new life circumstances.

The person who returns from the initiation is not the same as the one who entered the initiation process. Having undergone a deep psychospiritual transformation, he or she has a personal connection with the numinous dimensions of existence, as well as a new and greatly expanded worldview, a better self-image, more self-confidence, and a different system of values. All this is the result of a deliberately induced crisis that reaches the very core of the initiate's being and is at times terrifying, chaotic, and disorienting. For some time, the initiate can be in a confusing state that the anthropologists refer to as *"betwixt and between"*—having lost their old identity and not yet attained the new one. The rites of passage thus provide another example of a situation in which a period of temporary disintegration and turmoil leads to greater sanity and well-being. Polish psychiatrist Kazimierz Dabrowski observed this process occurring spontaneously in his patients and coined for it the term "positive disintegration" (Dabrowski 1964).

The two examples of "positive disintegration" we have discussed so far—the shamanic initiatory crisis and the experience of the rite of passage—have many features in common, but they also differ in some important respects. The shamanic crisis invades the psyche of the future shaman unexpectedly and without warning; it is spontaneous and autonomous in nature. By comparison, the rites of passage are a product of the culture and follow a predictable time schedule. The experiences of the initiates are the result of specific "technologies of the sacred," developed and perfected by previous generations.

In cultures that venerate shamans and also conduct rites of passage, the shamanic crisis is considered to be a form of initiation that is much superior to the rite of passage. It is seen as the intervention of a higher power and thus an indication of divine choice and a special calling. From another perspective, rites of passage represent a further step in cultural appreciation of the positive value of holotropic states of consciousness. Shamanic cultures accept and hold in high esteem both holotropic states that occur spontaneously during initiatory crises and the healing trance experienced or induced by recognized shamans. Rites of passage introduce holotropic states into the culture on a large scale, institutionalize them, and make them an integral part of ritual and spiritual life.

Ancient Mysteries of Death and Rebirth

Holotropic states also played a critical role in the ancient mysteries of death and rebirth, sacred and secret procedures that were widespread all over the ancient world. These mysteries were based on mythological stories about deities who symbolized death and transfiguration. In ancient Sumer, it was Inanna and Dumuzi, in Egypt, Isis and Osiris, in Greece the deities

Attis, Adonis, Dionysus, and Persephone, and in Italy, the Iranian-Roman Mithra. Their Mesoamerican counterparts were the Aztec Quetzalcoatl, or the Plumed Serpent, and the Mayan Hero Twins, as depicted in the Popol Vuh. These mysteries were particularly popular in the Mediterranean area and in the Middle East, as exemplified by the Sumerian and Egyptian temple initiations, the Mithraic mysteries, as well as the Greek Corybantic rites, Bacchanalia, and the mysteries of Eleusis.

The key to the powerful transformation that the initiates experienced in the course of the Eleusinian mysteries was the sacred potion *kykeon*, capable of inducing visions of the afterlife so powerful that it changed the way participants saw the world and their place in it. They were freed from the fear of death through the recognition that they were immortal souls temporarily in mortal bodies. An impressive testimony for the power and impact of what transpired in these events is the fact that the mysteries conducted in the Eleusinian sanctuary near Athens took place regularly and without interruption every five years for a period of almost 2000 years. They were observed regularly from ca. 1600 BC until 392 AD. Even then, they did not simply cease to attract the attention of the antique world. The ceremonial activities in Eleusis were brutally interrupted when the Christian Emperor Theodosius interdicted participation in the myster-

Ruins of the Telestrion, the giant hall that hosted the Eleusinian mysteries. In the background is the cave with the entrance into the underworld, which—according to the legend—Hades used to abduct Persephone.

ies and all other pagan cults. Shortly afterward, in 395 AD, the invading Goths destroyed the sanctuary.

In the telestrion, the giant initiation hall in Eleusis, more than 3,000 neophytes at a time experienced powerful experiences of psychospiritual transformation. The cultural importance of these mysteries for the ancient world and their as yet unacknowledged role in the history of European civilization becomes evident when we realize that there were many famous and illustrious figures of antiquity among the initiates. The list of neophytes included the philosophers Plato, Aristotle, and Epictetus, the military leader Alkibiades, the playwrights Euripides and Sophocles, and the poet Pindaros. Another famous initiate, emperor Marcus Aurelius, was fascinated by the eschatological hopes offered by these rites. The Roman statesman and philosopher Marcus Tullius Cicero took part in these mysteries and wrote an exalted report about their effects on Greek and Roman civilization.

In De Legibus (About Laws), Cicero wrote:

> *"For among the many excellent and indeed divine institutions which your Athens has brought forth and contributed to human life, none, in my opinion, is better than those mysteries. For by their*

Model of the Eleusinian sanctuary during the Roman period. The Telestrion, the hall where the mysteries took place; on the right the Lesser and Greater monumental gateways.

> *means we have been brought out of our barbarous and savage mode of life and educated and refined to a state of civilization; and as the rites are called 'initiations,' so in very truth we have learned from them the beginnings of life, and have gained the power not only to live happily, but also to die with a better hope"* (Cicero 1977).

Mithraism is another example of the great respect and influence the ancient mystery religions had in the antique world. It began to spread throughout the Roman Empire in the first century A.D., reached its peak in the third century, and succumbed to Christianity at the end of the fourth century. At the cult's height, the underground Mithraic sanctuaries *(mithraea)* could be found from the shores of the Black Sea to the mountains of Scotland to the border of the Sahara Desert. The Mithraic mysteries represented the sister religion of Christianity and its most important competitor (Ulansey 1989).

The specifics of the consciousness-expanding procedures involved in these secret rites have remained for the most part unknown, although three respectable scientists—mycologist Gordon Wasson, discoverer of LSD-25 Albert Hofmann, and Greek scholar Carl Ruck—collected impressive evidence that the sacred potion *kykeon* used in the Eleusinian mysteries was a concoction containing alkaloids of ergot similar to LSD. They described their meticulous research in the book *The Road to Eleusis: Unveiling the Secret of the Mysteries* (Wasson, Hofmann and Ruck 1978). It is also highly probable that psychedelic materials were also involved in the bacchanalia and other types of rites. Ancient Greeks did not know distillation of alcohol and could not ferment drinks with a higher concentration than 14%, which stops the fermentation process. But according to the reports, the wines used in Dionysian rituals had to be diluted three to twenty times, and just three cups of it "brought some initiates to the brink of insanity."

Spiritual Practices of the Great Religions

In addition to the ancient and aboriginal technologies of the sacred mentioned earlier, many great religions developed sophisticated psychospiritual procedures specifically designed to induce holotropic experiences. This includes, for example, different systems of yoga, meditations and movement meditations used in Vipassana, Zen, and Tibetan Buddhism, and spiritual exercises of the Taoist tradition, along with complex Tantric rituals. I should also mention various elaborate approaches used by the Sufis, the mystics of Islam. They regularly used intense breathing, devotional chants, and a trance-inducing whirling dance in their sacred ceremonies, or dhikrs.

From the Judeo-Christian tradition, we can mention the breathing exercises of the Essenes and their baptism, which involved half-drowning. Included in this list are the Jesus prayer *(hesychasm),* the exercises of Ignatius of Loyola, and Hasidic dances, as well as Kabbalistic meditations, which use letters of the Hebrew alphabet, reciting the name of God, breathing, and music. Approaches designed to induce or facilitate direct spiritual experiences are characteristic of the mystical branches of the great religions, their monastic orders, and fringe sects like the Pentecostals and Snake Handlers, or Holy Ghost People.

Ritual Use of Psychedelic Medicines

The most powerful means of inducing holotropic states of consciousness are psychedelic plants and substances, and the history of their ritual use can be traced back thousands of years. In the Rig Veda, more than one hundred stanzas are dedicated to the plant and sacred potion called soma. The Ninth Mandala of the Rig Veda, known as the Soma Mandala, consists entirely of hymns addressed to Soma Pavamana ("purified soma") (Jamison and Brereton 2014). The power of soma is evident from statements describing its effect, such as "half of us is on earth, the other half in Heaven, we have drunk soma" or "we have drunk Soma and become immortal; we have attained the light, the Gods discovered." In the Zoroastrian Zend Avesta, the same sacred drink is known as *haoma.*

The first historical record about the healing power of cannabis can be found in the writings of the Chinese Emperor Shen Neng from the year 2737 BC. Different varieties of hemp have been smoked and ingested under various names *(hashish, charas, bhang, ganja, kif, marijuana)* in India, the Middle East, Africa, and the Caribbean area for recreation, pleasure, and during religious ceremonies. They have represented an important sacrament for such diverse groups as the Brahmans, certain Sufi orders, ancient Scythians, and the Jamaican Rastafarians.

According to some controversial theories, psychedelics might have played an important role in Judeo-Christian history. Dan Merkur suggested in his book *The Mystery of Manna: The Psychedelic Sacrament of the Bible* that manna was a psychedelic substance (Merkur 2000). Dead Sea Scrolls scholar John Allegro argued in his book *The Sacred Mushroom and the Cross* that Christianity started as a shamanic cult using the fly agaric mushroom *(Amanita muscaria)* as a sacrament (Allegro 1970). John Lash Lamb found numerous depictions of stylized mushrooms in the Paris Eadwine Psalter (Lash Lamb 2008).

Mike Crowley concluded, in his well-documented book *Secret Drugs of Buddhism: Psychedelic Sacraments and the Origins of the Vajrayana,* that consciousness-expanding substances played an important role in Tibetan Buddhism. Drawing on sacred scriptures, iconography, botany, and pharmacology, Crowley amassed impressive evidence that psychedelic substances from soma to amrita deeply influenced the development of Indian religions (Crowley 2010). He suggested that Cintamani, the wish-fulfilling gem, might have been a mushroom related to the genus Psilocybe, and that trees associated with the goddess Tara, such as the acacia, might have been used to produce drinks containing DMT, which is similar to ayahuasca ("indohuasca").

Mycologist Gordon Wasson carried out meticulous research concerning the meal that, according to the Maha-parinibbana Sutra, the metalworker Cunda prepared for Buddha before Buddha entered parinirvana. There are scriptural differences about the meaning of the word *sukara maddava,* the name of the food that Buddha ate. The literal translation of this word is "swine bits" (from sukara, meaning pig and maddava, meaning tender or delicate). Theravada Buddhists believe that what the Buddha ate was pork, while the Mahayana Buddhists believe that this name refers to some sort of truffle or another kind of mushroom—something that pigs or boars like to eat. Wasson's research brought support for the Mahayana version. He concluded that the term "swine bits" likely referred to an entheogenic mushroom (Wasson 1982).

Ceremonial use of various psychedelic materials also has a long history in Central America. Highly effective consciousness-expanding plants were well-known in several pre-Hispanic cultures, including the Aztecs, Mayans, and Toltecs. The most famous of these plants are the Mexican cactus peyote *(Lophophora williamsii),* the sacred mushroom teonanacatl *(Psilocybe mexicana),* and ololiuqui, which are seeds of different varieties of the morning glory plant *(Ipomoea violacea and Turbina corymbosa).* These materials are still used as sacraments by the Huichol, Mazatec, Chichimeca, Cora, and other Mexican tribes, as well as the Native American Church.

The famous Aztec sculpture of Xochipilli (Lord of Flowers), god of flowers, maize, beauty, song, and dance, which was excavated in the foothills of Popocatepetl and exhibited in the National Archeological Museum in Mexico City, is richly decorated with carvings of floral designs. Harvard ethnobotanist Richard Schultes identified all but one as representing psychedelic plants—tendrils of morning glory *Rivea corymbosa, Psilocybe coerulea aztecorum, Nicotiana tabacum,* and *Heimia solicifolia.* He concluded that the posture of the head and body and the flexion of the toes indicate that the sculpture portrays the deity in an entheogenic ecstatic trance.

Powerful consciousness-expanding procedures played an important role in the ancient Mayan culture. Many reliefs on stone stelae, sculptures, and paintings on funeral ceramics show that the Mayans also used—besides peyote, magic mushrooms, and diviner's' sage *(Salvia divinatorum)*—the secretions of the skin and parotid glands of the toad *Bufo marinus.* A specifically Mayan mind-altering technique was massive bloodletting caused by piercing the tongues, earlobes, and genitals by lancets made of stingray spines, flint, or obsidian (Schele and Miller 1986, Grof 1994).

The famous South American *yajé* or *ayahuasca,* which has been used for centuries by various Amazonian tribes for healing and initiation rituals, is a decoction from a jungle liana *(Banisteriopsis caapi)* combined with other plant additives *(Psychotria viridis* and others). Ayahuasca is legal in Brazil and is being used by individual ayahuasqueros, in group sessions of the União do Vegetal, a religious society that seeks to promote peace and to work for spiritual development of the human beings, and by the Santo Daime, a syncretistic religious movement with a similar mission.

The origins of the use of ayahuasca are shrouded in great mystery. This sacred potion is a jungle brew that requires a combination of two different plants that makes perfect chemical sense. Psychotria and some other

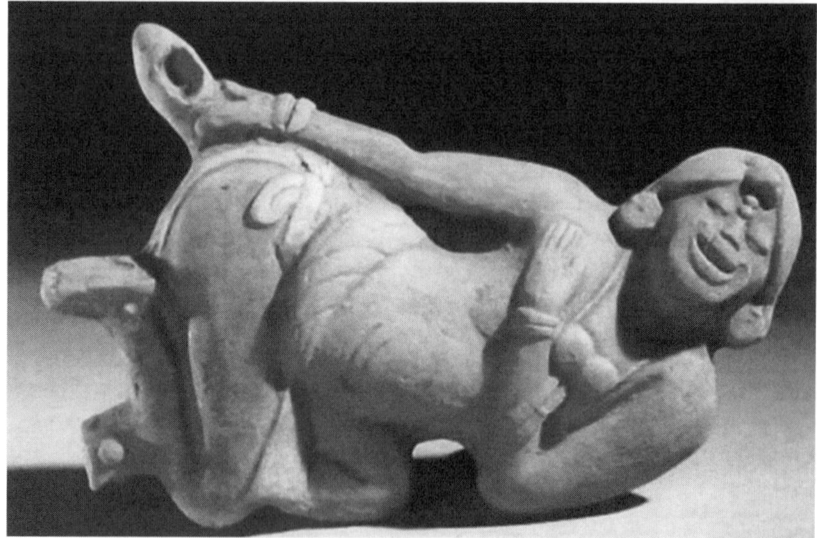

Lophophora Williamsii, Mexican cactus containing the psychedelic alkaloid mescaline (top); administration of a peyote enema, Mayan vase, Guatemala, Mayan Classic Period, AD 600 (center); peyote enema, ancient Mayan terracotta (bottom).

Psilocybe Mexicana var. *aztecorum,* "magic" mushroom of the Mazatecs (top left); mushroom stone, Guatemala City, ca. 2,000 years old (top right); psychoactive mushroom user and the death god Mictlantecuhtli. Detail from a leaf of an Aztec codex from the years immediately following the Spanish conquest. Codex Magliabecchi, Mexico (bottom).

Bufo alvarius, a toad producing psychedelic secretions with the skin and parotid glands (top); Mayan vase in the shape of a toad.

Anita Hofmann, wife of Albert Hofmann, with a bouquet of the psychedelic plant *Salvia divinatorum* (top); *Ipomoea violacea* (morning glory), source of the psychedelic seeds ololiuqui (bottom left); *Brugmansia* (angel trumpet), a plant from the *Solanaceae* family containing psychoactive substances atropine, scopolamine, and hyoscyamine (bottom right).

Quetzalcoatl, pre-Hispanic god of death and rebirth, as Plumed Serpent. Quetzal, a colorful parrot-like bird represents the spiritual element in human beings and coatl, the snake, represents their earth-bound nature. Aztec, fourteenth-sixteenth century.

additives used in the preparation of ayahuasca contain psychoactive tryptamines, and the Banisteriopsis liana contributes a mono-amino-oxidase (MAO) inhibitor that protects monoamines from fast degradation in the gastrointestinal tract.

It is easy to imagine that a hungry person finds a mushroom in the woods and, by tasting it, discovers its psychedelic property. It is less likely, but still conceivable, that somebody tries to eat a peyote cactus in spite of its prohibitive taste. However, the probability of accidentally discovering, among thousands of Amazonian plants, two that ideally complement each other's chemical effects to produce a psychedelic potion seems astronomically low. In addition, the fact that the hard woody liana requires many hours of cooking to extract the alkaloid makes the accidental discovery of this procedure close to impossible. The natives claim that the plants themselves told them how they should be used.

In recent decades, the Santo Daime people and the União do Vegetal have been introducing the ritual use of ayahuasca to industrial civilization in an effort to counteract alienation, loss of spirituality, and the ecological degradation of our planet. The Amazonian area and the Caribbean islands are also known for a variety of psychedelic snuffs. Aboriginal tribes in Africa ingest and inhale preparations from the bark of the iboga shrub *(Tabernanthe iboga)*. They use them in small quantities as stimulants during lion hunts and long canoe trips, and in larger doses for initiation rituals for men and women.

Scientific Interest in Psychedelic Plants

Compared to the millennia of human use of psychedelic plants and compounds as sacraments and sacred medicines, the period of scientific interest in them has been relatively short. The era of scientific research of psychedelics began at the turn of the twentieth century by the isolation of mescaline, the active principle of peyote, by Arthur Heffter. This was followed by three decades of experiments with this substance, culminating in the publication of the book *Meskalin Rausch* by Kurt Beringer (Beringer 1927). It is surprising that during this period of experimentation, researchers did not discover and describe mescaline's therapeutic potential and its capacity to induce mystical experiences. They concluded that this substance caused toxic psychosis and focused primarily on the remarkable effects that it had on sensory perception and artistic creativity.

The active alkaloid from *Tabernanthe iboga* was isolated in 1901 by Dybowski and Landrin and called ibogaine. From the 1930s to 1960s, ibogaine was sold in France in the form of Lambarène, an extract of the plant *Tabernanthe manii,* and promoted as a mental and physical stimulant; it was withdrawn from the market in 1966. Active alkaloids have also been isolated from *Peganum harmala, Banisteria caapi* and harmaline (also called banisterine, yageine, telepathine). The active principles in the secretions of Bufo alvarius were identified as tryptamine derivatives dimethyltryptamine (DMT) and 5-methoxy-DMT; the psychedelic properties of bufotenine (5-hydroxy-DMT) remained uncertain. The same tryptamines also turned out to be the active principles of the Caribbean psychedelic snuffs.

Arthur Heffter, a German chemist who isolated mescaline, the active principle of peyote.

Albert Hofmann and the Golden Era of Psychonautics

The golden era of psychonautics began with Albert Hofmann's synthesis of the ergot alkaloid LSD-25 and his discovery of its psychedelic effects. This discovery is usually described as accidental, but it was more complicated than that. Albert Hofmann himself preferred to call it "serendipitous." This word comes from an old Persian fairy tale, *Three Princes of Serendip (Sri Lanka),* a story of three brothers who travel together and discover, through accidents and sagacity, the nature of a lost camel. They are able to deduce from subtle environmental clues that a camel who walked on the road before them had had only one eye, was missing a tooth, was lame, and carried a pregnant woman, with honey on his one side and butter on the other.

Albert Hofmann synthesized LSD-25 for the first time in 1938 as the twenty-fifth substance in a series of derivatives of lysergic acid, an essential component of ergot alkaloids. The name of this acid reflects the fact that it is created by dissolution (Greek *lysis)* of ergot. The ergot compounds are used in medicine to stop gynecological bleeding, relieve migraine headaches, and improve blood circulation in the brains of geriatric patients. The psychedelic LSD-25 is thus an apple that fell far from the tree.

Following the routine protocol, Albert sent the sample to the pharmacological department for testing. The report that came back from the laboratory was very discouraging. It described LSD-25 as a substance that was not particularly interesting and did not deserve further research. In the following years, Albert continued to synthesize various other derivatives of lysergic acid, but he somehow could not get LSD-25 off his mind. He could not get rid of a pervasive feeling that, with this particular substance, the researchers in the laboratory must have overlooked something.

He reviewed the laboratory report and discovered that some of the mice showed psychomotor agitation after the administration of LSD-25. He came to the conclusion that because of its structural similarity with nikethamide, a central nervous system stimulant, it might be interesting to test it as a potential analeptic. Finally, in 1943, this feeling became so strong that he decided to synthesize another sample of LSD and have it tested. No matter how sophisticated these new tests would have been, experiments with animals would not have been able to reveal that it had

Albert Hofmann with a model of the LSD-25 molecule.

psychedelic effects. And this is where the remarkable accident came in.

As Albert was working on this synthesis, he started feeling strange; he was experiencing strong waves of emotions, seeing strange colors, and his perception of his surrounding environment was profoundly affected. He was initially afraid that he was having a psychotic episode, but when two and a half hours later he returned to normal, he came to the conclusion that he might have accidentally intoxicated himself by the substance he was working with. Three days later, he decided to test this idea with an auto-experiment. He prepared his work for the day and took a measured dose of LSD-25. Being very conservative, as he described himself, he took what he considered to be a miniscule dose of 250 micrograms (millions of a gram or gamma), only 25% of the dose commonly used with the other ergot alkaloids.

He naturally could not have known the enormous psychoactive power of the substance he had created. Later, when we were using LSD-25 therapeutically, 250 mcg was considered a dose that required several hours of preparation, a special environment, and preferably two sitters, one male and the other female, supervising the affected person for six-eight hours. We kept these clients overnight in the institute and talked with them in the morning before they went home. Albert took this dose casually, expecting that he would work as usual and close his eyes every half an hour to find out if anything was happening.

Within forty-five minutes, the substance started having an effect. This time, it was incomparably stronger. Albert had to stop working and asked his assistant to take him home, but it was wartime and there were restrictions on the use of cars, so many people in Basel used bicycles to get around. Albert's description of his ride through the streets of Basel has become legendary; it seemed to him that it would never stop (Hofmann 2005). When they finally arrived home, Albert was in a very bad condition. He suspected his neighbor was a witch and was hexing and killing him. He thought he was dying and asked his assistant to call a doctor. By the time the doctor arrived, though, the situation had changed. Albert had relived his birth and felt wonderful, like a newborn.

He wrote a report about this extraordinary experiment to his boss, Dr. Walter Stoll. It just happened that Dr. Stoll's son Werner was a psychiatrist and agreed to conduct a pilot study with this fascinating new substance.

He administered LSD-25 to a group of normal subjects and a group of patients with psychiatric diagnoses. In 1947, he published a paper on this study entitled *LSD-25: A Fantasticum from the Ergot Group* (Stoll 1947). After the publication of this study, this new semisynthetic ergot derivative practically became an overnight sensation in the world of science.

It is not generally known that it was not the psychedelic effect of LSD that caused the sensation. Anthropologists and historians had known for a long time that many ancient and native cultures used plants with psychedelic effects in their ritual and spiritual life and for healing. By the time of Albert's discovery, chemists had already isolated the active principles from some of these plants. It was the incredible intensity of the effects of LSD-25 that was sensational; it is effective in minute quantities—millionths of a gram, micrograms, or gammas. Just for comparison: we need about 100 mg of mescaline for a good session. Approximately the same intensity can be achieved with 100 mcg of LSD-25, about one thousandth of that dose.

It was therefore conceivable that the human body could produce a similar substance ("toxin X") and that serious mental diseases, or psychoses, would actually be chemical aberrations that could be treated by an appropriate antidote, a substance that would neutralize its effects. This would have been a test-tube solution for schizophrenia, the Holy Grail of psychiatry. In the early stages of LSD research, psychedelics were referred to as hallucinogens, psychotomimetic substances, and even delirogens, and the states induced by them as "experimental psychoses." It took psychotherapeutically oriented clinicians to overcome this preconception. The discovery of LSD and the hunt for "toxin X" started what has been called a "golden era of psychopharmacology."

During a relatively short period of time, the joint efforts of biochemists, pharmacologists, neurophysiologists, psychiatrists, and psychologists succeeded in laying the foundations of a new scientific discipline that can be referred to as the "pharmacology of consciousness." The active substances from several remaining psychedelic plants were chemically identified and prepared in chemically pure forms. A particularly important and exciting chapter of the history of psychonautics was in solving the mystery of the effects of the "magic mushrooms" of the Mazatecs, indigenous people of the Mexican state Oaxaca.

The Ethnomycological Research of Gordon and Valentina Pavlovna Wasson

Gordon Wasson and his wife, Russian pediatrician Valentina Pavlovna, were important protagonists during this chapter of history. Gordon was the most unlikely person to become involved with anything related to psychonautics; he was a successful New York banker and Vice-President of the J. P. Morgan Trust Company. This remarkable story began in 1927, when he and his young wife were on their belated honeymoon in the Catskill Mountains. During one of their strolls in the forest, Valentina Pavlovna collected wild mushrooms and insisted on preparing them for dinner.

As a typical Anglo-Saxon, Gordon was a *mycophobe*—a term that he later coined for people who believe that the only edible mushrooms are those found in the supermarket and who refer to any kind of wild mushrooms as "toadstools." He was horrified at the prospect of eating wild mushrooms and tried unsuccessfully to dissuade his wife from cooking them. Valentina, being a *mycophile*—the term Gordon later used for Eastern European mushroom enthusiasts—prevailed and prepared a delicious dinner with wild mushrooms as the main ingredient. Gordon reluctantly tasted her dish and liked it very much.

The next morning, when he discovered to his great surprise that both he and Valentina were still alive and well, he experienced a dramatic conversion from a mycophobe to a mycophile. This experience awakened a profound lifelong interest in mushrooms, and he became a world-famous amateur ethnomycologist. Gordon and Valentina spent the next twenty years studying the role mushrooms had played in human history, archaeology, comparative religion, folklore, and mythology. This extensive research culminated in the publication of their colossal, lavishly produced bibliophile opus, *Mushrooms, Russia and History* (Wasson and Wasson 1957), in which the Wassons concluded that mushroom worship was a significant component of preliterate humanity's religious life in most of Eurasia and the Americas.

They were particularly fascinated by the ritual use of the psychoactive mushroom *Amanita muscaria* by the shamans of the Finno-Ugrians and other far-north Eurasian peoples. This interest led them to eventually discover the writings of Bernardino de Sahagún, a Franciscan missionary priest involved in the Catholic evangelization of New Spain, and to the ritual use of "magic mushrooms" in pre-Hispanic cultures, as well as contemporary Central America. After three field trips to Mexico, they found Maria Sabina, a Mazatec curandera (medicine woman), who was using psychoactive mushrooms, known in Mesoamerica as *teonanacatl,* or the Flesh of Gods, in her healing ceremonies.

In June 1955, the Wassons and their friend, New York photographer Allan Richardson, became the first known Westerners allowed to participate in Maria Sabina's mushroom ritual, called *velada.* Their book *Mushrooms, Russia and History* gave the first account of the Wassons' encounter with Maria Sabina and their experience with magic mushrooms. They were deeply impressed by the powerful effects of the mushrooms from Maria Sabina's velada. They collected samples of the mushrooms and sent them to Europe for botanical identification.

The Wassons sought the help of Roger Heim, a famous French botanist specializing in mycology and tropical phytopathology, who identified the teonanacatl mushrooms as *Psilocybe mexicana* and its congeners. Heim was able to cultivate some of these mushrooms in his laboratory, and he and Gordon sent samples to the laboratories of the Swiss pharmaceutical company Sandoz for chemical analysis. In a brilliant chemical *tour de force,* Albert Hofmann was able to identify and synthesize two active alkaloids responsible for the effect of Psilocybe mushrooms, and gave them the names psilocybin and psilocin. Sandoz produced large quantities of dragées of the two new psychedelics and made them available for laboratory and clinical research worldwide.

Albert Hofmann's next contribution to the history of psychonautics was the isolation of the active principle from the seeds of the morning glory *Rivea corymbosa,* known among the natives as *ololiuqui,* which Gordon Wasson obtained from a Zapotec native. To Albert's great surprise, the active alkaloid turned out to be monoethylamid of lysergic acid (LAE-32), only one ethyl group different from LSD-25. It was so unlikely that lysergic acid derivatives could be produced by plants that far apart on the evolutionary ladder—the fungus ergot and the flowering plant Rivea corymbosa—that Albert's colleagues accused him of contaminating his sample of ololiuqui with lysergic acid from his lab. However, the identification of

New York banker and mycologist Gordon Wasson with a pre-Hispanic mushroom effigy in his office (top left); Stanislav Grof visiting Wasson in 1973 at his home in Danbury, Connecticut (top right). Pre-Hispanic mushoom effigies. Similar sculptures were found in Southern Mexico, Guatemala, and San Salvador, dating from 1,000 BC to 500 AD (bottom left). Terracotta sculpture representing celebrants dancing around a mushroom effigy, possibly a World Tree (axis mundi). Colima, 200 BC to 100 AD, Mexico (bottom right).

the alkaloid proved to be correct and Albert concluded that LSD should be considered a member of the group of pre-Hispanic sacraments.

As we saw earlier, mescaline, ibogaine, and harmine (banisterine) had already been isolated and chemically identified earlier in the twentieth century. The armamentarium of psychedelic substances was further enriched by psychoactive derivatives of tryptamine—DMT (dimethyl-tryptamine), DET (diethyl-tryptamine), and DPT (dipropyl-tryptamine)—synthesized and studied by the Budapest group of chemists, headed by Stephen Szara and Zoltan Böszörményi. DMT and 5-methoxy-DMT were recognized as the active principles of the psychedelic secretions of the parotid glands and skins of the toad *Bufo alvarius,* and as an important ingredient of ayahuasca (meaning soga de los muertos, or vine of the dead). For centuries, this remarkable potion has had the reputation of a miraculous medicine in the native cultures of South America.

In 1964, Israeli chemist Raphael Mechoulam made another important contribution to psychonautics when he isolated, identified, and synthesized tetrahydrocannabinol (THC), the psychoactive principle from cannabis (marijuana and hashish) (Mechoulam 1970). Mechoulam's original experiments were conducted in the early 1960s on hashish acquired from a local police station. His research revealed the extraordinary psychoactive and medicinal potential of this unique plant compound. Mechoulam also successfully elucidated and isolated the second most abundant cannabinol, cannabidiol (CBD), which turned out to be a powerful analgesic. It has other therapeutic effects, but does not induce a holotropic state of consciousness.

Raphael Mechoulam is still continuing his research and, along with his coworkers, has isolated and identified a large number of cannabinols with a broad range of useful clinical effects. He realized that it is not happenstance that humans use cannabis. In 1992, he found that the human body naturally produces its own internal cannabinoids that regulate human mood, pain, memory and more. For his research, he has received many national and international awards, and earned the name the Grandfather of Cannabis. His work is becoming increasingly important with the progress in the decriminalization of marijuana.

By the 1960s, a wide range of psychedelic alkaloids in pure form was available to researchers. It became possible to study their properties in the laboratory and explore the phenomenology of the experiences that they induce, as well as their therapeutic potential. The psychopharmacological revolution triggered by Albert Hofmann's serendipitous discovery of LSD and the hunt for toxin X were underway. In 1954, Wooley and Shaw formulated a biochemical theory of schizophrenia based on the antagonism between LSD-25 and serotonin (5-hydroxy-tryptamine) (Woolley and Shaw 1954, Grof 1959).

Abram Hoffer and Humphry Osmond proposed that schizophrenia might be caused by the abnormal metabolism of adrenaline, resulting in the psychedelic derivatives adrenochrome and adrenolutine (Hoffer and Osmond 1954, 1999). The influence of LSD on the Siamese fighting fish *Betta splendens* led to a hypothesis suggesting that its effects (and schizophrenia) might be explained by interference with the transfer of oxygen on the subcellular level (Abramson and Evans 1954, Abramson, Weiss, and Baron 1958). This was based on the observation that adding LSD-25 to the tank with these fish elicited several types of characteristic abnormal behavior similar to those caused by cyanide compounds.

"Albert's Wonder Child"

Although these biochemical theories of schizophrenia were eventually refuted and abandoned, LSD remained at the center of attention for researchers. Never before had a single substance held so much promise in such a wide variety of fields. For psychopharmacologists and neurophysiologists, the discovery of LSD meant the beginning of a golden era of research that could solve many puzzles concerning neuroreceptors, synaptic transmitters, chemical antagonisms, and the intricate biochemical interactions underlying cerebral processes.

For historians and art critics, the LSD experiments provided extraordinary new insights into the psychology and psychopathology of art. This was particularly true for paintings and sculptures of various native, so-called "primitive" cultures, psychiatric patients, and outsider art (l'art brut), as well as various modern movements, such as abstractionism, impressionism, cubism, pointillism, surrealism, fantastic realism, and dadaism. For professional painters who participated in LSD research, the psychedelic session often marked a radical change in their artistic expression. Their imagination became much richer, their colors more vivid, and their style considerably freer. They could also often reach into the deep recesses of their unconscious psyche and tap archetypal sources of inspiration. On occasion, people who had never painted before were able to produce extraordinary pieces of art (Masters and Houston 1968, Grof 2015).

LSD experimentation also produced fascinating observations that were of great interest to spiritual teachers and scholars of comparative religion. The mystical experiences frequently observed in LSD sessions offered a radically new understanding of a wide variety of phenomena from the spiritual domain, including shamanism, rites of passage, ancient mysteries of death and rebirth, Eastern religions and philosophies, and mystical traditions of the world. The fact that LSD and other psychedelic substances were able to trigger a broad range of spiritual experiences became the subject of heated scientific discussions.

These debates revolved around the fascinating problem concerning the nature and value of this "instant" or "chemical mysticism." As Walter Pahnke demonstrated in his famous Good Friday experiment, mystical experiences induced by psychedelics are indistinguishable from those described in mystical literature (Pahnke 1963). This finding, which was recently confirmed in a meticulous study by Roland Griffiths and Bill Richards, researchers at Johns Hopkins University, has important theoretical and legal implications (Griffith, Richards, McCann, and Jesse 2006).

LSD was highly recommended as an extraordinary unconventional teaching device that would make it possible for psychiatrists, psychologists, medical students, and nurses to spend a few hours in a world resembling that of their patients. As a result of this experience, they would be able to understand them better, communicate with them more effectively, and be more successful in their treatment. Thousands of mental health professionals took advantage of this unique opportunity. These experiments brought surprising and astonishing results. They not only provided deep insights into the inner world of psychiatric patients, but also revolutionized the understanding of the vast dimensions of the human psyche and the nature of consciousness.

As a result of their experiences, many professionals realized that the current model of the psyche, limiting the psyche to postnatal biography and the Freudian individual unconscious, is superficial and inadequate. My own attempt to create a map of the psyche that would adequately portray the experiential spectrum of psychedelic sessions required a radical expansion of the model of the psyche used by mainstream psychiatry by adding two large regions. The first of them, the perinatal domain, is closely related to the memory of biological birth, and the second, the transpersonal domain, overlaps to some extent with C. G. Jung's historical and archetypal collective unconscious, although it expands and modifies it. The perinatal and transpersonal domains will play an important role in later chapters of this book.

Early experiments with LSD and other psychedelics also showed that the roots of emotional and psychosomatic disorders were not limited to traumatic memories from childhood and infancy, as traditional psychiatrists assume, but reach much deeper into the psyche, into the perinatal and transpersonal regions. Reports from psychedelic psychotherapists revealed LSD's unique potential as a powerful tool that can deepen and accelerate the psychotherapeutic process. With LSD as a catalyst, psychotherapy can be useful for categories of patients that previously had been difficult to reach—alcoholics, narcotic drug addicts, criminal recidivists, and sexual deviants (Grof 1980).

LSD psychotherapy also proved to be particularly useful in terminal cancer patients. In a large percentage of these patients, LSD alleviated or even eliminated difficult emotional symptoms, such as depression, general tension, anger, and insomnia. In the studies with cancer patients, LSD also showed remarkable analgesic properties; it often relieved severe physical pain, sometimes even in those patients who had not previously responded to medication with narcotics. In some instances, the analgesic effect of LSD was not limited to the duration of the pharmacological action of the substance, but continued for several weeks.

The most important effect that LSD had in dying cancer patients was the significant reduction or even disappearance of their fear of death. This happened in spite of the fact that they knew they would die within days or months. As a result, the quality of their life was greatly enhanced during their remaining days and their experience of dying was positively transformed (Grof 2006). After forty years, during which clinical use of psychedelics was blocked by irrational and ignorant legislation, these results

Raphael Mechoulam (1930–), the "Father of Cannabis," an Israeli chemist who isolated the active principle tetrahydrocannabinol (THC) and many other cannabinols (top left). Walter Pahnke (1931–1971), psychiatrist, psychologist, minister, and pioneer in psychedelic therapy, who conducted the famous "Good Friday Experiment" (top right). Bill Richards, psychologist and psychedelic pioneer, member of the staff of the Maryland Psychiatric Research Center in the late 1960s and early 1970s. Currently a psychedelic researcher at The Johns Hopkins University (bottom left). Roland Griffith, psychopharmacologist and psychedelic researcher at Johns Hopkins University (bottom right).

are now being confirmed by a new generation of researchers with the use of LSD and psilocybin.

The most interesting and important development in the first decades of psychedelic research was the shift from the reductionist laboratory perspective to the understanding of a much larger revolutionary and paradigm-breaking potential of psychedelics. It became obvious to those therapists who had the privilege of working with them that these substances are unique tools for consciousness research and the exploration of the deep recesses of the human psyche, as well as extraordinary therapeutic agents. The far-reaching philosophical implications of this research are now supported by revolutionary evidence from other disciplines, including cosmology, quantum-relativistic physics, systems theory, and biology (Barrow and Tipler 1986, Sheldrake 1981, Laszlo 2003, 2007, 2016, Goswami 1995).

My own early work with psychedelics was laboratory research comparing the changes in psychological, biochemical, and electrophysiological tests after the administration of psychedelics to psychotic patients (Vojtěchovský and Grof 1960). The most intriguing finding in this stage of research was the extraordinary interindividual and intraindividual variability in the experiences of the participants in the study. The same substance administered in the same dosage and in the same set and setting resulted in radically different experiences in each of the subjects. Some sessions consisted mostly of beautiful abstract geometrical visions, while others brought the reliving of childhood memories and interesting psychological insights. In some sessions, the only symptoms were unpleasant physical sensations; in others, experiences of emotional and physical well-being or even ecstatic rapture. Some subjects had episodes with a paranoid perception of the environment, or a tendency toward manic behavior.

The same variability could be observed in a series of psychedelic sessions of the same individuals. Each of the serial sessions was different, sometimes quite significantly, and even in diametrically opposite ways. This unpredictability of the effects made me realize that we were not doing ordinary pharmacological research, that is, working with substances that have predictable effects, but doing something much more interesting. We were exploring the deep domains of the human psyche with the help of powerful catalysts. As a result, I lost interest in the laboratory research of

Humphry Osmond (1917–2004), English-Canadian psychiatrist and pioneer of psychedelic therapy, who coined the term "psychedelic" (top left). Aldous Huxley (1894–1963), British-American writer, novelist, and philosopher, and his second wife Laura Archera Huxley (1911–2007) (top right). Claudio Naranjo (1932–), Chilean-born psychiatrist of Arabic-Moorish, Spanish, and Jewish descent, and pioneer of psychedelic therapy (bottom left). Ralph Metzner (1935–2019), psychologist, psychotherapist, writer, and psychedelic pioneer, who conducted early psychedelic research at Harvard University with Richard Alpert and Timothy Leary (bottom right).

psychedelics and started exploring their potential as tools for exploration of the psyche and adjuncts to psychotherapy.

In my first book, *Realms of the Human Unconscious,* I suggested that the potential significance of LSD for psychiatry and psychology is comparable to the importance of the microscope for biology and medicine, or the telescope for astronomy. The microscope revealed the existence of the microworld and the telescope revealed the depth of the universe, domains which had been previously unknown. LSD makes it possible to study deep processes in the psyche that are not normally available for observation (Grof 1975).

For the general population, the turning point in the attitude toward psychedelics was the correspondence between Aldous Huxley and Humphrey Osmond, in which they were trying to find an appropriate, non-clinical name for the new category of substances. This competition was carried out in an exchange of poems. Aldous Huxley sent Humphry Osmonda rhyme containing his own suggestion for a new name: *"To make this trivial world sublime, take half a gram of phanerothyme."* Humphry Osmondcountered with: *"To fathom Hell or soar angelic, just take a pinch of psychedelic."*

Huxley's term "psychedelic," the winner in this contest, all but replaced the terms *hallucinogenic, psychotomimetic,* or *delirogenic,* and *experimental psychosis,* all of which suggest pathology, with a much friendlier and more appropriate name. Psychedelic (from the Greek *psyche* and *deloun,* meaning make visible) literally means "revealing" or "manifesting the psyche." The use of this word by the counterculture of the 1960s played a decisive role in the naming process. Today, we see terms like hallucinogens and psychotomimetics only in the articles of researchers who need to be seen as serious scientists by conservative and biased authorities.

Shifting the focus from the reductionist and pathological orientation to the exploration of consciousness and the farther reaches of the human psyche made it possible to amass fascinating insights into many different areas: the architecture of emotional and psychosomatic disorders, human sexuality, the ritual and spiritual life of ancient and native cultures, the great religions of the world, mystical traditions, death and dying, the psychology of art and artists, and archetypal astrology, as well as other problems. We will explore these insights in future chapters of this encyclopedia.

The interest in the therapeutic potential of psychedelics generated by clinical experimentation with LSD-25 and psilocybin also inspired some therapists to take a closer look at the less known psychoactive substances which had been known since the beginning of the twentieth century, but primarily only from the chemical and pharmacological point of view. Chilean-American psychiatrist Claudio Naranjo, taking advantage of the favorable legal situation in his native country, conducted a pioneering clinical study with pure alkaloids from psychedelic plants ibogaine and harmaline, and with MDA and MMDA, two amphetamine derivatives structurally similar to mescaline.

Claudio described this study in his book *The Healing Journey: New Approaches to Psychedelic Therapy* (Naranjo 1974). He paid special attention to the spiritual and psychotherapeutic potential of these substances. To distinguish them from classical psychedelics such as LSD, mescaline, and psilocybin, Naranjo coined for them the terms "emotion-enhancers" and "fantasy-enhancers." In later years, most researchers preferred the name "entheogens" (literally: generating God within).

Psychonautics Driven Underground by Irrational Legislation

Psychedelic research seemed to be on its way to fulfill its initial promises and expectations until the unfortunate Harvard affair involving Tim Leary, Richard Alpert, and Ralph Metzner, as well as the unsupervised mass self-experimentation and counterculture of the young generation, which turned Albert Hofmann's "wonder child" into a "problem child" (Hofmann 2005). The problems associated with this development were also blown out of proportion by sensation-hunting journalists.

The ignorant administrative and political sanctions against psychedelics in the 1960s were effective only against law-obeying scientists, but famously failed to stop the street use of psychedelic substances. The draconian legal sanctions against psychedelics and the deceptive and mendacious anti-drug propaganda actually motivated the rebellious young generation to experiment with them. This also encouraged a black market filled with dangerous products of uncertain quality and dosage, creating an absurd situation in which an average teenager knew more about psychedelics, consciousness, and the human psyche than mainstream psychiatrists and psychologists.

Robert Kennedy, whose wife had been treated with LSD and benefitted from the experience, brought up this issue in a 1966 hearing of his own subcommittee on LSD. He questioned the officials of the Federal Drug and Food Administration (FDA) and National Institute of Mental Health (NIMH) officials why so many LSD research projects were getting scrapped. Defending LSD research, he pointed out that it was bizarre to stop legitimate scientific research with psychedelic substances at a time when millions of Americans were using them. This situation should have made it imperative to acquire as much reliable information about them as possible.

The drastic legislation that killed serious legitimate research of psychedelics for four decades was not based on any scientific evidence, but actually ignored the existing clinical data. For example, in 1960, Los Angeles psychedelic pioneer Sidney Cohen published an article entitled *Lysergic acid diethylamide: Side Effects and Complications,* based on 25,000 administrations of LSD-25 and mescaline. He showed that problems associated with psychedelics, such as flashbacks, prolonged reactions, psychotic breaks, and suicidal attempts were actually minimal in the responsible use of these substances (Cohen 1960). They compared very favorably with other procedures routinely used by mainstream psychiatrists, such as insulin comas and electroconvulsive therapy; for both of them, 1% mortality was considered an acceptable medical risk. Edgar Moniz's widely used Nobel Prize-winning prefrontal lobotomy, causing irreversible ravaging damage to vast areas of the brain, and occasionally turning much of the hemisphere into a hemorrhagic cyst, is in a category of its own in this regard.

Those of us who were privileged to have personal experiences with psychedelics, and to use them in our work, were aware of the great promise that they represented, not only for psychiatry, psychology, and psychotherapy, but also for modern society in general. We were deeply saddened by the mass hysteria that pervaded not only the lay population, but also the clinical and academic circles. One aspect of this national hysteria deserves special attention because it shows the mendacious nature of the anti-drug propaganda and the role dishonest sensation-hunting journalists played in it.

Timothy Leary (1920–1996), Harvard Professor of Psychology who became a psychedelic pioneer and guru advocating mass experimentation with mind-expanding substances.

Sidney Cohen (1910–1987), Los Angeles psychiatrist, psychedelic pioneer and author of a comprehensive study on the safety of psychedelic substances.

In the late 1960s, Maimon Cohen and his colleagues, researchers from the State University of New York in Buffalo, NY, observed structural changes in the chromosomes of children whose mothers had taken LSD during pregnancy (Cohen et al 1968). Structural changes in chromosomes had also been observed in earlier experiments with commonly used drugs, such as aspirin, caffeine, and tetracyclic antibiotics. Dr. Cohen himself was very cautious in interpreting these results and emphasized that all these children were born healthy and normal.

An irresponsible journalist published an article with a large blurred photograph of a baby and the headline: "IF YOU TAKE LSD ONLY ONCE, YOU CAN HAVE A DEFORMED BABY." The absurdity of this statement is obvious, since a certain number of babies can be born unhealthy no matter what the mother does or does not do. The method used in this study was itself flawed, as we discovered in a joint study with Joe Hin Tjio, the Indonesian-American NIH cytogeneticist who had developed the method. In this joint study, Dr. Tjio was not able to distinguish the blood of our patients, who had taken high doses of LSD, from the blood of controls. Walter Houston Clark, who worked in our institute for several months as a volunteer, was able to obtain the blood of Timothy Leary after Leary had taken many hundreds of doses of LSD, and sent it Dr. Tjio as one of the samples. Dr. Tjio was not able to detect anything unusual in Tim Leary's blood. I included an extensive review of the literature on LSD, chromosomes, and genetics as an appendix in my book *LSD Psychotherapy* (Grof 1980).

The national hysteria involving psychedelics tragically compromised and criminalized tools with extraordinary therapeutic potential that, properly understood and used, had the power to counteract the destructive and self-destructive tendencies of industrial civilization. It was particularly heartbreaking to see the reaction of Albert Hofmann, the father of LSD and other psychedelics, as he watched his prodigious "wonder child" turn into a "problem child" and his vision of a New Eleusis rapidly fade away (Hofmann 2005).

Some of the psychedelic researchers resigned themselves to the situation and returned reluctantly to routine psychiatric practice that now seemed lifeless and dull after they had experienced the excitement of the new therapeutic perspectives. Others, aware of the limitations of verbal therapy, decided to use experiential approaches that do not use substances. A large number of therapists convinced of the value of psychedelics decided not to deprive their clients of the benefits offered by these substances, and continued their work underground (Stolaroff 1997, Schroder 2014) or found legal loopholes that allowed them to continue their work legally or semi-legally. Thanks to this development, the expertise of assisting in psychedelic sessions did not become an extinct trade.

The Shulgins and the Era of Entheogens

Despite all the legal difficulties, the four decades during which mainstream research was made virtually impossible became an extremely important chapter in the history of psychonautics. The credit for this goes to Alexander Theodore "Sasha" Shulgin, a brilliant Californian organic chemist, psychopharmacologist, and author. Sasha developed a new method for the synthesis of 3,4-methylenedioxy-N-methylamphetamine (MDMA, later called XTC, or Ecstasy), a substance developed in the early 1900s in Germany by Merck, intended as a parent compound to be used to synthesize other pharmaceuticals. In 1976, he introduced the substance to Leo Zeff, a Jungian psychologist from Oakland, CA.

Leo introduced the substance to hundreds of psychologists and lay therapists around the nation (Stolaroff 1997). In the late 1970s, MDMA became very popular as a psychotherapeutic tool, particularly effective for work with couples and with people suffering from post-traumatic stress. Due to its proclivity to induce experiences of empathy, sympathy, emotional closeness, openness, and oneness, MDMA has been often referred to as an *empathogen* or *entactogen* (from the Greek en, meaning in and the Latin tactus, meaning touch). It has the reputation of having saved many threatened relationships and marriages.

Sasha Shulgin embarked on a phenomenal *tour de force* during which he synthesized a large number of psychoactive substances. Starting in 1960, he and his wife Ann enlisted a small group of friends with whom he regularly tested his creations. They developed a systematic way of ranking the effects of various substances, known as the *Shulgin Rating Scale,* with a vocabulary to describe their visual, auditory, and physical effects. Sasha personally tested hundreds of drugs, mainly analogues of various phenethylamines—a group containing MDMA, mescaline, and the 2C family of psychedelics (phenethylamines that have methoxy groups on the 2 and 5 positions of a benzene ring) and tryptamines N,N-dimethyltryptamine (DMT) and 4-methoxy-DMT psilocybin, and psilocin). There exists a large number of slight chemical variations with differences in effect, all of which are meticulously recorded in the Shulgins' laboratory notebooks.

In 1991 and 1997, Sasha and his wife Ann published the findings from many years of their unparalleled research in two volumes with the esoteric names *PiHKAL* and *TiHKAL*. These books are treasure troves of information for psychonauts and have, since the time of their publication, become classics in the field. The cryptic titles of these volumes combine the technical information about their content with a testimony for the Shulgins' passion for their extraordinary quest. *PiHKAL* stands for *Phenethylamines I Have Known and Loved* and *TiHKAL* is an acronym for *Tryptamines I Have Known and Loved* (Shulgin and Shulgin 1991 and 1997). Thanks to his remarkable work in the field of psychedelic research and the rational drug design of psychedelic substances, Sasha has since been dubbed the "Godfather of Psychedelics."

Sasha was and is admired and loved by thousands of people who benefitted from his work and had their lives positively transformed by the substances he developed. Those of us who had the chance to visit his home and see his laboratory could not believe that it was the place where he produced scores of psychoactive substances. This place, probably not larger than twelve feet by twelve feet, looked more like the workshop of a medieval alchemist than a modern laboratory. The Shulgin project generated less enthusiasm in official circles. Richard Meyer, spokesman for the DEA's San Francisco Field Division, stated: "It is our opinion that those books are pretty much cookbooks on how to make illegal drugs. Agents tell me that in all clandestine labs that they have raided, they have found copies of those books."

During the forty years when irrational legislation killed all legitimate research, fascinating new psychoactive substances would not have been synthesized, discovered, and explored had it not been for dedicated individuals like the Shulgins, as well as other groups of researchers convinced of the scientific, psychological, and spiritual importance of psychedelics and entheogens. They carried on the informal exploration of these medicines and sacraments without official permission, taking advantage of legal loopholes and the slow pace of the criminalization of new substances.

These enthusiastic explorers have amassed a large amount of invaluable information that could, in the future, serve as a basis for well-designed and organized research projects. During the last thirty years, Ralph Metzner, an experienced therapist and pioneer of psychedelic research, kept in contact with some of these groups in the USA and in Europe, and collected data about their experiences with entheogenic tryptamine derivatives. He made this information available in his groundbreaking book, *The Toad and the Jaguar* (Metzner 2014). The main focus of this book is on a substance that seems particularly fascinating and promising, 5-methoxy-DMT, an active alkaloid of South American psychoactive snuffs and of the secretions of the parotid glands of the toad *Bufo alvarius.*

The book provides detailed information concerning the phenomenology of the experiences, therapeutic effects, modes of administration, the dose-effect relationship, impact of various settings, combination of entheogenic sessions with various forms of spiritual practice, and the comparison of 5-methoxy-DMT with its cousins DMT and bufotenine. What is particularly interesting seems to be the potential of 5-methoxy-DMT as a future therapeutic agent, because it is sufficiently powerful to induce therapeutic and transformative effects within a time period that does not put unreasonable demands on the therapists' schedule and makes it easier to contain the experience. With this substance, significant healing and transformation can often be achieved in not much longer than one session of psychoanalysis.

The Toad and the Jaguar is an extraordinary contribution to psychedelic literature that will one day be considered a classic. The information that it brings is sufficiently convincing to inspire clinical research of 5-methoxy-DMT. What immediately comes to mind is a study that would test the effects of this substance in the treatment of PTSD in veterans. It may have a good chance at approval because of the enormity of the psychiatric, economic, and political problems connected with this diagnostic category. Another important source of information about psychedelic therapy based on illicit clinical research is the book *Therapy with Substance: Psycholytic Psychotherapy in the Twenty-First Century* by German physician Friederike

Meckel Fischer, who was living in Switzerland (2015). She paid a great toll for her dedication to her patients; when it became known what work she was doing, she had to face tedious legal procedures and almost lost her medical license.

The Global Renaissance of Interest in Psychedelic Research

We are currently experiencing a remarkable worldwide renaissance of interest in the scientific research of psychedelic substances. This is an unexpected change after four decades during which official, legally sanctioned clinical work was virtually impossible. The credit for this remarkable turn of events goes to Rick Doblin and his enthusiastic team at the Multidisciplinary Association for Psychedelic Studies (MAPS) and their relentless effort to change this dismal situation. At present, new psychedelic research is being conducted at a number of American universities, including Harvard, Johns Hopkins, University of California in Los Angeles (UCLA), State University of New York (SUNY), University of California in San Francisco (UCSF), University of Arizona in Tucson, Arizona, and others.

Rick Doblin, (1953–), founder and executive director of the Multidisciplinary Association for Psychedelic Studies (MAPS).

The positive results of the groundbreaking research of MDMA-assisted psychotherapy with veterans suffering from Post-Traumatic Stress Disorder (PTSD), spearheaded by Michael and Annie Mithoefer in South Carolina, is of special interest (Mithoefer et al. 2014). According to official reports, more American soldiers stationed in Iraq and Afghanistan commit suicide because of PTSD than are killed by the enemy. And their suicidal and violent behavior continues after the soldiers return home. Since the formidable problems associated with this dangerous disorder resist traditional forms of therapy, this project might open the door for psychedelics into mainstream psychiatry. Phase 2 clinical trials of MDMA-assisted psychotherapy for PTSD have been conducted in South Carolina, Colorado, Canada, and Israel, and Phase 3 clinical trials are beginning in 2018. New research projects involving various cannabinoids, ibogaine, ketamine, and other psychedelic substances have been initiated worldwide.

Recently, unexpected justification for the work of the therapists who had decided to follow their own judgment and conscience rather than ignorant and misguided legislation, came in the form of an open letter from a prominent former government official. Dr. Peter Bourne, who had been the White House Drug Czar during Jimmy Carter's presidency, wrote a remarkable letter to the editor after reading an article in *The New Yorker* by Michael Pollan. This article, "The Trip Treatment," was about the use of psilocybin in medical treatment (Pollan 2015). In the letter, Bourne expressed his regret about the Carter government's unfortunate drug policy, and apologized to researchers who had continued to work with psychedelics in spite of a wrong administrative decision. This is his letter:

> *"Pollan's article about using psychedelics in medical treatments offers a sad commentary on how government funding for scientific research is influenced heavily by political and cultural values that are unrelated to science. With few exceptions, federal support for research on so-called drugs of abuse has taken into consideration only their adverse effects, reinforcing the bias of policymakers and funders. As a former director of the White House Office of Drug Abuse Policy, I now feel a sense of shame at having failed to try to reverse the Nixon-Ford policy that placed most psychedelics on the D.E.A.'s Schedule 1 list, prohibiting their use. Congress would*

almost certainly have blocked this change, but had we been able to lift the ban on scientific research into medical applications, doctors would probably now have a far better understanding of brain function, and the unnecessary suffering of many terminally ill patients could have been alleviated. We should applaud the heroic scientists and clinicians Pollan mentions, who are clearly committed to advancing the frontiers of science."

This letter might bring some satisfaction to the brave therapists who decided to be guided by scientific evidence and by their conviction that psychedelics were extremely useful therapeutic tools, rather than by irrational legislation engendered by mass hysteria. However, it cannot undo the damage that has been done to scientific progress and to the many thousands of patients who were deprived of the benefits of psychedelic treatment.

I am very proud of my brother Paul, professor of psychiatry at the University of Toronto, who as Chairman of the Expert Committee on Psychotropic Substances of the World Health Organization (WHO), opposed the decision to place MDMA in Schedule I, a category of substances with great abuse potential and no therapeutic value. Paul pointed out the many reports of therapists who had used MDMA informally and had observed significant improvement in their clients with post-traumatic stress disorder. His suggestion to not reclassify MDMA and to conduct more research before a final decision was made represents the only situation in the history of WHO in which the committee did not reach a unanimous decision. As there was no precedent for such a situation, the WHO had to call two lawyers, who debated for an hour and a half, about how to deal with this situation. Finally, they came up with the solution that the Chair can attach and publish an opposing position.

Search for a Manchurian Candidate

The history of psychonautics would not be complete without mentioning its shadow side. Not all inner journeys were taken with benevolent intentions, taken voluntarily, or even with the knowledge that it was happening. LSD, a colorless, tasteless, and incredibly potent substance, attracted the attention of secret services, intelligence agencies, and militaries worldwide. The CIA explored the potential of LSD to compromise foreign politicians and diplomats and to conduct brainwashing. In the infamous MK-ULTRA program, CIA agents introduced LSD into the San Francisco urban underworld and instructed hired prostitutes to secretly slip it into the drinks of their clients. They then observed through one-way screens how the substance changed the clients' behavior. They also surreptitiously added LSD into the drinks of people in various public places and observed how they responded. The justification that the CIA gave for its agents' criminal behavior was that the information was needed because Communist Russia, North Korea, and China were using psychedelics to brainwash captured Americans.

The military circles of various countries have been interested in LSD as a potential chemical weapon. One of the uses that was seriously considered was to contaminate the municipal water supply and use the resulting confusion to invade the afflicted cities. In experiments conducted with unsuspecting troops, soldiers secretly intoxicated with LSD and equipped with cameras attached to their guns were given specific tasks. Trained observers were assessing how accurate they were in aiming their guns, as well as other military activities. A different plan involved using LSD in aerosols and spraying the enemy's soldiers in the field.

When I was working in the Psychiatric Research Institute in Prague, we had the opportunity to realize how widespread the interest was in the military use of LSD. We conducted a clinical study of Niamid, a tricyclic antidepressant produced by Pfizer Pharmaceutical Company. We observed that the patients from this study showed no response to LSD for a period of three weeks after the treatment was discontinued. We thought this was an interesting observation and published a small article about it in an obscure Czech journal called *Activitas nervosa superior* (Grof and Dytrych 1965). Within a few weeks, we received, to our great surprise, more than one hundred requests for reprints from different countries of the world, mostly from facilities related to the military. We could imagine a scenario in which this information could be seen as valuable: soldiers pre-medicated with Niamid could operate safely in a territory contaminated by LSD.

Laboratory Psychonautics

So far, we have only explored psychonautics using psychedelic medicines. We should also add to this list the journeys mediated by various laboratory techniques for expanding consciousness. John Lilly, world famous researcher of dolphin intelligence and experimenter with psychedelic substances, developed a sensory isolation (sensory deprivation) tank, which induces holotropic states of consciousness by the significant reduction of meaningful sensory stimuli (Lilly 1977).

John Lilly's research was initially conceived to provide important information for the military. It was based on the observation that soldiers placed in solitary outposts can experience profound changes in consciousness, and pilots on solitary flights develop irrational behavior ("break-out phenomenon," or "empty cockpit syndrome"). Isolation was also known as one of the techniques used for interrogation and brainwashing. The early research of this phenomenon was inspired by the book *Alone,* written by Admiral Richard Byrd, American naval officer and polar explorer who spent six months alone in an Antarctic station, gathering weather data and fulfilling his desire "to taste peace and quiet long enough to know how good they really are." But early on, he began suffering inexplicable mental and physical disturbances (Byrd 2007).

In the extreme form of the sensory deprivation tank, which John Lilly built at the Maryland Psychiatric Research Center, the person in the experiment is deprived of sensory input by submersion in a large, dark and soundproof tank (about two meters high), filled with water at body temperature. Wearing a custom-made watertight mask and breathing through a plastic pipe, one can float in this tank for many hours like an embryo and experience a profound holotropic state of consciousness.

A smaller version of the Lilly tank is in the shape of a large box lined with plastic, containing a solution of Epsom salt (magnesium sulphate), which makes it possible to float on its surface. A thermostat ensures the temperature is close to that of the human body. John Lilly also designed a luxury version in the shape of a flying saucer for private experimentation, called the White Whale. It has become very popular among modern psychonauts.

Another well-known laboratory method of changing consciousness is biofeedback, developed by Elmer and Alyce Green, Barbara Brown, and others (Green and Green 1978, Brown 1974). The subject is attached to an EEG machine and asked to relax and meditate. He or she is guided by electronic feedback signals into holotropic states of consciousness, characterized by the preponderance of certain specific frequencies of brainwaves (alpha, theta, delta). The original machines were used for the feedback of acoustic signals of various frequencies.

Using acoustic stimuli is not a very engaging method and can even interfere with the experiment. Barbara Brown made the biofeedback method more interesting by using a Plexiglass lotus blossom with built-in electric lights of different colors assigned to specific frequencies. This lotus blossom starts glowing in darkness in a specific color when the subject produces a certain amount of waves of the desired frequency. In a version for children, the feedback could be provided by linking the production of a certain frequency of the brainwaves with the movement of an electric train. We could also mention here the techniques of sleep and dream deprivation, studied by William Dement and of lucid dreaming, developed by Stephen La Berge, as well as various devices combining stroboscopic

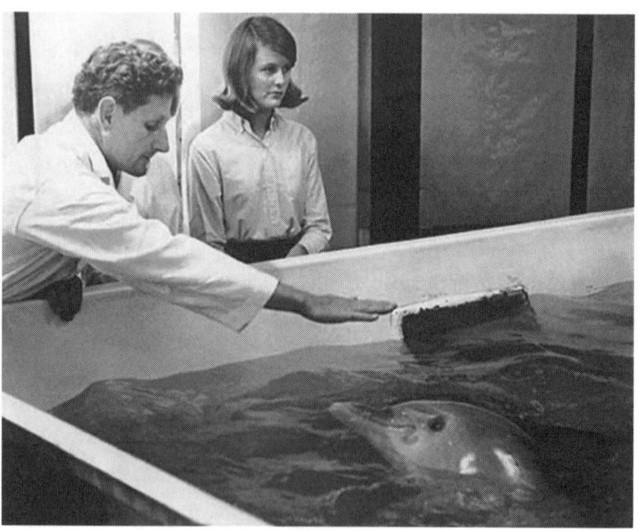

John Lilly (1915–2001), researcher of dolphin intelligence, sensory deprivation, and effects of psychedelic substances.

light, sound technology, body vibrations, kinesthetic stimulations, and others (Dement 1960, La Berge 1985).

It is important to emphasize that episodes of holotropic states of varying duration can also occur spontaneously (psychospiritual crises or spiritual emergencies). They are currently seen as a manifestation of mental illness (psychoses). Correctly understood and properly supported and treated, however, they can result in emotional and psychosomatic healing, positive personality transformation, and consciousness evolution. We will dedicate a special chapter later in the book to this important topic.

Literature

Abramson, H. A. and Evans, L. T. 1954. LSD-25: II. Psychobiological Effects on the Siamese Fighting Fish. *Science* 120:990-991.

Abramson, H. A., Weiss,B., and Baron, M. O. 1958. Comparison of Effect of Lysergic Acid Diethylamide with Potassium Cyanide and Other Respiratory Inhibitors on the Siamese Fighting Fish." *Nature* 181:1136-1137.

Allegro, J. 1970. *The Sacred Mushroom and the Cross: A Study of the Nature and Origin of Christianity within the Fertility Cults of the Ancient Near East.* New York: Doubleday.

Barrow, J. D. and Tipler, F. J. 1986. *The Anthropic Cosmological Principle.* Oxford: Clarendon Press.

Beringer, K. 1927. *Der Maskalinrausch (Mescaline Intoxication).* Berlin: Springer Verlag.

Brown, B. 1974. *New Mind, New Body: Bio Feedback: New Directions for the Mind.* New York:. Harper & Row.

Byrd, R. 2007. *Alone in the Antarctic.* Boston, MA: Sterling Point Books.

Campbell, J. 1968. *The Hero with A Thousand Faces.* Princeton, NJ: Princeton University Press.

Campbell, J. 1984. *The Way of the Animal Powers: The Historical Atlas of World Mythology.* San Francisco, CA: Harper.

Cicero, M.T. 1977. *De Legibus Libri Tres.* New York: Georg Olms Publishers.

Cohen, M. et al. 1968. The Effect of LSD-25 on the Chromosomes of

Children Exposed in Utero. *Pediat.Res.* 2; 486-492.

Cohen, S. 1960 Lysergic Acid Diethylamide: Side Effects and Complications. *J. Nervous and Mental Diseases* 130: 30-40.

Crowley, M. 2010. *Secret Drugs of Buddhism: Psychedelic Sacraments and the Origins of the Vajrayana.* United Kingdom: Psychedelic Press.

Dabrowski, K. 1964. *Positive Disintegration.* Boston, MA: Little Brown.

Dement, W. 1960. *Effect of Dream Deprivation.* Washington, DC: American Association for Advancement of Science.

Gennep, A. van 1960. *The Rites of Passage.* Chicago, IL: The University of Chicago Press.

Goswami, A. 1995. *The Self-Aware Universe: How Consciousness Creates the Material World.* Los Angeles, CA: J.P. Tarcher.

Green, E. E. and Green, A. M. 1978. *Beyond Biofeedback.* New York: Delacorte Press.

Griffiths, R. R., Richards, W. A., McCann, U., and Jesse, R. 2006. Psilocybine Can Occasion Mystical-Type Experience Having Substantial and Sustained Personal Meaning and Spiritual Meaning. *Psychopharmacology* 187-3: 268–283. |

Grof, S. 1959. Serotonin and Its Significance for Psychiatry (in Czech). *Csl. Psychiat.* 55:120.

Grof, S. and Dytrych, Z. 1965: Blocking of LSD Reaction by Premedication with Niamid. *Activ. nerv. super.* 7:306.

Grof, S. 1972. LSD and the Cosmic Game: Outline of Psychedelic Cosmology and Ontology. *Journal for the Study of Consciousness* 5:165.

Grof, S. 1975. *Realms of the Human Unconscious.* New York: Viking Press.

Grof, S. 1980. *LSD Psychotherapy.* Pomona, CA: Hunter House. Republished 2005, Santa Cruz, CA: MAPS Publications.

Grof, S. 1985. *Beyond the Brain: Birth, Death, and Transcendence in Psychotherapy.* Albany, NY: State University of New York Press.

Grof, S. and Grof, C. (eds.) 1989. *Spiritual Emergency: When Personal Transformation Becomes a Crisis.* Los Angeles, CA: J.P. Tarcher.

Grof, C. and Grof, S. 1990. *The Stormy Search for the Self: A Guide to Personal Growth through Transformational Crisis.* Los Angeles, CA: J. P. Tarcher.

Grof, S. (with Bennett, H. Z.) 1992. *The Holotropic Mind.* San Francisco, CA: Harper Publications.

Grof, S. 1994. *Books of the Dead: Manuals for Living and Dying.* London: Thames and Hudson.

Grof, S. 1998. *The Cosmic Game: Explorations of the Frontiers of Human Consciousness.* Albany, NY: State University of New York (SUNY) Press.

Grof, S. 2000. *Psychology of the Future: Lessons from Modern Consciousness Research.* Albany, N.Y: State University of New York (SUNY) Press.

Grof, S. 2006a. *When the Impossible Happens: Adventures in Non-Ordinary Realities.* Louisville, CO: Sounds True.

Grof, S. 2006b. *The Ultimate Journey: Consciousness and the Mystery of Death.* Santa Cruz, CA: MAPS Publications.

Grof, S. 2015. *Modern Consciousness Research and the Understanding of Art.* Santa Cruz, CA: MAPS Publications.

Hoffer, A. Osmond, H. and Smythies, J. 1954. Schizophrenia: A New Approach. II. Results of A Year's Research. *J. nerv.ment. Dis.* 100:29.

Hoffer, A. and Osmond, H. 1999. The Adrenochrome Hypothesis and Psychiatry. *The Journal of Orthomolecular Medicine* Vol. 14.

Hofmann, A. 2005. *LSD: My Problem Child.* Santa Cruz, CA: MAPS Publications.

Jamison, S. W. and Brererton, J. P. 2014. *Rig Veda Translation.* Oxford: Oxford University Press.

LaBerge, S. 1985. *Lucid Dreaming.* Los Angeles, CA: J.P. Tarcher.

Lash Lamb, J. 2008. *The Discovery of a Lifetime.* http://www.metahistory.org/psychonautics/Eadwine/Discovery.php.

Laszlo, E. 1993. *The Creative Cosmos.* Edinburgh: Floris Books.

Laszlo, E. 1995. *The Interconnected Universe: Conceptual Foundations of Transdisciplinary Unified Theory.* Singapore: World Scientific Publishing Company.

Laszlo, E. 2003. *The Connectivity Hypothesis: Foundations of An Integral Science of Quantum, Cosmos, Life, and Consciousness.* Albany, NY: State University of New York (SUNY) Press.

Laszlo, E. 2007. *Science and the Akashic Field: An Integral Theory of Everything.* Rochester, VT: Inner Traditions.

Laszlo, E. 2016. *What is Reality?: The New Map of Cosmos, Consciousness, and Existence.* Bayfield, CO: New Paradigm Publishers.

Lilly, J. 1977. *The Deep Self: Profound Relaxation and the Tank Isolation Technique.* New York: Simon and Schuster.

Masters, R. E. L., and Houston, J. 1968. *Psychedelic Art.* New York: Grove Press.

Mechoulam R. 1970. Marijuana Chemistry. *Science* 168:1159–66.

Meckel-Fischer, F. 2015. *Therapy with Substance: Psycholytic Psychotherapy in the Twenty-First Century.* London: Muswell Hill Press.

Merkur, D. 2000. *The Mystery of Manna: The Psychedelic Sacrament of the Bible.* Rochester, VT: Park Street Press.

Metzner, R. 2014. *The Toad and the Jaguar: A Field Report on Underground Research on a Visionary Medicine: Bufo Alvarius and 5-Methoxy-Dimethyltryptamine.* Verano, CA: Green Earth Foundation and Regent Press.

Mithoefer, M. et al. 2014. Durability of Improvement in Posttraumatic Stress Disorder Symptoms and Absence of Harmful Effects or Drug Dependency After 3,4-Methylene-Dioxy-Meth-Amphetamine-Assisted Psychotherapy: A Prospective Longterm Follow-Up Study. *Journal of Psychopharmacology* 27:28.

Naranjo, C. 1974. *The Healing Journey: New Approaches to Psychedelic Therapy.* New York: Pantheon Books.

Pahnke, W. N. 1963. "Drugs and Mysticism: An Analysis of the Relationship Between Psychedelic Drugs and the Mystical Consciousness." Ph. D. Dissertation, Harvard University.

Pollan, M. 2015. The Trip Treatment. *The New Yorker,* February 9 issue.

Schele, L. and Miller, M.E. 1986. *The Blood of Kings.* New York: George Brazille.

Sheldrake, R. 1981. *New Science of Life: The Hypothesis of Formative Causation.* Los Angeles, CA: J.P. Tarcher.

Shroder, T. 2014. *Acid Test: LSD, Ecstasy, and the Power to Heal.* New York: Blue Rider Press/Penguin Group.

Shulgin, A. and Shulgin, A. 1991. *PiHKAL: A Chemical Love Story.* Berkeley, CA: Transform Press.

Shulgin, A. and Shulgin, A. 1997. *TiHKAL: A Continuation.* Berkeley, CA: Transform Press.

Stolaroff, M. 1997. *The Secret Chief.* Santa Cruz, CA: MAPS Publications.

Stoll, W. A. 1947. "LSD-25, ein Phantastikum aus der Mutterkorngruppe" (LSD, A Fantasticum from the Ergot Group). Schweiz.Arch. *Neurol. Psychiat.* 60:279.

Teilhard de Chardin, P. 1975. *The Human Phenomenon.* New York: Harper and Row.

Ulansey, D. 1989. *Origins of the Mithraic Mysteries: Cosmology and Salvation in the Ancient World.* Oxford: Oxford University Press.

Vojtěchovský, M. and Grof, S. 1960. Similarities and Differences Between Experimental Psychoses After LSD and Mescaline (in Czech). *Csl. Psychiat.* 56:221.

Wasson, G., Hofmann, A., and Ruck, C. A. P. 1978. *The Road to Eleusis: Unveiling the Secret of the Mysteries.* New York: Harcourt, Brace Jovanovich.

Wasson, G. and Wasson, V.P. 1957. *Mushrooms, Russia, and History.* New York: Pantheon Books.

Wasson, R. G. 1982. The Last Meal of the Buddha. *Journal of the American Oriental Society* Vol. 102, No. 4.

Watts, A. 1973. *The Book on the Taboo Against Knowing Who You Are.* London: Sphere Books.

Weil, A. 1972. *The Natural Mind.* Boston: Houghton Mifflin.

Woolley, D.W. and Shaw, E. 1954. A Biochemical and Pharmacological Suggestion about Certain Mental Disorders. *Proceedings of the National Academy of Sciences* 40, 228–231.

II

The Revision and Re-Enchantment of Psychology: *Legacy from a Half Century of Consciousness Research*

The history of psychonautics explored at the beginning of this book examined the pivotal role that holotropic states of consciousness played in the spiritual, ritual, and cultural life of ancient societies and aboriginal cultures. We also reviewed the detrimental effect that the periods of the Industrial and Scientific Revolution and the Ages of Enlightenment and Reason had on the image, status, and cultivation of these states. This year, we are celebrating the seventy-fifth anniversary of Albert Hofmann's discovery of the psychedelic effects of LSD-25, an event that became a critical turning point in the history of psychonautics.

The initial excitement engendered by the consciousness revolution that LSD and other psychedelics brought into modern society was unfortunately short-lived. Irrational legal and administrative sanctions effectively terminated all scientific research and drove the experimentation with psychedelics underground. Albert Hofmann's vision of a New Eleusis, a society that would succeed in integrating the responsible use of psychedelic medicines into mainstream life for the benefit of all humanity, seemed like a sad pipe dream.

After a dark era of psychonautics that lasted several decades, we are currently experiencing a global renaissance of interest in the scientific research of psychedelic medicines, as well as lay self-experimentation with them. One way of looking at this renaissance is to see it as rectifying the errors of ignorant legislators and correcting the course of the evolution of psychiatry. From another perspective, though, it means rejoining the rest of humanity in appreciating and using the extraordinary potential of holotropic states. Our industrial civilization has so far been the only group in human history that has not recognized and utilized their value. This surprising development inspired me to write this Encyclopedia for Inner Journeys, so that the information about consciousness and the human psyche that I have amassed during sixty years of research is available for the new generation of researchers and for future psychonauts. I believe this information is essential for maximizing the positive potential of these states and minimizing their risks.

Discovering Holotropic States: A Journey Down Memory Lane

My own interest in consciousness research began in the fourth year of my medical studies, when I began spending my free time working as a student volunteer at the Psychiatric Clinic of the Medical Faculty in Prague. I was fascinated by the lectures of Professor Vladimír Vondráček, a brilliant, charismatic man with a physical resemblance to George Bernard Shaw or Moulin Rouge's Valentin le Désossé. Professor Vondráček's special interest was to find and present the cases of psychiatric patients whose personalities and clinical symptoms resembled those of famous historical figures, particularly saints, prophets, and founders of religions.

It was not until twenty years later, when my wife Christina and I developed the concept of "spiritual emergency," that I became critical of Professor Vondráček's book *The Phantastical and Magical from the Point of View of Psychiatry* (Vondráček 1968). Another book of his, however, became important for my professional development. It was his classic *Pharmacology of the Soul* that brought a group of psychoactive substances that later became known as psychedelics to the attention of Czech psychiatrists (Vondráček 1935).

At the time, there was another source of information related to psychedelics available in Czech literature—the essays by psychiatrist and phar-

Hunting scene from the Lascaux cave showing a wounded eviscerated bison pierced with a spear and a lying figure with an erect penis, most likely a shaman in trance (top).

Two clay bison effigies from the Tuc d'Audoubert cave surrounded by a circle of foot-prints.

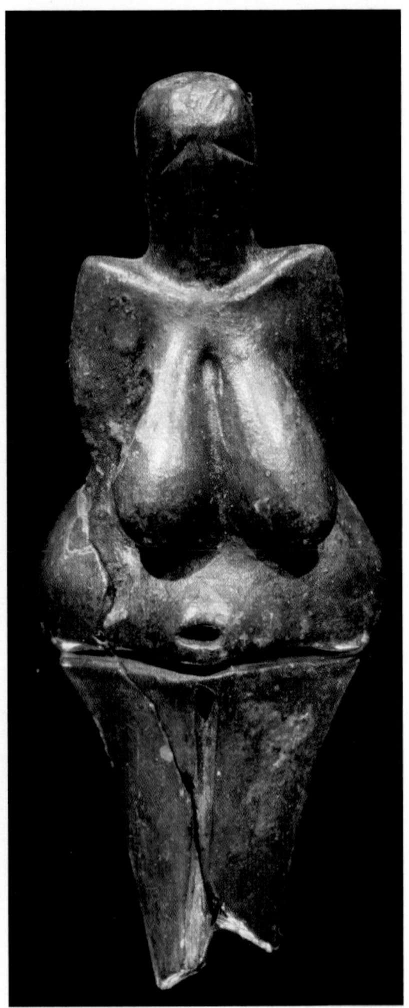

Venus of Willendorf, limestone figure from the Upper Paleolithic, ca. 25,000 BC (left).

Venus of Dolní Věstonice, a Paleolithic statuette, found in Moravia, one of the oldest ceramic pieces in the world, ca. 29,000 – 25,000 BC.

Venus of Laussel, an Upper Paleolithic limestone bas-relief ca. 25,000 years old, found in a rock shelter in the Dordogne region.

Pinax of Persephone and Hades from Locri. Reggio Calabria, National Museum of Magna Graecia (top).

Mithras killing the bull from ca. 150 AD, Louvre-Lens.

Sermon on Mushroom Mountain. Eadwine Psalter, National Library in Paris, twelfth century.

Jesus tempted by an antlered shaman-devil in a mushroom grove. Eadwine Psalter, National Library in Paris, twelfth century.

Buddha's Parinirvana. All of nature mourning the death of the Buddha.

Xochipilli, Lord of Flowers, god of flowers, love, and dance, in an enthogenic trance. The sculpture is decorated with reliefs of psychedelic plants (tendrils of *Ipomoea violacea, Nicotiana tabacum, Rivea corymbosa, Psilocybe aztecorum,* and *Heimia solicifolia).* National Museum of Anthropology, Mexico City.

Bird Jaguar and his wife Lady Balam-Ix performing a blood-letting ritual. Bird Jaguar is perforating his penis and his wife her tongue. Yaxchilan, Chiapas, Mexico. Mayan Late Classic Period, AD 770.

King Shield Jaguar holds a large torch illuminating the dark place where his wife, Lady Choc is performing a blood-letting ritual by perforating her tongue with a thorn-lined rope. Yaxchilan, Chiapas Mexico. Mayan Late Classic Period, AD 725.

Lady Choc, wife of Shield Jaguar, encountering the vision of an ancestor emerging from the Vision Serpent, Mayan symbol for visionary experiences. Yaxchilan, Chiapa, Mexico, Mayan Late Classic Period, AD 770.

Scene of death and rebirth from a turtle carapace. This tripod shows Hun Hunahpu, the father of the Hero Twins, with a headdress of quetzal feathers, emerging from a cracked turtle carapace decorated by a skull. Attending him are his sons Hunahpu and Xbalanque. Mayan Ceramic Codex, Mayan Late Classic Period.

Tlalocan, paradise of the Aztec Rain God Tlaloc. Tlaloc is pouring rain from both hands; he is flanked by two priests making offerings and planting seeds. Harvard ethnobotanist Richard Schultes identified the mushrooms lining the streams of seeds as caps of *Psilocybe* mushrooms. One of the ways to get into Tlaloc's earthly paradise was to ingest these "magic mushrooms." (Teotihuacan, Mexico, fourth-eighth century).

Stanislav Grof visiting Albert Hofmann in the Hofmann residence in Berg, a village on the Swiss-French border (top).

Stanislav and Christina Grof and visionary artists Martina Hoffmann and Roberto Venosa visiting Albert Hofmann in his home in Berg.

Swiss fantastic realist Hansruedi Giger guiding Albert Hofmann and Stanislav Grof through his museum in Gruyères in September 2005, four months before Hofmann's 100th birthday (top).

H. R. Giger and Stanislav Grof visiting Albert Hofmann in Berg four weeks before his death at the age of 102.

Anne and Sasha Shulgin, pioneering researchers of psychedelic and entheogenic substances and authors of *PiHKAL* and *TiHKAL* (top).

Stanislav Grof visiting biochemist and psychopharmacologist Sasha Shulgin in his laboratory in Lafayette, California, where Shulgin synthesized over 200 psychoactive substances.

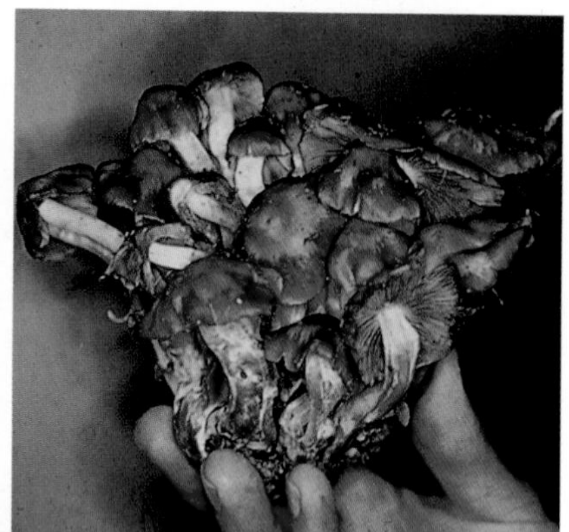

The house of Mazatec curandera Maria Sabina in the Mexican village Huautla de Jimenez in Oaxaca, where she conducted her magic mushroom ceremony, called *velada* (top left); *Psilocybe caerulescens,* var. *aztecorum,* "magic mushroom" of the Mazatecs (top right); Gordon Wasson buying *Psilocybe* mushrooms in a Mazatec market in Huautla de Jimenez (bottom).

Facing page: Maria Sabina giving Gordon Wasson his dose of mushrooms (top); Gordon Wasson in the middle of his mushroom experience in the syncretistic setting of the sacred ceremony *velada* (center); Gordon and Valentina Pavlovna Wasson sampling the mushrooms for the transport to Europe (bottom).

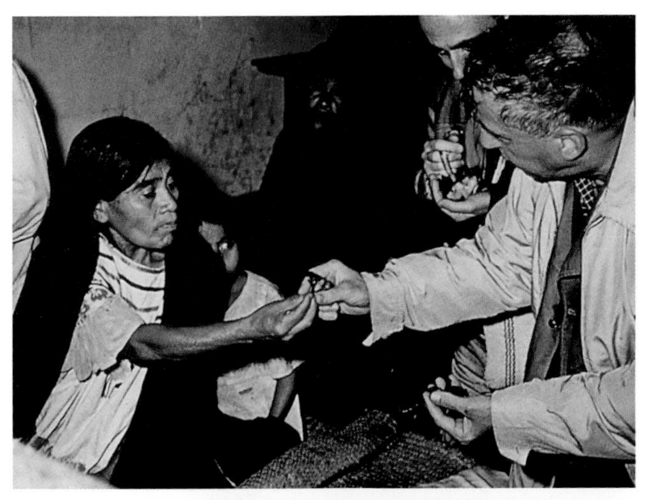

Leo Zeff (right) the "Secret Chief," Jungian analyst, and pioneering psychedelic therapist, who introduced LSD and MDMA to hundreds of his fellow therapists, with Rick Doblin (top).

Michael and Annie Mithoefer, psychedelic therapists conducting pioneering research of MDMA psychotherapy in patients with PTSD.

Czech President Václav Havel and his wife Dagmar, along with Stanislav Grof and his late wife Christina with the Vision 97 Award—a copy of the crossier of tenth century Bohemian martyred Christian Saint Adalbert of Prague (top); astronomy professor Jiří Grygar, dressed in an antique robe while performing the Delusional Boulder ceremony (middle); three mock awards of the Prague Sisyfos Club: the Bronze, Silver, and Golden Delusional Boulders (bottom).

Brigitte and Stan Grof visiting Richard Alpert (Ram Dass) in Maui, Hawaii. Ram Dass (1931–), is a former Harvard Professor of Psychology who became a psychedelic pioneer and world-renowned spiritual teacher.

Brigitte and Stanislav Grof with Ervin Laszlo and Maria Sági at the International Transpersonal Conference in Prague in September 2017 (top).

Raymond Moody (1944 –), psychologist, philosopher, and thanatologist, pioneer in the research of near-death experiences (NDE) with Stanislav Grof at the 2017 International Transpersonal Conference in Prague.

Three paintings depicting Katia Solani's experiences in Holotropic Breathwork: identification with a turtle carrying on her belly the image of a child needing nourishment (top left); the image of a beautiful landscape decorating the back of the turtle's shell (top right); picture of the same landscape as it appeared in a dream on the night following the session (bottom).

Amniotic universe, a painting representing a blissful episode of intrauterine life (BPM I) in a high-dose LSD session. Regression to prenatal life mediates access to the experience of oneness with the cosmos. The shape of the galaxy resembling a female breast ("Milky Way") suggests simultaneous experiential connection with the memories of the "good breast" (top).

Hostile Womb, a painting from an LSD session depicting the experience of a womb that is attacking the fetus. The aggressive immunological forces take the form of archetypal animals. (Robin Maynard-Dobbs)

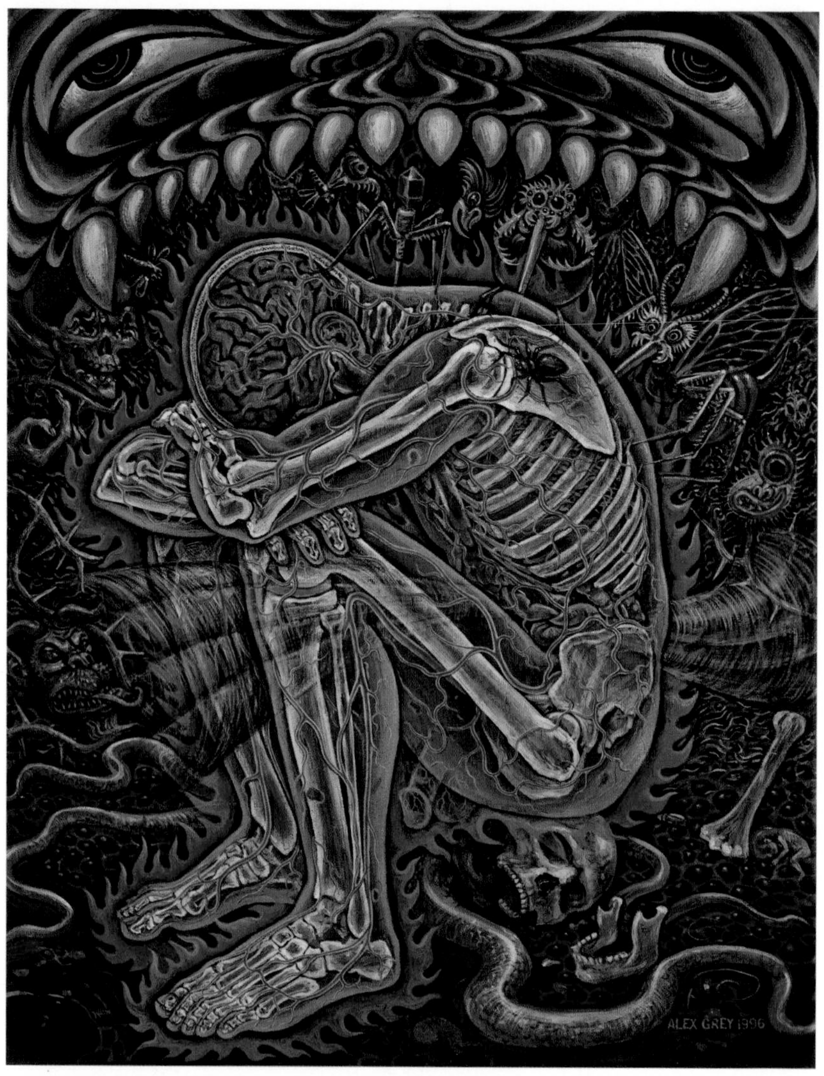

Despair, a painting by visionary artist Alex Grey, inspired by psychedelic medicine. This image has classic features of BPM II—crushing no-exit atmosphere, skull, jaws, fangs, bones, snakes, and spiders.

Biomechanoid II, a self-portrait by Swiss visionary artist and fantastic realist H. R. Giger. He created this painting as a poster for the Sydow-Zirkwitz Gallery. Inspired by the memory of his birth, the artist portrayed himself as a helpless Indian warrior, with a steel ring on his forehead, and encased in a heavy metal cage.

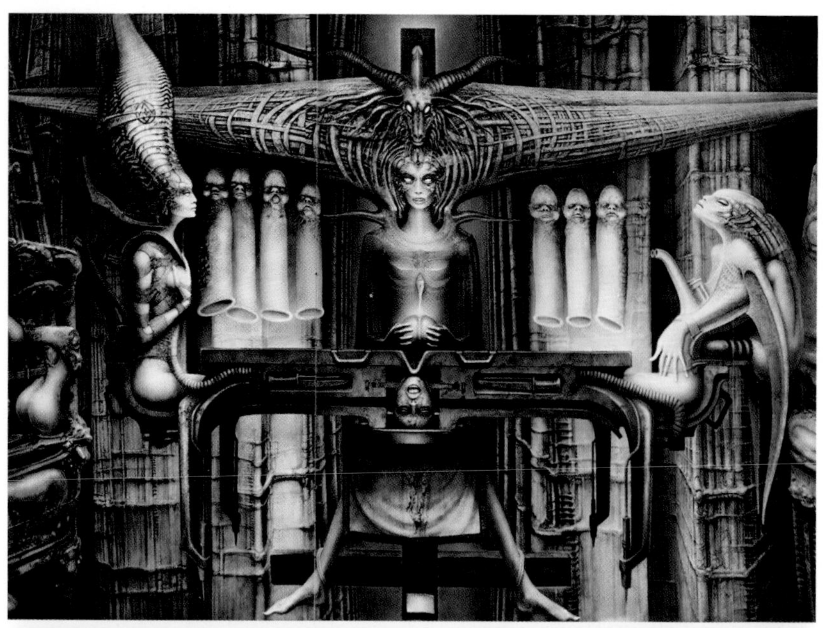

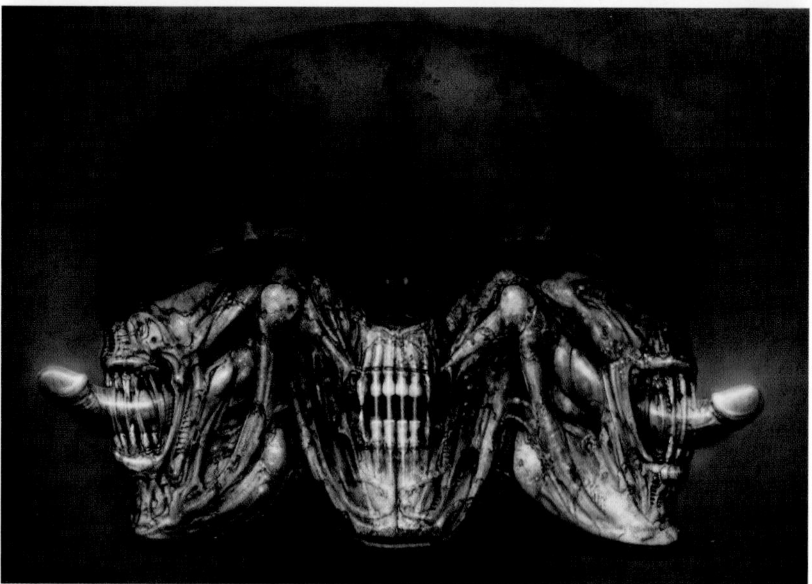

Spell, from a series by H. R. Giger, shows many characteristic motifs of BPM III. A Kaliesque female deity with the head of Baphonet above her, and below her a human head crushed in a vice, flanked by a skeletal hairdo, and phallic condom fetuses (top).

Necronom II, by H. R. Giger. This composition has all the characteristics of BPM III—soldier's helmets, skulls, fangs, and phalluses.

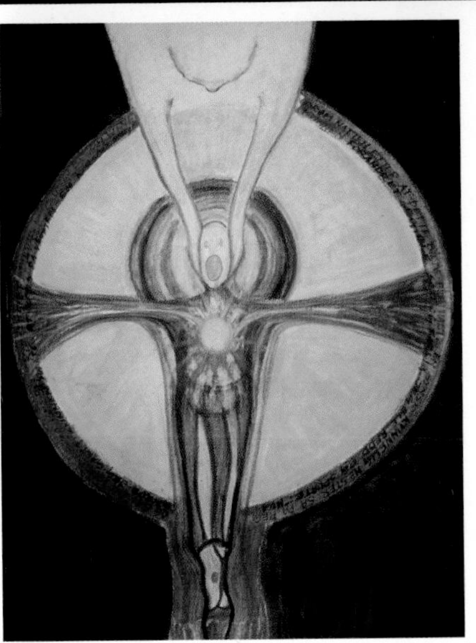

Nuclear Crucifixion by Alex Grey. Experience of death and rebirth in a psychedelic session connected to BPM II–IV. A vision of crucified Christ appears in a gigantic expanse (top).

A painting from a Holotropic Breathwork session, in which reliving of manual help during the final stages of birth was associated with experiential identification with crucified Christ.

Experience from a high-dose LSD session featuring a wild carnival scene during the transition from BPM III to BPM IV—symbols of death are not frightening any more, but appearing in an atmosphere of exuberant celebration and release of sexual and aggressive energy (top).

A painting from a psychedelic session, capturing the experience of the last seconds before being re/born. The triangle in the center is the place where the vortex of the fetus' head breaks through and the fiery red, yellow, and orange colors represent the explosive energies involved in this situation.

Out of Darkness, a painting representing the combined experience of being born and giving birth in a session of Holotropic Breathwork. Experiences of this kind typically result in a sense of giving birth to a new self (or Self) and can be very transformative and healing (Jean Perkins) (top).

Liberation, from an experience of psycho-spiritual death and rebirth in a Holotropic Breathwork session. The old personality structure has fallen apart and out of it emerges a new self (or Self), connected to the spiritual domain. Dismemberment is a frequent motif in the initiatory experiences of novice shamans. (Jaryna Moss)

Painting from an LSD session, depicting the experience of psychospiritual rebirth. Fire emerges from the vagina of the Great Mother Goddess, supported by nourishing Cosmic Hands. The upper part of the painting represents BPM IV, and the lower part the star-filled sky. The nourishing hands represent BPM I: a symbol of the uterus providing nourishment and safety (top). A painting from a psychedelic session depicting experiential identification with the Phoenix, an archetypal symbol of psychospiritual death and rebirth mediated by fire.

A painting depicting the final stage of the psychospiritual process of death and rebirth in a psychedelic session. The body of the newborn is still in the birth canal consumed by flames, but its head emerges into a peacock heaven of the Great Mother Goddess.

Psychospiritual death and rebirth from a Holotropic Breathwork session. Through the air flies a powerful swan toward the sun.The swan is a spirit bird that plays an important role in Siberian shamanism (top).

Mother Kundalini, a painting from a Holotropic Breathwork session. A woman with a fiery garment and wrapped in a star mantle. A small Divine Child rests in a papoose on her back. The artist wrote: "I was both the mother and the child. I loved this Great Mother deeply, I loved my mother, I loved every creature, every sentient being" (Katia Solani).

macologist Svetozar Nevole, *Apropos of Four-Dimensional Vision: Study of Physiopathology of the Spatial Sense with Special Regard to Experimental Intoxication with Mescaline* (Nevole 1947) and *Apropos of Sensory Illusions and Their Formal Genesis* (Nevole 1949). I was thus already familiar with and interested in psychedelics before LSD came into my life. After Albert Hofmann's discovery of LSD's psychedelic effects and the publication of Werner Stoll's pilot study, the Sandoz Pharmaceutical Company was sending free samples of LSD to universities, psychiatric institutes, and individual researchers and therapists all over the world.

My preceptor at the psychiatric clinic, Dr. George Roubíček, was one of the people who received a large package of 25 mcg dragees and a big box of 100 mcg ampoules of LSD-25 with the trade name Delysid. The letter accompanying the package described Albert Hofmann's discovery of the psychedelic effects of LSD and the results of Werner Stoll's pilot study. It asked the recipients if they would be interested in conducting research with this substance and to give Sandoz feedback about its effects, as well as its potential use in psychiatry and psychology.

Dr. Stoll's paper pointed out some interesting similarities between the LSD experience and the symptomatology of naturally occurring psychoses. It seemed plausible that the study of such "experimental psychoses"

Dr. Vladimir Vondráček (1895–1978), leading Czech psychiatrist, long-term head of the Psychiatric Clinic of the medical faculty in Prague, one of the founders of Czech psychopharmacology and sexology, and popularizer of psychiatry.

could provide interesting insights into the causes of naturally occurring psychotic states, particularly schizophrenia, the most enigmatic of psychiatric disorders. Werner Stoll also suggested that LSD should be tested as a possible therapeutic agent.

The letter from Sandoz also contained a little note that became my destiny and profoundly changed my personal and professional life. It suggested that this substance might be used as a revolutionary, unconventional educational tool for mental health professionals working with psychotic patients. The possibility of experiencing a reversible "experimental psychosis" seemed to provide a unique opportunity for psychiatrists, psychologists, psychiatric nurses, social workers, and students of psychiatry to gain intimate personal knowledge of the inner world of their clients. It would make it possible to understand them better, be able to communicate with them more effectively, and, as a result, treat them more successfully. New therapeutic strategies were sorely needed at a time when the treatments were truly medieval—insulin comas, electroconvulsive therapy, cardiazol shocks, and prefrontal lobotomy.

I was at that point becoming disillusioned by psychoanalysis, realizing the amount of time and money it required and how unimpressive the results were. I was extremely excited about such an extraordinary training opportunity and asked Dr. Roubíček if I could have an LSD session. Unfortunately, the staff of the psychiatric clinic decided that, for a variety of reasons, students would not be accepted as volunteers. Dr. Roubíček was very interested in the new substance, but too busy to spend hours at a time in the LSD sessions of his experimental subjects. He needed help, and there were no objections against me supervising the psychedelic sessions of others and keeping records of their experiences.

I thus had sat in the LSD sessions of many Czech psychiatrists and psychologists, prominent artists, and other interested persons before I myself qualified as an experimental subject. By the time I graduated from the medical school and was myself eligible for a session, my appetite had been repeatedly whetted by fantastic accounts of the experiences of others that I had witnessed. In the fall of 1956, after my graduation from the medical school, I was finally able to have my own LSD session.

Dr. Roubíček's area of special interest was research of the electrical activity of the brain. One of the conditions for participating in the LSD study was to agree to have an EEG recording taken before, during, and after the session. In addition, at the time of my session, he was particularly fascinated by what was called "driving" or "entraining" the brain waves. This involved exposure to various frequencies of a strong flashing stroboscopic light and finding out to what extent the brain waves in the suboccipital area of the brain (the optical cortex) could be "entrained," that is, forced to pick up the incoming frequency. Eager to have the LSD experience, I readily agreed to have my EEG taken and my brain waves "driven."

My brother Paul, who was at that time a medical student and was also deeply interested in psychiatry, agreed to supervise my session. I started feeling the effects of LSD about forty-five minutes after the ingestion. At first, there was a feeling of slight malaise, lightheadedness, and nausea. Then these symptoms disappeared and were replaced by a fantastic display of incredibly colorful abstract and geometrical visions unfolding in rapid kaleidoscopic sequences. Some of them resembled exquisite stained glass windows in medieval Gothic cathedrals, others arabesques from Muslim mosques. To describe the exquisite nature of these visions, I made references to Sheherezade and *A Thousand and One Nights* and to the stunning beauty of Alhambra and Samuel Taylor Coleridge's fantastic description of Kubla Khan's legendary Xanadu.

At the time, these were the only associations I was able to make. Today, I believe that my psyche somehow managed to produce a wild array of fractal images, similar to the graphic representations of nonlinear equations that can be created by modern computers. As the session continued, my experience moved through and beyond this realm of exquisite aesthetic rapture and changed into an encounter and confrontation with my unconscious psyche. It is difficult to find words for the intoxicating fugue of emotions, visions, and illuminating insights into my life, and existence in general, that became available to me on this level of my psyche. It was so profound and shattering that it instantly overshadowed my previous interest in Freudian psychoanalysis. I could not believe how much I learned in those few hours.

The breathtaking aesthetic feast and the rich plethora of psychological insights would have been sufficient in and of themselves to make my first encounter with LSD a truly memorable experience. However, all that paled in comparison with what was yet to come. Between the third and fourth hour of my session, when the effect of the LSD was culminating, Dr. Roubiček's research assistant appeared and announced that it was time for the EEG experiment. She took me to a small room, carefully pasted electrodes on my scalp, and asked me to lie down and close my eyes. She then placed a giant stroboscopic light above my head and turned it on.

The effects of the LSD immensely amplified the impact of the strobe and I was hit by a vision of light of incredible radiance and supernatural beauty. It made me think of the accounts of mystical experiences I had read about in spiritual literatures, in which the visions of divine light were compared with the incandescence of "millions of suns." It crossed my mind that this was what it must have been like at the epicenter of the atomic explosions in Hiroshima or Nagasaki. Today, I think it was more like Dharmakaya, or the Primary Clear Light, the luminosity of indescribable brilliance that, according to *The Tibetan Book of the Dead, Bardo Thödol,* appears to us at the moment of our death.

I felt that a divine thunderbolt had catapulted my conscious self out of my body. I lost my awareness of the research assistant, the laboratory, the psychiatric clinic, Prague, and then the planet. My consciousness expanded at an inconceivable speed and reached cosmic dimensions. I lost the connection with my everyday identity. There were no more boundaries or difference between me and the universe. I felt that my old personality was extinguished and that I ceased to exist. And I felt that by becoming nothing, I became everything.

The research assistant carefully followed her protocol for the experiment. She gradually shifted the frequency of the strobe from two to sixty hertz (frequencies per second) and back again, and then put it for a short time to the middle of the alpha band, theta band, and finally the delta band. While this was happening, I found myself at the center of a cosmic drama of unimaginable dimensions. In the astronomical literature that I read over the following years, I found names for some of the phenomena that seemed like what I experienced during those extraordinary ten minutes—the Big Bang, passage through black holes, white holes, and wormholes, as well as exploding supernovas and collapsing stars.

Although I had no adequate words for what had happened to me, there was no doubt in my mind that my experience was very close to those I knew from the great mystical scriptures of the world. Even though my psyche was deeply affected by the effects of LSD, I was able to see the irony and paradox of the situation. The Divine manifested and took me over in the middle of a serious scientific experiment, involving a substance produced in the test tube of a twentieth-century Swiss chemist, and conducted in a psychiatric clinic in a country that was dominated by the Soviet Union and had a Communist regime. I could see how experiences of this kind would make people lose interest in bloody revolution and become the "opium of the masses."

This day marked the beginning of my radical departure from traditional thinking in psychiatry and from the monistic materialism of Western science. I emerged from this experience touched to the core and immensely impressed by its power. Not believing at that time, as I do today, that the potential for a mystical experience is the natural birthright of all human beings, I attributed everything that happened to the combined effect of LSD and the stroboscopic light. But I felt strongly that the study of non-ordinary states of consciousness, in general, and those induced by psychedelics, in particular, was by far the most interesting area of psychiatry I could imagine. I realized that, under the proper circumstances, psychedelic experiences could become a "royal road into the unconscious," to a much greater degree than dreams were for Freud. And right there and then, I decided to dedicate my life to the study of non-ordinary states of consciousness. For the rest of my life, this research has been my profession, vocation, and passion.

The Emperor's New Clothes: Struggle with the Dominant Paradigm

The six decades that I have dedicated to consciousness research have been an extraordinary adventure of discovery and self-discovery. I spent the first two of them conducting psychotherapy with psychedelic substances, initially as principal investigator at the Psychiatric Research Institute in Prague, Czechoslovakia, and then at the Maryland Psychiatric Research Center in Baltimore, Maryland, where I participated in the last surviving official American psychedelic research program. Beginning in 1975, my wife Christina and I worked with Holotropic Breathwork, a powerful method of therapy and self-exploration that we jointly developed at the Esalen Institute in Big Sur, California. Over the years, we also supported many people undergoing spontaneous episodes of holotropic states of consciousness—psychospiritual crises or "spiritual emergencies," as we called them (Grof and Grof 1989, Grof and Grof 1991).

In psychedelic therapy, holotropic states are brought about by administering consciousness-expanding substances, such as LSD, psilocybin, mescaline, and tryptamine or amphetamine derivatives. In Holotropic Breathwork, consciousness is changed by a combination of faster breathing, evocative music, and energy-releasing bodywork. In spiritual emergencies, holotropic states occur spontaneously, in the middle of everyday life, and their cause is usually unknown. If they are correctly understood and supported, these episodes have an extraordinary healing, transformative, heuristic, and even evolutionary potential.

I have also been tangentially involved in many disciplines that are more or less directly related to holotropic states of consciousness. I have spent a lot of time exchanging information with anthropologists and have participated in sacred ceremonies of native cultures in different parts of the world, with and without the ingestion of psychedelic plants such as peyote, ayahuasca, Psilocybe mushrooms, and kava kava. This involved contact with various North American, Mexican, South American, African, and Ainu shamans and healers. I have also had extensive contact with representatives of various spiritual disciplines, including Vipassana, Zen, and Vajrayana Buddhism, Siddha Yoga, Tantra, and the Christian Benedictine order.

In addition, I have closely followed the development of thanatology, the young discipline studying near-death experiences and the psychological and spiritual aspects of death and dying. In the late 1960s and early 1970s, I participated in a large research project, studying the effects of psychedelic therapy for individuals dying of cancer (Grof 2006b). I have also been privileged to personally know some of the great psychics and parapsychologists of our era, pioneers of laboratory consciousness research, and therapists who had developed and practiced powerful forms of experiential therapy that induce holotropic states of consciousness. Some of my clients and trainees have experienced UFO and alien abduction phenomena, so I closely followed the work of John Mack, Harvard psychoanalyst and dear friend of mine, who conducted a large, controversial and widely publicized study of the alien abduction syndrome.

My initial encounter with holotropic states was very difficult and challenging, both intellectually and emotionally. In the early years of my laboratory and clinical psychedelic research, I was bombarded daily with experiences and observations for which my medical and psychiatric training had not prepared me. As a matter of fact, I was experiencing and observing things that were considered impossible in the context of the scientific worldview I had obtained during my medical training. And yet, those supposedly impossible things were happening all the time. I have described these "anomalous phenomena" before in my articles and books (Grof 2000, 2006a).

It took me years of daily participation in sessions with my patients and dozens of my own sessions before I was able to finally overcome the last remnants of the awe and respect that medical students and novice psychiatrists have for university professors and other scientific authorities. The influx of revolutionary data was inexorable. I eventually came to a firm conviction that the proud edifice of traditional psychiatry, with its mechanistic materialistic philosophy, is a giant on clay legs that stands in the way of genuine understanding of the human psyche and has a damaging effect on many people diagnosed as mentally ill. So I decided to dedicate my life and work to a concerted effort aimed at changing the dominant paradigm.

Holotropic States of Consciousness and Psychiatry

Psychedelic research and the development of experiential therapeutic techniques in the second half of the twentieth century moved holotropic states of consciousness from the world of healers of ancient and native cultures into modern psychiatry and psychotherapy. Therapists who were open to these new approaches and used them in their practice or their own self-exploration like myself were able to confirm the extraordinary healing potential of holotropic states. We discovered their value as goldmines of revolutionary new information about consciousness, the human psyche, and the nature of reality. I have described these paradigm-breaking observations in a series of books published between the mid-1970s and the end of the 1990s.

In the late 1990s, I received a phone call from Jane Bunker, my editor at State University of New York (SUNY) Press, who had published several of my books exploring different aspects of my work. She asked me if I would consider writing a book in one volume that would summarize the observations from my research, and would also serve as an introduction to my earlier books. She also asked if I could specifically focus on the experiences and observations from my research that current scientific theories are not able to explain, and suggest the revisions in our thinking that would be necessary to account for these revolutionary findings. After some hesitation, she added an even more challenging request: she asked me if I could try sketching what psychiatry and psychology would look like if we integrate all these paradigm-breaking observations.

This was a tall order, but also a great opportunity. My seventieth birthday was rapidly approaching and a new generation of facilitators was conducting our Holotropic Breathwork training all over the world. We needed a manual covering the material that was taught in our training modules, and here was an unexpected opportunity to publish a guidebook that would bring homogeneity into our training. I decided to write the book Jane had asked for and gave it a deliberately provocative title: *Psychology of the Future.* I realized that if I gave it a name like my previous books—*Beyond the Brain, The Holotropic Mind,* or *The Stormy Search for the Self*—it might get lukewarm attention from potential readers.

A title proposing what psychology should look like in the future seemed to be more eye-catching and engaging. Potential readers would get either interested in what I might be offering or challenged and irritated by such a presumptuous title. By the time I wrote the book, though, I was convinced that my conclusions were correct and that they would be confirmed in the future research of holotropic states, however long that might take.

The new psychology that I outlined in the book *Psychology of the Future* is absolutely necessary and indispensable if we want to start practicing psychonautics or understand any problems or issues related to holotropic states of consciousness. In various chapters of this encyclopedia, I draw on the observations and experiences from the research of these states, so I will first outline—as a general frame of reference—the basic features of this new psychology. I will describe the radical changes in our thinking about the human psyche in health and disease, about consciousness, and even about the nature of reality that it requires.

Modern Consciousness Research and the Dawning of a New Paradigm

I would like to set the discussion about the necessary revision of thinking in psychiatry and psychology into a larger historical context. In 1962, Thomas Kuhn, one of the most influential philosophers of the twentieth century, published his groundbreaking book *The Structure of Scientific Revolutions* (Kuhn 1962). On the basis of fifteen years of intensive study on the history of science, he demonstrated that the development of knowledge about the universe in various scientific disciplines is not a process of gradual accumulation of data and the formulation of ever more accurate theories, as is usually assumed. Instead, it shows a clearly cyclical nature with specific stages and characteristic dynamics which can even be predicted.

The central concept of Kuhn's theory, which makes this possible, is that of a *paradigm*. A paradigm can be defined as a constellation of basic metaphysical assumptions, beliefs, values, and techniques shared by the members of the community at a particular historical period. It also determines what are legitimate areas and topics for scientific research and how to conduct it and evaluate it. During the period when a dominant paradigm guides the thinking and activity of the academic community, scientists are doing what Kuhn calls "normal science," which is essentially problem-solving within a set of established rules, similar to playing chess.

A dominant paradigm maintains its governing influence on scientists until some of its basic assumptions are seriously challenged by new observations. Initially, the scientific community dismisses the inconvenient findings as products of bad science, attributing them to lack of experience, mental derangement, or dishonesty of the individuals responsible for them. When the observations withstand the test of time and are independently confirmed or supported by other scientists, it results in the period of "abnormal science." In this critical period of conceptual crisis and confusion, it becomes permissible to propose radically new ways of viewing and interpreting the phenomena that the old paradigm is unable to explain.

Eventually, one of these alternatives satisfies the necessary requirements to become the new paradigm that then dominates the thinking in the next period of the history of science. At this time, the history of science is rewritten and new individuals become the heroes of science, geniuses who centuries ago had ideas that are now an important part of the new paradigm. Thus Democritus and Leucippus, Greek philosophers of the fifth century BC, wrote about atoms, or tiny indivisible particles, as the basic constituents of the material world.

Fritjof Capra showed in his book *The Tao of Physics* that the understanding of matter in quantum-relativistic physics had been anticipated millennia ago by ancient Indian sages (Capra 1975). The relationship between the part and the whole revealed by optical holography was an integral part of the concept of *jivas* in ancient Jain scriptures, of the teaching about mutual Interpenetration found in the seventh and eighth centuries AD in Avatamsaka (Hwa Yen) Buddhism, and of the book *Monadology*, by the seventeenth century German philosopher Gottfried Wilhelm Leibniz.

The most famous historical examples of paradigm shifts are the replacement of the Ptolemaic geocentric system by the heliocentric system of Nicolas Copernicus, Galileo Galilei, and Johannes Kepler; the overthrow of Johann Joachim Becher's phlogiston theory in chemistry by Antoine Lavoisier's and John Dalton's atomic theory; and the conceptual cataclysms in physics in the first three decades of the twentieth century that undermined the hegemony of Newtonian physics and gave birth to Einstein's theories of relativity and quantum physics.

The paradigm shifts usually come as a major surprise to the mainstream academic community, because its members tend to see the leading paradigm as an accurate and definitive description of reality, rather than the best possible organization of the information available at that time. Alfred Korzybski and Gregory Bateson called this error in thinking "confusing the map with the territory" (Korzybski 1973, Bateson 1972). Bateson, known for his wry British humor, illustrated this fallacy with a parallel from everyday life: "If a scientist thinks in this way, he might one day go to the restaurant and eat the menu instead of his dinner." A good example of this mistake is the address that Lord Kelvin gave in 1900, only decades before the advent of quantum-relativistic physics, to an assembly of physicists at the British Association for the Advancement of Science. He declared: "There is nothing new to be discovered in physics now. All that remains is more and more precise measurements."

In the last six decades, various avenues of modern consciousness research have revealed a rich array of "anomalous phenomena"—experiences and observations that have undermined some of the generally accepted assertions of modern psychiatry, psychology, and psychotherapy concerning the nature and dimensions of the human psyche, the origins of emotional and psychosomatic disorders, and effective therapeutic mechanisms. These "anomalous phenomena" came from field anthropology, thanatology, parapsychology, psychedelic research, and powerful experiential therapies. Many of these observations are so radical that they question the basic metaphysical assumptions of materialistic science concerning the nature of reality and of human beings, as well as the relationship between consciousness and matter.

Fritjof Capra (1939 –), Austrian-American physicist, systems theorist, and deep ecologist, author of *The Tao of Physics* and *The Web of Life.*

Psychology of the Future: Lessons from Modern Consciousness Research

During the last six decades, I have conducted psychedelic therapy with LSD, psilocybin, dipropyltryptamine (DPT), and methylenedioxyamphetamine (MDA), facilitated sessions with Holotropic Breathwork, and worked with people experiencing spiritual emergencies. In these sessions, I have observed and experienced countless paradigm-breaking phenomena, indicating an urgent need for a radical revision of the most fundamental assumptions of mainstream psychiatry, psychology, and psychotherapy. I have identified seven areas which require substantial and far-reaching changes in our understanding of consciousness and the human psyche in health and disease:

1. *The Nature of Consciousness and Its Relationship to Matter*
2. *New Cartography of the Human Psyche: As Above, So Below*
3. *Architecture of Emotional and Psychosomatic Disorders*
4. *Effective Therapeutic Mechanisms*
5. *Strategy of Psychotherapy and Self-Exploration*
6. *The Role of Spirituality in Human Life*
7. *The Importance of Archetypal Astrology for Psychology*

Unless we change our thinking in these areas, our understanding of psychogenic emotional and psychosomatic disorders will remain superficial, unsatisfactory, and incomplete, and their therapy ineffective and disappointing. Psychiatry and psychology will be unable to genuinely comprehend the nature and origin of spirituality and appreciate the important role that it plays in the human psyche, human history, and in the universal scheme of things. These revisions are therefore essential for understanding the ritual, spiritual, and religious history of humanity—shamanism, rites of passage, the ancient mysteries of death and rebirth, and the great religions of the world. Without these radical changes in our thinking, potentially healing, transformative, and heuristically invaluable spontaneous holotropic experiences ("spiritual emergencies") will be misdiagnosed as psychotic and treated by suppressive medication.

A large array of the experiences and observations from the research of holotropic states will remain mystifying "anomalous phenomena," events that according to the current scientific paradigms should not be possible. A good definition of anomalous phenomena is: "What is left when you apply a bad theory." An avalanche of anomalous phenomena in modern consciousness research indicates an urgent need for a radical paradigm shift. Without this revision, mental health professionals will also have difficulty accepting the therapeutic power of psychedelic substances, because it is mediated by profound experiences that are currently seen as psychotic. This can be demonstrated by looking at the terms that mainstream clinicians and academicians use to describe psychedelics: experimental psychoses, hallucinogens, psychotomimetics, and even delirogens. This view reflects their inability to recognize the true nature of holotropic experiences as germane expressions of the deep dynamics of the psyche.

Even I have felt a strong resistance to the bewildering experiences and observations from the research of holotropic states, as well as the phenomena associated with them, such as astonishing synchronicities. It is not surprising, therefore, that the changes I am proposing have not been enthusiastically embraced by the academic community during the past fifty years since I started talking about them. I found them very challenging intellectually in spite of the fact that I was personally present in a large number of sessions and had the opportunity to experience them in my own sessions. This is understandable, considering the scope and radical nature of the necessary conceptual revisions. We are not talking about a minor patchwork, known as *ad hoc hypotheses,* but a major fundamental overhaul.

The resulting conceptual cataclysm would be comparable in its nature and scope to the revolution that physicists had to face in the first three decades of the twentieth century when they were forced to move from Newtonian physics to Einstein's theories of relativity and then to quantum physics. In fact, the conceptual changes I am proposing in the understanding of consciousness and the human psyche would represent a logical complement to the radical changes in our understanding of matter that have already occurred in physics. I have found that my friends and acquaintances who are quantum-relativistic physicists are much more open to these new ideas than mainstream psychiatrists and psychologists. Physicists are rapidly becoming avant-garde in the research of consciousness, leaving psychiatrists far behind.

The history of science abounds with examples of individuals who dared to challenge the dominant paradigm. Typically, their ideas were initially dismissed as products of ignorance, poor judgment, bad science, fraud, or even insanity. I can actually give a good personal example of the nature and intensity of the emotional exchanges during this period of abnormal science. In Prague on October 5, 2007, I received The Vision 97 Award from the Foundation of Václav Havel and his wife Dagmar. Former recipients of this prestigious award, which was given every year on the birthday of the Czech president Havel to a selected laureate, include American neurosurgeon and thinker Karl Pribram, former US Secretary of Labor Robert Reich, Phillip G. Zimbardo, the Stanford psychologist known for his 1971 prison experiment, MIT professor of computer science and pioneer in artificial intelligence Joseph Weizenbaum, and semiotician and writer Umberto Eco.

Seven years earlier, in the year 2000, I received a mock award called the "Delusional Boulder" from the Prague Sisyphus Club. This club is a group of scientistic Czech academicians and self-appointed arbiters of the purity of science similar to Carl Sagan's American CSICOP Group. This organization, like its American model, was headed by an astronomer (Dr. Jiří Grygar). Their annual award is intended to express the club members' ridicule of "silly individuals" who have spent years of hard labor (like Sisyphus) and produced something utterly futile and absurd that makes no sense to rational thinkers. In 2008, after I had received the Vision 97 Award, the enraged board members of the Sisyphus Club declared that my ideas were so outrageous and ridiculous that they had decided to create for me a special category—the "Diamond Arch-Delusional Boulder." Interested readers can read this entire history, with photos, on my personal website: stanislavgrof.com, in the section CV/BIO.

I am now in the ninth decade of my life, a time when researchers often try to review their professional career and summarize the conclusions they have reached. More than half a century of research into holotropic states—my own, as well as that of many of my transpersonally oriented colleagues—has amassed so much supportive evidence for a radically new understanding of consciousness and of the human psyche that I have decided to describe this new vision in its full form without trying to soften its controversial nature in any way. The fact that the new findings challenge the most fundamental metaphysical assumptions of materialistic science should not be a sufficient reason for rejecting them. Whether this new vision will ultimately be refuted or accepted by the academic community should be determined by the unbiased future research of holotropic states of consciousness.

The Nature of Consciousness and Its Relationship to Matter

According to the current scientific worldview, consciousness is an epiphenomenon of material processes; it allegedly emerges out of the complexity of the neurophysiological processes in the brain. This thesis is presented with great authority as if it has been scientifically proven beyond any reasonable doubt. On closer inspection, though, we discover that it is a basic metaphysical assumption of monistic materialistic science that is not supported by facts and actually contradicts the findings of modern consciousness research. Very few people, including scientists, realize that we actually do not have any proof that consciousness is generated in the brain.

More careful and discriminating materialistic philosophers and scientists refuse to wholeheartedly embrace the belief of the hardliners. They recognize that at least some aspects of our experience of the world cannot be explained as functions of the human brain. Following the ideas that Australian philosopher and cognitive scientist David Chalmers outlined in his 1996 book *The Conscious Mind: In Search of a Fundamental Theory*, they differentiate between the "hard" and the "easy problems" of consciousness (Chalmers 1996).

The "hard problem" is to explain why we can have subjective experiences, and how and why sensations acquire certain characteristics, such as colors, tastes, and smells. In other words, how something as tangible as a set of neurons can generate something as intangible as feelings, sensations, intuitions, and volitions. This contrasts with the "easy problems" of accounting for the ability to discriminate, integrate information, report mental states, focus attention, and so on. These are easy problems because all that is required for their solution is to specify a mechanism that can perform the function. The proposed solutions can be entirely consistent with the materialistic conception of natural phenomena.

There are many scientists who have refused to accept that consciousness can be explained by brain mechanisms. Wilder Penfield, famous Canadian-American neurosurgeon who successfully treated hundreds of epileptic patients by excising the areas of their brains in which the seizures originated, amassed vast amounts of experimental data. While performing brain surgery on these patients using only local anesthesia, he studied their reactions to electric stimulation of various parts of their brain. He mapped the functions of various regions of the brain, such as the memory cortex of the temporal lobe and the motor cortex of the gyrus, lying in front of the central fissure of the brain (the "homunculus"). In the book *Mystery of the Mind*, written toward the end of his life, he concluded that there was no good evidence that the brain alone can carry out the work that the mind does:

"Throughout my own scientific career, I, like the other scientists, have struggled to prove that the brain accounts for the mind. But now, perhaps, the time has come when we may profitably consider the evidence as it stands, and ask the question: *'Do brain mechanisms account for the mind?'* Can the mind be explained by what is now known about the brain? If not, which is the more reasonable of the two possible hypotheses: that man's being is based on one element, or on two? I conclude that it is easier to rationalize man's being on the basis of two elements than on the basis of one (Penfield 1975)."

Anesthesiologist and brain researcher Stuart Hameroff initially suggested that the solution of the problem of consciousness might lie in the quantum processes in the "cytoskeletal microtubules," nanometer-sized cylindrical structures found on the molecular and supramolecular level inside the brain cells (Hameroff 1987). Hameroff's idea was based on his observation that some of the more puzzling aspects of consciousness resembled equally puzzling aspects of quantum properties.

Even this conclusion, based on the sophisticated research of the brain, falls painfully short of bridging the formidable gap between matter and consciousness. In a video entitled "Through the Wormhole" that aired on the TV channel Science, Hameroff himself admitted it when he made this surprising statement: "I believe that consciousness, or its immediate precursor proto-consciousness, has been in the universe all along, perhaps from the Big Bang" (Hameroff 2012).

The origin of consciousness from matter is simply taken for granted as an obvious and self-evident fact, based on the metaphysical assumption of the primacy of matter in the universe. In fact, in the entire history of science, nobody has ever offered a plausible explanation for how consciousness could be generated by material processes, or even suggested a viable approach to the problem. Consider, for example, the book by Francis Crick, *The Astonishing Hypothesis: The Scientific Search for the Soul* (Crick 1994)—the book's jacket carried a very exciting promise: "Nobel Prize-winning Scientist Explains Consciousness."

Crick's "astonishing hypothesis" was succinctly stated at the beginning of his book: "You, your joys and your sorrows, your memories and your ambitions, your sense of personal identity and free will, are in fact no more than the behavior of a vast assembly of nerve cells and their associated molecules. Who you are is nothing but a pack of neurons." At the beginning of the book, "to simplify the problem of consciousness," Crick narrows his discussion by focusing on optical perception. He presents impressive experimental evidence showing that visual perception is associated with distinct physiological, biochemical, and electrical processes in the optical system from the retina through the optical tract to the suboccipital cortex. And there the discussion ends, as if the problem of consciousness had been satisfactorily solved.

In reality, this is where the problem begins. What exactly is capable of transforming biochemical and electric processes in the brain into a conscious experience of a reasonable facsimile of the object we are observing, in full color, and project it into three-dimensional space? The formidable problem of the relationship between *phenomena*—things as we perceive them (Erscheinungen)—and *noumena*—things as they truly are in themselves *(Dinge an sich)* was clearly articulated by seventeenth century German philosopher Immanuel Kant in the book *Critique of Pure Reason* (Kant 1999). Scientists focus their efforts on the aspect of the problem where they can find answers: the material processes in the brain. The much more mysterious problem—how physical processes in the brain generate consciousness—does not receive any attention, because it is incomprehensible and cannot be solved.

The attitude that Western science has adopted in regard to this issue resembles the famous Sufi story. On a dark night, Nasruddin, a satirical Sufi figure representing crazy wisdom, is crawling on his knees under a street lamp. His neighbor sees him and asks: "What are you doing? Are you looking for something?" Nasruddin answers that he is searching for a lost key and the neighbor offers to help. After some time of unsuccessful joint effort, the neighbor becomes confused and feels the need for clarification. He says: "I don't see anything! Are you sure you lost it here?" Nasruddin shakes his head and points his finger to a dark area outside of the circle illuminated by the street lamp and replies: "No, not here, over there!" The neighbor is puzzled and inquires further: "So why are we looking for it here and not over there?" Nasruddin explains: "Because it is light here and we can see. Over there it's dark and we would not have a chance!"

Similarly, materialistic scientists have systematically avoided the problem of the origin of consciousness because this riddle cannot be solved within the context of their conceptual framework. The idea that consciousness is a product of the brain is naturally not completely arbitrary. Its proponents usually refer to a vast body of very specific clinical and experimental evidence from neurology, neurosurgery, and psychiatry to support their position. The evidence for close correlations between the anatomy, neurophysiology, and biochemistry of the brain and states of consciousness is unquestionable and overwhelming. What is problematic is not the nature of the presented evidence, but the conclusions that are drawn from these observations. In formal logic, this type of fallacy is referred to as a *non sequitur*—an argument wherein the conclusion does not follow from the premises. While the experimental data clearly show that consciousness is closely connected with the neurophysiological and biochemical processes in the brain, they have very little bearing on the nature and origin of consciousness.

A simple analogy is the relationship between a TV set and the television program. The situation here is much clearer, since it involves a system that is human-made and its operation is well known. The reception of the television program—the quality of the picture and the sound—depends on the proper functioning of the TV set and on the integrity of its components. Malfunctions of various parts coincide with distinct and specific changes in the quality of the program. Some of them lead to distortions of form, color, or sound, others to interference between the channels, and so on. Like the neurologist who uses changes in consciousness as a diagnostic tool, a television mechanic can infer from the nature of these anomalies which parts of the set and which specific components are malfunctioning. When the problem is identified, repairing or replacing these elements will correct the distortions.

Since we know the basic principles of television technology, it is obvious to us that the set simply mediates the program and that it does not generate it. We would laugh at somebody who would try to scrutinize all the transistors, relays, and circuits of the TV set and analyze its wires in an attempt to figure out how it creates the programs. Even if we carried this misguided effort to a molecular, atomic, or subatomic level, we would have absolutely no clue as to why, at a particular time, a Mickey Mouse cartoon, a Star Trek sequence, or a Hollywood classic appear on the screen. The close correlation between the functioning of the TV set and the quality of the program does not necessarily mean that the entire secret of the program is in the set itself. Yet this is exactly the kind of conclusion that traditional materialistic science has drawn from comparable data about the brain and its relation to consciousness.

Ample evidence suggests exactly the opposite, namely that under certain circumstances, consciousness can operate independently of its material substrate and can perform functions that reach far beyond the capacities of the brain. This is most clearly illustrated by the existence of out-of-body experiences (OBEs), which can occur spontaneously, or in various facilitating situations—shamanic trances, psychedelic sessions, spiritual practice, hypnosis, experiential psychotherapy, and particularly in near-death experiences (NDEs). In all these situations, consciousness can separate from the body and maintain its sensory capacity, while moving freely to various close and remote locations.

In the *Bardo Thödol*, the *Tibetan Book of Death*, the disembodied form of consciousness that develops at the time of death is called the bardo body. Bardos are the intermediate states between incarnations. The consciousness can travel out of the physical body and get experiential access to any location in the world. The *Bardo Thödol* mentions only two exceptions—Bodh Gaya and the mother's womb. The reference to Bodh Gaya, the place where Buddha reached enlightenment, suggests that reaching enlightenment terminates the journey through the bardos. In *Bardo Thö-*

dol, the same happens when in the third bardo *(Sidpa bardo),* we enter our future mother's womb.

Veridical OBEs are particularly interesting, because independent consensual verification confirms that the perception of the environment by disembodied consciousness is accurate. In near-death situations, veridical OBEs can occur even in people who are congenitally blind for organic reasons (Ring 1982, 1985; Ring and Valarino 1998; Ring and Cooper 1999). Many other types of transpersonal phenomena can also mediate accurate information about various aspects of the universe that had not been previously received and recorded in the brain—other people, animals, plants, historical events, and archetypal figures and realms (Grof 2000).

In 2016, the world's foremost systems theorist and philosopher of Hungarian origin Ervin Laszlo published a book entitled *What Is Reality? The New Map of Cosmos, Consciousness, and Existence.* Addressing the problem of the nature and origin of consciousness, he described the answers to this question as they developed historically and subjected them to logical analysis in the light of existing clinical and experimental evidence. He showed how the concept of consciousness shifted from that of a local, to a nonlocal, and then to a cosmic phenomenon (Laszlo 2016).

In the mainstream materialistic worldview, consciousness is generated in, and confined to, the human brain. According to this theory, there is nothing mysterious about the presence of consciousness in human experience; the stream of experience we call consciousness is a byproduct of the neurophysiological processes in the brain. This idea was expressed in the most blatant way in a statement by the French physician and materialistic philosopher of the Enlightenment, Julien Offray de La Mettrie, best known for his work *L'homme machine* (Man As A Machine). He said, "There is nothing special about consciousness; the brain secretes consciousness like the kidney excretes urine" (Offray de La Mettrie, 1865).

Laszlo called this understanding of consciousness the turbine theory: the stream of consciousness is generated by the living brain, much as a stream of electrons is generated by a working turbine. As long as the turbine functions, it generates a stream of electrons: electricity. As long as the brain functions, it generates a stream of sensations: consciousness. When they shut down, the streams they generate vanish. Consciousness no more exists in a dead brain than electric charge exists in a stopped or destroyed turbine.

Laszlo pointed out some serious problems that the turbine theory has encountered. Thanatological research has brought overwhelming evidence that consciousness does not cease to operate when the brain activity stops. There exist many reports about NDEs of individuals in a state of clinical death, with a flat cardiogram (ECG) or even electroencephalogram (EEG). This phenomenon has been supported by thousands of clinical observations and proven beyond any reasonable doubt (Ring 1982, van Lommel 2010, Sabom 1982). Laszlo also refers to other interesting evidence that remains controversial. There are indications that conscious experience persists in some form, not just during the temporary cessation of brain function, but also in its permanent absence: when the subject is fully and irreversibly dead.

The problems with the turbine model could be overcome if we compare this to a networked computer—a computer with memory and a link to other computers and information systems. Here the information entered in a computer is identified by a particular code and can be recalled from the system with that code. When recalled, it will appear precisely as entered in the computer, displayed on another device. This information is then present in a universally accessible data system, such as the Cloud. This system stores and integrates all items of information regardless of their origin and allows their recall.

This type of integral memory function could account for transpersonal psychiatrists' observations that in holotropic states, consciousness can expand to retrieve information from almost anything in space and time, as we will see in a later section of this book (see table). It could also explain the experiences of individuals who are biologically related or have strong emotional bonds. Such people, like mothers and children, twins, and lovers, seem to be tuned into each other's consciousness. Mediums also seem able to tune into the consciousness of the person they contact. The networked computer theory of consciousness suggests that the traces of the consciousness present in the brain are also present beyond the brain. According to this model, consciousness is not a personal and local phenomenon, but a transpersonal and nonlocal one.

Ervin Laszlo described such a natural memory field in his book *The Creative Cosmos: Towards a Unified Science of Matter, Life and Mind,* and called it PSI-Field (Laszlo 1993). In his later work, he changed this name to Akashic field. This concept, of a subquantum field containing a holographic record of everything that happens in the universe, was the first scientific theory to address the baffling problems encountered in the research of holotropic states: how was it possible to experience convincing time travel to ancient Egypt, Japan during the time of the samurais, Paris during the French Revolution, or authentic identification with other people and animals? As the title of his more recent book, *Science and the Akashic Field,* suggests, Ervin Laszlo has been able to formulate not only a unifying conceptual framework for a number of scientific disciplines, but also to create a bridge that connects the best of hard science quite explicitly to the great Eastern spiritual philosophies, and to transpersonal psychology (Laszlo 2007).

A computer permanently linked with a universal information system that saves the uploaded information and integrates it into an overall information system adequately models consciousness not as a personal and local phenomenon, but a transpersonal and nonlocal one. Traces of consciousness present in the brain are also present beyond the brain. However, Laszlo pointed out that even the networked computer theory of consciousness does not explain the full extent of the evidence from holotropic states. It seems that in some instances, the units of consciousness that persist beyond the brain are not mere traces or copies of the elements that were experienced in the everyday state of consciousness; they seem to be autonomous units of living consciousness. Sometimes an individual does not just recall the experience of a deceased person, but enters into communication with it.

An example of this phenomenon is the "welcoming committee" experienced by people in near-death situations. Here the subject encounters deceased relatives and friends who appear to be intelligent beings able to provide information and answer questions (Ring and Valarino 1998). C. G. Jung had a similar experience with his spirit guide Philemon, who kept appearing to him during his spiritual emergency and was capable of answering questions to which Jung himself did not know the answers. Jung actually credited Philemon as the source of significant aspects of his psychology (Jung 2009).

This is Jung's description of his interactions with Philemon in his own words: "Philemon and other figures of my fantasies brought home to me the crucial insight that there are things in the psyche which I do not produce, but which produce themselves and have their own life. Philemon represented a force which was not myself. In my fantasies I held conversations with him, and he said things which I had not consciously thought."

Jung also had a dramatic experience of spirits visiting his house, at which time he channeled a text that came from the Alexandrian Gnostic philosopher Basilides. This text, one of the most remarkable works Jung wrote, was published with the title *Septem Sermones ad Mortuos* (Seven Sermons for the Dead); today it is seen as a summary revelation of the *Red Book* (Jung 2009). During one of my visits to Florence, I had the chance to spend a day with Roberto Assagioli several months before his death. He told me that he had channeled important ideas for his psychotherapeutic system, known as psychosynthesis, from a spirit guide who called himself "The Tibetan." It was allegedly the same entity from whom Alice Bailey received the metaphysical teachings that she described in a series of her books.

Quasi-experimental evidence for the survival of consciousness after death can be found in the literature on spiritism and mental or trance mediumship. Reports about spiritistic séances abounded in the nineteenth and beginning of the twentieth century. Although some of the professional mediums (including the famous Eusapia Palladino) were occasionally caught cheating, others (such as Mrs. Piper, Mrs. Leonard, and Mrs. Verrall) withstood all the tests and gained the high esteem of careful and reputable researchers (Grosso 1994). The best mediums were able to accurately reproduce the deceased's voice, speech patterns, gestures, mannerisms, and other characteristic features.

On occasion, the information received by the medium was unknown to any of the people present, or even to anyone living at all. Uninvited "drop-in" entities suddenly intruded into the séances and in some cases, their identities were later confirmed. In other instances, relevant messages were received in "proxy sittings," where a distant and uninformed party has sought information in lieu of a close relative or friend of the deceased. In cases of "cross correspondence," bits and pieces of a comprehensive message were conveyed through several mediums. Participants in some of these séances were Nobel Prize-winning scientists. There is no other area in which the testimonies of thinkers of such high caliber have been so easily dismissed.

In his paper entitled *Xenoglossy: Verification of the Speech of An Unlearned Language,* William Kautz presented the results of his analysis of a 90-year-old abandoned British case of mediumship involving foreign speech. The analysis showed that the examples of the extensive phonetic transcription (5,000 phrases over thirty years) are genuine Late Egyptian, a language that has been dead for 1,600 years. This result provides a confirmed example of the alleged phenomenon of *xenoglossy,* the speaking of a real foreign language by a person who never learned it (Kautz 2017). This case has important implications in psychology, egyptology, linguistics and the use of intuitive methods for obtaining detailed and accurate information of any kind. It offers especially what is perhaps the best evidence yet, though not a full proof, for the continuation of human consciousness beyond bodily death, the classic *survival problem.*

In our Esalen month-long workshops, we repeatedly had the opportunity to witness the remarkable abilities of the American psychic Anne Armstrong. A good example was a reading that Anne did for a German participant about her deceased father. After giving this woman highly relevant and accurate information about her father, Anne suddenly announced that she was getting a word that she did not understand. It happened to be a German term of endearment for little children that this woman's father used for her in her childhood. Anne was surprised by the intensity with which this word was entering her consciousness; she had no idea what it meant, since she did not speak any German.

In another Esalen month-long workshop entitled *Energy: Physical, Emotional, and Psychic,* we had an extraordinary experience which involved Brazilian spiritist and psychologist Luiz Gasparetto. Luiz had the reputation of being able to channel the spirits of famous deceased painters and paint in their style. He was a member of the Christian Spiritist Church, and was inspired by nineteenth-century French educator and physician Allan Kardec's writing in *The Spirits Book* and *The Mediums' Book* (Kardec 2011, 2012).

Working in a darkened room, lit only by weak red light (which makes it impossible to differentiate colors) and listening to Antonio Vivaldi's music, Luiz painted twenty-six impressive large paintings in the style of

Henri de Toulouse-Lautrec, Pablo Picasso, Amedeo Modigliani, Claude Monet, Rembrandt van Rijn, and other famous artists, all in the course of one hour. He painted most of them without looking, once while painting simultaneously with both hands, and one upside down with his bare feet under the table. Both stories are described in detail in my book *When the Impossible Happens* (Grof 2006a).

Raymond Moody, American psychologist, whose international best-seller *Life After Life* (Moody 1975) inspired the field of thanatology, provided another piece of controversial evidence to the issue of the survival of consciousness after death. In his book *Reunions: Visionary Encounters with Departed Loved Ones,* Moody described a *psychomanteum,* an environment that supposedly facilitated contact between survivors and their deceased friends and relatives. It consisted of a room draped with black velvet and a large mirror. Moody reported instances in which the apparitions not only appeared in the mirror, but also occasionally emerged from the mirror and freely moved around the room as three-dimensional holographic images (Moody 1993).

Luiz Gasparetto, Brazilian psychologist and spiritist painter.

A fascinating and truly incredible development in the attempts to communicate with the spirits of discarnate people is Interdimensional Transcommunication (ITC), an approach which involves modern electronic technology. This research could easily be dismissed as outrageous and ridiculous, if it were not for the fact that it has been conducted under rigorously controlled conditions by an international group of serious researchers, including Ernest Senkowski, George Meek, Mark Macy, Scott Rogo, Raymond Bayless, and others (Senkowski 1994). They reported that they were able to receive messages from the dead through instrumental means, appearing as anomalous voices and images on message machines, computers, radios, and TV monitors. This research also attracted the attention of senior scientists at the Institute of Noetic Sciences (IONS). Interestingly, Thomas Alva Edison is alleged to have worked for many years on a machine that could communicate with the spirit world. However, Edison died in 1931, before he had a chance to publish any of his notes.

Ervin Laszlo showed, through his thoughtful analysis of the data related to the problem of the origin and nature of consciousness, that neither the turbine theory nor the information field theory, modeled by the computer network, can adequately account for the observed facts. His conclusion was that "the consciousness we experience as a stream of sensations, feelings, intuitions and volitions is an integral part of the consciousness that pervades the cosmos. There is only one consciousness in the universe, and the consciousness that appears in us is an integral part of it." After decades of clinical work, C. G. Jung came to a similar conclusion: "The psyche is not a product of the brain and is not located within the skull; it is part of the generative, creative principle of the cosmos, of the *unus mundus*" (Jung 1964).

Materialistic scientists have not been able to produce any convincing evidence that consciousness is a product of the neurophysiological processes in the brain. They have been able to maintain this conviction only by ignoring, misinterpreting, and even ridiculing a vast body of observations indicating that consciousness can exist and function independently of the body and of the physical senses. This evidence comes from parapsychology, field anthropology, LSD research, experiential psychotherapy, thanatology, and the study of spontaneously occurring holotropic states of consciousness ("spiritual emergencies"). All these disciplines have amassed impressive data which clearly demonstrates that human consciousness operates in a way that lies far beyond the capacity of the brain, as it is understood by mainstream science, and that it is a primary and irreducible aspect of existence—an equal partner of matter or possibly superordinate to it.

In his groundbreaking book *The Tao of Physics,* Fritjof Capra demonstrated that after three hundred years of intensive research, Western science reached an understanding of the world of matter—quantum-relativistic physics—that bore striking similarity with the worldview which the ancient Indian sages foresaw millennia ago in their meditations (Capra 1975). A few decades later, psychedelic therapy, transpersonal psychology, and other avenues of modern consciousness research came to the same conclusion in regard to our understanding of consciousness and the human psyche.

A New Cartography of the Human Psyche: As Above, So Below

In the late 1950s, when I took my psychedelic research from the laboratory to my clinical practice, I was equipped with the knowledge instilled in me by my medical study, traditional psychiatric training, and Freudian psychoanalysis. This turned out to be very inadequate preparation for understanding the LSD experiences of my patients, as well as my own, and dealing with the situations that arose in psychedelic sessions.

When I started conducting serial sessions with medium dosages of LSD with my psychiatric patients, many of their early experiences seemed to involve the territory I was familiar with—postnatal biography and the Freudian individual unconscious. However, sooner or later, each of them moved into an entirely new experiential realm, which was at the time unknown to me. I was witnessing intense emotional and physical experiences of my patients that were frightening for them and also, initially, alarming for me.

Many of these clients had episodes of choking, strong tremors, pressure headaches, pains in various parts of their bodies, and occasional nausea. This was accompanied by a dismal triad of emotions—fear of death, of insanity, and of never coming back from this nightmarish world. The pulse was often significantly accelerated and sometimes bruises and various color changes spontaneously appeared in my patients' faces without any apparent physical cause.

I was aware that there was not a good way to stop an LSD experience which was taking the form of a "bad trip." Administering tranquilizers in the middle of a terrifying session would just freeze the distressing experience and prevent its positive resolution, so I provided support and encouragement for my patients as they were going through these challenging experiences. I discovered that many of them experienced a positive breakthrough which took the form of psychospiritual death and rebirth. At this time, I also scheduled my own LSD sessions, experimenting with higher dosages. My patients reported that in these sessions, they relived their own biological birth. I was able to confirm this in my personal experiences; there was no doubt in my mind that what we were experiencing were authentic and convincing memories of all the stages of our birth, with all the emotions and physical sensations.

I was even able to distinguish four experiential patterns related to the consecutive stages of childbirth, and called them Basic Perinatal Matrices (BPM I-IV). BPM I is related to the advanced stage of pregnancy before the onset of the delivery; BPM II portrays the stage of pregnancy when the uterus is contracted, but the cervix is not yet open; and BPM III reflects the propulsion through the birth canal after the cervix is fully dilated. BPM IV features the experience of birth—emerging from the birth canal and having the umbilical cord cut. I will be returning to this important concept repeatedly in various sections of this encyclopedia.

The discovery of the existence of the memory of birth in the unconscious and its paramount implications for psychology came as a big surprise to me, and represented the first major intellectual challenge that I encountered in my psychedelic research. In medical school, I had been taught that the fetus and the newborn are not yet conscious; they are not able to experience pain and their immature brain is not capable of forming the memory of birth. Until as recently as the 1980s, physicians assumed that infants did not have fully developed pain receptors; they believed that the infants' responses to physical insults were merely muscular reactions and their screaming was dismissed as "just a reflex." Medical procedures, from circumcision to heart surgeries, were routinely conducted without anesthesia.

There is actually a personal reason why accepting the existence of birth memory was particularly difficult for me. As a second year medical student, I attended a lecture on memory by professor William Laufberger, a Czech physiologist who had developed one of the first artificial chess players. He had also become world famous for achieving maturation in axolotls, Mexican salamanders *(Ambystoma mexicanum),* by giving them thyroid hormones. During the discussion period, I asked professor Laufberger how far back human memory can reach and if it is possible to remember birth. He laughed, gave me a scathing look like I was an absolute idiot, and with great certainty and authority ridiculed me for my question: "Of course not, the cortex of the newborn is not myelinized!"

Eventually, under the impact of numerous observations in my clients' sessions as well as my own, I was able to accept the existence of the birth memory as an unquestionable clinical fact and left it up to the brain researchers to find where this memory might be recorded. As my research continued, much more formidable challenges emerged. On the perinatal level, the fetal memories were often accompanied or alternated with scenes described in spiritual scriptures and historical books—past life experiences, visions of mythological beings, and visits to archetypal realms. In some of the advanced sessions of the series, the transpersonal motifs dominated the experience and the fetal elements were missing.

My initial tendency was to see the historical and mythological experiences as derivatives of the birth memories for which I could see a solid material basis—the highly developed brain of the newborn. The myelinization argument seemed at this point absurd and irrelevant. My attitude to these observations was similar to Otto Rank's tendency to interpret the archetypal Terrible Mother Goddesses, such as Medusa, Hekate, or Kali, as images inspired by the trauma of birth.

I initially thought that I had discovered a logical explanation for the fact that the belief in heaven, paradise, hell, and purgatory is so universal in the great religions of the world and in the mythology and creeds of ancient and native cultures. The blissful experience of the undisturbed prenatal existence without the concept of linear time (BPM I) seemed to be a perfect template for the concepts of Paradise and Heaven, the transition from BPM I to BPM II for Paradise Lost, and the extreme emotional and physical suffering without end in BPM II for Hell. Extreme suffering with hope and perspective of a better future (BPM III) corresponded with the descriptions of Purgatory and the emergence into numinous bright light and psychospiritual death and rebirth of BPM IV had all the features of divine epiphany as it is reported in the scriptures of various religions.

The existence of perinatal matrices also seemed to offer new revolutionary insights into a variety of other areas which were previously inadequately understood by Freudian psychoanalysis and other schools of depth psychology, with the models limited to postnatal biography and the individual unconscious. Salient examples are emotional and psychosomatic disorders, the ritual and spiritual history of humanity, the psychology and psychopathology of art, and the unbridled violence and insatiable greed of the human species, which leads to wars, bloody revolutions, concentration camps and genocide. We will explore these fascinating topics in future sections of this encyclopedia.

However, as I continued my research, I became convinced about the independent existence of a yet deeper domain of the human unconscious psyche that I called *transpersonal.* It involved authentic identification with the consciousness of other people, groups of people, animals of different species, and even plants. Other types of transpersonal experiences involved ancestral, collective, karmic, and phylogenetic memories, as well as sequences from the mythologies of various cultures—even those of which my clients and I had no previous intellectual knowledge.

When I was making these observations, Czechoslovakia was controlled by the Soviet Union. We were unable to buy books from the West and even our access to books in public libraries was censored and limited. Psychoanalytic literature was on the list of *"libri prohibiti;"* it was kept in separate compartments and available only for members of the Communist party writing critical books and articles about psychoanalysis. In 1967, when I immigrated to the United States, I was able to receive independent confirmation of many of my findings when I was able to read the works of C. G. Jung and become acquainted with his concept of the collective unconscious and its historical and archetypal domains. Jung's deepest and most convincing new insights came from spontaneous holotropic experiences that he had during his psychospiritual crisis ("spiritual emergency"), mine from my high-dose LSD sessions.

The final and most radical shift in my thinking about psychedelic experiences and other types of holotropic experiences came from more than forty years of cooperation with my close friend and colleague Richard Tarnas, which led to the discovery of astonishing correlations between the archetypal content and timing of holotropic states of consciousness and planetary transits, both collective and personal (Tarnas 1995, 2006, Grof 2006a). We have been discussing these findings in our joint classes at the California Institute of Integral Studies (CIIS) in San Francisco, in our seminars in the United States and Europe, and in telecourses.

According to my present understanding, when we are in a holotropic state induced either by psychedelic substances, powerful non-pharmacological means (such as Holotropic Breathwork), or occurring spontaneously, we tune experientially into the archetypal fields of the planets transiting our natal chart. The content of our session will then consist of a selection of biographical memories, fetal memories of one of the BPMs, and transpersonal experiences that have the archetypal qualities associated with the transiting planets.

The depth of the unconscious material manifesting in the session will then depend on the archetypal power of the transit, the method that triggered the experience, the type of substance and its dose—if it is a psychedelic session—and previous experience of the subject with holotropic states. In the following section, I will describe and discuss the extended cartography of the psyche as it emerged from my work with holotropic states of consciousness—psychedelic psychotherapy, Holotropic Breathwork, and work with individuals experiencing spiritual emergency.

From Freud to Cosmic Consciousness

Traditional psychiatrists and psychologists use a model of the human psyche that is limited to postnatal biography and to the individual unconscious described by Sigmund Freud. According to Freud, the newborn is a *tabula rasa* (clean slate); nothing that precedes birth is of interest for psychologists, including the birth process itself. Who we become is determined by an interplay between biological instincts and influences that have shaped our life since we came into this world—the quality of nursing, the nature of toilet training, various psychosexual traumas, development of the superego, our reaction to the Oedipal triangle, and conflicts and traumatic events in later life.

The Freudian individual unconscious is a derivative of our postnatal history—a repository of what we have forgotten, rejected as unacceptable, and repressed. This underworld of the psyche (the *Id* as Freud called it) is a realm dominated by primitive instinctual forces. Many aspects of psychoanalysis have been subjected to severe criticism by following generations and rejected or modified, but Freud's idea that psychological history begins after we are born has withstood the test of time and has been integrated into mainstream thinking.

To describe the relationship between the conscious psyche and the unconscious, Freud used his famous image of the submerged iceberg. In this simile, what was assumed to be the totality of the psyche was only a small part of it, like the portion of the iceberg showing above the surface of the water. Psychoanalysis discovered that a much larger part of the psyche, comparable to the submerged part of the iceberg, is unconscious and, unbeknownst to us, governs our thought processes and behavior.

Later contributions to depth psychology added the development of object relationships and interpersonal dynamics in the nuclear family as etiological factors, but maintain the exclusive emphasis on postnatal life, just like Freudian psychoanalysis (Blanck and Blanck 1974, 1979, Sullivan 1953, Satir 1983, Bateson et al. 1956). Even with these additions and modifications, this model proves to be painfully inadequate when we work with holotropic states of consciousness, whether induced by psychedelics and various non-drug means, or those occurring spontaneously. To account for all the phenomena occurring in these states, we must drastically revise our understanding of the dimensions of the human psyche.

In the early years of my psychedelic research, I sketched a vastly expanded cartography of the psyche that seems to meet this challenge. This map contains, beside the usual biographical level, two transbiographical realms: *the perinatal domain,* related to the trauma of biological birth; and *the transpersonal domain,* which accounts for such phenomena as experiential identification with other people, animals, plants, and other aspects of nature.

The transpersonal realm is also the source of ancestral, racial, phylogenetic, and karmic memories, as well as visions of archetypal beings and visits to mythological regions. The ultimate experiences in this category are an identification with the Universal Mind and with the Supracosmic and Metacosmic Void. Perinatal and transpersonal phenomena have been described throughout the ages in the religious, mystical, and occult literature of various parts of the world.

In view of the observations from holotropic states of consciousness, we can expand Freud's simile of the iceberg: the parts of the psyche discovered and described by classical psychoanalysis represent, at best, still only the

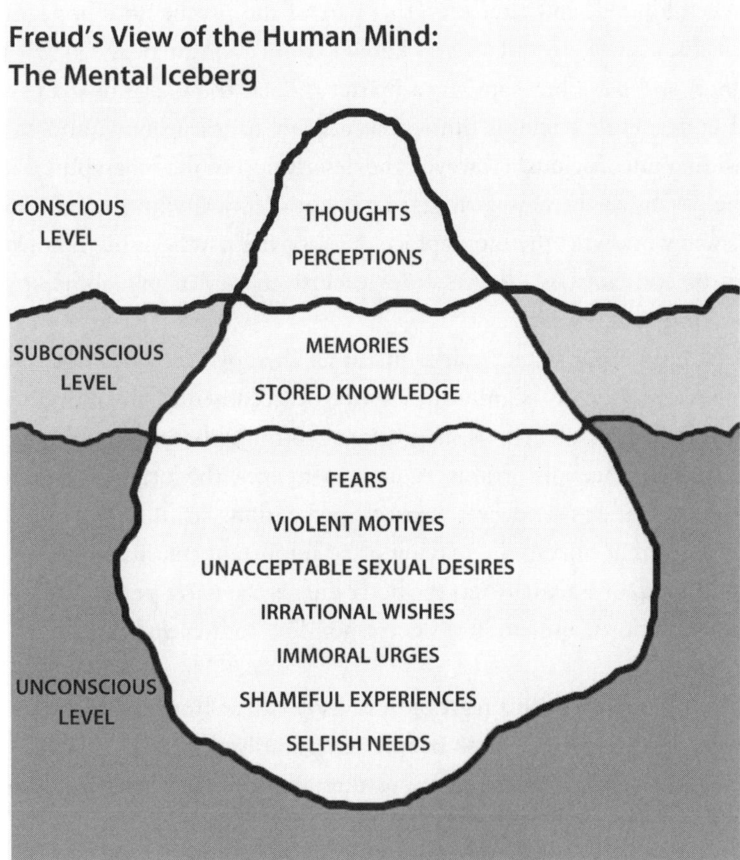

Freud's simile of the iceberg: what we considered to be the psyche is just a small fraction of it, comparable to the tip of the iceberg that shows above the water's surface. Psychoanalysis discovered a vast domain of the psyche that is unconscious like the submerged part of the iceberg.

tip of the iceberg; modern consciousness research revealed vast regions of the unconscious that—like the submerged parts of the iceberg—escaped the attention of Freud and his disciples, with the exception of Otto Rank and C. G. Jung. Joseph Campbell, with his incisive Irish humor, described this situation very concisely: "Freud was fishing while sitting on a whale."

Postnatal Biography and the Individual Unconscious

The biographical domain of the psyche consists of our memories from infancy, childhood, and later life. This part of the psyche does not require much discussion, since it is well known from traditional psychiatry, psychology, and psychotherapy. As a matter of fact, the image of the psyche used in academic circles is limited exclusively to this domain and to the individual unconscious. However, the description of the biographical level of the psyche in the new cartography is not identical with the traditional one. The work with the biographical level of the psyche using holotropic states of consciousness differs from exclusively verbal psychotherapy in several important ways:

1) In holotropic states, unlike in verbal therapy, one does not just remember emotionally significant events or reconstruct them indirectly from the analysis of dreams, neurotic symptoms, slips of the tongue, or from transference distortions. One experiences the original emotions, physical sensations, and even sensory perceptions in full age regression. That means that during the reliving of an important trauma from infancy or childhood, one actually has the body image, the naïve perception of the world, sensations, and emotions corresponding to the age he or she was at that time.

The authenticity of this regression is also evident from the fact that the wrinkles in the faces of these people temporarily disappear, giving them an infantile expression, and their postures, gestures, and behavior become childlike. They might hypersalivate, suck their fingers, or even show the sucking reflex and Babinski's reflex (fanning of the toes when the side of the sole is scratched by a pin). I have heard from men that when they were regressed and went to the bathroom to urinate, they felt that their penis had shrunk to the size of that of a little boy. In the same vein, women reported that during regression, they felt that their breasts disappeared from their body image.

2) The second difference between working on the biographical material using a holotropic state of consciousness and doing it with verbal psychotherapy is that it reveals the psychotraumatic impact of physical traumas and makes it possible to heal them. It should be obvious that physical suffering is also a psychotrauma, but it is not acknowledged and discussed in handbooks of psychology and psychotherapy. The only other approach that recognizes the powerful psychotraumatic impact of physical traumas is Ron Hubbard's *Dianetics* (Scientology). Scientologists use a process of exploration and therapy called *auditing,* during which the psychological intensity of emotions and thus the significance of traumas is assessed objectively by galvanometers measuring skin resistance (Hubbard 1950, Gormsen and Lumbye 1979).

Hubbard referred to imprints of physical traumatizations as *engrams* and saw them as primary sources of emotional problems. In his terminology, the usual psychological traumas are called *secondaries*; they borrow their emotional power from their associations with engrams. Scientology recognizes not only the role of physical traumas in postnatal life, but also the impact of somatic traumatization during birth and in past lives. Unfortunately, the abuse of scientological knowledge for the unethical pursuit of power and money by the Church of Scientology and Hubbard's wild fantasies about the Galactic Federation, the role of extraterrestrials on our planet, Clears, and Operating Thetans discredited his important theoretical contributions.

As I mentioned earlier, until as recently as the 1980s, the psychotraumatic impact of pain was not acknowledged by the medical profession. This was the case not only for memories of painful events, but also for current injuries in infants. Anesthesia was not used in infants during normally painful interventions, and circumcision is even today conducted in many places without anesthesia. For people with common sense, the 2015 report from Oxford University entitled "British Scientists Prove that Newborns Experience Pain" sounded almost like a joke. One could expect that the next research project would be "scientists prove that dogs and cats experience pain." The reason for the failure to recognize that physical insults are psychotraumas might be the fact that remembering and mentioning physical traumas in verbal psychotherapy is not associated with the experience of pain or other physical signs.

In experiential therapy, the memory of pain is relived in its full intensity, even if its source is surgical intervention conducted under general anesthesia. Many people undergoing psychedelic or holotropic therapy relive experiences of near drowning, operations, accidents, and discomfort during childhood diseases. Of particular importance seem to be memories of events associated with suffocation, such as diphtheria, whooping cough, strangling, or aspiration of a foreign object. This material emerges quite spontaneously and without any programming. As it surfaces, we realize that these physical traumas have a strong psychotraumatic impact and that they play a significant role in the psychogenesis of emotional and psychosomatic problems.

A history of physical traumas can regularly be found in clients suffering from asthma, migraine headaches, psychosomatic pains, panic anxiety attacks, phobias, sadomasochistic tendencies, or depression and suicidal tendencies. Reliving traumatic memories of this kind and their integration can have far-reaching therapeutic consequences. In my experience, psychosomatic symptoms and disorders can always be traced back to situations involving physical assaults or traumas.

This fact contrasts sharply with the position of academic psychiatry and psychology, which do not recognize the psychotraumatic impact of physical traumas. It also seriously questions the explanations of psychosomatic disorders as expressions of psychological problems and conflicts in body language. For example, pain in the shoulders has been interpreted as symbolizing the patient's feelings that he or she carries too much responsibility, pain in the stomach and nausea as meaning that the client is not able to "stomach something," and psychogenic asthma as dramatizing the "cry for the mother."

The psychotraumatic impact of physical pain and the resolution of this trauma can be illustrated by the story of Katia, a 49-year-old psychiatric nurse participating in our training for Holotropic Breathwork facilitators. Before she enrolled in the training, Katia had suffered from intense chronic back pain and episodes of depression. In her breathwork sessions, she was able to trace back her symptoms to a traumatic experience in early childhood—immobilization in a cast lasting many weeks—and resolve the armoring. Here is Katia's report in her own words:

> *Intense breathing at the beginning of the session made me feel that my body was blocked and frozen in a supine position. I tried desperately to turn on my belly, but was not able to do it. I experienced myself as a helpless turtle turned on her back, unable to escape her dangerous predicament. I began to cry for not being able to change my position, because it seemed that my life depended on it. I noticed that this turtle had on her belly the image of a child needing nourishment and I felt that there was some connection between this experience and my own inner child. I kept crying for a long time without consolation.*
>
> *After a long time, something changed and I felt that this turtle's shell had on it the image of a beautiful landscape. Then my experience changed again and I became a small child, who could not change her position and needed help from someone else in order to do it. After some time and with great effort, I finally succeeded to turn on my belly and saw myself in a beautiful landscape—running on the beach and diving and swimming in crystal-clear water.*
>
> *I realized that the landscape in which I found myself was the same as the one that was depicted on the turtle's shell. I felt free and enjoyed the scent of the flowers, the rushing cascades, and the air filled with the fragrance of the pines. I felt old like the earth and young like the Eternal Puppy (a playful reference to the Jungian archetype of Puella Eterna). I saw a small pond and I went to drink; as I did, I felt deeply relaxed and the sense of health and great well-being filled my body and my mind.*
>
> *Some time later, I shared this experience with my mother and she told me that when I was a year old, my pediatrician decided that I had to be put in a cast with my legs apart, because of an imperfect structure of my hip joints. I had to stay immobilized for forty days.*

The second example is from psycholytic therapy with LSD that I conducted at the Psychiatric Research Institute in Prague; the name psycholytic refers to serial administrations of medium dosages of the substance. Milan was a 36-year-old architect who enrolled in the LSD program with the diagnosis of psychogenic asthma after unsuccessful conventional therapy.

A series of LSD sessions revealed a major multilevel memory constellation underlying this disorder. The most superficial layer of this system was a memory of near-drowning at the age of seven that brought Milan close to death. A deeper layer of the same system was constituted by memories of being repeatedly choked and smothered by his two years older brother at the age of around four and five.

On an even deeper layer were memories of severe whooping cough at the age of two with episodes of choking. These biographical layers of this memory constellation were linked to an episode of perinatal crisis when his shoulder got stuck behind the pubic bone of his mother. The deepest layer of this complex system was transpersonal; it was what he identified as a past life experience of death on the gallows. It was a punishment for participating in a rebellion against a British king in medieval times.

Milan relived all the above experiences in his serial LSD sessions; it was associated with anxiety, strong coughing, flailing around, and intense tremors. In the course of this therapy, his clinical condition oscillated, but a major relief of his symptoms did not occur until his experience of death in the past life in England.

3) The story of Milan, besides showing the psychotraumatic effect of physical traumas, illustrated another important feature of the biographical/recollective level of the psyche. The work with holotropic states has shown that emotionally relevant memories are not stored in the unconscious as a mosaic of isolated imprints, but in the form of complex dynamic constellations. I have coined for these memory aggregates the name *COEX systems,* which is short for "systems of condensed experience." This concept is of such theoretical and practical importance that it deserves special discussion.

A COEX system consists of *emotionally charged memories from different periods of our life that resemble each other in the quality of emotions or physical sensations that they share.* Each COEX has a basic theme that permeates all its layers and represents their common denominator. The individual layers then contain variations on this basic theme that occurred at different periods of the person's life. The unconscious of a particular individual can contain several major COEX constellations. Their number, intensity, and the nature of the central themes varies considerably person to person.

The layers of a particular system can, for example, contain all the major memories of humiliating, degrading, and shaming experiences that have damaged our self-esteem. In another COEX system, the common denominator can be anxiety experienced in various shocking and terrifying situations, or claustrophobic and suffocating feelings evoked by oppressive and confining circumstances. Rejection and emotional deprivation, damaging the ability to trust men, women, or people in general, is another common motif. Situations that have generated profound feelings of guilt and a sense of failure, events that have resulted in a conviction that sex is dangerous or disgusting, and encounters with aggression and violence can be added to the above list as characteristic examples. Particularly important are COEX systems that contain memories of encounters with situations endangering life, health, and the integrity of the body.

This could leave the impression that COEX systems always contain painful and traumatic memories. However, it is the intensity of the experience and its emotional relevance that determines whether a memory will be included into a COEX, not its unpleasant nature. In addition to negative constellations, there are also those that comprise memories of very pleasant or even ecstatic events—memories of loving and fulfilling relationships, episodes of harmony in the family, stays in beautiful natural settings, major accomplishments and achievements, and so on.

COEX systems involving painful emotions and unpleasant physical feelings are, however, more common than the positive ones. This concept emerged from psychotherapy with clients suffering from serious forms of psychopathology, where the work on traumatic aspects of life plays a very important role. This accounts for the fact that constellations involving painful experiences receive much more attention. The spectrum of negative COEX systems is also considerably richer and more variegated than that of the positive ones. As Joseph Campbell pointed out, the misery in our life can have many different forms, while happiness depends on the fulfillment of a few basic conditions. However, a general discussion requires emphasizing that the COEX dynamics is not limited to constellations of traumatic memories.

In the early stage of my psychedelic research, when I first discovered the existence of COEX systems, I described them as principles governing the dynamics of the biographical level of the unconscious. At that time, my understanding of psychology was based on a very narrow biographical model of the psyche inherited from teachers, particularly my Freudian analyst. It was also true that, in the initial psychedelic sessions of a therapeutic series, especially when lower dosages (15–200 mcg) were used, the biographical material often dominated the picture.

This stage proved to be very important for the exploration of various layers of the psyche and their relationship to the dynamics of the symptoms, deemed "chemoarcheology," or the "onion-peeling of the unconscious," as some of my clients called it. Since my patients were allowed to keep their eyes open for significant parts of their sessions, I also gained important insights into the dynamics of their optical illusions and visions. I described these findings in some detail in my book *Realms of the Human Unconscious* (Grof 1975). I found out that keeping the eyes open was not the most effective therapeutic strategy, but it was essential for the discovery of the COEX systems and their influence on the phenomenology of the psychedelic experiences.

In the course of this research, it became clear to me that the COEX systems were not limited to the biographical level, but reached much deeper into the unconscious. In my present understanding, each of the COEX constellations seems to be superimposed over and anchored in a particular aspect of the birth process (a basic perinatal matrix or BPM). The experience of biological birth is so complex and rich in emotions and physical sensations that it contains in a prototypical form the elementary themes of most conceivable COEX systems. However, a typical COEX system reaches even further and its deepest roots consist of various forms of transpersonal phenomena, such as ancestral, collective, and karmic memories, Jungian archetypes, conscious identification with various animals, phylogenetic memories, and others.

I now see the COEX systems as general organizing principles of the human psyche. During our joint research, now extending over a period of more than forty years, Richard Tarnas and I have discovered that the phenomenology of holotropic states in general, and of the COEX systems in particular, can best be understood through the lens of archetypal dynamics. As we will see at a later date, that makes archetypal astrology what I call the "Rosetta Stone" of consciousness research." The concept of the COEX system has some similarity to C. G. Jung's ideas about "psychological complexes" (Jung 1960b) and Hanscarl Leuner's notion of "transphenomenal dynamic systems," (tdysts) (Leuner 1962), but it has many features that differentiate it from both of them. Before continuing the discussion about COEX systems, I would like to briefly outline the similarities and differences between these three concepts.

C. G. Jung's concept of "complex" emerged from his work with the association experiment. He inferred it on the basis of disturbances of the association process—prolonged reaction time and gaps or falsification of memory during repetition of the experiment. Jung described the complex as a mass of memories and other psychological content that share a definite feeling tone (irritation, fear, anger, etc). Every complex has a "nuclear element," a vehicle of meaning, and a number of associations stemming from personal experience.

The Rosetta Stone is a granodiorite stele found in 1799 in the Nile delta by a French soldier. It was inscribed with three versions of a decree issued at Memphis by Ptolemy 5 in 196 BC. These versions were written in ancient Egyptian hieroglyphic script, demotic script, and ancient Greek. This helped Jean François Champollion solve, in 1820, the secret of the Egyptian hieroglyphs.

Jung pointed out the resemblance of complexes with Richard Wagner's use of "leitmotifs," distinct musical themes characterizing *dramatis personae,* animals, objects, and situations: "The leitmotifs are the feeling tones of our complexes, our actions and moods are modulations of the leitmotifs." At the bottom of each complex, Jung found a universal governing principle, or an "archetype." For Jung, this complex was comprised

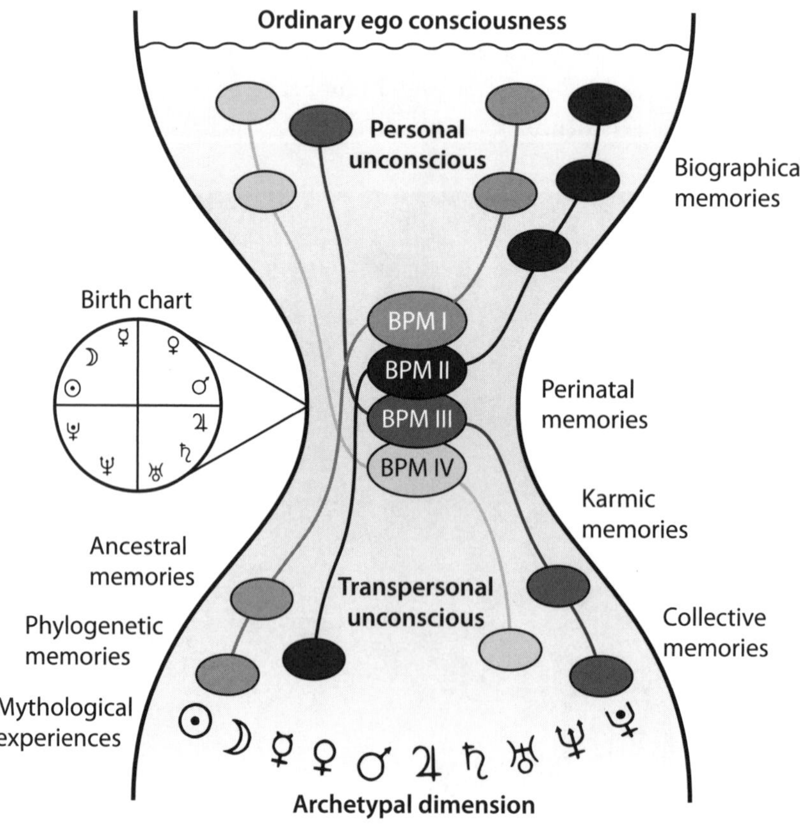

Diagram of a COEX system showing layers of postnatal memories from different periods of life (upper part) and transpersonal experiences (karmic, ancestral, and phylogenetic memories and archetypal motifs) (lower part). In the center are the Basic Perinatal Matrices (BPMs I–IV); what connects all the constituents within the COEX systems is that they share the same archetypal-thematic quality.

of biographical and archetypal material. He did not include in it any perinatal elements, since he did not believe that biological birth was of any relevance for psychology.

Jung assigned to complexes the central role in depth psychology. Complexes, not the dreams as Freud thought, were for him the *"via regia* to the unconscious." In humans, complexes manifest as involuntary fantasy images, attitudes, and actions that are specific for them. They can be found everywhere and at all epochs; they are "numinous" and can be detected above all in the realm of religious ideas. According to Jung, complexes have not only an obsessive, but often possessive, character: "Everybody knows nowadays that people 'have complexes.' What is not so well known, though far more important theoretically, is that complexes can have us." Complexes behave like sabotaging imps and give rise to all sorts of annoying, ridiculous, and revealing actions; they are behind the phenomena that Freud called "psychopathology of everyday life"—slips of the tongue and falsifications of memory and judgment. Intellectual knowledge of a complex is useless; its harmful action will continue until we discharge it. Then it rises into consciousness and can be assimilated.

Hanscarl Leuner's concept of the transphenomenal dynamic systems (tdysts) came from his work with the serial administration of low doses of psychedelics. My concept of COEX systems was formulated and described independently from Leuner's tdysts. (At that time in Prague, we could not get hard currency to buy foreign literature and did not have contact with researchers from the West). In his book *Die Experimentelle Psychose,* Leuner described tdysts as "layered constellations of emotionally charged memories from different periods of postnatal life—infancy, childhood, and adulthood." Leuner developed this concept specifically to explain the phenomenology of LSD sessions; he did not try to apply it to other areas (Leuner 1962).

According to Leuner, the tdysts determine the nature and content of LSD sessions. The layer of the tdyst emerging into consciousness influences the individual's thoughts, feelings, behavior, and the illusive transformations of the therapist and environment to the patient. Up to this point, the tdyst resembles the COEX system. But Leuner's model is based on Freudian psychoanalysis and is limited to postnatal biography; it does not include the perinatal and transpersonal levels of the psyche.

Leuner claimed that when all the layers of a tdyst emerge into consciousness and its emotional charge is dissipated, it loses its power over the individual's behavior and experience of the world. According to my observations, the archetypal field of the COEX usually reaches deeper into the psyche, to the perinatal and transpersonal levels. Leuner's model of the psyche remained limited to the postnatal biographical level. Having used low doses of LSD (75mcg), he did not discover the perinatal domain of the unconscious and reduced the transpersonal to the infantile ("the transcendental equals the primary narcissistic").

The COEX systems play an important role in our psychological life: they can influence the way we perceive ourselves, other people, and the world, as well as how we feel and act. They are the dynamic forces behind our emotional and psychosomatic symptoms, difficulties in relationships with other people, and irrational behaviors. And whereas Leuner's concept of tdysts does not imply a two-way interaction with the environment, I found that there exists a dynamic interplay between the COEX systems

Hanscarl Leuner (1919–1996), German psychiatrist and psychedelic pioneer, author of a psychotherapeutic method called Guided Affective Imagery (GAI).

and the external world. External events in our life can specifically activate corresponding COEX systems and, conversely, active COEX systems can determine how we perceive ourselves and the world, and make us behave in such a way that we recreate their core themes in our present life.

This mechanism can be observed very clearly in experiential work. In holotropic states, the content of the experience, the perception of the environment, and the behavior of the client are determined in general terms by the COEX system that dominates the session and, more specifically, by the layer of this system that is momentarily emerging into consciousness. All the characteristics of COEX systems can best be demonstrated by a practical example. I have chosen, for this purpose, Peter, a 37-year-old tutor who had been intermittently hospitalized and unsuccessfully treated in our department in Prague prior to his psychedelic therapy.

At the time we began with the experiential sessions, Peter could hardly function in his everyday life. He was almost constantly obsessed with the idea of finding a man with certain physical characteristics, preferably dressed in black clothes. He wanted to befriend this man and tell him about his urgent desire to be locked in a dark cellar and be exposed to various diabolic physical and mental tortures. Unable to concentrate on anything else, he wandered aimlessly through the city, visiting public parks, lavatories, bars, and railroad stations searching for the "right man."

He succeeded on several occasions to persuade or bribe various men who met his criteria to promise or do what he asked for. Having a special gift for finding persons with sadistic traits, he was almost killed twice, several times seriously hurt, and once robbed of all his money. On those occasions, where he was able to experience what he craved, he was extremely frightened and actually strongly disliked the tortures. In addition to this main problem, Peter suffered from suicidal depression, impotence, and infrequent epileptiform seizures.

Reconstructing his history, I found out that his major problems started at the time of his involuntary employment in Germany during World War II. The Nazis used people brought to Germany from occupied territories for work in places threatened by air raids, such as foundries and ammunition factories. They referred to this form of slave labor as *Totaleinsetzung*. At that time, two SS officers repeatedly forced him at gunpoint to engage in their homosexual practices. When the war was over, Peter realized that these experiences created in him a strong preference for homosexual intercourse experienced in the passive role. This gradually changed into fetishism for black male clothes and finally into the complex obsessive-compulsive masochistic behavior described above.

Fifteen consecutive psychedelic sessions revealed a very interesting and important COEX system underlying his problems. In its most superficial layers were Peter's more recent traumatic experiences with his sadistic partners. On several occasions, the accomplices he recruited actually bound him with ropes, locked him in a cellar without food and water, and tortured him by flagellation and strangulation, according to his wish. One of these men hit him on his head, bound him with a string, and left him lying in a forest after stealing his money.

Peter's most dramatic adventure involved a man who claimed he had just the kind of cellar Peter wanted in his cabin in the woods and promised to take him there. When they were traveling by train to this man's weekend house, Peter was struck by his companion's strange-looking bulky backpack. When the latter left the compartment and went to the bathroom, Peter stepped up on the seat and checked the suspicious baggage. He discovered a complete set of murder weapons, including a gun, a large butcher knife, a freshly sharpened hatchet, and a surgical saw used for amputations. Panic-stricken, he jumped out of the moving train and suffered serious injuries. Elements of the above episodes formed the superficial layers of Peter's most important COEX system.

A deeper layer of the same system contained Peter's memories from the Third Reich. In the sessions where this part of the COEX constellation manifested, he relived his experiences with the homosexual SS officers in detail, with all the complicated feelings involved. In addition, he relived several other traumatic memories from World War II and dealt with the entire oppressive atmosphere of this period. He had visions of pompous Nazi military parades and rallies, banners with swastikas, ominous giant eagle emblems, scenes from concentration camps, and many others.

Then came layers related to Peter's childhood, particularly those involving punishment by his parents. His alcoholic father was often violent when he was drunk and used to beat him with a large leather strap. His mother's favorite method of punishing him was to lock him into a dark cellar without food for long periods of time. Peter recalled that throughout his childhood, she always wore black dresses; he did not remember her ever wearing anything else. At this point, he realized that one of the roots of his obsession seemed to be craving suffering that would combine elements of punishment inflicted on him by his parents.

However, that was not the whole story. As we continued with the sessions, the process deepened and Peter confronted the trauma of his birth with all its biological brutality. This situation had all the elements that he expected from the sadistic treatment he was so desperately trying to receive: dark enclosed space, confinement and restriction of physical movement, and exposure to extreme physical and emotional tortures. Reliving the trauma of his birth finally resolved his difficult symptoms to such an extent that he could once again function in life.

In a holotropic state, when a COEX system is emerging into consciousness, it assumes a governing function and determines the nature and content of the experience. Our perceptions of ourselves and of the human and physical environment are distorted and illusively transformed in correspondence with the basic motif of the emerging COEX constellation, and with the specific features of its individual layers. This mechanism can be illustrated by describing the dynamics of Peter's holotropic process.

When Peter was working through the most superficial layers of the described COEX system, he saw me transformed into his past sadistic partners or into figures symbolizing aggression, such as a butcher, murderer, medieval executioner, Inquisitor, or cowboy with a lasso. He perceived my fountain pen as an Oriental dagger and expected to be attacked with it. When he saw on the table a knife with a stag horn handle used for opening envelopes, he immediately saw me changing into a violent-looking forester. On several occasions, he asked to be tortured and wanted to suffer "for the doctor" by withholding urination. During this period, the treatment room and the view from the window were illusively transformed into various settings where Peter's adventures with his sadistic partners took place.

When the older layer from World War II was the focus of his experience, Peter saw me transformed into Hitler and other Nazi leaders, a concentration camp commander, SS member, and Gestapo officer. Instead of ordinary noises outside the treatment room, he heard ominous sounds of parading soldiers' boots, music from the Nazi rallies and parades by the Brandenburg Gate, and the national anthem of Nazi Germany. The treatment room was successively transformed into a room in the Reichstag with eagle emblems and swastikas, a barrack in a concentration camp, a jail with heavy bars in the window, and even a death row.

When the core experiences from childhood were emerging in these sessions, Peter perceived me as punishing parental figures. At this time, he tended to display toward me various anachronistic behavior patterns characteristic of his relationship with his father and mother. The treatment room was changing into various parts of his home setting in childhood, particularly into the dark cellar in which he was repeatedly locked up by his mother.

The mechanism described above has its dynamic counterpart: the tendency of external stimuli to activate corresponding COEX systems of persons in holotropic states and to facilitate the emergence of the content of these systems into consciousness. This happens in those instances where specific external influences, such as elements of the physical setting, interpersonal environment, or therapeutic situation bear a resemblance to the original traumatic scenes or contain identical components. This seems to be the key for understanding the extraordinary significance of set and setting for the holotropic experience. A sequence from one of Peter's LSD sessions illustrates the activation of a COEX system by specific external stimuli accidentally introduced into the therapeutic situations.

One of the important core experiences that Peter uncovered in his LSD therapy was a memory of being locked by his mother into a dark cellar and denied food while the other members of the family were eating. The reliving of this memory was triggered quite unexpectedly by the angry barking of a dog that ran by the open window of the treatment room. The analysis of this event showed an interesting relationship between the external stimulus and the activated memory. Peter recalled that the cellar his mother used for punishment had a small window overlooking the neighbor's courtyard. The neighbor's German Shepherd, chained to his doghouse, used to bark almost incessantly on the occasions when Peter was confined in the cellar.

In holotropic states, people often manifest seemingly inappropriate and highly exaggerated reactions to various environmental stimuli. Such overreacting is specific and selective, and can usually be understood in terms of the dynamics of the governing COEX systems. Thus, patients are particularly sensitive to what they consider uninterested, cold, and "professional" treatment when they are under the influence of memory constellations that involve emotional deprivation, rejection, or neglect by their parents or other relevant figures in their childhood.

When they are working through the problems of rivalry with their siblings, patients may attempt to monopolize the therapist and want to be the only or at least the favorite patient. They find it difficult to accept that the therapist has other patients, and can be extremely irritated by any sign of interest paid to somebody else. Patients, who on other occasions do not mind or even wish to be left alone during a session, cannot bear for the therapist to leave the room for any reason when they are connecting with memories related to abandonment and childhood loneliness. These are just a few examples of situations in which oversensitivity to external circumstances reflects an underlying COEX system.

The common denominator in the COEX systems we have described so far is the quality of emotions or physical feelings that their layers share. There also exists a different category of COEX systems that can be referred to as interpersonal COEX systems. In these dynamic constellations, the common denominator is a certain type of relationship to a specific category of people—authority figures, sexual partners, or peers. Knowledge of these systems is extremely important for understanding the dynamics of the therapeutic process and the interpersonal problems that might develop between therapists/sitters and individuals who are in holotropic states of consciousness. It is also one of the most important therapeutic mechanisms in psychotherapy.

In the world of psychotherapy, there are many schools, which show a disturbing lack of agreement about some fundamental issues: what are the dimensions of the human psyche; what are its most important motivating forces; why do emotional and psychosomatic symptoms develop, what do they mean, and why do they take a specific form; and what techniques and strategy should be used in the work with clients. As a result, the psychotherapeutic procedures and the interpretations of the same psychological content are very different from school to school.

Studies of therapeutic results have shown some difference between being in psychotherapy and being on the waiting list, but failed to demonstrate any significant differences between the results of different schools (Frank and Frank 1991). The differences are instead found inside the schools rather than between them. In each of the schools, there are individuals who are known as better therapists than their colleagues. This brings up some interesting questions: what are the effective mechanisms in psychotherapy, when can verbal therapy help and why, and what are its limits?

It is clear that the answer is not to have a better understanding of the psyche and more accurate and better-timed interpretations, because these are factors that vary from one school to another. Some factors that have been mentioned as effective, on the other hand, are the quality of the human encounter between the therapist and client, compatibility and resonance between the personalities of the therapist and patient, and the feeling of being unconditionally accepted by another human being, often for the first time in one's life. Astrologers would talk about harmonious alignment between the charts of the two individuals.

It seems that breaking repetitive traumatic patterns in interpersonal relations (or interpersonal COEX systems) might play a critical role in successful therapy. An interesting study we conducted at the Psychiatric Research Institute in Prague about fifty years ago demonstrated this. This study focused on the following problem: when we look at the lives of people who have emotional or psychosomatic disorders, we discover that they tend to repeat the same kind of dysfunctional patterns in relationships with certain categories of relationships—figures in positions of authority, men, women, sexual partners, or peers. Their partners in these relationships might have very different personalities, but these clients tend to eventually develop the same kind of problems. Our study was an attempt to understand the mechanisms involved.

The research that we conducted at the Psychiatric Research Institute in Prague was called *Study of the Development of Interpersonal Relationships.* We selected eighteen patients from our outpatient department, nine men and nine women. None of these patients knew any of the others before the beginning of the study. We emptied our open-door, in-patient department and admitted all these patients on the same day. In the afternoon on the first day, they sat down in three randomly selected circles of six and were given questionnaires based on Timothy Leary's *Interpersonal Diagnostic Test of Personality.* This was a personality test that made Leary famous long before he took any psychedelic substances (Leary 1957).

Leary's questions about interpersonal relationships can be arranged on a system of coordinates where the vertical axis (ordinate) is dominance/submission and the horizontal axis (abscissa) is hate/love. They describe various combinations of these four attributes. For our project, the questions in the questionnaires describing the nature of the relationships of the patients to their co-patients were formulated in the future tense. They were thus guessing what kind of relationships they would have with their co-patients before they knew anything about them.

Following their admission, these patients then lived together in our institute for four weeks. They had a rich program consisting of various sports, artistic activity, occupational therapy, walks in nature, games, cultural events, etc. At the end of each week, they were again given the same interpersonal questionnaires, this time formulated in the present tense, describing the actual relationships they were having with their co-patients.

After the patients chose the statements describing the nature of their relationship (e.g. he/she is criticizing me, trying to control me, is supporting me, is affectionate with me, etc), the results were entered into a graph with the two coordinates and concentric circles, resembling a target for archery. According to Leary, the resulting pattern of a person with healthy relationships would be relatively balanced. Dysfunctional relationships would result in patterns heavily loaded in some of the quadrants.

This research brought some interesting results. It showed that in patients whose initial graphs showed strong expectations of dysfunctional relationships with specific co-patients, future descriptions of the actual relationships showed strong convergence with the initial expectations ("self-fulfilling prophecy"). The next step in the study was then asking the patients to use the same questionnaire in the past tense and describe their relationships with the members of their family of origin.

Dysfunctional repetitive patterns could be traced to the dynamics of the nuclear family: issues with authority figures (teachers, bosses, military officers, etc.) were connected to parents who imposed discipline in the family, problems in sexual relationships to one of the parents or the pattern of their marriage, and conflicts with the peer group to sibling rivalry. The critical period was the age of five or six, when the children start to apply patterns of interpersonal behavior established within a very unrepresentative sample of the population (nuclear family) to a larger community (teachers, schoolmates, and various acquaintances).

The question then was: are these patterns going to be corrected or reinforced? Since human relationships are complementary, an average person tends to respond in a predictable and expected way and thus reinforces a dysfunctional pattern. The task of a good teacher, ideal boss, and eventually the therapist is to respond in an atypical and unexpected way, to break the repetitive pattern and provide a corrective experience. The task of the therapist is particularly challenging and critical. By the time the client comes to a therapist, the dysfunctional patterns have been reinforced through many repetitions. Psychotherapy cannot be neutral; it either reinforces the client's dysfunctional patterns or provides a corrective experience. In psychotherapy, this is known as the Jean Valjean phenomenon.

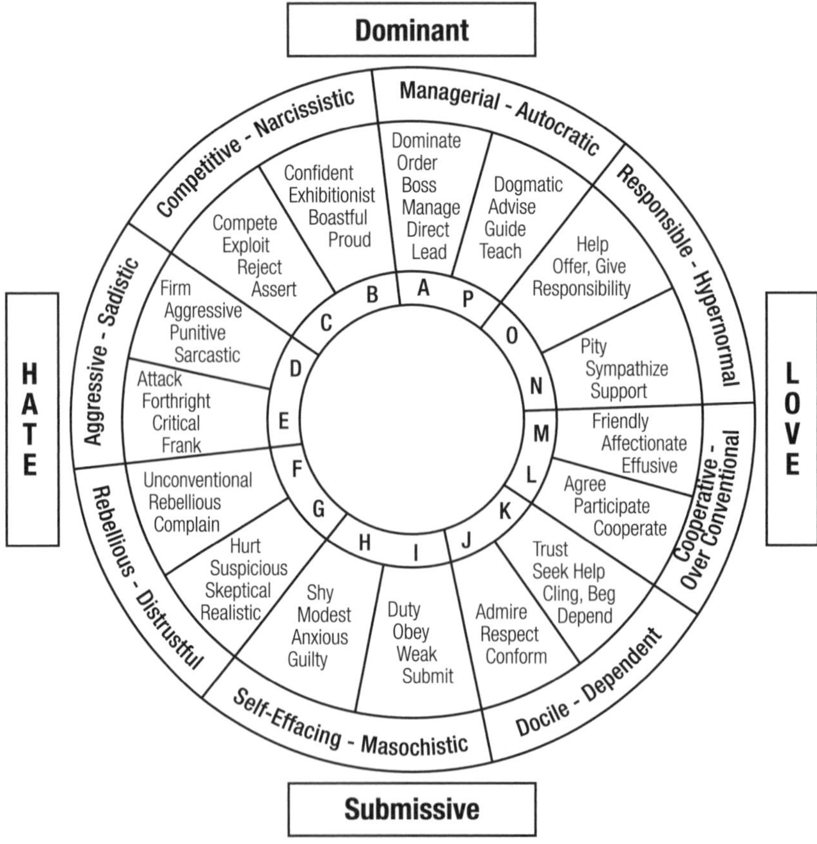

A diagram showing the structure of Timothy Leary's Interpersonal Diagnostic Questionnaire.

Here is the story from Victor Hugo's *Les Misérables* that gave it the name.

The convict Jean Valjean is released from a French prison after serving nineteen years for stealing a loaf of bread and for subsequent attempts to escape from prison. When Valjean arrives in a town, no one is willing to give him shelter because he is an ex-convict. Desperate, Valjean knocks on the door of a kind bishop who treats Valjean with great kindness as a valued guest. Valjean repays the bishop by stealing his silverware and taking off. When the policemen arrest Valjean, they recognize the initials on the silverware and take him back to the bishop's house. The bishop covers for him, claiming that the silverware was a gift. The gendarmes release Valjean and the bishop makes him promise to become an honest man. Under an assumed name, Valjean invents an ingenious manufacturing process that brings the town prosperity. He becomes an honest man and is eventually voted the town's mayor.

When we are working with holotropic states, it is important to be aware of the clients' repetitive interpersonal patterns, because these can become activated and amplified and create difficult situations in therapy. However, regression in holotropic states also provides an extraordinary opportunity for a corrective experience on a very deep level. The presence of a strong and loving male or female, the simultaneous presence of a male and female who get along unlike one's parents, and the satisfaction of unmet anaclitic needs experienced in deep regression can have an extraordinary healing and transformative effect on the previously afflicted categories of interpersonal relationships.

The Perinatal Level of the Unconscious

When our process of deep experiential self-exploration moves beyond the level of memories from childhood and infancy and reaches back to birth, we start encountering emotions and physical sensations of extreme intensity, often surpassing anything we previously considered possible. At this point, the experiences become a strange mixture of being born and dying. They involve a sense of severe, life-threatening confinement and a desperate and determined struggle to free ourselves and survive.

Due to the close connection between this domain of the unconscious and biological birth, I have chosen for it the name *perinatal.* It is a Greek-Latin composite word in which the prefix *peri,* means "near" or "around," and the root *natalis* signifies "pertaining to childbirth." This word is commonly used in medicine to describe various biological processes occurring shortly before, during, and immediately after birth. The obstetricians talk, for example, about perinatal hemorrhage, infection, or brain damage. However, since according to traditional medicine, the child does not consciously experience birth and this event is not recorded in memory, one never hears about perinatal experiences. The use of the term *perinatal* in connection with consciousness reflects my own findings and is entirely new (Grof 1975).

The strong representation of birth and death in our unconscious psyche and the close association between them might surprise mainstream psychologists and psychiatrists, since it challenges their deeply ingrained beliefs. According to the traditional medical view, only a birth so difficult that it causes irreversible damage to the brain cells can have psychopathological consequences, and even then mostly of a neurological nature, such as mental retardation or hyperactivity.

The official position of academic psychiatry is that biological birth is not recorded in memory and does not constitute a psychotrauma. The usual reason for denying the possibility of birth memory is that the cerebral cortex of the newborn is not mature enough to mediate the experiencing and recording of this event. More specifically, the cortical neurons are not yet fully "myelinized"—which means completely covered with the protective sheaths of a fatty substance called *myelin.* Surprisingly, this same argument is not used to deny the existence and importance of memories from the time of nursing, a period that immediately follows birth.

The psychological significance of the experiences of nursing and even bonding—the exchange of looks and physical contact between the mother and child immediately after birth—is generally recognized and acknowledged by mainstream obstetricians, pediatricians, and child psychiatrists (Klaus, Kennell, and Klaus 1985, Kennel and Klaus 1988). The image of the newborn as an unconscious and unresponsive organism is also in sharp conflict with the growing body of literature describing the remarkable sensitivity of the fetus during the prenatal period (Verny and Kelly 1981, Tomatis 1991, Whitwell 1999, Moon, Lagercrantz, and Kuhl 2010).

The denial of the possibility of birth memory based on the fact that the cerebral cortex of the newborn is not fully myelinized is particularly absurd considering that the capacity for memory exists in much lower life forms that do not have a cerebral cortex at all. In 2001, an American neuroscientist of Austrian origin, Eric Kandel, received a Nobel Prize in physiology for his research of the memory mechanisms of the sea slug Aplysia, an organism incomparably more primitive than the newborn human child. And it is well known that certain primitive forms of protoplasmic memory exist even in unicellular organisms. The most likely explanation of this striking logical inconsistency occurring in individuals trained in rigorous scientific thinking is the psychological repression of the terrifying memory of biological birth.

The amount of emotional and physical stress involved in childbirth clearly surpasses that of any postnatal trauma in infancy and childhood discussed in psychodynamic literature, with the possible exception of extreme forms of physical abuse. Various forms of experiential psychotherapy have amassed convincing evidence that biological birth is the most profound trauma of our life and an event of paramount psychospiritual importance. It is recorded in our memory in miniscule details down to the cellular level and it has a profound effect on our psychological development.

Reliving various aspects of biological birth can be very convincing and the process often replays in photographic detail. This can occur even in people who have no intellectual knowledge about their birth and lack elementary obstetric information. All these details can be confirmed if good birth records or reliable personal witnesses are available. For example, we can discover through direct experience that we had a breech birth, that forceps were used during our delivery, or that we were born with the umbilical cord twisted around the neck. We can feel the anxiety, biological fury, physical pain, and suffocation that we experienced during birth and even accurately recognize the type of anesthesia used when we were born.

This is often accompanied by various postures and movements of the body, arms, and legs, as well as rotations, flexions and deflections of the head that accurately recreate the mechanics of a particular type of delivery. When we are reliving birth, bruises, swellings, and other vascular changes can unexpectedly appear on the skin in the places where the forceps were applied or where the umbilical cord was constricting the throat. These observations suggest that the record of the trauma of birth reaches all the way down to the cellular level.

The intimate connection between birth and death in our unconscious psyche makes eminent sense. It reflects the fact that birth is a potentially or actually life-threatening event. The delivery brutally terminates the intrauterine existence of the fetus. The fetus "dies" as an aquatic organism and is born as an air-breathing, physiologically and even anatomically different form of life. Its collapsed lungs expand and, together with the kidneys and the gastrointestinal system, take over the functions previously performed by the placenta—breathing, excretion of urine, and elimination of the waste products.

The passage through the birth canal is, in and of itself, a difficult and potentially dangerous process that can bring us close to death. Various complications of birth, such as a serious discrepancy between the size of the child and the pelvic opening, the transversal position of the fetus, breech birth, or placenta praevia can further increase the emotional and physical challenges associated with this process. The child and the mother can lose their lives during delivery and children might be born severely blue from asphyxiation, or even dead and in need of resuscitation.

The conscious reliving and integration of the trauma of birth plays an important role in the process of experiential psychotherapy and self-exploration. The experiences originating on the perinatal level of the unconscious appear in four distinct experiential patterns, each of which is characterized by specific emotions, physical feelings, and symbolic imagery. These patterns are closely related to the experiences that the fetus has before the onset of birth and during the three consecutive stages of biological delivery. These experiences leave deep unconscious imprints in the psyche that later in life have an important influence on the individual. I refer to these four dynamic constellations in the deep unconscious as *Basic Perinatal Matrices* or *BPMs.*

The spectrum of perinatal experiences is not limited to those that can be derived from the biological and psychological processes involved in childbirth. Perinatal matrices form integral parts of COEX systems that also contain postnatal memories and transpersonal experiences with which they share the same archetypal qualities. These can alternate with the reliving of the fetal memories or appear simultaneously with them in various combinations. The BPMs represent important gateways to the collective unconscious described by C. G. Jung. Identification with the infant facing the ordeal of the passage through the birth canal seems to provide access to experiences involving people from other times and cultures, various animals, and even mythological figures. It is as if by connecting with the fetus struggling to be born, one connects in an intimate, almost mystical way with other sentient beings who are in a similar predicament.

The connections between the experiences of the consecutive stages of biological birth and various symbolic images associated with them are very specific and consistent. The reason why they emerge together is not understandable in terms of conventional logic. However, that does not mean that these associations are arbitrary and random. They have their own deep order that can best be referred to as "experiential logic." What this means is that the connection between the experiences characteristic for various stages of birth and the concomitant symbolic themes are not based on some formal external similarity, but on the fact that they share the same emotional feelings and physical sensations.

Perinatal matrices are rich and complex and have specific biological and psychological features, as well as archetypal connections. Experiential confrontation with birth and death seems to result automatically in a spiritual opening and the discovery of the mystical dimensions of the psyche and of existence. Once the age regression reaches the perinatal level, a new expe-

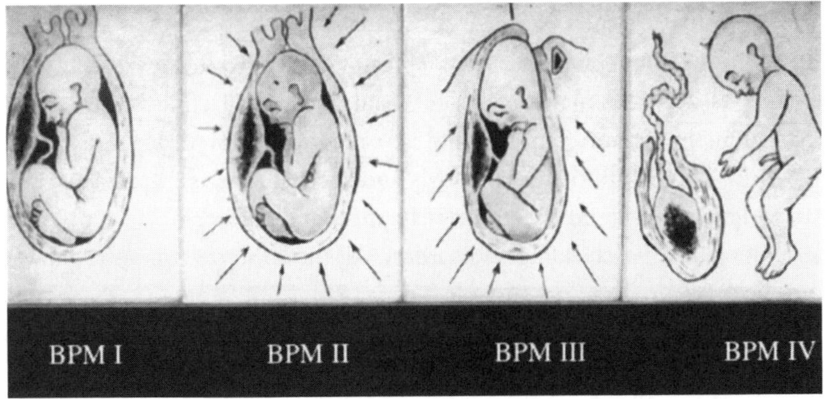

A model portraying the stages of biological birth underlying the four Basic Perinatal Matrices (BPM I–BPM IV).

riential quality enters the experience: C. G. Jung used the name *numinosity*, a term that he borrowed from Rudolf Otto. This neutral term makes it possible to avoid words with a similar meaning that have been used in various contexts and could be easily misunderstood, such as religious, sacred, spiritual, mystical or magical.

The encounter with perinatal matrices can occur in sessions with psychedelic substances, during Holotropic Breathwork, in the course of spontaneous psychospiritual crises ("spiritual emergencies"), or in actual life situations, such as during childbirth or in near-death experiences (NDEs) (Ring 1982). The specific symbolism of these experiences comes from the collective unconscious, not from the individual memory banks. It can thus draw on any historical period, geographical area, and spiritual tradition of the world, quite independently from the subject's cultural or religious background.

Individual perinatal matrices have connections with certain categories of postnatal experiences that share the same archetypal qualities and belong to the same COEX systems. They also have associations with the archetypes of Mother Nature, the Great Mother Goddess, Heaven, and Paradise (BPM I); the Terrible Mother Goddess and Hell (BPM II); Sabbath of the Witches and satanic rituals (BPM III); Purgatory and deities from different cultures representing death and rebirth (BPM III-IV), and divine epiphany, the alchemical *cauda pavonis* (peacock tail), and rainbow arc (BPM IV). Later in the book, we will explore the remarkable parallels between the phenomenology of BPMs I-IV and the astrological archetypes Neptune, Saturn, Pluto, and Uranus.

Additional types of experiences that can be included in the same COEX system as perinatal matrices are ancestral, racial, collective, karmic, and phylogenetic memories. We should also mention theoretically and practically important links between BPMs and specific aspects of physiological activities in the Freudian erogenous zones, and to specific categories of emotional and psychosomatic disorders. All these interrelations are shown on the synoptic paradigm in table 2 (pp. 171).

Reinforced by strong, emotionally charged experiences from infancy, childhood, and later life, perinatal matrices can shape our perception of the world, profoundly influence our everyday behavior, and contribute to the development of various emotional and psychosomatic disorders. On a collective scale, perinatal matrices play an important role in religion, art, mythology, philosophy, and various sociopolitical phenomena, such as totalitarian systems, wars, revolutions, and genocide. We will explore these broader implications of perinatal dynamics in later chapters.

First Basic Perinatal Matrix: BPM I (Primal Union with the Mother)

This matrix is related to the intrauterine existence before the onset of the delivery. The experiential world of this period can be referred to as the "amniotic universe." When we identify with the fetus in the womb, we do not have the awareness of boundaries and do not differentiate between the inner and the outer. This is reflected in the nature of the experiences associated with reliving the memory of the prenatal state. During episodes of undisturbed embryonic existence, we typically have experiences of vast regions with no boundaries or limits—interstellar space, galaxies, or the entire cosmos. A related experience is floating in the sea, identifying with various aquatic animals, such as fish, jellyfish, dolphins, or whales, or even becoming the ocean. This seems to reflect the fact that the fetus is essentially an aquatic creature.

Positive intrauterine experiences can also be associated with archetypal visions of Mother Nature—safe, beautiful, and unconditionally nourishing like a good womb. We can envision fruit-bearing orchards, fields of ripe corn, agricultural terraces in the Andes, or unspoiled Polynesian islands. Mythological images from the collective unconscious that often appear in this context portray various celestial realms and paradises as they are described in mythologies of different cultures, even those of which we have no intellectual knowledge. The type of ecstasy associated with BPM I can be called *Apollonian* or *oceanic;* it is characterized by the transcendence of time and space, feelings of peace, tranquility, clarity, and cosmic unity.

When we are reliving episodes of intrauterine disturbances, memories of the "bad womb," we have a sense of a dark and ominous threat and often feel that we are being poisoned. We might see images that portray polluted waters and toxic dumps. This reflects the fact that many prenatal disturbances are caused by toxic changes in the body of the pregnant mother. Sequences of this kind can be associated with archetypal visions of frightening demonic entities or with a sense of insidious all-pervading evil. Those of us who are reliving episodes of more violent interference with prenatal existence, such as an imminent miscarriage or attempted abortion, usually experience some form of universal threat or bloody apocalyptic visions of the end of the world. This again reflects the intimate interconnections between events in our biological history and the Jungian archetypes.

The following account of a high-dose psychedelic session can be used as a typical example of a BPM I experience, opening at times into the transpersonal realm.

> *All that I was experiencing was an intense sense of malaise resembling a flu. I could not believe that a high dose of LSD, which in my previous sessions had produced dramatic psychological changes, could evoke such a minimal response. I decided to close my eyes and observe carefully what was happening. At this point, the experience seemed to deepen and I realized that what with my eyes open appeared to be an adult experience of a viral disease now changed into a realistic situation of a fetus suffering some strange toxic assaults during its intrauterine existence.*
>
> *I was greatly reduced in size, and my head was considerably bigger than the rest of my body and my extremities. I was suspended in a liquid milieu and some harmful chemicals were being channeled into my body through the umbilical area. Using some unknown receptors, I was detecting these influences as noxious and hostile to my organism. While this was happening, I was aware that these toxic "attacks" had something to do with the condition and activity of the body of my mother. Occasionally, I could distinguish influences that appeared to be due to the ingestion of alcohol, inappropriate food, or smoking. A different kind of discomfort seemed to be caused by chemical changes accompanying my mother's emotions—anxieties, nervousness, anger, and conflicting feelings about pregnancy.*
>
> *Then the feelings of sickness and indigestion disappeared, and I was experiencing an ever-increasing state of ecstasy. This was accompanied by a clearing and brightening of my visual field. It was as if multiple layers of thick, dirty cobwebs were being magically*

torn and dissolved, or a movie projection or television broadcast was brought into focus by an invisible cosmic technician. The scenery opened up, and an incredible amount of light and energy enveloped me and streamed in subtle vibrations through my whole being.

On one level, I was still a fetus experiencing the ultimate perfection and bliss of a good womb or a newborn fusing with a nourishing and life-giving breast. On another level, I became the entire universe. I was witnessing the spectacle of the macrocosm with countless pulsating and vibrating galaxies and, at the same time, I was it. These radiant and breathtaking cosmic vistas were intertwined with experiences of the equally miraculous microcosm, from the dance of atoms and molecules to the origins of life and the biochemical world of individual cells. For the first time, I was experiencing the universe for what it really is—an unfathomable mystery, a divine play of Absolute Consciousness.

For some time, I was oscillating between the state of a distressed, sickened fetus and a blissful and serene intrauterine existence. At times, the noxious influences took the form of insidious demons or malevolent creatures from the world of spiritual scriptures or fairy tales. During the undisturbed episodes of fetal existence, I experienced feelings of basic identity and oneness with the universe; it was the Tao, the Beyond that is Within, the "Tat tvam asi" (Thou art That) of the Upanishads. I lost my sense of individuality; my ego dissolved, and I became all of existence.

Sometimes this experience was intangible and contentless, sometimes it was accompanied by many beautiful visions—archetypal images of Paradise, the ultimate cornucopia, golden age, or virginal nature. I became a dolphin playing in the ocean, a fish swimming in crystal-clear waters, a butterfly floating over mountain meadows, and a seagull gliding over the sea. I was the ocean, animals, plants, the clouds—sometimes all these at the same time.

Nothing concrete happened later in the afternoon and in the evening hours. I spent most of this time feeling at one with nature and the universe, bathed in golden light that was slowly decreasing in intensity.

Second Perinatal Matrix: BPM II (Cosmic Engulfment, No Exit or Hell)

While reliving the onset of biological birth, we typically feel that we are being sucked into a gigantic whirlpool or swallowed by some mythic beast. We might also experience the entire world or cosmos being engulfed. This can be associated with images of devouring or entangling archetypal monsters, such as leviathans, dragons, whales, giant snakes, tarantulas, or octopuses. The sense of overwhelming vital threat can lead to intense anxiety and general mistrust bordering on paranoia. Another experiential variety of the beginning of the second matrix is the theme of descending into the depths of the underworld, the realm of death, or Hell. As Joseph Campbell so eloquently described, this is a universal motif in the mythologies of the hero's journey (Campbell 1968, 1972).

In the fully developed first stage of biological birth (the basis of BPM II), the uterine contractions periodically constrict the fetus, and the cervix is not yet open. Each contraction causes compression of the uterine arteries, and the fetus is threatened by lack of oxygen. Reliving this stage of birth is one of the worst experiences we can have during self-exploration that involves holotropic states. We feel caught in a monstrous claustrophobic nightmare, exposed to agonizing emotional and physical pain, and have a sense of utter helplessness and hopelessness. Feelings of loneliness, guilt, the absurdity of life, and existential despair reach metaphysical proportions. A person in this predicament typically loses their sense of linear time and becomes convinced that this situation will never end, and that there is absolutely no way out. An experiential triad characteristic for this state is fear of dying, going crazy, and never coming back.

Reliving this stage of birth is usually accompanied by transpersonal experiences that involve people, animals, and even mythological beings in a painful and hopeless predicament similar to that of the fetus caught in the relentless grip of the contracting uterus. We can experience identification with prisoners in dungeons, victims of the Inquisition, and inmates in concentration camps or insane asylums. Our suffering can take the form of the pain of animals caught in traps or even reach dimensions that are archetypal.

We can experience the torture of sinners in Hell, the agony of Jesus on the cross, or the excruciating torments of Greek archetypal figures representing endless suffering—Sisyphus rolling his boulder up the mountain in the deepest pit of Hades, Prometheus chained to a rock in the Caucasus mountains and having his liver eaten by an eagle, Tantalus vexed by hunger and thirst with luscious fruit and fresh water just out of his reach, and Ixion attached to a fiery wheel spinning through the air in the underworld.

While we are under the influence of this matrix, we are selectively blinded and unable to see anything positive in our life and in human existence in general. The connection to the divine dimension seems to be irretrievably severed and lost. Through the prism of this matrix, life seems to be a meaningless Theater of the Absurd, a farce staging of cardboard characters and mindless robots, or a cruel circus sideshow. In this state of mind, existential philosophy appears to be the only true and unabashed description of existence. It is interesting in this regard that Jean Paul Sartre's work was deeply influenced by a badly managed and unresolved mescaline session dominated by BPM II (Riedlinger 1982). Samuel Beckett's preoccupation with death and birth and his search for Mother also reveal strong perinatal influences.

It is only natural that someone confronted with this abysmal aspect of the psyche would feel a great reluctance to face it. Going deeper into this experience seems like meeting eternal damnation. Yet, paradoxically, the fastest way of ending this unbearable state is to fully experience the depth of suffering and despair that we once had to face in the birth canal, surrendering to it completely and accepting it. That changes the seemingly hopeless situation of BPM II into BPM III, reliving the stage of birth where the dilated cervix makes escape and the termination of suffering possible. St. John of the Cross gave this shattering experience of terrifying darkness and utter despair the name Dark Night of the Soul and C. G. Jung called it the Night Sea Journey. In her autobiography, St. Teresa described Hell as a suffocating place of unendurable torments, which she experienced while she was cramped in a small hole. BPM II is an important stage of spiritual opening that can have an immensely purging and liberating effect.

The most characteristic features of BPM II can be illustrated by the following account from a high dose psychedelic session:

The atmosphere seemed increasingly ominous and fraught with hidden danger. It seemed that the entire room started to turn and I felt drawn into the very center of a threatening whirlpool. I thought about Edgar Allan Poe's chilling description of a similar situation in his story "A Descent into the Maelstrom." As the objects in the room seemed to be flying around me in a rotating motion, another image from literature emerged in my mind—the cyclone in Frank Baum's Wonderful Wizard of Oz *that sweeps Dorothy away from the monotony of her life in Kansas and sends her on a strange journey of adventure. My experience also had something to do with entering the rabbit hole in* Alice in Wonderland *and I awaited with great trepidation what world I would find on the other side of the looking glass. The entire universe seemed to be closing in on me and there was nothing I could do to stop this apocalyptic engulfment.*

As I was sinking deeper and deeper into the labyrinth of my own unconscious, I felt an onslaught of anxiety turning to panic. Everything became dark, oppressive, and terrifying. It was as if the weight of the whole world was encroaching on me, exerting incredible hydraulic pressure that threatened to crack my skull and reduce my body to a tiny compact ball. A rapid fugue of memories from my past cascaded through my brain, showing me the utter futility and meaninglessness of my life and existence in general. We are born naked, frightened, and in agony and we will leave the world the same way. The existentialists were right! Everything is impermanent, life is nothing else but waiting for Godot! Vanity of vanities, all is vanity!

The discomfort I felt turned to pain and the pain increased to agony. The torture intensified to the point where every cell in my body felt like it was being bored open with a diabolic dentist's drill. Visions of infernal landscapes and devils torturing their victims suddenly brought to me the awareness that I was in Hell. I thought of Dante's Divine Comedy: *"Abandon all hope ye who enter!" There seemed to be no way out of this diabolical situation; I was forever doomed without the slightest hope for redemption.*

Third Perinatal Matrix: BPM III (The Death-Rebirth Struggle)

Many aspects of this rich and colorful experience can be understood from its association with the second clinical stage of biological delivery: the propulsion through the birth canal after the cervix opens and the head descends into the pelvis. In this stage, the uterine contractions continue, but the cervix is now dilated and allows the gradual propulsion of the fetus through the birth canal. This involves crushing mechanical pressures, pains, and often a high degree of anoxia and suffocation. A natural concomitant of this highly uncomfortable and life-threatening situation is an experience of intense anxiety.

Besides the interruption of blood circulation caused by uterine contractions and the ensuing compression of uterine arteries, the blood supply to the fetus can be further compromised by various complications. The umbilical cord can be squeezed between the head and the pelvic opening or be twisted around the neck. The placenta can detach during delivery or actually obstruct the way out *(placenta praevia)*. In some instances, the fetus can inhale various forms of biological material that it encounters in the final stages of this process, including its own feces *(meconium),* which further intensifies the feelings of suffocation. The problems in this stage can be so extreme that they require instrumental intervention, such as the use of forceps, suction cup, or even an emergency Cesarean section.

BPM III is an extremely rich and complex experiential pattern. Besides the actual realistic replay of the fetus' struggle in the birth canal, it can be accompanied by a wide variety of transpersonal imagery drawn from history, nature, and archetypal realms. The most important of these are the atmosphere of titanic fight, aggressive and sadomasochistic sequences, experiences of deviant sexuality, demonic episodes, scatological involvement, and encounters with fire. Most of these aspects of BPM III can be meaningfully related to certain anatomical, physiological, and biochemical characteristics of the corresponding stage of birth.

The *titanic aspect* of BPM III is quite understandable in view of the enormity of the forces operating in the final stage of childbirth—powerful contractions of the uterus compressing the fetus, whose head is wedged in the narrow pelvic opening. When we encounter this facet of the third matrix, we experience streams of energy of overwhelming intensity rushing through our body and building up to explosive discharges. At this point, we might identify with raging elements of nature, such as volcanoes, electric storms, earthquakes, tidal waves, or tornadoes.

The experience can also involve technology with enormous energy—tanks, rockets, spaceships, lasers, electric power plants, or even thermonuclear reactors and atomic bombs. The titanic experiences of BPM III can reach archetypal dimensions and portray battles of gigantic proportions, such as the cosmic battle between the forces of Light and Darkness, angels and devils, the Olympic gods and the Titans, or the Devas and Asuras from Tibetan Vajrayana Buddhism.

The aggressive and sadomasochistic aspects of this matrix reflect the biological fury of the organism whose survival is threatened by suffocation, as well as the introjected destructive onslaught of the uterine contractions. Facing this aspect of BPM III, we might experience cruelties of astonishing proportions, manifesting in scenes of violent murder and suicide, mutilation and automutilation, massacres of various kinds, and bloody wars and revolutions. They often take the form of torture, execution, ritual sacrifice and self-sacrifice, bloody man-to-man combat, and sadomasochistic practices. In these experiences, violent, destructive and self-destructive impulses are associated with strong sexual arousal.

The experiential logic of the sexual aspect of the death-rebirth process is not as immediately obvious. It seems that the human organism has an inbuilt physiological mechanism that translates inhuman suffering, and particularly suffocation, into a strange kind of sexual arousal and eventually into ecstatic rapture. This can be seen in the experiences of the martyrs and flagellants described in religious literature. Additional examples can be found in material from concentration camps, from the reports of prisoners of war, and from the files of Amnesty International. It is also well known that men dying of suffocation on the gallows typically have an erection and even ejaculate. In medieval lore, mandrake *(Mandragora officinarum),* a psychoactive plant used in magic rituals, grew under the gallows, in places sprayed by the semen of dying criminals.

Sexual experiences that occur in the context of BPM III are characterized by the enormous intensity of the sexual drive, by their mechanical and unselective quality, and their exploitative, pornographic, or deviant nature. They depict scenes from red light districts and from the sexual underground, extravagant erotic practices, and sadomasochistic sequences. Equally frequent are episodes portraying incest and episodes of sexual abuse or rape. In rare instances, the BPM III imagery can involve the gory and repulsive extremes of criminal sexuality—erotically motivated murder, dismemberment, cannibalism, and necrophilia.

The fact that, on this level of the psyche, sexual arousal is inextricably connected with highly problematic elements—extreme danger, threats, anxiety, aggression, inflicting pain on another organism, suffering pain from another organism, and various forms of biological material—forms a natural basis for the development of the most common types of sexual dysfunctions, variations, deviations, and perversions (Krafft-Ebing's psychopathia sexualis). The close connection between sexuality and aggression oriented both inward and outward found in sadomasochism was a problem that Freud struggled with and had not satisfactorily resolved before his death. To find a plausible explanation for this condition, one has to reach beyond the Freudian model into the perinatal domain.

The *demonic aspect* of BPM III can present specific problems for the subjects, as well as therapists and facilitators. The uncanny and eerie nature of the manifestations involved often leads to a reluctance to face it. The most common themes observed in this context are scenes of the Sabbath of the Witches *(Walpurgis Night),* satanic orgies and Black Mass rituals, and temptation by evil forces. The common denominator connecting this stage of childbirth with the themes of the Sabbath or with the Black Mass rituals is the peculiar experiential amalgam of death, deviant sexuality, pain, fear, aggression, scatology, and distorted spiritual impulses that they share. This observation seems to have great relevance for the experiences of satanic cult abuse reported by clients in various forms of regressive therapy.

The *scatological aspect* of the death-rebirth process has its natural biological basis in the fact that, in the final stage of the delivery, the fetus can come into close contact with various forms of biological material—blood, vaginal secretions, urine, and even feces. However, the nature and content of these experiences by far exceed what the newborn might have actually experienced during birth. Experiences of this aspect of BPM III can involve such scenes as crawling in offal or through sewage systems, wallowing in piles of excrement, drinking blood or urine, or participating in repulsive images of putrefaction. It is an intimate and shattering encounter with the worst aspects of biological existence.

When the experience of BPM III comes closer to resolution, it becomes less violent and disturbing. The prevailing atmosphere is that of extreme passion and driving energy of intoxicating intensity. The imagery portrays exciting conquests of new territories, hunts of wild animals, extreme sports, and adventures in amusement parks. These experiences are clearly related to activities that involve an "adrenaline rush"—parachuting, bungee jumping, car racing, acrobatic diving, dangerous stunts or circus performances, etc.

At this time, we can also encounter archetypal figures or deities, demigods, and legendary heroes representing death and rebirth. We can have visions of Jesus, his torment and humiliation, the Way of the Cross, and crucifixion, or even actually experience full identification with his suffering. Whether or not we intellectually know the corresponding mythologies, we can experience such mythological themes as the descent of the Sumerian goddess Inanna to the Underworld to obtain the elixir of Immortality for her deceased lover Dumuzi, the resurrection of the Egyptian god Osiris, or the death and rebirth of the Greek deities Dionysus, Attis, or Adonis. The experiences can portray Persephone's abduction by Hades, the immolation of the Plumed Serpent Quetzalcoatl and his journey through the underworld, or the ordeals of the Mayan Hero Twins as described in the Popol Vuh.

Just before the experience of psychospiritual rebirth, it is common to encounter the element of fire. The motif of fire can be experienced either in its ordinary everyday form or in the archetypal form of purgatorial fire *(pyrocatharsis).* We can have the feeling that our body is on fire, have visions of burning cities and forests, and identify with the victims of immolation. In the archetypal version, the burning seems to radically destroy whatever is corrupted in us and prepare us for spiritual rebirth. A classical symbol of the transition from BPM III to BPM IV is the legendary Phoenix, a bird who dies in fire and rises, resurrected, from the ashes.

The pyrocathartic experience is a somewhat puzzling aspect of BPM III, since its connection with biological birth is not as direct and obvious as is the case with the other symbolic elements. The biological counterpart of this experience might be the explosive liberation of previously blocked energies in the final stage of childbirth or the overstimulation of the fetus with indiscriminate "firing" of the peripheral neurons. It is interesting that this encounter with fire has its experiential parallel in the delivering mother, who at this stage of delivery often feels that her vagina is on fire.

Several important characteristics of the third matrix distinguish it from the previously described no-exit stage. The situation here is challenging and difficult, but it does not seem hopeless and we do not feel helpless. We are actively involved in a fierce struggle and have the feeling that the suffering has a definite direction, goal, and meaning. In religious terms, this situation is related to the concept of Purgatory rather than Hell.

In addition, we do not just play the role of helpless victims. At this point, three different roles become available to us. Besides being observers of what is happening, we can also identify with both the aggressor and the victim. This can be so convincing that it might be difficult to distinguish and separate the roles. Also, while the no-exit situation involves suffering, the experience of the death-rebirth struggle represents the borderline between agony and ecstasy and the fusion of both. It seems appropriate to refer to this type of experience as *Dionysian* or *volcanic ecstasy* in contrast to the *Apollonian* or *oceanic ecstasy* of the cosmic union associated with the first perinatal matrix.

The following account from a high-dose LSD session illustrates many of the typical themes associated with BPM III as described above:

> *Although I never really clearly saw the birth canal, I felt its crushing pressure on my head and all over, and I knew with every cell of my body that I was involved in the birth process. The tension was reaching dimensions that I had not imagined were humanly possible. I felt unrelenting pressure on my forehead, temples, and occiput, as if I were caught in the steel jaws of a vise. The tensions in my body had a brutally mechanical quality. I imagined myself passing through a monstrous meat grinder or a giant press full of cogs and cylinders. The image of Charlie Chaplin victimized by the world of technology in* Modern Times *briefly flashed through my mind.*
>
> *Incredible amounts of energy seemed to be flowing through my entire body, condensing and releasing in explosive discharges. I felt an amazing mixture of feelings; I was suffocated, frightened, and*

helpless, but also furious and strangely sexually aroused. Another important aspect of my experience was a sense of utter confusion. While I felt like an infant involved in a vicious struggle for survival and realized that what was about to happen was my birth, I was also experiencing myself as my delivering mother. I knew intellectually that being a man I could never give birth, yet I felt that I was somehow crossing that barrier and that the impossible was becoming a reality.

There was no question that I was connecting with something primordial—an ancient feminine archetype of the delivering mother. My body image included a large pregnant belly and female genitals with all the nuances of biological sensations. I felt frustrated by not being able to surrender to this elemental process, to give birth and be born, to let go and to let the baby out. An enormous reservoir of murderous aggression emerged from the underworld of my psyche. It was as if an abscess of evil had suddenly been punctured by the cut of a cosmic surgeon. A werewolf or a berserk was taking me over; Dr. Jekyll was turning into Mr. Hyde. There were many images of the murderer and the victim as being one and the same person, just as earlier I could not distinguish between the child who was being born and the delivering mother.

I was a merciless tyrant, the dictator exposing his subordinates to unimaginable cruelties, and also a revolutionary, leading the furious mob to overthrow the tyrant. I became the mobster who murders in cold blood and the policeman who kills the criminal in the name of the law. At one point, I experienced the horrors of the Nazi concentration camps. When I opened my eyes, I saw myself as an SS officer. I had a profound sense that he, the Nazi, and I, the Jew, were the same person. I could feel the Hitler and the Stalin in me and felt fully responsible for the atrocities in human history. I saw clearly that humanity's problem is not the existence of vicious dictators, but this Hidden Killer that we all harbor within our own psyches, if we look deep enough.

Then the nature of the experience changed and reached mythological proportions. Instead of the evil of human history, I now sensed the atmosphere of witchcraft and the presence of demonic elements. My teeth were transformed into long fangs filled with some mysterious poison, and I found myself flying on large bat wings through the night like an ominous vampire. This soon changed into wild, intoxicating scenes of a Witches' Sabbath. In this strange, sensuous ritual, all the usually forbidden and repressed impulses seemed to surface and were experienced and acted out. I was aware of participating in some mysterious sacrificial ceremony celebrating the Dark God.

As the demonic quality gradually disappeared from my experience, I still felt tremendously erotic and was engaged in endless sequences of the most fantastic orgies and sexual fantasies, in which I played all the roles. All through these experiences, I simultaneously continued being the child struggling through the birth canal and the mother delivering it. It became very clear to me that sex and birth were deeply connected and that satanic forces had important links with the propulsion through the birth canal. I struggled and fought in many different roles and against many different enemies. Sometimes I wondered if there would ever be an end to my misery.

Then a new element entered my experience. My entire body was covered with some biological filth, which was slimy and slippery. I could not tell if it was the amniotic fluid, urine, mucus, blood, or vaginal secretions. The same stuff seemed to be in my mouth and even in my lungs. I was choking, gagging, making faces, and spitting, trying to get it out of my system and off my skin. At the same time, I was getting a message that I did not have to fight. The process had its own rhythm and all I had to do was surrender to it. I remembered many situations from my life where I felt the need to fight and struggle and, in retrospect, that too felt unnecessary. It was as if I had been somehow programmed by my birth to see life as much more complicated and dangerous than it actually is. It seemed that this experience could open my eyes in this regard and make my life much easier and more playful than before.

Fourth Perinatal Matrix: BPM IV (The Death-Rebirth Experience)

This matrix is related to the third clinical stage of delivery, to the final expulsion from the birth canal and the severing of the umbilical cord. Experiencing this matrix, we complete the preceding difficult process of propulsion through the birth canal, achieve explosive liberation, and emerge into light. This can often be accompanied by concrete and realistic memories of various specific aspects of this stage of birth. These can include the experience of anesthesia, the pressure of the forceps, and the sensations associated with various obstetric maneuvers or postnatal interventions.

Reliving biological birth is not experienced as a simple mechanical replay of the original biological event, but also as a psychospiritual death and rebirth. As the fetus is completely confined during the birth process and has no way of expressing the extreme emotions and reacting to the intense physical sensations involved, the memory of this event remains psychologically undigested and unassimilated.

Our self-definition and our attitudes toward the world in our postnatal life are heavily contaminated by this constant reminder of the vulnerability, inadequacy, and weakness that we experienced at birth. In a sense, we were born anatomically but have not caught up with this fact emotionally. The "dying" and the agony during the struggle for rebirth reflect the actual pain and vital threat of the biological birth process. However, the ego death that precedes rebirth is the death of our old concepts of who we are and what the world is like, which were forged by the traumatic imprint of birth, and are maintained by the memory of it that stays alive in our unconscious.

As we clear these old programs by letting them emerge into consciousness, they lose their emotional charge and do, in a sense, die. We have identified with them so much, though, that approaching the moment of the ego death feels like the end of our existence, or even like the end of the world. As frightening as this process is, it is actually very healing and transforming. Paradoxically, while only a small step separates us from an experience of radical liberation, we still have a sense of all-pervading anxiety and impending catastrophe of enormous proportions.

What actually dies in this process is the false ego that, up to this point in our life, we have mistaken for our true self. As we lose all the reference points we know, we have no idea what is on the other side, or even if there is anything there at all. This fear tends to create an enormous resistance to continue and complete the experience. As a result, without appropriate guidance, many people can remain psychologically stuck in this problematic territory.

When we overcome the metaphysical fear encountered at this important juncture and decide to let things happen, we experience total annihilation on all imaginable levels—physical destruction, emotional disaster, intellectual and philosophical defeat, ultimate moral failure, and even spiritual damnation. During this experience, all reference points, everything that is important and meaningful in life, seem to be mercilessly destroyed. Immediately following the experience of total annihilation—hitting "cosmic bottom"—we are overwhelmed by visions of white or golden light of supernatural radiance and exquisite beauty that appears numinous and divine.

Having survived what seemed like an experience of total annihilation and the apocalyptic end of everything, we are blessed only seconds later with fantastic displays of magnificent rainbow spectra, peacock designs, celestial scenes, and visions of archetypal beings bathed in divine light. Often, this is the time of a powerful encounter with the archetypal Great Mother Goddess, either in her universal form or in one of her culture-specific forms. Following the experience of psychospiritual death and rebirth, we feel redeemed and blessed, experience ecstatic rapture, and have a sense of reclaiming our divine nature and cosmic status. We are overcome by a surge of positive emotions toward ourselves, other people, nature, and existence in general.

It is important to emphasize that this kind of healing and life-changing experience occurs when birth was not too debilitating or confounded by heavy anesthesia. If that was the case, we do not have a sense of triumphant emergence into light and radical resolution. Instead, the postnatal period might feel like a slow recovery from a crippling disease or awakening from a hangover. Anesthesia at birth can also have profound adverse psychological consequences for postnatal life and create a disposition for addiction, including a tendency to solve problems in life by escaping into a drug state.

Another condition that can obscure the experience of triumphant emergence from the birth canal is Rh incompatibility between the mother and the fetus. When the mother is Rh negative and the father Rh positive, the fetus is treated by the maternal organism as an invader and is subjected, from conception, to immunological attacks. The strength or titer of the antibodies increases with each pregnancy and can become fatal without radical medical interventions. The immunological pollution of the prenatal state represents a serious challenge in the process of inner exploration. It can involve a number of sessions with extremely unpleasant BPM I experiences—general malaise, severe nausea, and vomiting. In this case, reliving birth does not bring clean resolution, because the blood of the newborn continues to be poisoned by antibodies.

The following account of a death-rebirth experience from a high-dose psychedelic session describes a typical sequence characteristic of BPM IV.

> *However, the worst was yet to come. All of a sudden, I seemed to be losing all my connections to reality, as if some imaginary rug was pulled from under my feet. Everything was collapsing and I felt that my entire world was shattered to pieces. It was like puncturing a monstrous metaphysical balloon of my existence; a gigantic bubble of ludicrous self-deception had burst open and exposed the lie of my life. Everything that I ever believed in, everything that I did or pursued, everything that seemed to give my life meaning, suddenly appeared utterly false. These were all pitiful crutches without any substance with which I tried to patch up the intolerable reality of existence. They were now blasted and blown away like the frail feathered seeds of a dandelion, exposing a frightening abyss of ultimate truth—the meaningless chaos of the existential Void.*
>
> *Filled with indescribable horror, I saw a gigantic figure of a deity towering over me in a threatening pose. I somehow instinctively recognized that this was the Hindu god Shiva in his destructive aspect. I felt the thunderous impact of his enormous foot that crushed me, shattered me to smithereens, and smeared me like an insignificant piece of excrement all over what I felt was the bottom of the cosmos. In the next moment, I was facing a terrifying giant figure of a dark Indian goddess whom I identified as Kali. My face was being pushed by an irresistible force toward her gaping vagina that was full of what seemed to be menstrual blood or repulsive afterbirth. I sensed that what was demanded of me was absolute surrender to the forces of existence and to the feminine principle represented by the goddess. I had no choice but to kiss and lick her vagina in utmost submission*

and humility. At this moment, which was the ultimate and final end of any feeling of male supremacy I had ever harbored, I connected with the memory of the moment of my biological birth. My head was emerging from the birth canal with my mouth in close contact with the bleeding vagina of my mother.

In the next moment, I was flooded with a divine light of supernatural radiance and indescribable beauty; its golden rays were exploding into thousands of exquisite peacock designs. From this brilliant golden light emerged a figure of the Great Mother Goddess, who seemed to embody love and protection for all ages. She spread her arms and reached toward me, enveloping me into her essence. I merged with this incredible energy field, feeling purged, healed, and nourished. What seemed to be some divine nectar and ambrosia, some archetypal essence of milk and honey, was pouring into me in absolute abundance.

Then the figure of the goddess gradually disappeared, absorbed by an even more brilliant light. It was abstract, yet endowed with definite personal characteristics and radiating infinite intelligence. It became clear to me that what I was experiencing was the merging with and absorption into the Universal Self, or Brahman, as I have read about in books of Indian philosophy. This experience subsided after about ten minutes; however, it transcended any concept of time and felt like eternity. The flow of the healing and nourishing energy and the visions of golden glow with peacock designs lasted through the night. The resulting sense of heightened well-being stayed with me for days, yet the memory of the experience has remained vivid for years and has profoundly changed my entire life philosophy.

The Transpersonal Domain of the Psyche

When we work with holotropic states of consciousness, we have to expand the cartography of the human psyche used by mainstream psychiatrists and psychologists by adding a vast transbiographical domain. The experiences that belong to this category were known in all ancient and aboriginal cultures and played an important role in their ritual and spiritual life. Modern psychiatrists are familiar with these experiences, but they see them as products of an unknown pathological process, rather than genuine and germane constituents of the human psyche.

When I amassed sufficient evidence that these experiences are normal manifestations of the deep recesses of the psyche and parted from the official position of mainstream psychiatry, I coined for them the name *transpersonal.* This term means literally "reaching beyond the personal" or "transcending the personal." The common denominator in this rich and ramified group of experiences is the realization that our consciousness has expanded beyond the usual boundaries of the body/ego and has transcended the limitations of linear time and three-dimensional space.

In the everyday ("normal") state of consciousness, we experience ourselves as existing within the boundaries of our physical body (the body image) and our perception of the external world is restricted by the range of our sensory organs, as well as by the physical characteristics of our environment. Our experiences are also clearly defined by the categories of three-dimensional space and linear time. Under ordinary circumstances, we vividly experience only our present situation and our immediate environment; we *recall* past events and *anticipate* the future or fantasize about it. In transpersonal experiences, one or several of the above limitations appear to be transcended.

The best way to describe transpersonal experiences is to compare them with our everyday experiences of ourselves and the world. In the ordinary state of consciousness, we experience ourselves as material objects separated from the rest of the world by our skin. The British-American writer and philosopher Alan Watts referred to this experience of oneself as identifying with the "skin-encapsulated ego." We cannot see objects from which we are separated by a solid opaque wall, ships that are beyond the horizon, or the other side of the moon. If we are in Prague, we cannot hear what our friends are talking about in San Francisco. We cannot feel the softness of the lambskin unless the surface of our body is in direct contact with it.

In transpersonal states of consciousness, none of the above limitations are absolute; any of them can be transcended. There are no limits to the spatial reach of our senses. We can experience, with all the sensory qualities, episodes that occurred at any place and any time in the past and, occasionally, even those that have not yet happened. The spectrum of

Table 2. Varieties of Transpersonal Experiences

Experiential Extension within Spacetime

Transcendence of Spatial Boundaries

Experience of dual unity
Experiential identification with other persons
Experience of group consciousness
Experience of identification with animals
Identification with plants and botanical processes
Identification with life and all creation
Experience of inorganic materials and processes
Experiences of extraterrestrial beings and worlds
Psychic phenomena involving transcendence of space (telepathy, OBEs, astral projection, horizontal clairvoyance)

Transcendence of Temporal Boundaries

Fetal and embryonal experiences
Ancestral experiences
Racial and collective experiences
Past life experiences
Phylogenetic experiences
Experiences of the evolution of life
Cosmogenetic experiences
Psychic phenomena involving transcendence of time (psychometry, vertical clairvoyance, past life reading)

Experiential Exploration of the Microworld

Organ and tissue consciousness
Cellular consciousness
Experience of DNA
Experiences of the molecular, atomic, and subatomic worlds

Experiential Extension beyond Spacetime and Consensus Reality

Energetic phenomena of the subtle body (auras, nadis, chakras, meridians)
Experiences of animal spirits (power animals)
Encounters with spirit guides and suprahuman beings
Experiences of universal archetypes
Sequences involving specific blissful and wrathful deities
Intuitive understanding of universal symbols
Creative inspiration and the Promethean impulse
Experience of the Demiurge and insights into cosmic creation
Experience of Absolute Consciousness
The Supracosmic and Metacosmic Void

Transpersonal Experiences of a Psychoid Nature

Synchronicities (interplay between intrapsychic experiences and spacetime)

Spontaneous Psychoid Events

Supernormal physical feats
Spiritistic phenomena and physical mediumship
Recurrent spontaneous psychokinesis (Poltergeist phenomena)
UFOs and alien abduction experiences

Intentional Psychokinesis

Ceremonial magic
Healing and hexing
Yogic siddhis
Laboratory psychokinesis

transpersonal experiences is extremely rich and includes phenomena from several different levels of consciousness. In Table 2, I attempted to list and categorize the various types of experiences that, in my opinion, belong to the transpersonal domain (pp. 171).

In my own psychedelic and Holotropic Breathwork sessions, I have experienced most of the phenomena that are listed in this synoptic table, and have also repeatedly observed them in my work with others. In the context of this encyclopedia, I will not be able to provide definitions and descriptions of all these types of experiences and illustrate them with clinical examples. For this, I have to refer the interested readers to my previous publications (Grof 1975, 1980, 1985, 2006a).

As the table shows, transpersonal experiences can be divided into three large categories. The first one primarily involves transcendence of the usual spatial and temporal barriers. An experiential extension beyond the spatial limitations of the "skin-encapsulated ego" leads to experiences of merging with another person into a state that can be called "dual unity," assuming the identity of another person, or identifying with the consciousness of an entire group of people. As impossible and absurd as it seems to our rational mind and common sense, we can have an experience of becoming all mothers or children of the world, warriors of all ages, the entire population of India, or all the inmates of prisons and concentration camps. Our consciousness can even expand to such an extent that it seems to encompass all of humanity. Descriptions of experiences of this kind can be found in spiritual literature all over the world.

In a similar way, we can transcend the limits of the specifically human experience and identify with the consciousness of various animals and plants on the Darwinian evolutionary tree—becoming an eagle, silver back gorilla, dinosaur, or amoeba, a sequoia tree, kelp, or a carnivorous plant. We can even experience a form of consciousness that seems to be related to inorganic objects and processes—such as the consciousness of a diamond, granite, or a burning candle.

In the extremes, it is possible to experience consciousness of the biosphere, of our entire planet, or the whole material universe. Incredible as it might seem to a Westerner subscribing to monistic materialism, these experiences suggest that everything we can experience as an object in the everyday state of consciousness has, in the holotropic state of consciousness, a corresponding subjective representation. It is as if everything in the universe has its objective and subjective aspect as it is described in the great spiritual philosophies of the East. For example, the Hindus see all that exists as a manifestation of Brahman, and the Taoists consider everything in the universe to have been created by transformations of the Tao.

Other transpersonal experiences in this first category are characterized primarily by overcoming temporal rather than spatial boundaries, as in the transcendence of linear time. We have already talked about the possibility of reliving important memories from infancy and childhood, and of the memory of biological birth and prenatal existence. According to the materialistic worldview, memories require a material substrate. However, as the temporal regression continues farther back into history, it becomes increasingly difficult to find a believable material medium for these memories. It seems more plausible to see them as involving transcendence of time or some immaterial substrate, such as Laszlo's Akashic field, Sheldrake's morphogenetic field, von Foerster's memory without a material substrate, or the field of consciousness itself (Laszlo 2016, Sheldrake 1981, von Foerster 1965).

It is possible to experience authentic memories from different periods of early embryonic development and even identification with the sperm and the ovum at the time of conception on the level of cellular consciousness. The process of the experiential retracing of creation does not stop here, though. In holotropic states, we can experience episodes from the lives of our human or animal ancestors, or even those that seem to be coming from the racial and collective unconscious, as described by C. G. Jung. Quite frequently, experiences that seem to be happening in other cultures and historical periods are associated with a sense of personal remembering, a convincing feeling of déjà vu or déjà vecu (something that one has already seen or experienced). People then talk about reliving memories from past lives, or from previous incarnations.

Experiences in holotropic states can also take us into the microworld, to structures and processes that are ordinarily not accessible to our unaided senses. These can be reminiscent of Isaac Asimov's film *Fantastic Voyage,* which portrays the world of our inner organs, tissues, and cells, or can even involve full experiential identification with them. Particularly fascinating are experiences of the DNA, which are associated with insights into the ultimate mystery of life, reproduction, and heredity. Occasionally, this type of transpersonal experience can take us into the inorganic world of molecules, atoms, and subatomic particles.

The content of transpersonal experiences described so far consists of various phenomena existing in spacetime. They involve elements of our everyday familiar reality—other people, animals, plants, materials, and events from the past. As far as these phenomena themselves are concerned, there is nothing here that we would ordinarily consider unusual. They belong to a reality that we know; we accept their existence and take it for granted. What surprises us in regard to the two categories of transpersonal experiences described above is not their content, but the fact that we can witness or fully identify with something that is not ordinarily accessible to our senses.

We know that there are pregnant whales in the world, but we should not be able to have an authentic experience of actually being one. We readily accept that there once was the French Revolution, but we should not be able to have a vivid experience of actually being there and lying wounded on the barricades of Paris. We know that there are many things happening in the world in other places, but it is usually considered impossible to experience something that is happening elsewhere (without the mediation of a television camera, satellite, and TV set or computer). We may also be surprised to find consciousness associated with lower animals, plants, and with inorganic nature.

The second category of transpersonal phenomena is even stranger. In holotropic states, our consciousness can extend into realms and dimensions that the Western industrial culture does not consider "real." Here belong numerous visions of or identification with archetypal beings, deities, and demons of various cultures, as well as visits to fantastic mythological realms. They are often drawn from mythologies of which we previously had no intellectual knowledge. We can also achieve an intuitive understanding of universal symbols, such as the cross, the Nile cross or *ankh,* the swastika, the pentacle, the six-pointed star, or the yin-yang sign. It is possible to have an encounter and communicate with discarnate and suprahuman entities, spirit guides, extraterrestrial beings, or what appear to be inhabitants of parallel universes.

In its farthest reaches, our individual consciousness can transcend all boundaries and identify with Cosmic Consciousness, or the Universal Mind, also known under many different names: Brahman, Buddha, the Cosmic Christ, Keter, Allah, the Tao, the Great Spirit, and many others. The ultimate of all experiences appears to be identification with the Supracosmic and Metacosmic Void, the mysterious and primordial emptiness and nothingness, the Cosmic Abyss that is the ultimate cradle of all existence. It has no concrete content, yet it contains all there is in a germinal and potential form. It has the intelligence and the immense energy necessary to create universes.

The third category of transpersonal experiences comprises phenomena that I call *psychoid,* using the term coined by Hans Driesch, the founder of vitalism, and adopted by C. G. Jung. This group includes situations in which intrapsychic experiences are associated with corresponding events in the external world that are meaningfully related to them. Psychoid experiences cover a wide range from synchronicities, spiritual healing, and ceremonial magic to UFO encounters, psychokinesis, and other mind-over-matter phenomena known from the yogic literature as *siddhis* (Grof 2006a).

Transpersonal experiences have many strange characteristics that shatter the most fundamental metaphysical assumptions of the materialistic worldview and of the Newtonian-Cartesian paradigm. Researchers who have studied and/or personally experienced these fascinating phenomena realize that the attempts of mainstream science to dismiss them as irrelevant plays of human fantasy or as erratic hallucinatory products of a diseased brain are naïve and inadequate. Any unbiased study of the transpersonal domain of the psyche has to confirm that the phenomena encountered here represent a critical challenge not only for psychiatry and psychology, but also for the monistic materialistic philosophy of Western science.

Although transpersonal experiences occur in the process of deep individual self-exploration, it is not possible to interpret them simply as intrapsychic phenomena in the conventional sense. On the one hand, they appear on the same experiential continuum as the biographical and perinatal experiences and are thus coming from within the individual psyche. On the other hand, they seem to be tapping directly, without the mediation of the senses, into sources of information that are clearly far beyond the conventional reach of the individual.

Somewhere on the perinatal level of the psyche, a strange experiential switch seems to occur: what was, up to that point, deep intrapsychic probing becomes an extrasensory experience of various aspects of the universe at large. Some people who experienced this peculiar transition from the inner to the outer compared it with the graphic art of the Dutch painter Maurits Escher, while others talked about a "multidimensional experiential Moebius strip." The Emerald tablet *(Tabula smaragdina)* by Hermes Trismegistus, which became the basic tenet of esoteric systems such as Tantra, Kabbalah, or the Hermetic tradition, confirms these observations with its message: "as above so below" or "as without, so within." Each of us is a microcosm containing, in some mysterious way, the entire universe.

These observations indicate that we can obtain information about the universe in two radically different ways. The conventional mode of learning is based on sensory perception and analysis, as well as synthesis of the received information. The radical alternative that becomes available in holotropic states is learning by direct experiential identification with various aspects of the world.

In the context of old paradigm thinking, the claims of ancient esoteric systems that the microworld can reflect the macroworld, or that the part can contain the whole, seemed to be utterly absurd, since they seemed to offend common sense and violate the elementary principles of Aristotelian logic. This has changed radically after the discovery of the laser, which opened astonishing new ways of understanding the relationship between the part and the whole. The holographic or holonomic thinking has provided, for the first time, a conceptual framework for a scientific approach to this extraordinary phenomenon (Bohm 1980, Pribram 1971,1981, Laszlo 1993).

The reports from subjects who have experienced episodes of embryonic existence, the moment of conception, and elements of cellular, tissue, and organ consciousness abound with medically accurate insights into the anatomical, physiological, and biochemical aspects of the processes involved. Similarly, ancestral, racial and collective memories and past-incarnation experiences often provide very specific details about architecture, clothing, weapons, art forms, social structure, and religious and ritual practices of the corresponding cultures and historical periods, or even concrete historical events.

People who experienced phylogenetic experiences or identification with existing life forms not only found them unusually authentic and convincing, but often acquired extraordinary insights concerning animal psychology, ethology, specific habits, or unusual reproductive cycles. In some instances, this was accompanied by archaic muscular innervations not characteristic for humans, or even such complex behaviors as the enactment of a courtship dance of a particular species.

The philosophical challenge associated with the already described observations is further augmented by the fact that the transpersonal experiences reflecting the material world often appear on the same continuum as, and intimately interwoven with, others which contain elements that the Western industrial world does not consider to be real. This includes experiences involving deities and demons from various cultures, mythological realms such as heavens and paradises, and legendary or fairytale sequences.

We can have an experience, for example, of Shiva's heaven, the paradise of the Aztec rain god Tlaloc, the Sumerian underworld, or one of the Buddhist hot hells. It is also possible to communicate with Jesus, have a shattering encounter with the Hindu goddess Kali, or identify with the dancing Shiva. These episodes can impart accurate new information about religious symbolism and mythological motifs that were previously unknown to the person involved. Observations of this kind confirm C. G. Jung's idea that, besides the Freudian individual unconscious, we can also gain access to the collective unconscious that contains the cultural heritage of all humanity (Jung 1959).

The general concept of the Great Chain of Being, according to which reality includes an entire hierarchy (or *holarchy)* of dimensions that are ordinarily hidden to our perception, is very important and well-founded. It would be erroneous to dismiss this understanding of existence as primitive superstition or psychotic delusion, as has so frequently been done. Anybody attempting to do that would have to offer a plausible explanation for why the experiences that systematically support this elaborate and comprehensive vision of reality have occurred so consistently in people of various races, cultures, and historical periods.

Anybody trying to defend the monistic-materialistic position of Western science would also have to account for the fact that these experiences continue to emerge in highly intelligent, sophisticated, and otherwise mentally healthy people of our era (Grof 1998). This happens not only under the influence of psychedelics, but also under such diverse circumstances as sessions of various forms of experiential psychotherapy, meditations of people involved in systematic spiritual practice, in near-death experiences, and in the course of spontaneous episodes of psychospiritual crises ("spiritual emergencies").

It is not an easy task to summarize, in a few pages, conclusions from observations amassed in the course of more than sixty years of research of holotropic states and make those statements believable. Although I had the opportunity to hear the accounts of transpersonal experiences from thousands of people and had many of them myself, it took me years to fully absorb the impact of the cognitive shock that the discovery of their existence imparted on me. Due to space considerations, I am not able to present detailed case histories that could help illustrate the nature of transpersonal experiences and the insights they provide. However, I doubt that even that, in and of itself, would suffice to counteract the deeply ingrained programs that Western science has instilled into our culture. The conceptual challenges that are involved are so formidable that nothing short of a deep personal experience would be adequate for this task.

The existence and nature of transpersonal experiences violate some of the most basic assumptions of mechanistic science. They imply such seemingly absurd notions as relativity and the arbitrary nature of all physical boundaries, non-local connections in the universe, communication through unknown means and channels, memory without a material substrate, nonlinearity of time, and consciousness associated with all living organisms, even including inorganic matter. Many transpersonal experiences involve events from the microcosm and the macrocosm, realms that cannot normally be reached by unaided human senses, or from historical periods that precede the origin of the solar system, the formation of planet earth, the appearance of living organisms, the development of the nervous system, or the emergence of *homo sapiens.*

The study of transpersonal experiences reveals a remarkable paradox concerning the nature of human beings. Observed in the everyday (hylotropic or "oriented toward matter") state of consciousness, we appear to be separate Newtonian objects existing in three-dimensional space and in linear time. In a holotropic state, we function as infinite fields of consciousness transcending space and time. This complementary nature of human beings seems to have a distant analogue in the wave-particle nature of light described by the complementarity principle of the Danish physicist Niels Bohr. It is interesting that Bohr believed that the principle of complementarity will eventually be relevant for other scientific disciplines.

Similar paradoxical statements can be found in esoteric systems and mystical traditions: "The human being is a microcosm containing the macrocosm," and "As Above, so Below, as Without, so Within." Similar, seemingly absurd, pronouncements have been made by mystics about separation and oneness or identity and difference: "We know we are separate from each other, but we are all One," and "We know we are just insignificant parts of the universe, but each of us is the entire universe."

Optical Holography and the Mystical Worldview

An unexpected scientific explanation and clarification of these paradoxes was made possible in the 1960s by the development of optical holography. The understanding of the holographic principles is so important for transpersonal psychology and psychonautics that it deserves a separate section in this encyclopedia. As absurd and implausible as these ideas might appear to a traditionally trained scientist and to our common sense, they can be relatively easy to reconcile in the context of the new revolutionary developments in various scientific disciplines, which is usually referred to as the new or emerging paradigm.

The mathematics underlying holography was developed by Dennis Gabor, a Hungarian electrical engineer living in Great Britain. His original intention was to improve the resolution of the electronic microscope. Initially, it was not possible to create optical holograms because a coherent source of light had yet to be developed. In 1961, when the laser was invented in Malibu, California, Gabor's holographic principles could be used for creating optical holograms.

An optical hologram requires a *laser* (light amplification by stimulated emission of radiation): a source of monochromatic and coherent light. Monochromatic light means that all light rays are of the same wavelength

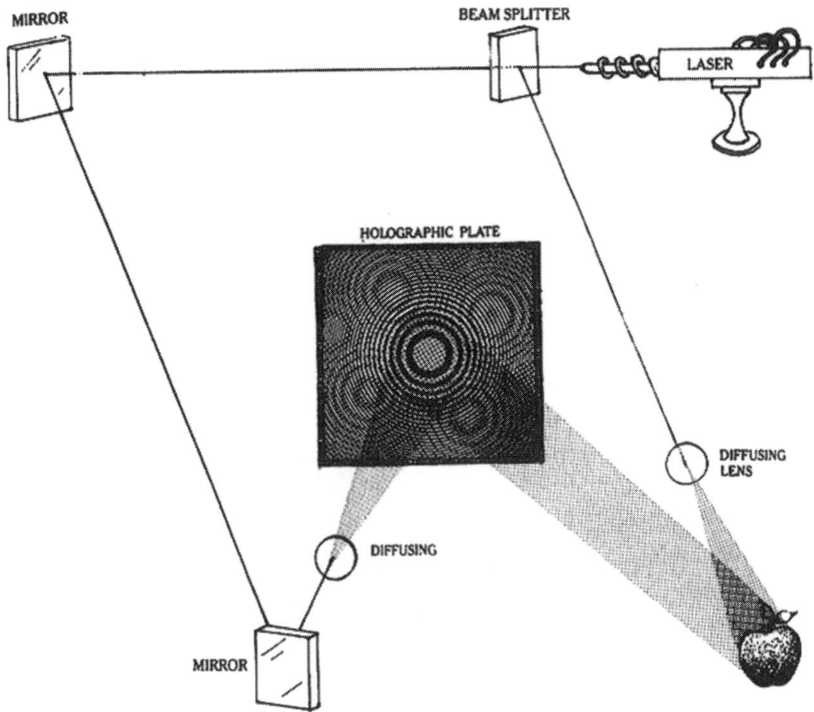

Optical holography provides a physical model for transpersonal experiences and clarifies seemingly paradoxical statements of mystics. An object is photographed using laser light, a beam splitter, diffusing lens, and holographic plate (top). Holograms have distributed information. Each of the fragments of a hologram illuminated by laser can retrieve the information from the entire image of the object. Similarly, in holotropic states of consciousness, every human psyche has potential to access to the entire field of cosmic consciousness (bottom). Mystics have discovered in their transpersonal experiences that objects which appear to be material and separate are parts of a unified and undifferentiated field of consciousness.

A hologram projection of newlyweds. Although they appear to be two separate entities, this illusion is created simply by interference patterns of light.

(or frequency, which is the reciprocal value of wavelength). Coherent light means that all light emitted by the laser is in phase.

A hologram thus needs a source of laser light, a film plate, and the object from which you are making the hologram. The laser beam is directed toward a glass pane *(beam splitter)* that is partially silver-plated, so that half of the beam is reflected from it and the other half penetrates through it (the same principle as the one-way screen). This is done in such a way that the reflected half of light is directed towards the object that is being photographed and then from it to the film plate *(the working beam).* The second half that penetrates through the glass *(the reference beam)* is reflected by mirrors and spread (by the *beam-spreader)* over the film plate, where it meets the light carrying the image of the object. What occurs is called interference.

The way to visualize interference is to imagine a pond as several pebbles are thrown into it. The concentric waves that this creates *(Huyghens waves)* travel and as they meet, they interact with each other. Two crests meeting each other would create a bigger crest, two crests of opposite direction would cancel each other, two troughs would create a deeper trough, etc. In the world of light, the amplitude of the light waves determines the intensity of the light; the larger the amplitude, the lighter those points in the hologram will be. The interference is then recorded in the film plate and the film is developed; this creates a hologram.

In traditional photography, we can tell from the negative what was photographed—trees, houses, people, etc. This is not possible when we work with holograms. No matter what objects are being photographed, all holograms look alike; they are large scale interference patterns *(moiré patterns).* But if the hologram is illumined by a laser, it recreates the wave front and produces a three-dimensional image of the object that was photographed. If we observe the image through the plate, we can see it from different angles, but only in a limited range. It is also possible to make a hologram of a hologram, which is called a *projection hologram.*

When a projection hologram is illumined by laser light, the resulting image appears to be floating freely in the air on the other side of the film plate. It is then possible to walk around it and watch it from a very wide range of angles (with the exception of the position that would block the stream of the laser light). When we observe a projection hologram from different angles, we experience a parallax, that is, the apparent displacement of the observed object due to the change in our position. If the person on the hologram has glasses, we would see in them different reflections replicating what they looked like in the original situation. If the person has a diamond ring, it would be changing the colors of its facets depending on which direction we looked at it.

Why would optical holography be of such interest for transpersonal psychologists? As we will see, we can use it to model visionary states and clarify some paradoxical statements from mystics. For example, holograms have enormous storage capacity. In conventional photography, we can store only one picture per frame (unless we are superimposing images for some artistic effect); in a single hologram, we can store a large number of images.

This can be done in two different ways. In the first one, we can change the angle of the laser with each of the objects we are photographing. When we develop the film and keep illuminating it with the laser, replicating the angles of the original exposure, each angle will "tease out" from the common matrix the image of the object that was photographed from that angle. The information about all of them would be in the hologram, but to actually see them, we would have to illuminate the hologram from the same angle that was used to create it.

The other way is to create the hologram in such a way that we use the same angle during sequential exposures of these objects. When we then illumine the resulting hologram, all of the photographed objects will appear simultaneously and occupy the same place. In the 1970s, when I was very interested in holography, I spent some time in Honolulu in the holographic laboratory at the University of Hawaii. In this lab, they created a hologram which was called *The Child of Hawaii.* They did it through the sequential exposure of a number of Hawaiian children without changing the angle of the laser. So the final hologram was occupying the space that is normally taken by one child, but the information about all the children was in it. As one looked at it, it seemed that different faces were emerging from it, one after another, and sometimes more than one at a time.

Another fascinating property of holograms is that the information is distributed in them in such a way that it can be retrieved from each of their parts. If we had a conventional photograph and cut it in two pieces, we would lose half of the information. A hologram can be cut into a large number of little pieces and, by illuminating each of the fragments with a laser, we can retrieve from it the information about the entire object. We will lose some of the resolution power, but still obtain the image of the whole.

The mechanisms that I just described can be used in a very interesting way in order to mimic the experiences in holotropic states. In one of the demonstrations of the hologram, I was sitting in a dark room and they projected sequentially holographic images of a number of people photographed with different angles of the laser. As the person who was illuminating this hologram was changing the angle of the laser, I would see one face after another emerging from darkness, disappearing, and being replaced by another, very much like the visions in psychedelic or Holotropic Breathwork sessions.

In another demonstration, they would illumine the hologram of a number of people photographed with the same angle of the laser, like *The Child of Hawaii.* I would see all of them in the space normally occupied by one. As I was looking at this composite hologram, I was seeing different faces in that same space. This mimicked another very interesting experience in holotropic states. For example, when I was having a psychedelic session and Christina was sitting for me, I would see her at one point as all women. For a moment, she seemed to be a lovely young girl and then in the next moment, she turned into a very old craggy crone. At one point, she looked like a Polynesian beauty, and then she transformed into a medieval witch. She was like an archetypal Woman with all possible manifestations of Femininity appearing in the space that is usually occupied by just one body.

The Hawaiian lab I was visiting offered to make newlyweds a wedding hologram as a gift. The couple could actually choose how they wanted this to be done. They could choose a more conventional hologram showing them as two persons, a bridegroom and a bride. That means that they would stand in front of the plate and there would be just one exposure. The other possibility was a hologram that would show them in a kind of Tantric fusion. They would see one body, but the images of both the bride and the bridegroom would be contained in it. This would be achieved by two sequential exposures without changing the angle of the laser.

The hologram showing the bridal couple as two separate objects can be used to illustrate a very interesting aspect of holograms. Let us imagine that we have in front of us the projection variety of this hologram. A well-made hologram could fool not only a child who had never seen a hologram, but also an educated adult who does not have the necessary technical information. They would perceive this situation as two persons, two separate Newtonian objects.

What we know about holography, however, is that the holographic images cannot exist on their own. To make a hologram, one has to have a laser source, something that gives the inflection to the light (in this case the holographic plate), and the undifferentiated field of light filling the space. The semblance of two separate objects is created by the interference patterns of light. It is a play of lights and shadows in which the brightness of various points is reflecting the amplitude of light resulting from the interference.

Quantum-relativistic physicist David Bohm, struggling with the paradoxes and challenges of this discipline, created a holographic model of the universe. According to him, the material world we experience in our usual state of consciousness is a complex holographic system *(the explicate or unfolded order).* Its creative matrix is in another dimension of reality that is not perceptible to our physical senses in our everyday state of consciousness *(the implicate or enfolded order).* In the example of the bridal hologram, we saw that perceiving it as two separate autonomous objects would be a naïve and false perception. David Bohm (like Albert Einstein) would say the same about our perception of the material world. It does not require any great intelligence to see the world as made of separate Newtonian objects. But to discover that this is ultimately a naïve and false pedestrian perception (like the Hindu *maya)* and realize that on a deeper level, it is an undifferentiated whole, requires quantum-relativistic physics, Whiteheadian philosophy, or a holotropic state of consciousness.

Why is optical holography such a useful model for illustrating certain important aspects of the mystical worldview? First of all, the basic tenet of many esoteric teachings, from the Emerald Tablet of Hermes Trismegistos, to Tantra, Kabbalah, and Gnosticism, is that each individual is a microcosm that contains the entire macrocosm: *as above so below, as without so within.* This does not seem to make any sense; one has to make a decision.

You have to be a part or the whole; Aristotelian logic asserts you cannot be something and at the same time something else.

However, in holography, this is not the case. If we are interested only in what we can measure and weigh—which is what science does since Galileo requested it—then a hundredth of a hologram is an insignificant part of it. But if we are not interested in what the part of the hologram weighs or measures, but in the information that it provides, one hundredth of the hologram can provide adequate information about the whole. Similarly, each of us is an insignificant part of the universe, but we can experientially identify with any of its components and in that sense, we are commensurate with it. In that case, the information about the whole can be contained in each of its parts.

In that same vein, we can look at another statement mystics make: "I know that you and I are separate from each other. But from another perspective, you and I are One." If we look again at the holographic model, we realize that seeing the two images as being part of a deeper undivided unified system is a more sophisticated perspective. And we can also see that these two statements are complementary; they are not mutually exclusive.

Psychonautics is ultimately about information, not about material things. In holotropic states, we can, for example, experientially identify with members of other species. If I experience myself as an elephant, I will have information about what it feels like to be an elephant. I will have a very convincing sense that I have become an elephant, which will go way beyond anything I have ever learned about elephants. This does not mean that when you put me on a scale, I will weigh three tons. This has nothing to do with the material aspect of the phenomena we are dealing with. We are talking about information about those phenomena. In that sense, one can be both part and the whole. One can be separate and be one at the same time. You can have a form and no form at the same time, even exist and not exist at the same time. Holography provides a very elegant way of solving some of the seeming paradoxes or even absurdities that we read about in mystical literature.

We have now gone through the extended cartography of the psyche, which is absolutely essential for anyone who gets involved in serious psychonautics and holotropic states for purposes such as self-exploration, the spiritual quest, therapeutic work, artistic inspiration, scientific curiosity, or the cultivation of intuition and extrasensory perception.

As I will try to demonstrate in future chapters of this book, the expanded cartography outlined above is also of critical importance for any serious approach to such phenomena as shamanism, rites of passage, mysticism, religion, mythology, parapsychology, near-death experiences, and psychedelic states. This new model of the psyche is not just a matter of academic interest. It has important revolutionary implications for the understanding of emotional and psychosomatic disorders, including many conditions currently diagnosed as psychotic, and offers new and revolutionary therapeutic possibilities.

Literature

Bateson, G, et al. 1956. Towards a Theory of Schizophrenia. *Behavioral Science* 1(4): 251-254.

Bateson, G. 1972. *Steps to An Ecology of Mind.* San Francisco: Chandler Publications.

Blanck, G. and Blanck, R. 1974. *Ego Psychology I: Theory and Practice.* New York: Columbia University Press.

Blanck, G. and Blanck, R. 1979. *Ego Psychology II: Psychoanalytic Developmental Psychology.* New York: Columbia University Press.

Bohm, D. 1980. *Wholeness and the Implicate* Order. London: Routledge & Kegan Paul.

Campbell, J. 1968. *The Hero with A Thousand Faces.* Princeton: Princeton University Press.

Campbell, J. 1972. *Myths to Live By.* New York: Bantam.

Capra, F. 1975. *The Tao of Physics.* Berkeley, CA: Shambhala Publications.

Chalmers. D. 1996 *The Conscious Mind: In Search of a Fundamental Theory.* Oxford: Oxford University Press.

Crick, F. 1994. *The Astonishing Hypothesis: The Scientific Search for the Soul.* New York: Scribner Publishing.

Foerster, H. von. 1965. *Memory Without A Record. In: The Anatomy of Memory* (D. P. Kimble, ed.). Palo Alto: Science and Behavior Books.

Frank, J. D. and Frank, J. B. 1991. *Persuasion and Healing: A Comparative Study of Psychotherapy.* Baltimore, MD: The Johns Hopkins University

Press.

Gormsen, K., and Lumbye, J. 1979. "A Comparative Study of Stanislav Grof's and L. Ron Hubbard's Models of Consciousness." Presented at the Fifth International Transpersonal Conference, Boston, MA, November.

Grof, S. 1975. *Realms of the Human Unconscious.* New York: Viking Press.

Grof, S. 1985. *Beyond the Brain: Birth, Death, and Transcendence in Psychotherapy.* Albany, N.Y: State University of New York (SUNY) Press.

Grof, S. 1987. Spirituality, Addiction, and Western Science. *Re-Vision J.* 10(2), 5-18.

Grof,, S. and Grof, C. (eds) 1989. *Spiritual Emergency: When Personal Transformation Becomes a Crisis.* Los Angeles, CA: J.P. Tarcher.

Grof,, C. and Grof, S. 1991. *The Stormy Search for the Self: A Guide to Personal Growth Through Transformational Crises.* Los Angeles, CA: J.P. Tarcher.

Grof, S. 1998. *The Cosmic Game: Explorations of the Frontiers of Human Consciousness.* Albany, NY: State University of New York Press.

Grof, S. 2000. *Psychology of the Future: Lessons from Modern Consciousness Research.* Albany, NY: State University of New York (SUNY) Press.

Grof, S. 2006a. *When the Impossible Happens: Adventures in Non-Ordinary Realities.* Louisville, CO: Sounds True.

Grof, S. 2006b. *The Ultimate Journey: Consciousness and the Mystery of Death.* Santa Cruz, CA: MAPS Publications.

Grosso, M. 1994. The Status of Survival Research: Evidence, Problems, Paradigms. A paper presented at the Institute of Noetic Sciences Symposium The Survival of Consciousness After Death, Chicago, IL, July.

Hameroff, S. 1987. *Ultimate Computing.* North Holland: Elsevier Publishing.

Hameroff, S. 2012. *Through the Wormhole,* Science Channel, season 2, narrated by Morgan Friedman, October 28).

Hubbard, L. R. 1950. *Dianetics: The Modern Science of Mental Health.* East Grinstead, Sussex, England: Hubbard College of Scientology.

Jung, C. G. 1959. *The Archetypes and the Collective Unconscious. Collected Works,* vol. 9,1. Bollingen Series XX, Princeton, N.J.: Princeton University Press.

Jung, C. G. 1960b. *A Review of the Complex Theory. Collected Works,* vol. 8,

Bollingen Series XX. Princeton: Princeton University Press.

Jung, C. G. (ed.) 1964. *Man and his Symbols*. New York: Doubleday.

Jung, C. G. 2009. *The Red Book*.

Kant, I. 1999. *Critique of Pure Reason*. Cambridge, MA: Cambridge University Press.

Kardec, A. 2012. *The Spirits' Book*. Norwich/Norfolk: Spastic Cat Press.

Kardec, A. 2011. *The Mediums' Book*. Miami Beach, FL: Edicei of America Spiritist Books, LLC.

Kautz, W. 2017. Xenoglossy: Verification of the Speech of An Unlearned Language. Paper presented at the International Transpersonal Conference in Prague, Czech Republic, September 2017.

Kennell, J. H. and Klaus, M. 1988. Bonding: Recent Observations That Alter Perinatal Care. *Pediatrics in Review*, 19, 4–1.

Klaus, M., Kennell, J. H. and Klaus, P. H. 1985. *Bonding: Building the Foundations of Secure Attachment and Independence*. Reading, MA: Addison Wesley.

Korzybski, A. 1973. *Science and Sanity: An Introduction to Non-Aristotelian Systems and General Semantics*. Lakeville, CT: Colonial Press.

Kuhn, T. 1962. *The Structure of Scientific Revolutions*. Chicago, Il.: University of Chicago Press.

Laszlo, E. 1993. *The Creative Cosmos*. Edinburgh: Floris Books.

Laszlo, E. 1995. *The Interconnected Universe: Conceptual Foundations of Transdisciplinary Unified Theory*. Singapore: World Scientific Publishing Company.

Laszlo, E. 2003. *The Connectivity Hypothesis: Foundations of An Integral Science of Quantum, Cosmos, Life, and Consciousness*. Albany, NY: State University of New York (SUNY) Press.

Laszlo, E. 2007. *Science and the Akashic Field: An Integral Theory of Everything*. Rochester, VT: Inner Traditions.

Laszlo, E. 2016. *What is Reality?: The New Map of Cosmos, Consciousness, and Existence*. A New Paradigm Book.

Leuner, H. 1962. *Experimentelle Psychose (Experimental Psychosis)*. Berlin: Springer Series #95.

Lommel, P. van 2010. *Consciousness Beyond Life. The Science of the Near-Death Experience*. New York: Harper Collins.

Moody, R. A. 1975. *Life After Life*. New York; Bantam.

Moody, R. A. 1993. *Reunions: Visionary Encounters with Departed Loved Ones.* New York: Villard Books.

Moon, C., Lagercrantz, H., and Kuhl, P. 2010. Phonetic learning in Utero. *The Journal of the Acoustical Society of America,* 127, 3, 2017.

Nevole, S. 1947. *O čtyřrozměrném viděni: Studie z fysiopathologie smyslu prostorového, se zvlástním zřetelem k experimentální otravě mezkalinem (Apropos of Four-Dimesional Vision: Study of Physiopathology of the Spatial Sense with Special Regard to Experimental Intoxication with Mescaline.)* Prague: Lékařské knihkupectví a nakladatelství.

Nevole, S. 1949. *O smyslových ilusích a o jejich formální genese (Apropos of Sensory Illusions and Their Formal Genesis).* Prague: Zdravotnické nakladatelství Spolku lékařů a vědeckých pracovníků J.E.Purkyně.

Offray de La Mettrie, J. 1865. *L'Homme Machine (Man the Machine).* Paris: Frederic Henry, Libraire-Editeur.

Penfield, W. 1975. The Mystery of the Mind : A Critical Study of Consciousness and the Human Brain. Princeton, NJ: Princeton University Press.

Pribram, K. 1971. *Languages of the Brain.* Englewood Cliffs, NJ: Prentice Hall.

Pribram, K. 1981. *Non-Locality and Localization: A Review of the Place of the Holographic Hypothesis of Brain Function in Perception and Memory.* Preprint for the Tenth ICUS, November.

Riedlinger, T. 1982. Sartre's Rite of Passage. *Journal of Transpersonal Psychol.* 14: 105.

Ring, K. 1982. *Life at Death: A Scientific Investigation of the Near-Death Experience.* New York: Quill.

Ring, K. 1985. *Heading Toward Omega: In Search of the Meaning of the Near-Death Experience.* New York, Quill.

Ring, K. and Valarino, E. E. 1998. *Lessons from the Light: What We Can Learn from the Near-Death Experience.* New York: Plenum Press.

Ring, K. and Cooper, S. 1999. *Mindsight: Near-Death and Out-of-Body Experiences in the Blind.* Palo Alto, CA: William James Center for Consciousness Studies.

Sabom, Michael. 1982. *Recollections of Death: A Medical Investigation.* New York: Harper & Row.

Satir, V. 1983. *Conjoint family therapy.* Palo Alto, CA: Science and Behavior Books.

Senkowski, E. 1994. Instrumental Transcommunication (ITC). An Institute for Noetic Sciences lecture at the Corte Madera Inn, Corte Madera, CA, July.

Sheldrake, R. 1981. *A New Science of Life*. Los Angeles: J. P. Tarcher.

Sullivan, H. S. 1953. *The Interpersonal Theory of Psychiatry.* New York: Norton.

Tarnas, R. 1995. *Prometheus the Awakener.* Woodstock, CT: Spring Publications.

Tarnas, R. 2006. *Cosmos and Psyche: Intimations of a New World View*. New York: Random House.

Tomatis, A. A. 1991. *The Conscious Ear: My Life of Transformation through Listening*. Barrytown, NY: Station Hill Press.

Verny, T. and Kelly, J. 1981. *The Secret Life of the Unborn Child.* Toronto: Collins Publishers.

Vondráček, V. 1935. *Farmakologie duše (Pharmacology of the Soul).* Prague: Lékařské knihkupectví a nakladatelství.

Vondráček, V. 1968. *Fantastické a magické z hlediska psychiatrie (Fantastic and Magical from the Viewpoint of Psychiatry.)* Prague: State Medical Publishing House.

Whitwell, G. E. 1999. Life Before Birth: Prenatal Sound and Music. Internet column reviewing the literature on prenatal effects of sound, http://www.birthpsychology.com.

III

Maps of the Psyche in Depth Psychology: *Toward an Integration of Approaches*

It is important to have a good map when we travel to new territories, and inner journeys to non-ordinary realities are no exception. Unfortunately, the cartography of the psyche currently used by Western mainstream psychiatrists and psychologists is painfully superficial and inadequate. It is useless as a guide for deep self-exploration and actually causes serious problems for psychonauts, because it considers perinatal and transpersonal experiences—which have great therapeutic and spiritual value—to be products of a pathological process.

During the mass self-experimentation of the 1960s, young psychonauts embarking on their inner journeys lacked a roadmap for their ventures into mysterious non-ordinary realities. They were thus like the early explorers traveling into unknown regions of our planet and discovering new worlds. The early travelers' maps charted the areas they had already visited and contained vast areas marked with the inscription: "HIC SUNT LEONES" ("here are lions"). The symbol of the lion, a wild and dangerous animal, was used as a reference to all the unexpected hardships and challenges that could be encountered in the as yet unexplored territories: savages, predatory animals, and poisonous plants and snakes. Conversely, there could also be pleasant surprises ahead: friendly and supportive inhabitants, useful fauna and flora, and natural sceneries of stunning beauty.

In this chapter, we will explore the history of depth psychology and review attempts to create a map of the human psyche. The world of psychotherapy consists of many competing schools that have serious disagreements about fundamental issues related to this task. These include the answers to what are the dimensions of the psyche; what are its principal motivational forces; why do symptoms develop and what do they mean; which aspects of the client's life experience play the key role in causing emotional and psychosomatic disorders; and what techniques should be used to work with the clients. This is true not only for schools coming from very different *a priori* philosophical positions (such as behaviorism and psychoanalysis), but also for those that originally started from the same source (such as the approaches created by the psychoanalytic renegades). Even deeper discrepancies can be found between the understanding of the psyche in the Western schools of psychology and psychotherapy and the great spiritual philosophies of the East, such as Hinduism, Buddhism, Taoism, or Sufism.

The work with holotropic states of consciousness has made it possible to bring clarity and simplification into the hopeless labyrinth of Western schools of psychotherapy and to create a comprehensive map of the psyche as described in an earlier chapter, which also provides a bridge to the spiritual traditions of the East. In this module, we will follow the development of the maps of the human psyche from a historical perspective. We will show which ideas from the founders of these schools withstood the test of time and have been supported by the findings of holotropic research, and which need to be modified or replaced.

Sigmund Freud

We will begin the story of the search for the map of the human psyche with the father of depth psychology, Austrian neurologist Sigmund Freud. Holotropic states played a crucial role in the early history of psychoanalysis and psychotherapy. In psychiatric handbooks, the roots of depth psychology are usually traced back to hypnotic sessions with hysterical patients conducted by Jean Martin Charcot at the Salpetrière Hospital in

Sigmund Freud (1856–1939), Austrian neurologist, founder of psychoanalysis and father of depth psychology.

Paris, and the research in hypnosis, which was carried out by Hippolyte Bernheim and Ambroise Liébault at the Nancy School. Sigmund Freud visited both places during his journey to France and learned the technique of inducing hypnosis. After returning from Paris, he used it in the work with his clients.

Freud's early ideas were inspired by his work with a patient whom he treated jointly with his friend Joseph Breuer, who had invited him as a neurological consultant for the case. The young woman, Bertha Pappenheim, whom Freud called Miss Anna O. in his writings, suffered from severe hysterical symptoms. During her therapeutic sessions, she was able to enter into an autohypnotic trance, during which she experienced spontaneous holotropic states of consciousness. She regressed to childhood and relived various traumatic memories underlying her neurotic disorder. This was accompanied by *abreaction*—the expression of pent-up emotions and blocked physical energies. She found these experiences very helpful and referred to them as "chimney sweeping."

The therapy with Anna O. ran into serious problems, though: she developed a strong transference on Breuer and repeatedly tried to embrace and kiss him. She started having symptoms of hysterical pregnancy *(pseudocyesis)* and claimed that Breuer was the father of her child. This led to a crisis

Salpêtrière, the famous teaching hospital of Sorbonne University in Paris, where Jean Martin Charcot conducted his experiments with hysterical patients.

A drawing showing Jean Martin Charcot (1825–1893), French neurologist and professor of pathological anatomy, demonstrating the effects of hypnosis on hysterical patients (top). Josef Breuer (1842–1925), Austrian physician and inventor of the "talking cure," who invited Sigmund Freud as consultant in the case of his patient, Bertha Pappenheim (bottom left). Bertha Pappenheim (1859–1936), an Austrian-Jewish feminist and socialite known as Anna O., who played an important role in the history of psychoanalysis as the patient of Josef Breuer and Sigmund Freud (bottom right).

in Breuer's marriage and the treatment had to be terminated. In their joint work, *Studies in Hysteria,* Freud and Breuer linked the origin of hysteria to psychotraumatic situations in childhood, primarily incest, during which the child could not adequately respond emotionally and physically. This resulted in a "jammed affect" ("abgeklemmter Affekt") that then became the source of energy for the symptoms (Freud and Breuer 1936).

As therapy for hysteria, Freud and Breuer recommended hypnotic regression, reliving the underlying childhood traumas, and emotional and physical abreaction. Freud and Breuer then went their separate ways due to differences about theoretical and practical issues. Breuer pursued physiological hypotheses and continued to use the hypnotic technique, while Freud abandoned the use of hypnosis, and became interested in psychological mechanisms. As Freud's ideas matured, he developed a novel set of theories and techniques that he called "psychoanalysis."

Freud felt increasingly uncomfortable having close contact with his patients, and moved from the direct emotional experience in a holotropic state and "making the unconscious conscious" to the use of free associations in the everyday state of consciousness. Freud got the inspiration for this method from Artemidoros of Daldianos, the ancient Greek who used it for the interpretation of his clients' dreams. However, while Artemidoros used his own free associations, Freud concluded that it made more sense to work with the associations of his patients. He also shifted his emphasis from the conscious reliving of unconscious psychotraumas and emotional abreaction to working with transference neurosis and transference analysis, and from actual traumas to Oedipal fantasies. In retrospect, these were unfortunate developments that sent psychoanalysis and Western psychotherapy in the wrong direction for the next fifty years (Ross 1989).

Using the method of free associations, Freud conducted groundbreaking research into the human psyche and laid the foundations of a new discipline—depth psychology. Many of his ideas are valuable for psychonauts: he discovered the existence of the unconscious and described its dynamics, developed the technique of dream interpretation, explored the psychological mechanisms involved in the genesis of psychoneuroses and psychosomatic disorders, brought attention to infantile sexuality, and depicted the phenomena of transference and countertransference. He created the first model and cartography of the human psyche, although it was limited to postnatal biography and the individual unconscious.

Since Freud singlehandedly explored the territories of the psyche previously unknown to Western scientists, it is understandable that his concepts kept changing as he confronted new problems. However, one element that remained constant during all these changes was Freud's deep need to establish psychology as a scientific discipline. He was profoundly influenced by his teacher Ernst Brücke, founder of the scientific organization known as the Helmholtz School of Medicine.

According to Brücke's view, all biological organisms are complex systems of atoms governed by strict laws, particularly the principle of the conservation of energy. The explicit goal and ideal of the Helmholtz School was to introduce the principles of Newton's scientific thinking into other disciplines to make them truly scientific. It was in the spirit of the Helmholtz School that Freud modeled his description of psychological processes after Newton's mechanics. The four basic principles of the psychoanalytic approach—dynamic, economic, topographical, and deterministic—exactly parallel the basic concepts of Newtonian physics. So, for example, the Id, Ego, and Superego had the properties of Newtonian objects—they were clashing, displacing each other, and where one of them was, the others could not be. Libido energy was flowing through the organism, in what resembled a hydraulic system, frequently jamming and causing congestion.

Freud's most important specific contributions can be divided into three thematic categories: the theory of instincts, the model of the psyche, and the principles and techniques of psychoanalytic therapy. Freud believed that the psychological history of the individual begins after birth and referred to the newborn as a *tabula rasa* (a "blank" or "erased" tablet). He ascribed a critical role in mental dynamics to instinctual drives, which he saw as forces bridging the psychic and somatic spheres. In his early work, Freud saw the human psyche as a battlefield with two rivaling forces—*libido* and the nonsexual *ego instinct* related to self-preservation. He believed that mental conflicts resulting from the clash between these instincts were responsible for psychoneuroses and a variety of other psychological phenomena. Of the two instincts, libido attracted much more of Freud's attention and received preferential treatment.

Freud discovered that the origins of sexuality are not in puberty, but lie in early childhood; drawing on his clinical observations, he formulated a developmental theory of sex. According to him, the psychosexual activities start during nursing when the mouth of the infant functions as an erogenous zone *(oral phase)*. During the period of toilet training the emphasis shifts, first, to sensations associated with defecation *(anal phase)* and, later, with urination *(urethral phase)*. Finally, around the age of four, these pregenital partial drives become integrated under the domination of genital interest involving the penis or clitoris *(phallic phase)*.

This also coincides with the development of the Oedipus or Electra complex, a predominantly positive attitude toward the parent of the opposite sex and an aggressive stance toward the one of the same sex. At this time, Freud attributed an important role to the overvaluation of the penis and the castration complex. The boy gives up his Oedipal tendencies because of castration fears. The girl moves from her primary attachment to her mother toward the father because she is disappointed by the "castrated" mother and hopes to receive a penis or child from her father.

Overindulgence in erotic activities or, conversely, frustrations, conflicts, and traumas interfering with them can cause fixation on different stages of libidinal development. Fixation and failure to resolve the Oedipal situation may result in psychoneuroses, sexual perversions, and other forms of psychopathology. Freud and his followers developed a detailed dynamic taxonomy linking different emotional and psychosomatic disorders to specific vicissitudes of libidinal development and the maturation of the ego (Fenichel 1945). Freud also traced difficulties in interpersonal relationships to factors interfering with the evolution from the stage of primary narcissism of the infant, characterized by self-love, toward differentiated object relations, where the libido is invested in other people.

During the early stages of his psychoanalytic explorations and speculations, Freud put great emphasis on the pleasure principle, or an inborn tendency to seek pleasure and avoid pain, as the main regulatory principle governing the psyche. He related pain and distress to an excess of neuronal stimuli and pleasure to the discharge of tension and reduction of excitation. The counterpart of the pleasure principle was the reality principle or ego instinct, a learned function reflecting the demands of the external world and requiring the postponement of immediate pleasure *(frustration by delay)*. In his later investigations, Freud found it increasingly difficult to reconcile clinical facts with the exclusive role of the pleasure principle in psychological processes.

He noticed that in many instances, aggressive impulses were not serving the purpose of self-preservation and, therefore, should not be attributed to the ego instinct. This was quite obvious in the inexplicable need to suffer in masochistic individuals, in the self-destructive tendencies of depressed patients, including suicide, in auto-mutilations occurring in certain emotional disorders, and in the repetition compulsion involving self-damaging behavior. Freud used the term "beyond the pleasure principle" for these phenomena.

Consequently, Freud decided to treat aggression as a separate instinct, the source of which was in the skeletal muscles, and its aim was destruction. This gave the final touch to an essentially negative image of human nature depicted by psychoanalysis. According to this view, the psyche is not only driven by base instincts, but it contains destructiveness as its intrinsic and essential component. In Freud's earlier writings, aggression was seen as a reaction to frustration and to the thwarting of libidinal impulses. In his late speculations, Freud postulated the existence of two basic instincts—the sexual instinct *(Eros),* which serves the goal of preserving life, and the death instinct *(Thanatos),* which counteracts it and tends to destroy the organism and return it to an inorganic condition.

Freud's final formulations concerning the role of the death instinct appeared in his last major work, *An Outline of Psychoanalysis.* There the basic dichotomy between two powerful forces, the sexual instinct (Eros or Libido) and the death instinct (Thanatos or Destrudo), became the cornerstone of his understanding of mental processes and disorders. In the newborn, Eros plays the predominant role and the role of Thanatos is negligible. In the course of life, the power of Thanatos increases and at the end of life, it destroys the organism and reduces it to the inorganic status (Freud 1964).

The concept of Thanatos helped Freud come to terms with the problem of sadism. He saw it as an attempt to direct Thanatos to another object rather than being its victim. However, he never found a good answer to the problem of sadomasochism, with its close connection between sex and aggression, and the link between the need to both inflict and experience pain. The image of the psyche as a battlefield with Eros and Thanatos as two rival forces was a concept that dominated Freud's thinking in the last years of his life.

This major revision of psychoanalytic theory generated little enthusiasm among Freud's followers. Statistical research conducted by Brun showed that only 6% of Freudians accepted these late ideas of Freud. This version of psychoanalysis has never been fully incorporated into mainstream psychoanalytic thinking (Brun 1953). Even Freud's ardent followers were strong in their criticism of the late Freud: he was a brilliant observer as long as he talked about sex. When he started writing about death, his ideas were distorted by his personal problems. He lost too many relatives, he was distressed by the large number of people killed in WWI, and he suffered enormously because of a poorly fitted prosthetic device that he wore for sixteen years after a mutilating resection of his jaw for an osteoclastoma. At the end of his life, he developed cancer of the tongue and ended his suffering by asking his physician for euthanasia through an overdose of morphine.

Freud's early topographical model of the psyche, outlined at the beginning of the twentieth century in his *The Interpretation of Dreams* (Freud 1953), was derived from his analysis of dreams, the dynamics of psychoneurotic symptoms, and the psychopathology of everyday life. It distinguishes three regions of the psyche that are characterized by their relationship to consciousness—the unconscious, the preconscious, and the conscious.

The unconscious contains mental representations of instinctual drives that had once been conscious, but were unacceptable and therefore banned from consciousness and repressed. All the activity of the unconscious is to pursue the pleasure principle—to seek discharge and wish fulfillment. For this purpose, it uses *primary process thinking* that disregards logical connections; it has no conception of time, knows no negatives, and readily permits contradictions to coexist. It attempts to reach its goals by means of such mechanisms as condensation, displacement, and symbolization.

Eventually, Freud replaced the concept of system-conscious and system-unconscious with his famous model of the mental apparatus, which postulated the dynamic interplay of three separate structural components of the psyche: Id, Ego, and Superego. The Id represents a primordial reservoir of instinctual energies that are Ego-alien and governed by the primary process. The Ego is related to consciousness and governs the perception of external reality and reactions to it. The Superego is the youngest of the structural components of the mind; it comes fully into being with the resolution of the Oedipus complex. One of its aspects represents the introjected prohibitions and injunctions of the parents, backed by the castration complex; this is the conscience, or the inner "demon." The other aspect is what Freud called the Ego Ideal, which reflects the positive identification with the parents or their substitutes.

In addition, Freud noticed that a certain aspect of the Superego is savage and cruel, betraying its unmistakable origins in the Id. He deemed it responsible for the extreme self-punishing and self-destructive tendencies observed in certain psychiatric patients. More recent contributions to Freudian theory have emphasized the role of the drives and object attachments formed in the pre-Oedipal period in the development of the Superego. These pregenital precursors of the Superego reflect projections of the child's own sadistic drives and a primitive concept of justice based on retaliation. These features of the child's psyche were confirmed by Melanie Klein, using sandplay as a therapeutic tool (Klein 1960). However, research suggests that the violent impulses Klein observed in children's play might also have perinatal origins, as we shall see.

In general, the practice of psychoanalytic therapy reflects the Cartesian dichotomy between mind and body. This is expressed in psychoanalytic practice through its exclusive focus on mental processes; it involves no direct physical interventions. There is actually a strong taboo against any physical contact with the patient. Some psychoanalysts have even strongly advised against shaking hands with the patients, as it could be potentially dangerous for the transference/countertransference dynamics. Intense emotional expression and physical activity was referred to as "acting out" and seen as an impediment in the therapeutic process.

This outline of the basic concepts of classical psychoanalysis and its theoretical and practical vicissitudes provides a basis for considering Freud's contributions in light of the observations from deep experiential psychotherapy involving holotropic states of consciousness. In general, it is possible to say that psychoanalysis appears to be an adequate conceptual framework, as long as the sessions focus on the biographical level of the unconscious. The psychosexual dynamics and the fundamental conflicts of the human psyche as described by Freud manifest with unusual clarity and vividness even in sessions with naive subjects who have never been analyzed, have not read psychoanalytic books, and have not been exposed to any other forms of explicit or implicit indoctrination.

They experience regression to childhood and even early infancy, relive various psychosexual traumas and complex sensations related to infantile sexuality, and are confronted with conflicts involving activities in various libidinal zones. They have to face and work through the basic psychological problems described by psychoanalysis, such as the Oedipus or Electra complex, the trauma of weaning, castration anxiety, penis envy, and conflicts around toilet training. The work with holotropic states also confirms Freud's observations concerning the biographical roots of psychoneuroses and psychosomatic disorders, and their specific connections with various erogenous zones and stages of ego development.

However, two major revisions must be introduced into the Freudian conceptual framework to account for certain important aspects of the biographical level of the unconscious. The first of these is the concept of dynamic governing systems organizing emotionally relevant memories, for which I have coined the term COEX systems. The second revision involves the paramount psychotraumatic impact of physical traumas, such as operations, diseases, injuries, or near-drowning, which Freudian psychoanalysis did not recognize and take into consideration. Such memories play an important role in the genesis of various emotional and psychosomatic symptoms and provide an experiential bridge to corresponding elements of the perinatal level. We discussed these differences in an earlier chapter (pp. 128).

However, these are minor problems that could easily be corrected. The fundamental fallacy of psychoanalysis is its exclusive emphasis on postnatal biographical events and on the individual unconscious. It tries to generalize its findings, which are certainly relevant for one superficial and narrow band of consciousness, to other levels of consciousness and to the totality of the human psyche. Thus, its major shortcoming is that it has no genuine recognition of the perinatal and transpersonal levels of the unconscious. This makes psychoanalysis essentially useless as a conceptual framework for working with holotropic states of consciousness, such as psychedelic therapy, Holotropic Breathwork, and supporting individuals undergoing a spiritual emergency. Navigating these states requires knowledge of the perinatal and transpersonal domains of the psyche.

Being limited to postnatal biography, psychoanalysis provides a superficial and inadequate understanding of psychopathology. According to Freud, the etiology and dynamics of emotional disorders is almost entirely explainable from postnatal events. As we have discussed earlier, experiential therapies bring overwhelming evidence that childhood traumas do not represent the primary pathogenic causes for emotional and psychosomatic disorders. They represent superficial layers superimposed over emotions, physical energies, and contents from deeper levels of the psyche. Symptoms of emotional and psychosomatic disorders have an intricate multilevel and multidimensional dynamic structure (COEX systems). The biographical layers represent only one component of this complex network; important roots of the problems involved can almost always be found on the perinatal and transpersonal levels.

The incorporation of the perinatal level into the cartography of the unconscious has far-reaching consequences for psychoanalytic theory; it clarifies many of its problems and puts them in a very different perspective. The shift of emphasis from biographically determined sexual dynamics to the dynamics of the basic perinatal matrices (BPMs) is possible without rejecting most of the important findings of psychoanalysis because of the deep experiential similarity between the pattern of sexual orgasm and the orgasm of biological birth, and the simultaneous activation and engagement of all the erogenous zones (oral, anal, urethral, and phallic) during childbirth.

The awareness of perinatal dynamics and their incorporation into the cartography of the unconscious provides a simple, elegant, and powerful explanatory model for many phenomena that represented a crux for the theoretical speculations of Freud and his followers. In the realm of psychopathology, psychoanalysis has failed to provide satisfactory explanations for the phenomena of sadomasochism, automutilation, sadistic murder, and suicide. It did not adequately tackle the puzzle of the savage part of the Superego, which seems to be a derivative of the Id.

The concept of feminine sexuality, and femininity in general as outlined by Freud, represents without doubt the weakest aspect of psychoanalysis, and borders on the bizarre and ridiculous. It lacks any genuine understanding of the female psyche; it leaves out such critical elements of women's lives as pregnancy and birth, and treats women essentially as castrated males. Psychoanalysis also offers only superficial and unconvincing interpretations for an entire spectrum of other phenomena occurring in psychiatric patients.

Freud was unable to recognize the importance of perinatal dynamics, and misinterpreted transpersonal experiences by reducing them to basic biological facts. For this reason, he failed to provide a reasonable basis for understanding a number of phenomena from the ritual and spiritual life of humanity, such as shamanism, totemism, rites of passage, ancient mysteries of death and rebirth, the great religions of the world, and their mystical traditions.

Freud's definition of religion as the obsessive-compulsive neurosis of humanity and the obsessive-compulsive neurosis as a private religion completely missed the point by reducing the problem of religion to ritual (Freud 1907). The sources of all religions are the transpersonal experiences of the founders, prophets, and early followers. Rituals would be empty and meaningless without their connection with visionary experiences. Equally problematic was Freud's attempt to explain religion as a result of the guilt of young males who ganged up on their father, a dominant tyrannical male in the primordial horde, murdered him, and ate him (Freud 1989). Freud's misunderstanding of spirituality and religion is one of the main reasons why psychoanalysis is of little value for psychonautics, where the spiritual quest plays a central role.

Freud's attempts to use psychoanalysis to explain sociopolitical events also fell short of providing believable insights into such phenomena as wars, genocide, and bloody revolutions. As we will in see a later section of this book, none of these can be adequately understood without taking into consideration the perinatal and transpersonal levels of the psyche. The general lack of efficacy of psychoanalysis as a therapeutic tool should also be mentioned as one of the serious shortcomings of this otherwise intriguing system of thought.

However, on a number of occasions, Freud's genius came quite close to the discovery of the perinatal level of the unconscious. Many of his formulations dealt, although not explicitly, with problems closely related to birth and to the death-rebirth process. He was the first one to come up with the idea that the vital anxiety experienced during the passage through the birth canal might represent the deepest source and prototype of all future anxieties. But, for some reason, he did not pursue this exciting idea any further and did not make an attempt to incorporate it into psychoanalysis.

Later, he opposed the speculations of his disciple, Otto Rank, who published a drastic revision of psychoanalysis, emphasizing the paramount significance of the trauma of birth as the fundamental event of human life (Rank 1929). In the writings of Freud and his followers, a surprisingly clear line is usually drawn between the interpretation and evaluation of prenatal, or perinatal, and postnatal events. The material occurring in free associations or dreams that is related to birth or intrauterine existence is consistently called "fantasy," in contrast to material from the postnatal time, which is usually seen as possibly reflecting memories of actual events. Otto Rank, Nandor Fodor, and Lietaert Peerbolte are exceptions to this, as they had a genuine appreciation and understanding of perinatal and prenatal dynamics (Rank 1929, Fodor 1949, Peerbolte 1975).

Freud's development regarding the psychological importance of death was fascinating. In Freud's early writings and in mainstream classical psychoanalysis, death had no representation in the unconscious. Fear of death was interpreted alternately as fear of castration, fear of loss of control, fear of an overwhelming sexual orgasm, or as a death wish toward another person, redirected by the strict Superego back toward the subject. Freud was never quite satisfied with his thesis that the unconscious or Id does not know death, however, and he found it increasingly difficult to deny the relevance of death for psychology and psychopathology.

In his late formulations, after his recognition of the existence and importance of phenomena that lay "beyond the pleasure principle," Freud introduced into his theory the concept of the death instinct, or Thanatos, which he saw as being at least an equipotent counterpart to Eros or Libido. Freud's understanding of death did not accurately portray its role in the perinatal dynamics, however. He was far from the insight that, in the context of the death-rebirth process, birth, sex, and death form an inextricable triad, and that all of them can function as gateways to transcendence. However, Freud's recognition of the psychological significance of death was quite remarkable; here, as in many other areas, he was clearly far ahead of his followers.

The advantages of the model that includes perinatal dynamics are far-reaching. It not only offers a more adequate and comprehensive interpretation of many emotional and psychosomatic disorders and their dynamic interrelations, but it also logically links these to anatomical, physiological, and biochemical aspects of the birth process. The phenomenon of sadomasochism can be easily explained from the experience of BPM III, with its intimate connections between sexual arousal, pain, and aggression.

The mixture of sexuality, aggression, anxiety, and scatology, which is another important characteristic of the third perinatal matrix, provides a natural context for the understanding of other sexual disorders, deviations and perversions. On this level, sexuality and anxiety are two facets of the same process and neither of them can be derived from the other. This throws new light on Freud's frustrating attempts to explain anxiety as being caused by the repression of libidinal feelings and, in turn, describing anxiety as having a prominent role among negative emotions that cause repression.

BPM III is also characterized by an excessive generation of aggressive and sexual impulses, with a simultaneous blockage of external motor expression of any kind due to uterine constriction, all in the context of an extremely brutal, life-threatening, and painful situation. This appears to be the natural basis for the deepest roots of the Freudian savage Superego, which is cruel and primitive. Its connection to pain, masochism, self-mutilation, violence, and suicide (ego death) is easily comprehensible and constitutes no mystery if seen as an introjection of the merciless impact of the birth canal.

In the context of perinatal dynamics, the concept of *vagina dentata,* female genitals that can kill or castrate, was considered by Freud a product of primitive infantile fantasy, but it represents a realistic assessment based on the memory of birth. In the course of delivery, countless children have been killed, almost killed, or severely damaged by this potentially dangerous organ. The connection of the vagina dentata to castration fears becomes obvious when these can be traced back to their actual source—the memory of the cutting of the umbilical cord.

This clarifies the paradox of the occurrence of "castration fears" in both sexes, as well as the fact that, in their free associations, subjects in psychoanalysis equate castration with death, separation, the loss of an important relationship, suffocation, and annihilation. The image of vagina dentata thus represents an inappropriate generalization of a perception of this organ, which is correct when applied to a specific situation, namely childbirth rather than to everyday life. It is this generalization, not the perception itself, which is wrong.

The recognition of the perinatal level of the unconscious eliminates a serious logical gap in psychoanalytic thinking that is hard to explain in view of the otherwise intellectual acuity of psychoanalysts. According to Freud, his followers, and many theoreticians inspired by him, very early events that occurred during the oral period of the infant's life can have profound influence on later psychological development. This is generally accepted, even for relatively subtle influences.

Thus, Harry Stack Sullivan suggested that the nursing infant is able to distinguish experiential nuances in the oral erogenous zone, such as a "good nipple," "evil nipple," and "wrong nipple." A "good nipple" provides milk and the mother is behaving in a loving way; an "evil nipple" gives milk, but the mother is rejecting or anxious; the "wrong nipple," such as the infant's big toe, fails to give milk. Which kind of nipple the infant experiences can then have a profound impact on his or her entire life (Sullivan 1953). How, then, could the same organism that is a connoisseur of nipples possibly have missed experiencing, a few minutes or hours earlier, the extreme conditions of delivery—life-threatening anoxia, extreme mechanical pressures, agonizing pain, and a whole spectrum of other alarming signals of vital danger?

According to the observations from psychedelic therapy, various biological and psychological subtleties of nursing are of great importance. However, as one could expect from the above description, the relevance of the birth trauma is of a far higher order. The infant has to be certain about an adequate supply of life-giving oxygen before he or she can feel hunger or cold, notice whether the mother is present or absent, or distinguish the nuances of the nursing experience.

Birth and death are events of fundamental relevance that occupy a metaposition in relation to all the other experiences of life. They are the alpha and omega of human existence. A psychological system that does not incorporate them is bound to remain superficial, incomplete, and of limited relevance. The psychoanalytic model also fails to provide any useful clues for the understanding of the ritual and spiritual life of humanity, the phenomenology of psychotic experiences, world mythology, and serious social psychopathology, such as wars and revolutions, totalitarianism, and genocide. Any serious approach to all these phenomena requires knowledge of the perinatal and transpersonal dynamics; it is thus clearly beyond the reach of classical Freudian analysis.

The above discussion of psychoanalysis may not satisfy its contemporary practitioners, since it is limited to classical Freudian concepts and does not take into consideration important recent developments in this field. It seems therefore appropriate to offer a brief reference to the theory and practice of ego psychology. The origins of this discipline can be found in the writings of Sigmund Freud and Anna Freud. Its basic concepts were further developed and refined by Heinz Hartmann, Ernst Kris, Rudolph Loewenstein, Rene Spitz, Margaret Mahler, Edith Jacobson, Otto Kernberg, Heinz Kohut, and others.

The basic theoretical modifications of classical psychoanalysis include a sophisticated development of the concept of object relations, appreciation of their central role in the development of the personality, and focus on the problems of human adaptation. Additional important concepts explored by ego psychology are the conflict-free zones in the psyche, the inborn ego apparatus, and average expectable environment.

Ego psychology considerably expands the spectrum of psychoanalytic interests, including, on the one hand, normal human development and, on the other, severe psychopathologies—autistic and symbiotic infantile psychoses, narcissistic personality disorder, and borderline personality. These changes in theory have also found their reflection in the therapeutic techniques. Such technical innovations as ego building, drive attenuation, and the correction of distortion of structure make it possible to attempt psychotherapeutic work with patients who have precarious ego strength and show borderline psychotic symptomatology.

As significant as these developments are for psychoanalysis, they maintain the serious limitation of classical Freudian thought's narrow biographical orientation. Since they do not recognize the perinatal and transpersonal levels of the psyche, they cannot reach a true comprehension of psychopathology. Instead, they spin out refinements of concepts related to a layer of the psyche that is not sufficient for its understanding. Many borderline and psychotic states have significant roots in the negative aspects of perinatal matrices, or in the transpersonal domain.

By the same token, ego psychology cannot conceive of and utilize the powerful mechanisms of healing and personality transformation that are available through experiential access to transindividual realms of the psyche. In light of the therapeutic strategies presented in this encyclopedia, the main problem is not to protect and build up the ego through sophisticated verbal maneuvers, but to create a supportive framework within which it can be experientially transcended. The experience of ego death and the ensuing unitive experiences, both of a symbiotic-biological and transcendental nature, then become the sources of new strength and personal identity. Understanding the concepts and mechanisms of this kind and their utilization in therapy are as far beyond the reach of ego psychology as they were for classical Freudian analysis.

The Famous Renegades

Alfred Adler

In the dynamics of neurosis, Alfred Adler's individual psychology puts great emphasis on "feelings of inadequacy" and the "constitutional inferiority" of some organs or systems of organs, and the tendency to overcome these. Striving for superiority and success follows a strictly subjective pattern reflecting the circumstances of one's life, particularly one's biological endowment and early childhood environment (Adler 1932). Adler's concept of inferiority is broader than it appears at first sight though, as it includes insecurity and anxiety, among other elements. Similarly, the striving for superiority is a search for perfection and completion, but it also implies a search for meaning in life.

A deeper, hidden dimension behind the inferiority complex is the memory of infantile helplessness, and at its bottom is impotence in view of the dictate of death. This focus on infantile helplessness and death brings Adler's thinking close to the recognition of the importance of the trauma of birth, in which these are essential elements. The inferiority complex can lead, through the mechanism of overcompensation, to superior performance and, in extreme cases, create a genius. Adler's favorite example was

Demosthenes, a stammering Greek boy with a weak voice and a tic in his shoulder, who became the most powerful orator of all time. He practiced his speeches on the ocean shore with a stone under his tongue, trying to compete with the sound of the waves. A sword suspended from a tree above his shoulder hurt him every time he had a tic. In less fortunate cases, the same mechanism can create a neurosis.

Alfred Adler's individual psychology remained limited to the biographical level, like Freudian psychoanalysis, but its focus differed. In contrast with Freud's deterministic emphasis, Adler's approach was clearly teleological and finalistic. Freud explored historical and causal aspects of the pathogenesis of neurosis and other mental phenomena, whereas Adler was interested in their purpose and final goal. According to him, the guiding principle of every neurosis is the imaginary aim to be a "complete man."

Alfred Adler (1870–1937), Austrian medical doctor and psychotherapist, founder of the school of individual psychology.

According to Adler, the sexual drives and the tendencies toward sexual perversions of various kinds, as emphasized by Freud, are only secondary expressions of this guiding principle. The preponderance of sexual material in the fantasy life of the neurotic is simply a jargon, a *modus dicendi,* expressing strivings toward the masculine goal. This drive for superiority, totality, and perfection reflects a deep need to compensate for all-pervasive feelings of inferiority and inadequacy.

In his therapeutic practice, Adler emphasized the active role of the therapist. He interpreted society for the patient, analyzed his lifestyle and goals, and suggested specific modifications. He gave encouragement, instilled hope, restored the patient's faith in himself, and helped him to realize his strength and ability. In Adler's psychology, the therapist's understanding of the patient is considered to be essential for the successful reconstruction of the patient. The patient's insight into his own motivations, intentions, and goals is not seen as a prerequisite for therapeutic change. Adler saw the Freudian concept of transference as erroneous and misleading, and as an unnecessary obstacle to the therapeutic progress. He emphasized that the therapist should be warm, trustworthy, reliable, and interested in the patient's well-being in the here and now.

The observations from LSD work and other experiential approaches bring an interesting new perspective and insight into the theoretical conflict between Adler and Freud. In general, this controversy is based on the erroneous belief that the complexity of the psyche can be reduced to some simple fundamental principles. The human mind is so complex that many different theories can be constructed, all of which seem to be logical, coherent, and explain major facts of observation, yet at the same time are mutually incompatible or actually contradict each other.

More specifically, the disagreements between psychoanalysis and individual psychology reflect a lack of awareness of the spectrum of consciousness with its different levels. In this sense, both systems are incomplete and superficial, since they focus exclusively on the biographical level and do not acknowledge the perinatal and transpersonal realms. Consequently, projections of various elements from these neglected areas of the psyche appear in both systems in a distorted and diluted form.

The conflict between the emphasis on the sexual drive and on the will toward power and masculine protest appears to be important and irreconcilable only as long as one's knowledge of the psyche is limited to the biographical level. As we have already discussed, intense sexual arousal (including activation of the oral, anal, urethral, and genital erogenous zones) and feelings of helplessness, alternating with desperate attempts to mobilize one's strength and survive, represent integral and inseparable aspects of the dynamics of BPM III. Although in respect to the death-rebirth process, there may, temporarily, be more emphasis on the sexual or the power aspect of the perinatal unfolding, the two are inextricably interwoven.

As an example, the study *A Sexual Profile of Men in Power* by Sam Janus, Barbara Bess, and Carol Saltus is based on more than 700 hours of interviews with high-class call girls from the East Coast of the United States (Janus, Bess, and Saltus 1977). Unlike many other researchers, the authors were less interested in the personalities of the prostitutes than in the preferences and habits of their customers. Among these men were many prominent American politicians, presidents of large companies and law firms, and a Supreme Court judge.

The interviews revealed that only an absolute minority of the clients simply sought sexual intercourse. Most of them were interested in various alternative erotic practices that would qualify as "heavy kinky sex." Requests for bondage, whipping, and other forms of torture were very common. Some of these clients were willing to pay high prices for the psychodramatic staging of complex sadomasochistic scenes. One of the clients, for example, requested a realistic enactment of a situation in which he played the role of an American pilot shot down and captured in Nazi Germany during World War II. The prostitutes were asked to dress as bestial Gestapo women wearing high boots and military helmets. Their task was to subject the client to various ingenious tortures.

Among the frequently requested and highly priced practices were the "golden shower" and "brown shower," being urinated and defecated on during the sexual act. According to the accounts of the call girls, after the sadomasochistic and scatological experience culminated and their clients reached sexual orgasm, many of these extremely ambitious and influential men regressed to an infantile state. They wanted to be held, suck on the prostitutes' nipples, and be treated like babies. This behavior was in sharp contrast with the public image these men had been trying to project in their everyday life.

The interpretations of these findings offered in the book are strictly biographical and Freudian in nature. The authors link tortures to parental punishments, the golden shower and brown shower to problems related to toilet training, the need for sucking the breast to frustrated nursing and anaclitic needs, mother fixation, and the like. However, closer inspection reveals that the clients actually enacted classical perinatal scenes rather than postnatal childhood events. The combination of physical restraint, pain and torture, sexual arousal, scatological involvement, and subsequent regressive oral behavior are unmistakable indications of the activation of BPM III and IV.

The conclusions of Janus, Bess, and Saltus deserve special notice. The authors appealed to the American public not to expect their politicians and other prominent public figures to be models of sexual behavior. In the light of their research, this expectation would be highly unrealistic. Their findings indicated that the high degree of drive and ambition that it takes to become a successful public figure in today's society is inextricably linked with an excessive sexual drive and an inclination to deviant sexuality.

We thus should not be surprised by the scandals in the highest social and political circles, such as the affair of John Profumo, Secretary of State for War, with Christine Keeler, which shook the British parliament and discredited the Conservative Party; the escapades of Ted Kennedy that destroyed his chances for presidency; John Kennedy's naked swimming parties and sexual peccadilloes that threatened national security; Anthony Weiner's multiple sex scandals and pornographic sexting; and Bill Clinton's sexual extravaganzas that for many months paralyzed the U.S. government.

The deep roots of sexual pathology, Krafft-Ebing's *psychopathia sexualis,* can be found in the third perinatal matrix, where strong libidinal arousal is associated with anxiety, pain, aggression, and the encounter with biological material. Feelings of inadequacy, inferiority, and low self-esteem can be traced beyond the biographical conditioning in early childhood to the helplessness of the fetus in the life-threatening and overpowering situation of birth. Both Freud and Adler, because of an insufficient depth of their approach, focused selectively on two categories of psychological forces that, on a deeper level, represent two facets of the same process.

The awareness of death, the crucial theme of the perinatal process, had a powerful impact on both researchers. Freud postulated, in his final theoretical formulations, the existence of the death instinct (Thanatos) as an important force in the psyche. His biological emphasis prevented him from seeing the possibility of the psychological transcendence of death, and he created a gloomy and pessimistic image of human existence. The theme of death also played an important role in his personal life, since he suffered from severe thanatophobia.

Adler's life and work were also very strongly influenced by the problem of death. He saw the inability to prevent and control death as being the core of feelings of inadequacy. It is interesting that Adler was aware that his decision to become a physician—a member of the profession trying to control and conquer death—was deeply influenced by his near-death experience at the age of five. It is likely that the same factor also functioned as a prism that shaped his theoretical speculations.

From observations arising from deep experiential therapy, the determined striving for external goals and the pursuit of success do very little in overcoming feelings of inadequacy and low self-esteem, no matter the outcome of these endeavors. The feelings of inferiority cannot be resolved by mobilizing one's forces to overcompensate them, but by confronting them experientially and surrendering to them. They are then consumed in the process of ego death and rebirth, and a new self-image emerges from the awareness of one's cosmic identity. True courage lies in the willingness to undergo this awesome process of inner transformation, not in a heroic pursuit of external goals. Unless the individual succeeds in finding his or her true identity within, any attempts to give their life meaning by striving for external achievement will be a futile and ultimately self-defeating, quixotic crusade.

Wilhelm Reich

Another important psychoanalytic renegade was the Austrian psychiatrist and political activist Wilhelm Reich. Maintaining Freud's main thesis concerning the paramount importance of sexual factors in the etiology of neuroses, he modified Freud's concepts substantially by emphasizing "sex economy"—the balance between energy charge and discharge, or sexual excitement and release. According to Reich, the suppression of sexual feelings, together with the characterological attitude that accompanies it, constitutes the true neurosis; the clinical symptoms are only its overt manifestations.

The emotional traumas and sexual feelings are held in repression by complex patterns of chronic muscular tensions—the "character armor." The term "armoring" refers to the function of protecting the individual against painful and threatening experiences from without and within. For Reich, the critical factor that contributes to incomplete sexual orgasm and congestion of bioenergy is the repressive influence of society. A neurotic individual maintains balance by binding his excess energy in muscular tensions, and thus limiting sexual excitement. A healthy individual does not have such a limitation; his or her energy is not bound in muscular

Wilhelm Reich (1897–1957), Austrian medical doctor and psychoanalyst, one of the most radical figures in the history of psychoanalysis.

armoring and can flow freely.

Reich's contribution to therapy is of great significance and lasting value. His dissatisfaction with the methods of psychoanalysis led him to the development of a system called "character analysis" and, later, "character analytic vegetotherapy" (Reich 1949). It was a radical departure from classical Freudian techniques, because it concentrated on the treatment of neuroses from a biophysical point of view and involved physiological elements. Reich used hyperventilation, a variety of body manipulations, and direct physical contact to mobilize the jammed energies and remove the blocks. Reich's therapeutic experiments inspired the revolutionary experiential and physical therapies of the 1960s, many of which have been referred to as neo-Reichian—Alexander Lowen's bioenergetics, John Pierrakos' Core Energetics, Charles Kelly's Radix Therapy, Stanley Keleman's Formative Psychology, Arthur Janov's Primal Therapy, and others.

According to Reich, the goal of therapy was to ensure the patient was capable of fully surrendering to the spontaneous and involuntary movements of the body that are normally associated with the respiratory process. If this was accomplished, the respiratory waves produced an undulating movement in the body that Reich called the "orgasm reflex." He believed that those patients who achieve it in therapy are then capable of surrendering fully in the sexual situation, reaching a state of total satisfaction. The full orgasm discharges all the excess energy of the organism, and the patient remains free of symptoms (Reich 1961).

As he was developing his theories and trying to implement his ideas, Reich became increasingly controversial. Seeing the repressive role of society as one of the main factors in emotional disorders, he combined his innovative work in psychotherapy with radical political activity as a member of the Communist Party. This eventually ended in his break with both the psychoanalytic circles and the Communist movement. After Reich's conflict with Freud, his name was dropped from the roster of the International Psychoanalytic Association. The publication of his politically explosive book *Mass Psychology of Fascism* (Reich 1970), in which he described the Nazi movement as a social pathology caused by the repression of sexuality, led to his excommunication from the Communist Party.

In later years, Reich became increasingly convinced of the existence of a primordial cosmic energy that is the source of three large realms of existence, which arise through a complicated process of differentiation—mechanical energy, inorganic mass, and living matter. This energy that Reich called *orgone* could be demonstrated visually, thermally, electroscopically, and by the means of Geiger-Müller counters. It was different from electromagnetic energy, and one of its main properties was pulsation.

According to Reich, the dynamics of orgone and the relationship between "mass-free orgone energy" and "orgone energy that has become matter" is essential for any true functional understanding of the universe, nature, and the human psyche. The streaming of orgone and its dynamic superimpositions can explain such diverse phenomena as the creation of subatomic particles, tornadoes, the aurora borealis, and the formation of galaxies, as well as the origin of life forms, growth, locomotion, sexual activity and the reproductive processes, and psychological phenomena.

Reich designed special orgone accumulators, boxes that, according to him, collected and concentrated orgone for therapeutic use. He sent one of the devices to Albert Einstein, who spent five days studying it before he declared the orgone theory to be an illusion and tried to dissuade Reich from pursuing it. Orgone therapy was based on the assumption that the body and the psyche are both rooted bioenergetically in the pulsating pleasure system (blood and vegetative apparatus) as the common source of psychological and somatic functions. Orgone therapy was, therefore, not a psychological but rather a biological therapy dealing with disturbances of pulsation in the autonomic system.

Wilhelm Reich's work, which began originally as highly innovative therapeutic experimentation, moved gradually into increasingly remote areas—physics, biology, cellular biopathy, abiogenesis, meteorology, astronomy, extraterrestrial visitations, and philosophical speculations. The end of his stormy scientific career was tragic. Since he used and advocated for the use of orgone generators, which were denounced by the Food and Drug Administration, he got into serious conflicts with the U.S. government. After much harassment, he was twice imprisoned, and finally died in jail from a heart attack.

From the point of view of the concepts presented in this encyclopedia, Reich's major contribution seems to be in the areas of bioenergetic processes and the psychosomatic correlations in the genesis of emotional disorders and in their therapy. Reich was fully aware of the enormous blocked energies underlying neurotic symptoms and of the futility of purely verbal approaches to therapy. Also, his understanding of armoring and the role of musculature in neuroses is a contribution of lasting value. The observations from LSD work confirm the basic Reichian concepts of energetic blockages and the involvement of the muscular and the vegetative systems in neuroses.

A patient's experiential confrontation with his or her emotional symptoms is typically accompanied by intense tremors, shaking, jerks, contortions, the prolonged maintaining of extreme postures, grimacing, uttering sounds, and even occasional vomiting. It is quite clear that dramatic physiological manifestations and psychological aspects of this process, such as perceptual, emotional, and ideational manifestations, are intimately interconnected, representing two sides of the same coin. The basic difference between my own point of view and the Reichian theory lies in the interpretation of this process.

Wilhelm Reich put great emphasis on the gradual accumulation and congestion of sexual energy in the organism due to societal influences' interference with full sexual orgasm. As a result of repeated incomplete discharge, the libido jams in the organism and finally finds deviant expressions in a variety of psychopathological phenomena, from psychoneuroses to perversions and sadomasochism. Effective therapy, then, requires a release of pent-up libidinal energies, dissolution of the "body armor," and achievement of total orgasm. The observations from the work with holotropic states support Reich's concept of the body armor, but indicate clearly that this energetic reservoir is not a consequence of chronic sexual stasis resulting from incomplete orgasms.

Much of the energy released during experiential psychotherapy turns out to be the result of the hours of excessive neuronal excitation triggered by the stress, pain, fear, and suffocation experienced during the passage through the birth canal. The deepest basis of much of the character armor seems to be in the introjected dynamic conflict between the excessive neuronal overstimulation caused by the birth process and the unrelenting straitjacket of the birth canal, preventing adequate emotional and physical response and peripheral discharge. The dissolution of the armor coincides, to a great extent, with the completion of the death-rebirth process. However, some of its elements have even deeper roots in the transpersonal realms.

Perinatal energy can be easily mistaken for jammed libido because BPM III has a substantial sexual component and due to the similarity between the pattern of the sexual orgasm and the birth orgasm. Activated perinatal energy seeks peripheral discharge, and the genitals represent one of the most logical and important channels. This seems to form the basis for a vicious circle: the aggression, fear, and guilt associated with the third perinatal matrix interfere with full orgastic ability and, conversely, the absence or incompleteness of sexual orgasm blocks an important safety valve for the birth energies.

The situation is thus the opposite of what Reich postulated. It is not that societal and psychological factors interfering with full orgasm lead to the accumulation and stasis of sexual energy, but that deep-seated perinatal energies interfere with adequate orgasm and, at the same time, create psychological and interpersonal problems. To rectify this situation, these powerful energies must be discharged in a nonsexual, therapeutic context and reduced to a level that the patient and the partner can comfortably handle in a sexual interaction. Many phenomena discussed by Reich, from sadomasochism to the mass psychopathology of fascism, can be explained more adequately from perinatal dynamics than from incomplete orgasm and the jamming of sexual energy.

Reich's speculations, although unconventional and at times undisciplined, are, in their essence, often compatible with modern developments in science. In his understanding of nature, he came close to the worldview suggested by quantum-relativistic physics—emphasizing the unity underlying the world, focusing on process and movement rather than substance and solid structure, and acknowledging the active role of the observer. Reich's ideas about the joint origin of inorganic matter, life, consciousness, and knowledge are at times reminiscent of the philosophical speculations of David Bohm and Ervin Laszlo. His arguments against the universal validity of the principle of entropy and the second law of thermodynamics resemble the conclusions of Ilya Prigogine's careful and systematic research into dissipative structures and order out of chaos.

In the field of psychology, Reich came close, both theoretically and practically, to the discovery of the perinatal realm of the unconscious. His work on muscular armoring, his discussion of the dangers of sudden removal of the armor, and his concept of total orgasm clearly involve important elements of perinatal dynamics. However, he showed determined resistance to its most critical elements—the psychological significance of the experiences of birth and death. This is evident from his passionate defense of the primary role of genitality and his rejection of Otto Rank's concept of the birth trauma, Sigmund Freud's speculations about death, and Karl Abraham's assumptions of a psychological need for punishment.

In many ways, Reich also teetered on the edge of mysticism and transpersonal psychology. He was obviously close to the concept of cosmic consciousness and mystical awareness, which found its expression in his speculations about the orgone. True religion, for him, was unarmored oceanic merging with the dynamics of the universal orgone energy. However, in sharp contrast with perennial philosophy, Reich's understanding of this cosmic energy was quite concrete; orgone was measurable and had specific physical characteristics.

Reich never reached a true understanding and appreciation of the great spiritual philosophies of the world. In his passionate critical excursions against spirituality and religion, he tended to confuse mysticism with certain superficial and distorted versions of mainstream religious doctrines. In his polemics, he argued against the literal belief in devils with tails and pitchforks, winged angels, formless blue-gray ghosts, dangerous monsters, heavens, and hells. He then discounted these as projections of unnatural, distorted organ sensations and, in the last analysis, as misperceptions of the universal flow of the orgone energy. Similarly, Reich was also strongly opposed to Jung's interest in mysticism and his tendency to spiritualize psychology.

For Reich, mystical inclinations reflected armoring and a serious distortion of orgone economy. The mystical search, then, could be reduced to misunderstood biological urges. Thus: "Fear of death and dying is identical with unconscious orgasm anxiety, and the alleged death instinct, the longing for disintegration, for nothingness, is the unconscious longing for the orgastic resolution of tension." He also said, "God is the representation of the natural life forces, of the bio-energy in man, and is nowhere so clearly expressed as in the sexual orgasm. Devil then is the representation for the armoring that leads to perversion and distortion of these life forces." In direct contrast with psychedelic observations, Reich claimed that the mystical tendencies disappear if therapy succeeds in dissolving the armor. In his opinion, "orgastic potency is not found among mystics any more than mysticism is found among the orgastically potent" (Reich 1972).

Otto Rank

Otto Rank's major areas of disagreement with Freud were his emphasis on the paramount significance of the birth trauma as compared to sexual dynamics, negation of the crucial role of the Oedipus complex, and his concept of Ego as an autonomous representative of the will, rather than a slave of the Id. Rank also offered modifications of the psychoanalytic technique that were as radical as his theoretical contributions. He suggested that a verbal approach to psychotherapy is of limited value and that the main emphasis in therapeutic work should be on experience. According to

Otto Rank (1884–1939), Austrian psychoanalyst, author, lecturer, and teacher. Rank discovered the psychological importance of the trauma of birth.

Rank, it was essential for the patient to relive the trauma of birth in therapy; without it, treatment should not be considered complete. He actually gave his clients the date when psychoanalysis would end, and believed that coming close to this date would activate their unconscious material related to birth and bring it to the threshold of consciousness.

As far as the role of birth trauma in psychology is concerned, Freud was actually the first one to draw attention to the possibility that the fear associated with the "sensations and innervations" during the challenging passage through the birth canal might be the prototype and source of all future anxieties. This idea came to him when he was observing the obstetric nurses' medical examinations. One of the questions during the exam was: "When and why does meconium [fetal feces] appear during birth?" The correct answer would have been that it indicates a high degree of suffocation for the fetus. The nurse's answer was "because the fetus is scared shitless," thus putting the emphasis on the effect of fear on the anal sphincter.

The nurse did not pass the examination, but Freud took the reference to fear in connection to birth seriously. He thought about the linguistic similarity that exists in some languages between the words for fear and a narrow space, such as *angustiae* (narrow canyon) and *anxietas* (fear) in Latin, and *eng* (narrow) and *Angst* (anxiety) in German. In Czech, the word *úzkost* literally means both *narrowness* and *anxiety*. It is also well known that soldiers experiencing extreme fear in battles sometimes lose control over the anal sphincter and soil their pants. Freud discussed this issue in several of his writings, but did not pursue it any further.

Otto Rank became captivated by this idea and worked secretly on the book *The Trauma of Birth* (Rank 1929). He gave the finished work to Freud as a birthday gift, fresh from the press. Freud's principal biographer, Ernest Jones, said that after reading this book, Freud went into a state of emotional shock that lasted four months. His reaction was not an expression of criticism and anger about what Rank had written. As a matter of fact, it was exactly the opposite; he was afraid that future generations would see Rank's theory as more important than his own discovery of psychoanalysis.

Freud was very sensitive to this, because he had narrowly missed out on obtaining scientific priority for discovering the anesthetic properties of cocaine and its importance for medicine. This distinction went to his Viennese colleague Karl Koller. Once he recovered from his shock over Rank's book, Freud wrote a fair report about it. He referred to the book as a very important contribution to psychoanalytic theory, second in its importance only to his own discovery of psychoanalysis. He suggested that analysts should study the people born by Cesarean section and compare them with those who had normal and difficult births to see what differences they could find.

Later, Freud received letters from Berlin's influential psychoanalyst Karl Abraham and others, warning him that Rank's book would destroy the homogeneity of the psychoanalytic movement. They suggested that some of the members would enthusiastically embrace Rank's theory and others would reject it and refuse to accept Rank's extreme formulations. Freud yielded to the pressure, and the resulting conflict between him and Rank led to the termination of Rank's membership in the Psychoanalytic Association.

There was a major difference, though, between the concept of the birth trauma as seen by Freud and Rank. Holotropic research showed that during the short time that Freud thought about the trauma of birth, his understanding of birth was actually more accurate than Rank's. While Freud emphasized the extreme physiological challenges involved in the passage through the birth canal, Rank put more emphasis on losing the comfort of the maternal womb as a paradisean situation of unconditional and effortless gratification, and having to face the challenges of postnatal life.

Rank saw the trauma of birth as the ultimate reason why separation is the most painful and frightening human experience. According to him, all later frustrations of partial drives can be seen as derivatives of this primal trauma. Most of the events experienced by the individual as traumatic derive their pathogenic power from their similarity to biological birth. The entire period of childhood can be seen as a series of attempts at abreacting and psychologically mastering this fundamental trauma. Infantile sexuality can be reinterpreted as the child's desire to return to the womb, the anxiety associated with it, and curiosity about where he or she came from.

Rank did not stop here, though. He believed that the mental life of humans has its origin in the primal anxiety and primal repression precipitated by the birth trauma. The central human conflict consists of the desire to return to the womb and the fear of this wish. As a result of it, any change from a pleasurable situation to an unpleasant one will give rise to feelings of anxiety. Rank also offered an alternative to the Freudian interpretation of dreams. Sleep is a condition that resembles the intrauterine life, and dreams can be understood as attempts to relive the birth trauma and return to the prenatal state. Even more than the act of sleep itself, they represent a psychological return to the womb. The analysis of dreams provides the strongest support for the psychological significance of the birth trauma.

Similarly, Rank also reinterpreted the cornerstone of Freudian theory, the Oedipus complex, by putting emphasis on the trauma of birth and the desire to return to the womb. According to him, the core of the Oedipus myth is the mystery of the origin of man, which Oedipus tries to solve by returning to the mother's womb. This happens not only literally, in the act of marriage and sexual union with his mother, but also symbolically through his blindness and disappearance into the cleft rock leading into the Underworld (Mullahy 1948).

In Rankian psychology, the birth trauma also plays a crucial role in sexuality; its importance is based on the deep desire to return to the intrauterine existence that governs the human psyche. According to him, much of the difference between the sexes can be explained by women's ability to replay the reproductive process through their bodies and find their immortality in procreation, whereas for men, sex represents mortality and their strength lies in nonsexual creativity, such as technology, science, painting, music, and literature. Interestingly, males who explore the perinatal layer of their psyche can at times develop feelings of "womb envy," in sharp contrast with Freud's focus on "penis envy."

Analyzing human culture, Rank found the birth trauma to be a powerful psychological force behind religion, art, and history. Every form of religion ultimately tends toward the reinstitution of the original succoring and protective situation of the womb. The deepest root of art is the "autoplastic imitation" of one's own origin and growth from the maternal vessel. Art, being a representation of reality and at the same time a denial of it, is a particularly powerful means of coping with the primal trauma. The history of human dwellings, from the search for primitive shelters to elaborate architectural structures, reflects instinctive memories of the warm, protective womb. The use of implements and weapons is, in the last analysis, based on an "insatiable tendency to force one's way completely into the mother."

LSD psychotherapy and other forms of deep experiential work have brought strong support for Rank's general thesis about the paramount psychological significance of the birth trauma. However, substantial modifications of the Rankian approach are necessary to increase its compatibility with actual clinical observations. As I mentioned earlier, Rank's theory focuses on the problem of separation from the mother and loss of the womb as the essential traumatic aspects of birth. For him, the trauma consists of the fact that the postnatal situation is far less favorable than the prenatal one. Outside the womb, the child has to face the irregularity of the food supply, the absence of the mother, oscillations of temperature, and loud noises. He or she has to breathe, swallow food, and dispose of waste products.

In the work with holotropic states, the situation appears much more complicated. Birth is not traumatic just because the child is transferred from the paradise situation in the womb into the adverse conditions of the external world; the passage through the birth canal itself entails enormous emotional and physical stress and pain. This was emphasized in Freud's original speculations about birth, but almost entirely neglected by Rank. In a sense, Rank's concept of the birth trauma applied more to the situation of a person born by elective Cesarean section than to vaginal childbirth.

Most of the psychopathological conditions are rooted in the dynamics of BPM II and BPM III, which reflects the challenges experienced during the hours spent in the birth canal between the undisturbed intrauterine state and the postnatal existence in the external world. The impulse to exteriorize and discharge the pent-up feelings and energies generated during the birth struggle represents a deep motivational force for a broad spectrum of human behaviors.

Like Freud, Adler, and Reich, Rank also did not have a genuine understanding of the transpersonal realms. He saw religious and mythological motifs and figures as derivatives of the trauma of birth. For example, the crucified body of Jesus represented the polar opposite of the comfortable and relaxed body of the fetus in the womb and the images of terrifying female goddesses, such as Hekate or Medusa, were inspired by the anxiety experienced during birth. In spite of these shortcomings, Rank's discovery of the psychological importance of the birth trauma and its many ramifications was a truly remarkable achievement that preceded, by many decades, the confirmations of his findings in LSD psychotherapy. It is astonishing that one hundred years later, mainstream psychiatric academics and clinicians still refuse to accept that birth is a major psychotrauma, in spite of overwhelming evidence from experiential therapies.

We should mention that several other psychoanalysts also recognized the significance of various aspects of the birth trauma. Nandor Fodor, in his pioneering book *The Search For The Beloved* (Fodor 1949), described, in considerable detail, the relations between various facets of the birth process and many important psychopathological symptoms in a way that has extensive congruence with the LSD observations. Lietaert Peerbolte wrote a comprehensive book, *Prenatal Dynamics* (Peerbolte 1975), in which he discussed his unique insights into the psychological relevance of prenatal existence and the birth experience. This topic also received a great deal of attention in the work of Frank Lake and in original and imaginative, although more speculative and less clinically grounded, books by Francis Mott (Lake 2007, Mott 2012).

Carl Gustav Jung

The list of famous psychoanalytic renegades would not be complete without Carl Gustav Jung, who was initially one of Freud's favorite disciples and the designated "crown prince" of psychoanalysis. Jung's revisions were by far the most radical and his contributions were truly revolutionary. It is not an exaggeration to say that his work moved psychiatry as far beyond Freud as Freud's discoveries were ahead of his own time. Jung's analytical psychology is not just a variety or modification of psychoanalysis; it represents an entirely new concept of depth psychology and psychotherapy.

Jung was well aware that his findings could not be reconciled with Cartesian-Newtonian thinking and that they required a drastic revision of the most fundamental philosophical assumptions of Western science. He was deeply interested in the revolutionary developments of quantum-

Carl Gustav Jung (1875–1961), Swiss psychiatrist and psychoanalyst, founder of analytical psychology.

relativistic physics and had fruitful exchanges with some of its founders, including Wolfgang Pauli and Albert Einstein. Unlike the rest of the theoreticians of psychoanalysis, Jung also had a genuine understanding of the mystical traditions and a great respect for the spiritual dimensions of the psyche and of human existence. Jung was the first transpersonal psychologist, although he didn't call himself one.

Jung can also be considered the first modern psychologist. The differences between Freudian psychoanalysis and Jung's analytical psychology are representative of the differences between classical and modern psychotherapy. Although Freud and some of his followers proposed rather radical revisions of Western psychology, only Jung challenged its very core and its philosophical foundations—monistic materialism and the Cartesian-Newtonian paradigm. As June Singer so clearly pointed out, he stressed "the importance of the unconscious rather than of consciousness, the mysterious rather than the known, the mystical rather than the scientific, the creative rather than the productive, [and] the religious rather than the profane" (Singer 1994).

Jung's concept of the human psyche represented a major expansion beyond Freud's biographical model. His radical departure from Freud's psychoanalysis started when he was analyzing a collection of poetry and prose by the American writer Miss Frank Miller, which was published in Geneva by Theodore Flournoy and became known as the *Miller Fantasies* (Miller 1906). He discovered that many motifs in her writing had parallels in the literature of various countries around the world, as well as different historical periods. His book *Symbols of Transformation,* inspired by this research, is a work of major historical importance as a landmark of his break with Freud (Jung 1956).

These observations were further confirmed through the analysis of patients' dreams, fantasies, and the hallucinations and delusions of his schizophrenic patients, along with his own dream life. This convinced him that we do not have only the Freudian individual unconscious, a psychobiological junkyard of rejected instinctual tendencies, repressed memories, and subconsciously assimilated prohibitions, but also a collective unconscious, the manifestation of an intelligent and creative cosmic force, which binds us to all humanity, nature, and the entire cosmos.

Jung's collective unconscious has a historical domain, which contains the entire history of humanity, and the archetypal domain, which harbors the cultural heritage of mankind—mythologies from every culture that has ever existed. In holotropic states of consciousness, we can experience visions of characters and scenes from these mythologies, even if we do not have any previous intellectual knowledge of them. Exploring the collective unconscious, Jung discovered universal principles governing the dynamics of this domain of the psyche. He first referred to them as "primordial images"—using a term that he borrowed from Jacob Burckhardt; later he called them "dominants of the collective unconscious" and, finally, "archetypes." According to the understanding that has emerged from Jungian psychology, consciousness research, and scholarly mythological research, archetypes are timeless, primordial cosmic principles underlying and informing the fabric of the material world (Jung 1959).

Jung put great emphasis on the unconscious and its dynamics, but his concept of it was radically different from Freud's. Jung did not see the human being as a biological machine. He recognized that humans can transcend the narrow boundaries of their egos and of the personal unconscious and connect with the Self that is commensurate with the entire cosmos. Jung saw the psyche as a complementary interplay between its conscious and unconscious elements, with a constant energy exchange and flow between the two. According to him, the unconscious is not governed by historical determinism alone, but also has a projective, finalistic, teleological function. The Self has a specific goal or purpose for each of us and can guide us to it. Jung referred to this as the *individuation process.*

Studying the specific dynamics of the unconscious through the association experiment, Jung discovered its functional units, for which he coined the term *complexes*. Complexes are constellations of psychological elements—ideas, opinions, attitudes, and convictions—that are clustered around a nuclear theme and associated with distinct feelings (Jung 1960). Jung was able to trace complexes from biographically determined motifs to archetypes of the collective unconscious (Jung 1959).

In his early work, Jung saw a similarity between archetypes and animal instincts, and thought that they were hard-wired in the human brain. Later on, while studying instances of extraordinary coincidences, such as dreams or visions, with events in the external world *(synchronicities),* he concluded that the archetypes must be in some way influencing the very fabric of the world (Jung 1960a). As they seemed to represent a link between matter and psyche or consciousness, he referred to them as *psychoids,* borrowing a term coined by the founder of vitalism, Hans Driesch.

Comparative religion and world mythology can be seen as unique sources of information about the collective aspects of the unconscious. According to Freud, myths can be interpreted in terms of the characteristic problems and conflicts of childhood, and their universality reflects the commonality of human experience. Jung found this explanation unacceptable; he repeatedly observed that the universal mythological motifs *(mythologems)* occurred in individuals for whom all intellectual knowledge of this kind was absolutely out of the question. This suggested to him that there were myth-forming structural elements in the unconscious psyche that gave rise both to the fantasy lives and dreams of individuals and to the mythology of peoples. Dreams can thus be seen as individual myths, and myths as collective dreams.

Freud showed a very deep interest in religion and spirituality throughout his life. He believed that it was possible to get a rational grasp of the irrational processes and tended to interpret religion in terms of unresolved conflicts from the infantile stage of psychosexual development. In contrast to Freud, Jung was willing to accept the irrational, paradoxical, and even mysterious. He had many religious experiences during his lifetime that convinced him of the reality of the spiritual dimension in the universal scheme of things. Jung's basic assumption was that the spiritual element is an organic and integral part of the psyche. Genuine spirituality is an aspect of the collective unconscious and is independent of childhood programming and the individual's cultural or educational background. Thus, if self-exploration and self-analysis reach sufficient depth, spiritual elements emerge spontaneously into consciousness.

Jung also differed from Freud in his understanding of the central concept of psychoanalysis, that of the libido. He did not see it as a strictly biological force aiming for mechanical discharge, but as a creative force of nature—a cosmic principle comparable to Aristotle's *entelechy* or Henri Bergson's *élan vital.* Jung's genuine appreciation of spirituality and his understanding of libido as a cosmic force found their expression in a unique concept regarding the function of symbols. For Freud, a symbol was an analogous expression of, or allusion to, something already known; its function was comparable to that of a traffic sign. In psychoanalysis, one image is used instead of another one, usually of a forbidden sexual nature. Jung disagreed with this use of the term symbol and referred to Freudian symbols as signs. For him, a true symbol points beyond itself into a higher level of consciousness. It is the best possible formulation of something that is unknown, an archetype that cannot be represented more clearly or specifically.

What truly makes Jung the first modern psychologist is his scientific method. Freud's approach was strictly historical and deterministic; he was interested in finding rational explanations for all psychic phenomena and tracing them back to biological roots, following the chains of linear causality. Jung was aware that linear causality is not the only mandatory connecting principle in nature. He originated the concept of *synchronicity*—an acausal connecting principle that refers to meaningful coincidences of events separated in time and/or space. Jung's willingness to enter the realm of the paradoxical, mysterious, and ineffable also included an open-minded attitude toward the great Eastern spiritual philosophies. He studied and commented on the I Ching, Bardo Thödol, Secret of the Golden Flower, and awakening of Kundalini. Among his esoteric interests were also astrology, mediumship, and other psychic phenomena (Jung 1958, 1967, 1970, 1995, 1996).

The observations from psychedelic experiences and other types of holotropic states of consciousness have repeatedly confirmed most of Jung's brilliant insights. Although even Jung's analytical psychology does not adequately cover the entire spectrum of phenomena occurring in holotropic states, it requires the least revisions or modifications of all the schools of depth psychology. On the biographical level, Jung's description of psychological complexes bears some similarity to COEX systems, although the two concepts are not identical. Jung and his followers were aware of the importance of the death-rebirth process in mythology, and studied its various forms from ancient Greek mysteries to the rites of passage of aboriginal cultures. However, Jung was not able to see the close connection between this process and biological birth.

Jung, who discovered and described the vast domains of the historical and archetypal collective unconscious, was not able to accept that birth is a psychotrauma and plays an important role in the human psyche. In an interview, which is now available under the name *Jung on Film,* Richard I. Evans asked Jung what he thought about the theory of his colleague Otto Rank attributing psychological significance to the trauma of birth. Jung laughingly dismissed this idea: "Oh, birth is not a trauma, it is a fact; everybody is born" (Jung 1957).

Jung's most fundamental contribution to psychotherapy is his recognition of the spiritual dimensions of the psyche and his discoveries in the transpersonal realms. Observations from holotropic states have brought strong support for the existence of the collective unconscious and the archetypal world, Jung's understanding of the nature of libido, his distinction between the ego and the Self, the recognition of the creative and prospective function of the unconscious, and the concept of the individuation process.

All these elements can be independently confirmed by observations in psychedelic and Holotropic Breathwork sessions, even with unsophisticated subjects. Material of this kind also frequently emerges in sessions guided by therapists who are not Jungians, and even those who have no knowledge of Jungian psychology. In a more specific way, analytical psychology is very useful in understanding various archetypal images and themes that surface spontaneously in experiential sessions. Deep experiential work has also independently confirmed Jung's observations on the significance of synchronicity.

The differences between the concepts presented in this encyclopedia and Jung's theories are relatively minor as compared to the far-reaching correlations. It has already been mentioned that the concept of the COEX system is similar, but not identical to Jung's description of a psychological complex. Jungian psychology has a good general understanding of the process of psychospiritual death-rebirth as an archetypal theme, but does not recognize the perinatal level of the unconscious and the importance of the trauma of birth.

Perinatal phenomena, with their emphasis on birth and death, represent a critical interface between individual biography and the transpersonal realms. Deep experiential confrontation with this level of the psyche is typically associated with the sense of a serious threat to survival and with a life-death struggle. Death-rebirth experiences have an important biological dimension; they are often accompanied by a broad spectrum of intense physiological manifestations, such as feelings of suffocation, pain in different parts of the body, tremors, cardiovascular distress, hypersalivation, sweating, nausea and vomiting, and on rare occasions, unintentional urination.

In Jungian analysis, which uses more subtle techniques than psychedelic therapy or some of the new powerful experiential approaches, the emphasis is on the psychological, philosophical, and spiritual dimensions of the death-rebirth process, while the psychosomatic components are seldom, if ever, effectively dealt with. In experiential psychotherapy, one always encounters an amalgam of actual fetal memories of biological birth and concomitant themes from the archetypal and historical collective unconscious. Swiss psychologist Arny Mindell and his wife Amy have introduced the missing somatic elements into Jungian analysis by developing what they call process psychotherapy (Mindell 2001).

In the transpersonal realm, Jungian psychology seems to have explored certain categories of experiences in considerable detail, while entirely neglecting others. The areas that have been discovered and thoroughly studied by Jung and his followers include the dynamics of the archetypes and the collective unconscious, mythopoetic properties of the psyche, certain types of psychic phenomena, and synchronistic links between psychological processes and the world of matter.

There seem to be no references, however, to transpersonal experiences that involve authentic identification with other people, animals, plants, and inorganic processes that can mediate access to new information about these elements of the material world. Considering Jung's deep interest and scholarship in the Eastern spiritual philosophies, it is surprising that he seemed to pay very little attention to past incarnation memories, which are of critical importance in any form of deep experiential psychotherapy. Despite the above differences, Jungians seem, in general, to be the most conceptually equipped to deal with the phenomenology of holotropic states of consciousness, provided they can get used to the dramatic form the experiences take and become comfortable with them. Knowledge of Jungian psychology and mythology is essential for safe and rewarding psychonautics.

Sandor Ferenczi

It seems appropriate to conclude this brief journey through the world of depth psychology by mentioning the work of another prominent pioneer and member of Freud's Viennese circle, Sandor Ferenczi. Although he is not usually listed among the renegades, his original speculations and practices took him far beyond orthodox psychoanalysis. In his famous paper *The Confusion of the Tongues Between the Adults and the Child,* Ferenczi returned to Freud's original idea that real incest plays an important role in the genesis of psychoneurosis, not the child's incest fantasy (Ferenczi

Sándor Ferenczi (1873–1933), Hungarian neurologist and psychiatrist and member of Freud's Viennese circle.

1949). Another of his controversial contributions to psychoanalysis was his concept of "mutual analysis" that he conducted with his American patients Elizabeth Severn and Clara Thompson. Also, his support of Otto Rank clearly indicated that he was far from a conforming and docile follower of Freud.

In his theoretical framework, he seriously considered not only perinatal and prenatal events, but also phylogenetic memories. Being one of the few disciples of Freud who immediately accepted his concept of Thanatos, Ferenczi also integrated a metaphysical analysis of death into his conceptual system. In his remarkable essay, *Thalassa: A Theory of Genitality,* Ferenczi described the sexual drive as an attempt to return to the maternal womb and even beyond it. According to him, in sexual intercourse, the interacting organisms share in the gratification of the germ cells (Ferenczi 1938).

Men have the privilege of returning to the womb directly, while women entertain fantasy substitutes or identify with their children when they are pregnant. However, the essence of Ferenczi's "Thalassa regressive trend" is the striving to return to an even earlier situation—the original aquatic existence in the primeval ocean. In the last analysis, the amniotic fluid represents the water of the ocean filling a cavity in the maternal womb. According to Ferenczi, terrestrial mammals have a deep organismic craving to reverse the decision they once made when they left their oceanic milieu and return where they came from. This would be the solution the ancestors of today's whales and dolphins actually made millions of years ago.

However, the ultimate goal of all life might be to arrive at a state characterized by the absence of irritability and, finally, to attain the inertia of the inorganic world. It is thus possible that death and dying are not absolute and that germs of life and regressive tendencies lie hidden even within inorganic matter. One could then conceive of the entire organic and inorganic world as a system of perpetual oscillations between the will to live and the will to die, in which an absolute hegemony on the part of either life or death is never attained. Ferenczi thus clearly came close to the concepts of perennial philosophy and mysticism, although his formulations were expressed in the language of the natural sciences.

This historical review of the conceptual disagreements in the early psychoanalytic movement clearly demonstrates that many of the concepts which may appear surprisingly new in Western psychology were, in one form or another, seriously considered and passionately discussed by the early pioneers of psychoanalysis. The major contribution of this review is thus an evaluation of the various schools of depth psychology in light of the findings of modern consciousness research, as well as the integration of their contributions into a comprehensive cartography of the psyche that will serve the needs of psychonauts.

Literature

Adler, A. 1932. *The Practice and Theory of Individual Psychology.* New York: Harcourt, Brace & Co.

Brun, A. 1953. Ueber Freuds Hypothese vom Todestrieb (Apropos of Freud's Theory of the Death Instinct). *Psyche* 17:81.

Fenichel, O. 1945. *The Psychoanalytic Theory of Neurosis.* New York: W. W. Norton.

Ferenczi, S. 1968. *Thalassa.* New York: W. W. Norton and Company.

Ferenczi, S. 1949. Confusion of the Tongues Between the Adults and the Child. *The International Journal of Psychoanalysis,* 30:225-230.

Fodor, N. 1949. *The Search for the Beloved: A Clinical Investigation of the Trauma of Birth and Prenatal Condition.* New Hyde Park, NY: University Books.

Freud, S. 1907. "Obsessive Actions and Religious Practices." *The Standard Edition of the Complete Psychological Works of Sigmund Freud, Vol. 9.* London: The Hogarth Press & The Institute of Psychoanalysis.

Freud, S. and Breuer, J. 1936. *Studies in Hysteria.* New York: Nervous and Mental Diseases Publication Company.

Freud, S. 1953. "The Interpretation of Dreams." *The Standard Edition of the Complete Psychological Works of Sigmund Freud. Vol. 4.* London: The Hogarth Press & the Institute of Psychoanalysis.

Freud, S. 1964. "An Outline of Psychoanalysis." *The Standard Edition of the Complete Psychological Works of Sigmund Freud. Vol. 23.* London: The Hogarth Press & The Institute of Psychoanalysis.

Freud, S. 1989. *Totem and Taboo.* London: W.W. Norton.

Janus, S., Bess, B., and Saltus, C. 1977. *A Sexual Profile of Men in Power.* Englewood Cliffs, NJ: Prentice-Hall.

Jung, C. G. 1956. *Symbols of Transformation. Collected Works, vol. 5, Bollingen Series XX,* Princeton, NJ: Princeton University Press.

Jung, C. G. 1958. *Psychological Commentary on the Tibetan Book of the Great Liberation. Collected Works, vol. 11. Bollingen Series XX,* Princeton, NJ: Princeton University Press.

Jung, C. G. 1959. *The Archetypes and the Collective Unconscious. Collected Works, vol. 9,1. Bollingen Series XX,* Princeton, NJ: Princeton University Press.

Jung, C. G. 1960a. *Synchronicity: An Acausal Connecting Principle. Collected Works, vol. 8, Bollingen Series XX.* Princeton, NJ: Princeton University Press.

Jung, C. G. 1960b. *A Review of the Complex Theory. Collected Works, vol. 8, Bollingen Series XX.* Princeton, NJ: Princeton University Press.

Jung,C. G. 1967. *The I Ching or Book of Changes (Richard Wilhelm, translator). Collected Works, vol. Bollingen Series XIX,* Princeton, NJ: Princeton University Press.

Jung, C. G. 1970. *Commentary to The Secret of the Golden Flower: A Chinese Book of Life (Richard Wilhelm, translator).* New York: Harcourt, Brace, and Company.

Jung, C. G. 1996. *The Psychology of Kundalini Yoga: Notes on the seminars given in 1932 by C. G. Jung (Soma Shamdasani, ed.). Bollingen Series XCIX.* Princeton, NJ: Princeton University Press.

Klein, M. 1960. *The Psychoanalysis of Children.* New York: Grove Press.

Lake, F. 2007. *Clinical Theology: A Theological and Psychiatric Basis for Clinical Pastoral Care.* Lexington, KY: Emeth Press.

Miller, F. 1906. "Quelques Faits d'Imagination Créatrice." *Archives de psychologie (Geneva)* V 36-51.

Mindell, A. 2001. *Working with the Dreaming Body.* Portland, OR: Lao Tse Press.

Mott, F. J. 2012. *The Nature of the Self.* London: Starwalker Press.

Mullahy, P. 1948. *Oedipus Myth and Complex: A Review of Psychoanalytic Theory.* Trenton, NJ: Hermitage Press.

Peerbolte, L. 1975. *"Prenatal Dynamics" Psychic Energy.* Amsterdam, Holland: Servire Publications.

Rank, O. 1929. *The Trauma of Birth.* New York: Harcourt Brace.

Reich, W. 1949. *Character Analysis.* New York: Noonday Press.

Reich, W. 1961. *The Function of the Orgasm: Sex-Economic Problems of Biological Energy.* New York: Farrar, Strauss & Giroux.

Reich, W. 1970. *The Mass Psychology of Fascism.* New York: Simon & Schuster.

Reich, W. 1972. *Ether, God, and Devil and Cosmic Superimposition.* New York: Farrar, Straus & Giroux.

Ross, C. 1989. *Multiple Personality Disorder.* Indianapolis, IN: Wiley Publications.

Singer, J. 1994. *Boundaries of the Soul: The Practice of Jung's Psychology.* New York: Anchor Books.

Sullivan, H. S. 1953. *The Interpersonal Theory of Psychiatry.* New York: W. W. Norton.

IV

Architecture of Emotional and Psychosomatic Disorders

In order to comprehend the extensive implications that the study of holotropic states has had for understanding emotional and psychosomatic disorders, we must first examine the conceptual frameworks that are currently used in psychiatry. The attempts to explain the nature and origin of psychiatric disorders fall into two broad categories. Some academics and clinicians show a strong preference to see these disorders as resulting from causes that are primarily of biological nature, while others favor psychological explanations. In everyday clinical practice, psychiatrists also often choose an eclectic approach and assign different degrees of significance to elements from both categories, leaning to one side or the other of the argument.

The organically oriented psychiatrists believe that—since the psyche is a product of material processes in the brain—the final answers in psychiatry will come from neurophysiology, biochemistry, genetics, and molecular biology. According to them, these disciplines will one day be able to provide adequate explanations, as well as practical solutions, for most of the problems in their field. This orientation is usually associated with a rigid adherence to the medical model and with attempts to develop a fixed diagnostic classification for all emotional disorders, including those for which no organic basis has been found.

An alternative orientation in psychiatry emphasizes factors of a psychological nature, such as the role of traumatic influences in infancy, childhood, and later in life, along with pathogenic potentials of conflict, the importance of family dynamics and interpersonal relationships, and the impact of the social environment. In the extremes, this way of thinking is applied not only to neuroses and psychosomatic disorders, but also to those psychotic states for which medicine has no biological explanation: functional or endogenous psychoses.

A logical consequence of this approach is to seriously question the appropriateness of applying the medical model, including rigid diagnostic labels, to disorders that are not biologically determined and are thus clearly of a different order than the organic ones. From this perspective, psychogenic disorders reflect the complexity of the developmental factors to which we have been exposed over the course of our life. Transpersonal psychologists would expand the spectrum of these influences to our entire psychospiritual history. Since these influences differ widely from person to person, the efforts to squeeze the resulting disorders into the straitjacket of medical diagnosis makes little sense.

Although many professionals advocate for an eclectic approach that acknowledges a complex interplay of biology and psychology, or nature and nurture, the biological approach dominates the thinking in academic circles and routine everyday psychiatric practice. As a result of its complex historical development, psychiatry has become established as a subspecialty of medicine, which gives it a strong biological bias. Mainstream conceptual thinking in psychiatry, the approach to individuals with emotional disorders and behavior problems, the strategy of research, basic education and training, and forensic measures are all dominated by the medical model.

This situation is a consequence of two important sets of circumstances. Medicine has been successful in establishing etiology and finding effective therapy for a specific, relatively small group of mental abnormalities of organic origin. It has also demonstrated its ability to control, symptomatically, many of those disorders for which specific organic etiology could not be found. The initial successes in unraveling the biological causes of mental disorders, however astonishing, were really isolated and limited to a small fraction of the problems with which psychiatry deals. The medical approach to psychiatry has failed to find specific organic etiology for problems vexing the absolute majority of its clients: psychoneuroses, psychosomatic diseases, manic-depressive disorders, and functional psychoses.

The psychological orientation in psychiatry was inspired by the pioneering research of Sigmund Freud and his followers. Some of them, such as C. G. Jung, Otto Rank, Wilhelm Reich, and Alfred Adler, left the Psychoanalytic Association, or were expelled from it and started their own schools. Others stayed within the organization, but developed their own variations of psychoanalytic theory and technique. Over the course of the twentieth century, this collective effort resulted in a large number of schools of "depth psychology," which differ significantly from each other in terms of their understanding of the human psyche and the nature of emotional disorders, as well as the therapeutic techniques they use.

Most of these individuals have had minimal or no influence on mainstream thinking in psychiatry and references to their work appear in academic textbooks as a historical note or even footnote. Only Freud's early writings, the work of a few of his followers, and the modern developments in psychoanalysis known as "ego psychology" have had significant impact on the psychiatric field. As we have seen, Freud and his colleagues formulated a dynamic classification that explains and ranks emotional and psychosomatic disorders in terms of fixation on a specific stage of the libido development and the evolution of the ego.

One of Freud's major contributions was the discovery that sexuality does not start in puberty, but during nursing. The libidinal interests of the infant gradually shift from the oral zone (at the time of nursing) to the anal and urethral zone (at the time of toilet training) and finally, to the phallic zone (focus on the penis and clitoris at the time of the Oedipus and Electra complex). Traumatization or, conversely, overindulgence during these critical periods can cause specific fixation on one of these zones. This predisposes the individual to psychological regression to this area when in the future he or she encounters serious difficulties.

The understanding of psychopathology based on Freud's libido theory was summarized by German psychoanalyst Karl Abraham and graphically represented in Otto Fenichel's classic *The Psychoanalytic Theory of Neurosis* (Abraham 1927, Fenichel 1945). In his famous scheme, Abraham defined major forms of psychopathology in terms of the primary fixation of the libido. According to him, fixation on the passive oral stage (before teething occurs) predisposes the individual to schizophrenia and plays a critical role in the development of alcoholism and narcotic drug addiction. Fixation on the oral-sadistic or cannibalistic stage (after teething) can lead to manic-depressive disorders and suicidal behavior.

The primary fixation for the obsessive-compulsive neurosis and personality is on the anal level. Anal fixation also plays an important role in the genesis of so-called pregenital conversions, such as stammering, psychogenic tics, and asthma. These disorders are characterized by an obsessive-compulsive personality structure, but use the mechanism of hysterical conversion for the formation of symptoms. Urethral fixation is associated with shame and fear of blunder, and a tendency to compensate for it through excessive ambition and perfectionism. Anxiety hysteria (various phobias) and conversion hysteria (paralysis, anesthesia, blindness, loss of voice, and hysterical attack) result from a fixation on the phallic stage (see table pp. 245).

This aspect of psychopathology was elaborated in great detail in the later development of psychoanalysis. Modern ego psychology, inspired by the groundbreaking work of Anna Freud and Heinz Hartmann, revised and refined classical psychoanalytic concepts and added some important new dimensions (Blanck and Blanck 1974, 1979). Combining direct observations in infants and young children with a deep knowledge of psychoanalytic theory, René Spitz and Margaret Mahler laid the foundations for a deeper understanding of the ego development and establishment of personal identity. Their work brought attention to the importance of the evolution of object relationships and the difficulties associated with them.

Karl Abraham's scheme took into consideration not only the points of libidinal fixation, but also fixation on the stages of the ego's evolution from autoeroticism and primary narcissism to the establishment of object love. The description and definition of three phases in the evolution of the ego—the autistic, symbiotic, and separation-individuation phase—have important theoretical and clinical implications (Spitz 1965, Mahler 1961, 2008).

Margaret Mahler, Otto Kernberg, Heinz Kohut, and others expanded Karl Abraham's scheme by adding several disorders that, according to them, have their origin in the early disturbances of object relations—autistic and symbiotic infantile psychoses, narcissistic personality disturbance, and borderline personality disorders (Mahler 1961, Kernberg 1976, 1984, Kohut 1971). This new understanding of the dynamics of ego evolution and its vicissitudes also made it possible to develop techniques of psychotherapy for psychiatric patients in these categories who cannot be reached by methods of classical psychoanalysis.

There is no doubt that ego psychologists improved, refined, and expanded the psychoanalytic understanding of psychopathology. However, they share the superficial understanding of the psyche with classical psychoanalysis, which is limited to postnatal biography and the individual unconscious. The observations from the study of holotropic states of con-

Karl Abraham: Dynamic Classification of Neuroses

<table>
<tr><th colspan="2">Fixation of Libido</th><th colspan="2">Emotional and Psychosomatic Disorders</th></tr>
<tr><td rowspan="2">ORAL</td><td>Passive</td><td colspan="2">• Schizophrenia
• Alcoholism
• Addiction</td></tr>
<tr><td>Active</td><td colspan="2">• Manic-depressive disorders
• Suicide</td></tr>
<tr><td colspan="2">ANAL</td><td>• Obsessive-compulsive neurosis</td><td rowspan="3">• Pregenital conversions
• Stammering
• Tics
• Asthma</td></tr>
<tr><td colspan="2">URETHRAL</td><td>• Fear of blunder
• Perfectionism</td></tr>
<tr><td colspan="2">PHALLIC</td><td>• Conversion Hysteria
• Anxiety Hysteria</td></tr>
</table>

Karl Abraham's dynamic classification of neuroses (from Otto Fenichel's book *The Psychoanalytic Theory of Neuroses*).

sciousness show that emotional and psychosomatic disorders, including many states currently diagnosed as psychotic, cannot be adequately understood solely from difficulties in postnatal development, such as problems in the development of the libido or vicissitudes involving the formation of object relations.

The attempts of Freud and his followers to understand emotional and psychosomatic disorders were groundbreaking and generally moving in the right direction. However, because they were using narrow models of the psyche that were limited to postnatal biography and the individual unconscious, the explanations remained superficial and unconvincing. At times, they were even highly questionable, such as Freud's theory of the death instinct (Thanatos), Otakar Kučera's attempt to explain sadomasochism as a fixation on the active-oral stage of libido development in which the infant hurts himself or herself during aggressive attempts to bite with the newly grown teeth, or interpretation of suicide as killing the introjected bad breast (Freud 1964, Kučera 1959). More recent editions of the American Diagnostic and statistical Manual (DSM III-V) abandoned etiological considerations altogether and moved to simple descriptions of symptoms (the "neo-Kraepelinian approach").

The new, vastly expanded model of the psyche that has emerged from the research of holotropic states of consciousness makes it possible to continue the etiological quest of the psychoanalytic pioneers in the same direction and offer a much deeper and more convincing understanding of emotional and psychosomatic disorders. It also opens up exciting new perspectives for therapy. According to the new insights, these conditions have a multilevel, multidimensional structure with important roots in the perinatal and transpersonal levels of the unconscious.

The recognition of the perinatal and transpersonal roots of emotional disorders does not mean denying the significance of the biographical factors described by psychoanalysis and ego psychology. The events in infancy and childhood certainly play an important role in the overall picture. However, instead of being the primary causes of these disorders, the memories of traumatic events from postnatal biography function as important conditions for the emergence of elements from deeper levels of the psyche.

What gives neurotic, psychosomatic, and psychotic symptoms their extraordinary dynamic power and specific content are complex COEX constellations that are not limited to biographical layers, but reach deep into the perinatal and transpersonal domains. The pathogenic influences emphasized by Freudian analysis and ego psychology modify the content of the themes from deeper levels of the unconscious, add to their emotional charge, and mediate their access into conscious awareness.

We have already seen the relationship between symptoms and the underlying multilayer COEX system comprising biographical and perinatal elements earlier, in the case of Peter. The following example involves Norbert, a 51-year-old psychologist and minister who participated in one of our five-day workshops at the Esalen Institute.

During the group introduction preceding the first session of Holotropic Breathwork, Norbert complained about severe chronic pain in his shoulder and pectoral muscles that caused him great suffering and made his life miserable. Repeated medical examinations, including X-rays, had not detected any organic basis for his problem and all therapeutic attempts had remained unsuccessful. Serial Procaine injections had brought only brief, transient relief for the duration of the drug. He also described breathing difficulties for which no organic explanation had been found.

At the beginning of the session of Holotropic Breathwork, Norbert made an impulsive attempt to leave the room, since he could not tolerate the music, which he felt was "killing" him. It took great effort to persuade him to stay with the process and to explore the reasons for his discomfort. He finally agreed and, for almost three hours, experienced severe pains in his breast and shoulder, which intensified to the point of becoming unbearable. He struggled violently as if his life were seriously threatened, choked and coughed, and let out a variety of loud screams. Following this stormy episode, he quieted down and was relaxed and peaceful. With great surprise, he realized that the experience had released the tension in his shoulder and muscles and that he was free from pain. The breathwork experience also opened his respiratory pathways, allowing him to breathe much more easily.

Retrospectively, Norbert reported that there were three distinct layers in his experience, all of them related to the pain in his shoulder and associated with choking. On the most superficial level, he relived a frightening situation from his childhood in which he almost lost his life. When he was about seven years old, he and his friends were digging a tunnel on a sandy ocean beach. When the tunnel was finished, Norbert crawled inside to explore it. As the other children jumped around, the tunnel collapsed and buried him alive. He almost choked to death before he was rescued.

When the breathwork experience deepened, he relived a violent and frightening episode that took him back to the memory of biological birth. His delivery was very difficult, since his shoulder had been stuck for an extended period of time behind the pubic bone of his mother. This episode shared the combination of choking and severe pain in the shoulder with the previous one.

In the last part of the session, the experience changed dramatically. Norbert started seeing military uniforms and horses and recognized that he was involved in a battle. He was even able to identify it as one of the battles in Cromwell's England. At one point, he felt a sharp pain and realized that his shoulder had been pierced by a lance. He fell off the horse and experienced himself being trampled by the horses running over his body and crushing his chest.

Norbert's consciousness separated from the dying body, soared high above the battlefield, and observed the scene from a bird's eye view. Following the death of the soldier, whom he recognized as himself in a previous incarnation, his consciousness returned to the present and reconnected with his body, which was now pain-free for the first time after many years of agony. The pain relief brought about by these experiences turned out to be permanent. We saw Norbert more than twenty years after this memorable session and found out that the symptoms still had not returned.

The traumatic memory of certain aspects of birth seems to be an important component of psychogenic symptoms of all kinds. The unconscious record of the experience represents a universal pool of difficult emotions and physical sensations that constitute a potential source of various forms of psychopathology. Whether emotional and psychosomatic disorders actually develop and which form they take then depends on either the reinforcing influence of traumatic events in postnatal history or on the mitigating effect of favorable biographical factors.

The roots of emotional, psychosomatic, and interpersonal problems can include not only biographical and perinatal components, but also reach deep into the transpersonal domain of the psyche. They can take the form of past-life experiences or of mythological figures and motifs that share the same archetypal quality. It is also not uncommon to discover that the symptoms are related, on a deeper level, to elements drawn from the animal or botanical kingdoms. The symptoms of emotional and psychosomatic disorders are the result of a complicated interplay involving biographical, perinatal, and transpersonal elements.

It is interesting to speculate what factors might be responsible for the origination of COEX constellations and the relationship between their biographical layers, perinatal matrices, and transpersonal components. The similarity of some of the postnatal traumas and their resemblance to certain aspects of the perinatal dynamics might be attributed to chance. The life of some individuals might accidentally bring victimizing situations resembling BPM II, violent or sexual traumas with elements of BPM III, episodes involving pain and choking, and other insults similar to perinatal distress. However, when a COEX system is established, it has a self-replicating propensity and can unconsciously drive the individual to recreate situations of a similar kind and thus add new layers to the memory constellation, as we saw earlier in the case of Peter.

Many people involved in deep self-exploration reported some interesting insights concerning the relationship between past-life experiences and the birth trauma. The reliving of birth often coincides or alternates with various karmic episodes that share an emotional quality or certain physical sensations with it. This connection suggests the possibility that the way in which we experience our birth might be determined by our karma. This applies not only to the general nature of our birth experience, but also to specific details.

Being hanged or strangled in a past-life situation, for example, can translate to suffocation during birth caused by the umbilical cord twisted around the neck. Pains inflicted by sharp objects in karmic dramas can become pains caused by uterine contractions and pressures. The experience of being in a medieval dungeon, torture chamber of the Inquisition, or a concentration camp can fuse with the no-exit experience of BPM II, and so on. Karmic patterns can also underlie and shape traumatic events in postnatal biography.

Bearing in mind this history, our psychological understanding of the most important forms of psychopathology changes due to the observations made from holotropic states of consciousness. The following discussion focuses exclusively on the role of psychological factors in the formation of symptoms. It does not include the disorders that are clearly organic in nature and belong in the realm of medicine, such as those caused by tumors or fevers.

Before we explore the revolutionary new understanding of specific disorders, it seems appropriate to acknowledge Freud's inquisitive and brilliant intellect. He was not satisfied with his own interpretations of many conditions in terms of traumatic experiences in infancy and childhood, and with the efficacy of the free associations method as a therapeutic tool. He even made a statement in one of his last books, *An Outline of Psychoanalysis* (Freud 1964), that sounds almost like a prophetic intimation of the forthcoming psychedelic era:

> *"But here we are concerned with therapy only in so far as it works by psychological means; and for the time being we have no other. The future may teach us to exercise a direct influence, by means of particular chemical substances, upon the amounts of energy and their distribution in the apparatus of the mind. It may be that there are other undreamed of possibilities of therapy. But for the moment we have nothing better at our disposal than the technique of psychoanalysis and for that reason, in spite of its limitations, it is not to be despised."*

Since modern academics and clinicians seem to have given up on the quest of Freud and his early disciples for a more plausible explanation of psychogenic disorders, I will try to demonstrate the explanatory power of the new model by expanding, revising, and deepening the original Freudian concepts.

Freud's Classical Psychoneuroses

Most psychiatrists would probably agree that anxiety, whether in its free-floating variety, in the form of phobias involving specific persons, animals, and situations, or as a factor underlying various other symptoms and syndromes, represents one of the most common and basic psychiatric problems. Since anxiety is a response to situations that endanger survival or body integrity in nature, it makes sense that one of the primary sources of clinical anxiety is the trauma of birth, which is an actual or potentially life-threatening situation.

Freud himself briefly entertained the possibility that the frightening experience of birth might be the prototype for all future anxieties. He got the idea during an examination of obstetric nurses, as mentioned in an earlier chapter.

Anxiety Hysteria (Phobias)

In classical psychoanalysis, phobias were seen as conditions that began around the age of four and were the result of fixation at the phallic stage of libidinal development due to a psychosexual trauma. Work with holotropic states, however, has shown that the roots of phobias reach much deeper, to the perinatal level of the unconscious and often even further, to the transpersonal domain. The critical role that the trauma of birth plays in the genesis of phobias is most evident in ***claustrophobia*, *the fear of closed and narrow places*** (from Latin *claustrum,* meaning closed place and Greek *phobos,* meaning fear). It manifests in confined or crowded situations, such as elevators, subways, and small rooms without windows, and leads to an urgent need to leave the confined space and seek open air.

Individuals who are claustrophobic are under the selective influence of a COEX system that is associated with the onset of BPM II, when the uterine contractions begin to close in on the fetus. The biographical factors from postnatal life that contribute to this disorder are memories of situations that involve uncomfortable confinement or restriction of breathing—near drowning, respiratory diseases, immobilization by a plaster cast, and being locked in a dark space or bound (e.g. to prevent masturbation or scratching at eczema). From the transpersonal level, the elements that are most significant for this phobia are karmic memories involving imprisonment, entrapment, and suffocation. While the general tendency of claustrophobic patients is to avoid situations that intensify symptoms, a true therapeutic change requires the full experience of the underlying unconscious memories and opening of the breath through bodywork and abreaction.

Agoraphobia (from Greek *ágora,* meaning central square of a town), the fear of open places or of the transition from an enclosed space to a wide-open one, seems at first to be the opposite of claustrophobia. In actuality, agoraphobic patients are typically also claustrophobic, but the transition from an enclosed place to a large open space represents a stronger emotional challenge for them than staying in the enclosed space. On the perinatal level, agoraphobia is associated with the very final stage of BPM III, when the sudden release after many hours of extreme confinement is accompanied by the fear of losing all boundaries, being blown apart, exploding, and ceasing to exist.

When they are in the open space, agoraphobic patients behave like children. They are afraid to cross the street or a large square by themselves and need support from adults and to be led by the hand. Some of them are afraid that they will lose control, take off their clothes, and lie on the ground naked, exposed to the looks of bystanders and passersby. This is reminiscent of the situation of the newborn, who has just experienced birth and is inspected by adults. In holotropic therapy, the experience of ego death and psychospiritual rebirth tends to bring significant relief from this condition.

Patients suffering from ***thanatophobia*** (from Greek *thanatos,* meaning death) or the pathological fear of death, experience episodes of vital anxiety, which they interpret as the onset of a life-threatening heart attack, stroke, or suffocation. This phobia has deep roots in the extreme physical discomfort and sense of impending catastrophe associated with the trauma of birth. The COEX systems involved are typically related to situations that endanger life, such as operations, diseases, and injuries, particularly those that interfere with breathing. The radical resolution of thanatophobia requires the conscious reliving of the different layers of the underlying COEX system and an experiential confrontation with death.

Nosophobia (from Greek *nosos,* meaning disease), the pathological fear of having or contracting a disease, is closely related to thanatophobia and also to hypochondriasis, an unsubstantiated delusional conviction of having a serious illness. Patients suffering from this disorder have a variety of strange body sensations that they cannot account for and they tend to interpret them in terms of a present somatic disease. These symptoms involve pains, pressures, and cramps in different parts of the body, strange energy flows, paraesthesias, and other forms of unusual phenomena. They can also manifest as the dysfunction of various organs, such as breathing difficulties, dyspepsia, nausea and vomiting, constipation and diarrhea, muscular tremors, general malaise, weakness, and fatigue.

Repeated medical examinations typically fail to detect any organic disorder that would explain the subjective complaints. The reason for this is that the disturbing sensations and emotions are not related to a present physiological process, but to memories of past physical traumas. Patients with these problems often repeatedly demand various clinical and laboratory tests and can become a real nuisance in doctors' offices and hospitals. Many of them end up in the care of psychiatrists, where they often do not receive the compassionate acceptance they deserve.

Psychiatrists are medical doctors, and the absence of any organic basis for these patients' complaints can make them take the complaints of these patients less seriously. Physical symptoms that cannot be justified by appropriate laboratory findings are often dismissed as products of the clients' imagination or even as malingering. Nothing could be further from the truth. Despite the negative medical findings, the physical complaints of these patients are very real. However, they do not reflect a current medical problem but, rather, are caused by surfacing memories of serious physiological difficulties from the past. Their sources are various diseases, operations, and injuries. The trauma of birth is particularly important.

Three distinct varieties of nosophobia deserve special attention: cancerophobia, the pathological fear of developing or having cancer, bacillophobia, the fear of microorganisms and infection, and mysophobia, the fear of dirt and contamination. All these problems have deep perinatal roots, although their specific forms are biographically codetermined. In ***cancerophobia*** (from Greek *cancer,* meaning crab), the important element is the similarity between cancer and pregnancy. It is well known from psychoanalytic literature that the malignant growth of tumors is unconsciously identified with embryonic development. This similarity goes beyond the most obvious superficial parallel, that of a rapidly growing foreign object inside one's body. The connection can actually be supported by anatomical, physiological, and biochemical data. In many respects, the cancer cells resemble undifferentiated cells from the early stages of embryonic development.

In ***bacillophobia*** and ***mysophobia*** (from Latin *bacillus,* and Greek *musos* meaning dirt), the pathological fear focuses on biological material, body odors, and uncleanliness. The biographical determinants of these disorders usually involve memories from the time of toilet training, but their roots reach deeper, to the scatological aspect of the perinatal process. It is typically found in patients who came into contact with the mother's feces or inhaled the fetal feces *(meconium)* during birth. The key to understanding these phobias is the connection that exists within BPM III between death, aggression, sexual excitement, and various forms of biological material.

Patients suffering from these disorders are not only afraid that they themselves might get biologically contaminated, but they are also frequently preoccupied with the possibility of infecting others. Their fear of biological materials is thus closely associated with aggression that is oriented both inward and outward, which is precisely the situation characteristic of the final stages of birth. On a more superficial level, the fear of infection and bacterial growth is also unconsciously related to sperm and conception and therefore again connected to pregnancy and birth. The most important COEX systems related to the above phobias involve relevant memories from the anal-sadistic stage of libidinal development and conflicts around toilet training and cleanliness. Additional biographical material is represented by memories that depict sex and pregnancy as dirty and dangerous. Like all emotional disorders, these phobias often also have transpersonal components.

Deep entanglement and identification with biological contaminants are also the basis of a particular kind of low self-esteem that involves self-degradation and a sense of disgust with oneself, referred to colloquially as "shitty self-esteem." It is frequently associated with ritual behaviors aimed at getting rid of repulsive and disgusting material, and improving one's exterior. The most obvious of these rituals is the compulsive washing of hands or other parts of the body. It can be so excessive that it results in serious injuries to the skin and bleeding. Other rituals represent efforts to avoid or neutralize the biological contamination, such as wearing white gloves, using a clean handkerchief to touch doorknobs, or cleaning cutlery and plates before eating meals. This connects this problem with obsessive-compulsive neuroses.

A woman whose memory of perinatal events is close to the surface can suffer from a ***phobia of pregnancy and delivery***. Being in touch with the memory of the birth agony makes it difficult for a woman to accept her femininity and her reproductive role, because motherhood means inflicting pain and suffering. The idea of becoming pregnant and having to face the ordeal of delivery can, under these circumstances, be associated with paralyzing terror.

Aichmophobia (from Greek *aichmē*, meaning point) is a morbid fear of sharp things, such as knives, scissors, pencils, or knitting needles. This emotionally tormenting condition, which usually begins for a parent shortly after the child is born, is not a pure phobia, but involves obsessive-compulsive elements. It is a combination of violent impulses against the child along with the fear of actually hurting it. This is typically associated with a fear of mothering or overprotective behavior and unreasonable concerns that something might happen to the baby. Whatever the biographical determinants of this problem might be, the deeper source can be traced to the delivery of that child. This reflects the fact that the passive and active aspects of childbirth are intimately connected in the unconscious.

The states of biological symbiotic union between the mother and the child represent states of experiential unity. Women reliving their own birth typically experience themselves, simultaneously or alternately, as delivering. Similarly, memories of being a fetus in the womb are characteristically associated with an experience of being pregnant, and situations of being nursed with those of nursing. The deep roots of the phobia of mothering lie in the first clinical stage of delivery (BPM II) when the uterus is contracting and the cervix is closed. At this time, the mother and the child are trapped in a state of biological antagonism, inflicting pain on each other.

This situation tends to activate the mother's memory of her own birth, unleashing the aggressive potential associated with it, and directs it toward the child. The fact that delivering a child opens experiential access to perinatal dynamics represents an important therapeutic opportunity. This is a very good time for women who have just delivered their babies to do some unusually deep psychological work. On the negative side, the activation of the mother's perinatal unconscious can result in postpartum depressions, neuroses, or even psychoses, if the emerging emotions are not adequately processed.

Postpartum psychopathology is usually explained by vague references to hormonal changes. This does not make much sense considering that women's responses to delivery covers a very broad range from ecstasy to psychosis, while the hormonal changes follow a fairly standard pattern. In my experience, the perinatal memories play a crucial role in the phobias of pregnancy and mothering, as well as postpartum psychopathology. Experiential work on the trauma of birth and the early postnatal period seems to be a chosen method for these disorders.

Siderodromophobia, the phobia of traveling by train and subway (from Greek *sideron,* meaning iron, and *dromos,* meaning way), is based on certain similarities between the experience of birth and travel in these means of transportation. The most important common denominators of the two situations are the sense of entrapment and the experience of enormous forces and energies in motion without any control over the process. Additional influential elements are passing through tunnels and underground passages, and the encounter with darkness. In the time of the old-fashioned steam engine, the elements of fire, the pressure of the steam, and the noisy siren, conveying a sense of emergency, seemed to be contributing factors. For these situations to trigger the phobia, the perinatal memories must be easily available to consciousness, due to their intensity and the bridging effect of the postnatal layers of the underlying COEX system.

A phobia that is closely related to the above is ***fear of traveling by airplanes***. It shares the alarming sense of entrapment with the other situations, the fear of the powerful energy in motion, and the inability to have any influence on the course of events. An additional factor during bumpy flights seems to be the anxious efforts to stay in the same position and the inability to let oneself move. The lack of control seems to be an element of great importance in the phobias involving travel. This can be illustrated with ***the phobia of traveling by car***, which is a means of transportation in which we can easily play both the role of the passenger and that of the driver. This phobia typically manifests only when we are passively driven and not when we are in the driver's seat and can deliberately change or stop the motion.

It is interesting that ***seasickness*** and ***airsickness*** are also often related to perinatal dynamics and tend to disappear after the individual has completed the death-rebirth process. The essential element here seems to be the willingness to give up the need to be in control and the ability to surrender to the flow of events, no matter what they bring. Difficulties arise when the individual tries to impose his or her control on processes that have their own unrelenting dynamic momentum. The excessive need for control in a situation is characteristic for individuals who are under a strong influence of BPM III and related COEX systems, while the capacity to surrender to the flow of events shows a strong connection with the positive aspects of BPM I and BPM IV.

Acrophobia, or ***the fear of heights*** (from Greek *ákron*, meaning peak or summit) is not really a pure phobia. It is always associated with the compulsion to jump down or throw oneself from a high place—a tower, window, cliff, or bridge. The sense of falling with a simultaneous fear of destruction is a typical manifestation of the final stages of BPM III. The origin of this association is not clear, but it might involve a phylogenetic component. Some animals deliver standing and their birth can involve a significant drop (for example, the birth of a giraffe) and women in some native cultures deliver while suspended on branches, squatting, or on all fours *(a la vache)*. This was allegedly the case when queen Maya gave birth to Buddha, standing and holding onto a branch. Another possibility is that the moment of birth reflects the first encounter with the phenomenon of gravity, including the possibility or even an actual memory of being dropped.

In any case, it is very common that people, who in holotropic states are under the influence of BPM III, have experiences of falling, acrobatic diving, or parachuting. A compulsive interest in extreme sports and other activities that involve falling (parachuting, bungee-jumping, movie stunts, acrobatic flying) seems to reflect the need to exteriorize the feelings of impending disaster in situations that allow a certain degree of control (the bungee cord, the string of a parachute) or involve some other forms of safeguards (termination of the fall in water). The COEX systems responsible for the manifestation of this particular facet of the birth trauma include childhood memories of being playfully tossed in the air by adults and accidents involving falling.

Due to the somewhat enigmatic relationship between the phobia of heights, the experience of falling, and the final stages of birth, it may be useful to illustrate it with a specific example. It involves Ralph, a German immigrant to Canada, who many years ago had attended one of our Holotropic Breathwork workshops in British Columbia. Case histories related to other types of phobias can be found in my other publications (Grof 1975, 2000).

In his holotropic sessions, Ralph experienced a powerful COEX system that he felt was the cause of his serious phobia of heights. The most superficial layer of this COEX contained a memory from prewar Germany. This was the time of a hectic military build-up and of equally hectic preparations for the Olympic Games in Berlin, in which Hitler intended to demonstrate the superiority of the Nordic race.

Since the victory in the Olympics was, for Hitler, a matter of extreme political importance, many talented athletes were assigned to special camps for rigorous training. This was an alternative to being drafted into the Wehrmacht, the infamous German army. Ralph, a pacifist who hated the military, was selected for one of these camps. It was a welcome opportunity to avoid the draft.

The training involved a variety of sport disciplines and was incredibly competitive; all the performances were graded and those with the least points were sent to the army. Ralph was lagging behind and had one last opportunity to improve his standing. The stakes and his motivation to succeed were very high, but the challenge was truly formidable. The task he was supposed to perform was something he had never done in his life: a head-first dive into a swimming pool from a 30-foot-high tower.

The biographical layer of his COEX system consisted of reliving the enormous ambivalence and fear associated with the dive, as well as the sensations of falling. The deeper layer of the same COEX that immediately followed this experience was the reliving of Ralph's struggle in the final stage of birth, with all the emotions and physical sensations involved. The process then continued into what Ralph concluded must have been a past-life experience.

He became an adolescent boy in a native culture who was involved with a group of peers in a dangerous rite of passage. One after the other, they climbed to the top of a tower made of wooden poles tied together with flexible vegetable tendrils. Once there, they attached the end of a long liana to their ankles and fixed its other end to the edge of the platform at the top of the tower. It was a status symbol and matter of great pride to have the longest liana and not to get killed.

When he experienced the feelings associated with the jump in this rite of passage, he realized that they were very similar both to the feelings associated with his dive in the Olympic camp and to those he encountered in the final stages of birth. All three situations were clearly integral parts of the same COEX.

Zoophobia (from the Greek *zoon,* meaning animal or organism), the fear of various animals, can involve many different forms of life, both large and dangerous beasts, as well as small and harmless creatures. It is essentially unrelated to the actual danger that a particular animal represents for humans. In classical psychoanalysis, the feared animal was seen as a symbolic representation of the castrating father or the bad mother and always had a sexual connotation. The work with holotropic states has shown that such a biographical interpretation of zoophobias is inadequate and that these disorders have significant perinatal and transpersonal roots.

If the object of the phobia is a large animal, the most important elements seem to either be the theme of being swallowed and incorporated (wolf) or the relation to pregnancy and nursing (cow). It was mentioned earlier that the archetypal symbolism of the onset of BPM II is the experience of being swallowed and incorporated. This perinatal fear of engulfment can easily be projected on large animals, particularly predators. Classical examples of the relationship between a large animal and birth are the fairy tale about Little Red Riding Hood and the Biblical story of Jonah, with their perinatal symbolism of being swallowed.

Certain animals also have a special symbolic association with the birth process, such as gigantic tarantulas, which frequently appear in the initial phase of BPM II as symbols of the Devouring Feminine. This seems to reflect the fact that spiders catch free-flying insects in their webs, immobilize them, envelop, and kill them. It is not difficult to see a similarity between this sequence of events and the experiences of the child during biological delivery. This connection seems to be essential for the development of ***arachnophobia***, fear of spiders (from the Greek *arachne,* meaning spider).

Another zoophobia that has an important perinatal component is ***ophiophobia*** or ***serpentophobia***, the fear of snakes (from the Greek *ophis* and Latin *serpens,* meaning snake). Images of snakes, which on a more superficial level have a phallic connotation, are common symbols representing the birth agony and thus the terrifying and devouring feminine. Poisonous vipers represent the threat of imminent death and also the beginning of the initiatory journey (see the frescoes in Pompeii representing a Dionysian ritual), while large boa-type constrictors symbolize the crushing and strangulation involved in birth. The fact that large constrictor snakes swallow their prey and appear pregnant further reinforces the perinatal association.

The serpentine symbolism typically extends deep into the transpersonal realm, where it can have many different culturally specific meanings, such as the snake from the Garden of Eden who deceived Eve; the snake representing the Serpent Power Kundalini; the snake Muchalinda, protecting the Buddha against rain; Vishnu's endless snake Ananta; the Mesoamerican Plumed Serpent, Quetzalcoatl; the Rainbow Serpent of the Australian Aborigines, and many others.

Entomophobia, the phobia of insects (from the Greek *entomos,* meaning insect), can frequently be traced back to the dynamics of perinatal matrices. Bees, for example, seem to be related to reproduction and pregnancy because of their role in the transfer of pollen and fertilization of plants, as well as their ability to cause swelling in humans. Flies, as a result of their affinity for excrement and their propensity to spread infection, are associated with the scatological aspect of birth. As has already been pointed out, this has a close relation to phobias of dirt and microorganisms, and the compulsive washing of hands.

Keraunophobia, the pathological fear of thunderstorms, (from the Greek *keraunos,* meaning thunderbolt) is psychodynamically related to the transition between BPM III and BPM IV, and thus to the ego death. Lightning represents an energetic connection between heaven and earth, and electricity is a physical expression of divine energy. For this reason, an electric storm symbolizes the contact with the divine light that occurs at the culmination of the death-rebirth process. During psychedelic sessions in Prague, several of my patients relived electroshocks that had been administered to them in the past. They remained conscious throughout the entire experience, even though in the original situation, the electric shocks knocked them unconscious.

They had these experiences when their process of psychospiritual transformation had reached the point of the ego death. It is interesting that one of the theories trying to explain the therapeutic effect of electroshocks actually suggested that the procedure induced the experience of psychospiritual death and rebirth. The most famous keraunophobic was Ludwig van Beethoven. He succeeded in confronting the subject of his fear when he included a magnificent musical representation of a thunderstorm in his Pastoral Symphony.

Pyrophobia, the pathological fear of fire (from the Greek *pyr,* meaning fire), also has deep psychological roots in the transition from BPM III to BPM IV. When we discussed the phenomenology of the perinatal matrices, we saw that individuals approaching the ego death typically have visions of fire. They also often experience their body burning and feel like they are passing through purifying flames *(pyrocatharsis).* The motif of fire and purgatory is thus an important concomitant of the final stage of psychospiritual transformation. When this aspect of the unconscious dynamics reaches the threshold of consciousness, the liaison between the experience of fire and the impending ego death gives rise to pyrophobia.

In those individuals who are able to intuit the positive potential of this process, the fact that its final outcome would be psychospiritual death and rebirth, the effect can be exactly the opposite. They have the feeling that something fantastic would happen to them if they could experience the destructive force of fire. This expectation can be so strong that it results in an irresistible urge to actually start a fire. The observation of the resulting conflagration brings only transient excitement and tends to be disappointing. However, the feeling that the experience of fire should bring a phenomenal liberation is so convincing and compelling that these people try again and become arsonists. Pyrophobia is thus, paradoxically, closely related to pyromania (from Greek *mania,* meaning frenzy).

Hydrophobia, the pathological fear of water, also typically has a strong perinatal component. This reflects the fact that water plays an important role in connection to childbirth. If the pregnancy and delivery have a normal course, this connection is very positive. In that case, water represents the comfort of the amniotic existence or of the postnatal period, when receiving a bath indicates that the danger of birth is over. However, various prenatal crises, such as inhalation of the amniotic fluid during birth, or postnatal bathing accidents, can give water a distinctly negative charge. The COEX systems underlying hydrophobia also typically contain biographical elements (traumatic experiences with water in infancy and childhood) and transpersonal elements (shipwreck, flood, or drowning in a previous incarnation).

Conversion Hysteria

This psychoneurosis, much more prevalent in Freud's time than it is today, played an important role in the history and development of psychoanalysis. Several of Freud's patients and many his followers' patients belonged to this diagnostic category. The name of this disorder is derived from the Greek *hystera,* meaning uterus, because it was initially considered an exclusively female disorder; this belief was later disproved and abandoned. ***Conversion hysteria*** has a rich and colorful symptomatology and, according to the psychogenetic taxonomy constructed by Berlin psychoanalyst Karl Abraham, it is closely related to the group of phobias, or anxiety hysteria.

This means that the major fixation for this disorder is on the phallic stage of libidinal development, and that the psychosexual trauma which underlies it occurred at the time when the child was under a strong influence of the Electra or Oedipus complex. Of the several defense mechanisms involved in the psychogenesis of conversion hysteria, the most characteristic one is conversion, which gave this form of hysteria its name. This term refers to the symbolic transformation of unconscious conflicts and instinctual impulses into physical symptoms.

Examples of the physical manifestations which affect motor functions include paralysis of arms or legs (abasia, astasia), loss of speech (aphonia), and vomiting. Conversion that affects sensory organs and functions can result in temporary blindness, deafness, or psychogenic anesthesia. Conversion hysteria can also produce a combination of symptoms that convincingly imitate pregnancy. This false pregnancy, or pseudocyesis, involves amenorrhea, morning nausea and vomiting, and a sizable extension of the abdominal cavity caused by retention of gases in the intestines. Religious stigmata, simulating the wounds of Jesus, have also often been interpreted as hysterical conversions.

Freud suggested that, in hysterical conversions, repressed sexual thoughts and impulses find their expression in changes of physical functions. The affected organ is effectively "sexualized," that is, it becomes a symbolic substitute for genitals. For example, hyperemia and the swelling of various organs might symbolize erection, or abnormal feelings or physiological changes in these organs might imitate genital sensations.

Freud, for example, accepted the theory of his close friend, otorhinolaryngologist Wilhelm Fliess, who believed that blushing of the face is displaced sexual excitement and picking the nose is a surrogate for masturbation. Freud even sent some of his hysterical patients to have their nasal septum surgically broken, an intervention that Fliess recommended as treatment for this disorder. Freud also suggested that, in some instances, the emerging memory of a traumatic situation can be understood by the physical sensations that the individual was experiencing at that time.

The most complex and distinctive manifestation of hysteria is a specific psychosomatic syndrome, referred to as a ***major hysterical spell or attack.*** It is a condition characterized by fainting *(syncope),* breathing difficulties, extreme backward arching of the body on the floor *(arc de cercle, opisthotonus),* alternating crying and laughter, flailing around, and pelvic movements resembling sexual intercourse. According to Freud, hysterical spells are pantomimic expressions of forgotten events from childhood and of fantasy stories constructed around these events. These spells represent disguised sexual themes related to the Oedipus and Electra complex and their derivatives. Freud pointed out that the behavior during hysterical spells clearly betrays their sexual nature. He compared the loss of consciousness at the height of the attack to the momentary loss of consciousness during sexual orgasm.

Observations from holotropic states show that conversion hysteria, in addition to the biographical determinants, also has significant perinatal and transpersonal roots. Underlying conversion phenomena in general, and hysterical spells in particular, are powerful bioenergetic blockages which have conflicting innervations related to the dynamics of BPM III. The behavior of people reliving the final stage of birth, especially the characteristic deflection of the head and extreme backward arching, often resembles a hysterical spell.

The nature and timing of the biographical material involved in the psychogenesis of conversion hysteria are in basic agreement with the Freudian theory. Experiential work typically reveals psychosexual traumas from the period of childhood when the patient reached the phallic stage of development and was under the influence of the Oedipus or Electra complex. The movements in the hysterical attack can be shown to represent, in addition to the mentioned perinatal elements, symbolic allusions to certain specific aspects of the underlying childhood trauma.

The sexual content of the traumatic memories associated with conversion hysteria explains why they are part of a COEX system that also includes the sexual facet of BPM III. If we are not familiar with the fact that the memory of birth has a strong sexual element, it is easy to overlook the perinatal contribution to the genesis of conversion hysteria and attribute this disorder entirely to postnatal influences. It is interesting to mention, in this context, Freud's own observation and admission that the leading themes underlying hysterical spells often were often not sexual seduction or intercourse, but pregnancy or childbirth.

The involvement of BPM III in the psychogenesis of conversion hysteria explains many important aspects that have often been mentioned but never adequately explained in psychoanalytic literature. It is, above all, the fact that the analysis of hysterical symptoms reveals not only their connection to libidinal impulses and sexual orgasm, but also to "erection," generalized to the entire body (birth orgasm), and quite explicitly to childbirth and pregnancy. The same is true for strange links that exist in conversion hysteria between sexuality, aggression, and death. The struggle for breath is also a feature that hysterical attack has in common with reliving birth. This suggests that the best approach to a hysterical attack is to treat it as an experiential session—encourage the full expression of emotions and physical sensations. This might prove to actually be a therapeutic opportunity for treating the underlying condition.

The psychodynamic basis of conversion hysteria is quite similar to that of agitated depression. This becomes evident when we look at the most striking and dramatic expression of this disorder, the major hysterical spell. In general, agitated depression is a more serious disorder than conversion hysteria, and it manifests the content and dynamics of BPM III in a much purer form. Observing the facial expressions and behavior of a patient with agitated depression leaves no doubt that there are reasons for grave concern. This impression is supported by the high incidence of suicide and even murder combined with suicide that is found in these patients.

A major hysterical spell shows a superficial resemblance to agitated depression. However, the overall picture is obviously far less severe and it lacks the depth of despair. It appears stylized and contrived, and has definite theatrical features with unmistakable sexual overtones. In general, a hysterical attack has many basic characteristics of BPM III—excessive tension, psychomotor excitement and agitation, a mixture of depression and aggression, loud screaming, disturbances of breathing, and dramatic arching. However, the basic experiential template appears here in a considerably more mitigated form than in agitated depression and is substantially modified and colored by later traumatic events.

The dynamic connection between conversion hysteria, agitated depression, and BPM III becomes evident in the course of deep experiential therapy. At first, the holotropic states tend to trigger or amplify hysterical symptoms and the client discovers their source in specific psychosexual traumas from childhood. Typically, later sessions increasingly resemble agitated depression and eventually reveal the underlying elements of BPM III. Reliving birth and the connection to BPM IV then brings alleviation, or even disappearance of the symptoms. The deepest roots of hysterical conversions can reach to the transpersonal level and take the form of karmic memories or archetypal motifs.

Hysterical paralysis of the hands and arms, inability to stand *(abasia),* loss of speech *(aphonia)* and other conversion symptoms also have strong perinatal components. These conditions are not caused by lack of motor impulses, but by a dynamic conflict of antagonistic motor impulses that cancel each other. This situation comes from the painful and stressful experience of childbirth, during which the child's body responds with an excessive chaotic generation of neural impulses for which there is no adequate discharge.

A similar interpretation of hysterical conversion symptoms was first suggested by Otto Rank in his pioneering book *The Trauma of Birth* (Rank 1929). While Freud saw conversions as expressions of a psychological conflict in body language, Rank believed that their real basis was physiological, reflecting the original situation that existed during birth. The problem for Freud was how a primarily psychological problem could be translated into a physical symptom. Rank had to face the opposite problem—to explain how a primarily somatic phenomenon could acquire, through a secondary elaboration, psychological content and symbolic meaning.

Some serious manifestations of hysteria that border on psychosis, such as psychogenic stupor, uncontrolled daydreaming, and mistaking fantasy for reality *(pseudologia fantastica),* seem to be dynamically related to BPM I. They reflect a deep need to reinstitute the blissful emotional condition characteristic of the undisturbed intrauterine existence and the symbiotic union with the mother. While the component of emotional and physical satisfaction involved in these states can easily be detected as surrogates of the desired good womb and good breast situation, the concrete content of daydreaming and fantasies uses themes and elements related to the individual's childhood, adolescence, and adult life. In recent decades, classical conversion hysteria, which was a very common occurrence during my medical studies and early years of my psychiatric practice (1950s and 1960s), has become a very rare psychiatric disorder.

Obsessive-Compulsive Neurosis

Patients suffering from ***obsessive-compulsive disorders*** are tormented by intrusive irrational thoughts that they cannot get rid of, and they feel compelled to perform certain absurd and meaningless repetitive rituals. They are usually aware that their thought processes and behavior are irrational and even bizarre, but they are not able to control them. If they refuse to comply with these strange urges, they are overwhelmed by free-floating anxiety that can be excruciating.

The spectrum of obsessive-compulsive thinking and behavior covers a wide range, from innocent playful behavior and "psychopathology of everyday life" to torturous ordeals that make ordinary life impossible. Many people leaving for a vacation walk out of the house with a packed suitcase and suddenly experience a creeping feeling that they have forgotten an important item at home or did not turn off the light or stove. They have to go back to the house to check the situation and by doing so, they reach closure. A person suffering from OCD will have to keep returning again and again to check the checking and the checking of the checking and will miss the train or flight.

I was born in Prague and lived there until the age of thirty-six. The streets in much of the city had sidewalks decorated with beautiful patterns made of small black, grey, white, and red granite cubes. Many people walking on the streets had, on and off, an impulse to walk on the sidewalk in a particular, distinct pattern—stepping on areas of the same color, meandering in a specific way, or avoiding certain geometrical formations. But my OCD patients tended to get caught in this game for several hours, unable to leave, because they experienced an abysmal fear whenever they tried to stop.

The problem for one of my OCD patients was that he had to imagine a system of Cartesian coordinates whenever he encountered something that evoked a strong emotional reaction in him, such as meeting an attractive girl. He went through an agonizing process of trying to find a proper place in the correct quarter of the diagram for that person or event, with satisfying distances from the abscissa and ordinate. In his LSD session, he realized that this laborious thought process was reflecting the conflicting vectors involved in having his head caught and squeezed in the birth canal.

There seems to be a general agreement in psychoanalytic literature that conflicts related to homosexuality, aggression, and biological material form the psychodynamic basis of this disorder. Other common features are inhibition of genitality and a strong emphasis on pregenital drives, particularly those that are anal in nature. These aspects of the obsessive-compulsive neurosis point to a strong perinatal component, particularly to the scatological aspect of BPM III.

Another characteristic feature of this neurosis is strong ambivalence concerning religion and God. Many obsessive-compulsive patients live in a constant severe conflict about God and religious faith, and experience strong rebellious and blasphemous thoughts, feelings, and impulses. For example, they associate the image of God with masturbation or defecation or have an irresistible temptation to laugh aloud, scream obscenities, or pass gas in a church or at a funeral. This alternates with desperate desires to repent, expiate, and punish themselves to undo their transgressions, blasphemy, and sins.

As discussed in the section on the phenomenology of perinatal matrices, this close association of sexual, aggressive, and scatological impulses with the numinous and divine element is characteristic for the transition between BPM III and BPM IV. Similarly, a strong conflict between the rebellion against an overwhelming force alternating with a wish to surrender to it is characteristic for the final stages of the death-rebirth process. In holotropic states, this unrelenting authoritative force can be experienced in an archetypal figurative form.

It can manifest as a strict, punishing, and cruel God comparable to Yahweh of the Old Testament, or even a fierce pre-Columbian deity demanding bloody sacrifice. The biological correlate of this punishing deity is the restricting influence of the birth canal that inflicts extreme, life-threatening suffering on the individual and, at the same time, prevents any external expression of the instinctual energies of sexual and aggressive nature that are activated by the ordeal of biological birth.

The constricting force of the birth canal represents the biological basis for the part of the superego that Freud called "savage." It is a primitive and barbaric element of the psyche that can drive an individual to cruel self-punishment, automutilation, or even violent suicide. Freud saw this part of the superego as being instinctive in nature and thus a derivative of the Id. Postnatally, the restrictive and coercive influence takes far more subtle forms of injunctions and prohibitions, which come from parental authorities, legal institutions, and religious commandments. This is the polar opposite of yet another aspect of the superego, Freud's "ideal ego" (das ideale Ich), which expresses our wish to identify with and emulate the person whom we admire.

An important perinatal source of obsessive-compulsive neurosis is the unpleasant or even life-threatening encounter with various forms of biological material in the final stages of birth. The COEX systems that are psychogenetically associated with this disorder involve traumatic experiences related to the anal zone and to biological material, such as a history of strict toilet training, painful enemas, anal rape, and gastrointestinal diseases. Another important category of related biographical material includes memories of various situations representing a threat to genital organization (circumcision, operation for phimosis). Quite regularly, transpersonal elements with similar themes play an important role in the genesis of this difficult condition.

The obsessions, compulsions to ritual behavior, conflicts about religion and sexuality, and the anxiety which arises when the individual tries to resist and control these symptoms can be truly excruciating and torturous. After 1949, when the Portuguese neurosurgeon Edgar Moniz received a

Nobel Prize for a controversial mutilating neurosurgical procedure, prefrontal lobotomy (from Greek *lobos,* meaning cerebral lobe and *temnein,* meaning cut), severe cases of this disorder were (together with chronic schizophrenics) considered indications for this barbaric operation. On the positive side, a study conducted at the University of Arizona found a temporary alleviation of symptoms in patients suffering from obsessive-compulsive disorder after the administration of psilocybin (Moreno et al. 2006).

Depression, Mania, and Suicidal Behavior

Mainstream theories concerning the etiology of manic-depressive disorders have undergone many changes during the last several decades. The literature on this topic has been vast and speculations varied. They are well summarized in encyclopedic books by Goodwin and Jamison (Goodwin and Jamison 1990, Goodwin 2007). Here I make reference only to the main conceptual trends. In the 1940s and 1950s, much of the attention of mainstream professionals was focused on psychoanalytic theories of manic-depressive disorders. Classical psychoanalysis linked these disorders to fixation on the active oral phase and saw suicide as aggression toward introjected hated objects (e.g. killing of the introjected breast of the bad mother).

In the 1960s, the emphasis shifted to neurochemical explanations implicating, for example, low levels or an imbalance of neurotransmitters (catecholamines adrenaline and noradrenaline, serotonin, and dopamine), neuropeptides, signaling networks, and abnormal cellular metabolism. Later researchers concluded that the etiology of manic disorders is less specific and more complex, and that it depends on a combination of genetic and other biological factors, psychological influences, and the social/environmental situation. The most recent speculations attribute an important role in the genesis of affective disorders to the abnormal connectivity of neural networks in the brain's regulatory systems, oscillation patterns, and biological rhythms.

Various biological theories of manic-depressive disorders indicate only the propensity for manic and depressive episodes, but fail to explain why the episodes take the form of one or the other; they also offer no clues for understanding the specifics of the clinical symptomatology of either of them. Paradoxically, although the manic and depressive phases seem to represent polar opposites in their clinical picture, they both show increased activity as indicated by biochemical parameters of stress and peak oscillatory activity of biological rhythms. Observations from holotropic research, though, might help to understand and resolve these controversies.

The early Statistical and Diagnostic Manuals (DSM I and II) paid attention to etiological factors and showed strong psychoanalytic influences. Later versions of the manual intentionally avoided etiological, biological, and psychodynamic speculations and chose the "neo-Kraepelinian approach," which focuses only on the description of symptoms and syndromes. It would be impossible to relate the new insights from holotropic research to such vague concepts as the multifactorial etiology of manic-depressive disorders or a simple description of symptoms and syndromes. I have therefore decided to revise and deepen the original explanations of emotional and psychosomatic disorders in classical psychoanalysis, which was imperfect, but at least aimed in the right direction.

In classical psychoanalysis, ***depression*** and ***mania*** were seen as disorders that are related to serious problems in the active (sadistic or cannibalistic) oral period, such as interference with nursing, emotional rejection and deprivation, and difficulties in the early mother-child relationship. Suicidal tendencies were then interpreted as acts of hostility against an introjected object, the image of the "bad mother," primarily her breast (Fenichel 1945, Karl Abraham's scheme in Table 1 on pp. 245). In view of the observations from holotropic states, this picture has to be revised and substantially deepened. In its original form, it is implausible and unconvincing and does not explain some very fundamental clinical observations regarding depression.

For example, why do we have two radically different forms in which depression manifests, the inhibited and the agitated variety? Why are depressed people typically bioenergetically blocked, as exemplified by a high incidence of headaches, pressure on the chest and shoulders, psychosomatic pains, and retention of water? Why are they physiologically inhibited and show loss of appetite, gastrointestinal dysfunction, constipation, no interest in sex, and amenorrhea? Why do individuals who are depressed, including those who have an inhibited depression, show high levels of biochemical stress? Why do they feel hopeless and often describe themselves as "feeling stuck"? Why is depression so closely related to suicide and mania? Why do mania and depression, disorders that seem to be polar opposites to the extent that it is reflected in clinical terminology ("bipolar disorder") both show an increase in biochemical indicators of stress and in oscillatory activity of biological rhythms?

These questions cannot be answered by psychotherapeutic schools that are conceptually limited to postnatal biography and the Freudian individual unconscious. Even less successful in this regard are theories that try to explain manic-depressive disorders simply as results of chemical aberrations in the organism. It is highly unlikely that a chemical change could, in and of itself, account for the complexity of the clinical picture of depression, including its close link with mania and suicide. This difficult situation changes dramatically once we realize that these disorders have significant perinatal and transpersonal roots. We start seeing many of the problems mentioned earlier in an entirely new light, and many of the manifestations of depression suddenly appear logical.

Inhibited depressions have important roots in the second perinatal matrix. The phenomenology of the sessions governed by BPM II, as well as the periods immediately following poorly resolved experiences dominated by this matrix, exhibit all the essential features of deep depression. The person who is under the influence of BPM II experiences agonizing mental and emotional pain—hopelessness, despair, overwhelming feelings of guilt, and a sense of inadequacy. He or she feels deep anxiety, lack of initiative, loss of interest, and an inability to enjoy existence. In this state, life appears to be utterly meaningless, emotionally empty, and absurd.

One's own life, and the world itself, are seen as if through a negative stencil, with selective awareness of the painful, bad, and tragic aspects of life, and blindness toward anything positive. This situation appears to be utterly unbearable, inescapable, and hopeless. Sometimes this is accompanied by the loss of the ability to see colors; when that happens, the entire world is perceived as a black and white film. In spite of the extreme suffering involved, this condition is not associated with crying or any other dramatic external manifestations; it is characterized by a general motor inhibition.

As I mentioned earlier, inhibited depression is associated with bioenergetic blockages in various parts of the body and the severe inhibition of major physiological functions. Typical physical concomitants of this form of depression are feelings of oppression, constriction and confinement, a sense of suffocation, tensions and pressures in different parts of the body, and headaches. It's also very common to have retention of water and urine, constipation, cardiac distress, and a loss of interest in food and sex, as well as having a tendency toward hypochondriacal interpretations of various physical symptoms.

All these symptoms are consistent with the understanding of this type of depression as a manifestation of BPM II. This is further supported by paradoxical biochemical findings. People suffering from inhibited depression typically show a high degree of stress, as indicated by the elevation of catecholamines and steroid hormones in the blood and urine. This biochemical picture fits well with BPM II, which represents a highly stressful inner situation with no possibility of external action or manifestation ("sitting on the outside, running on the inside").

The theory of psychoanalysis links depression to early oral problems and emotional deprivation. Although this connection is correct, it does not account for important aspects of depression—the sense of being stuck, hopelessness with feelings of no exit, and bioenergetic blockage, as well as the physical manifestations, including the biochemical findings. The present model shows the Freudian explanation as essentially correct but partial. While the COEX systems associated with inhibited depression include biographical elements emphasized by psychoanalysis, a fuller and more comprehensive understanding has to include the dynamics of BPM II.

The early deprivation and oral frustration has much in common with BPM II, and the inclusion of both of these situations in the same COEX system reflects deep experiential logic. BPM II involves the interruption of the symbiotic connection between the fetus and the maternal organism, which is caused by uterine contractions and the resulting compression of the arteries. This severing and loss of the biologically and emotionally meaningful contact with the mother terminates the supply of oxygen, nourishment, and warmth to the fetus. Additional consequences of the uterine contractions are a temporary accumulation of toxic products in the body of the fetus and an exposure to an unpleasant and potentially dangerous situation.

It thus makes good sense that the typical constituents of COEX systems dynamically related to inhibited depression (and to BPM II) involve separation from and absence of the mother during infancy and early childhood and the ensuing feelings of loneliness, cold, hunger, and fear. They represent, in a sense, a "higher octave" of the more acute and disturbing deprivation caused during the delivery by the uterine contractions. More superficial layers of the relevant COEX systems reflect family situations that are oppressive and punishing for the child and permit no rebellion or escape. They also often include memories of playing the role of scapegoat in various peer groups, having abusive employers, and suffering political or social oppression. All these situations reinforce and perpetuate the role of helpless victim in the no-exit predicament characteristic of BPM II.

An important category of COEX systems that is instrumental in the dynamics of depression involves memories of events that constituted a physical insult and threat to survival or body integrity, and in which the individual was effectively a helpless victim. This observation is an entirely new contribution to the understanding of depressions, thanks to holotropic research. Psychoanalysts and psychodynamically oriented academic psychiatrists emphasize the role of psychological factors in the pathogenesis of depression and do not take psychotraumas from physical insults into consideration.

The psychotraumatic effects of serious diseases, injuries, operations, long-term confinement in a plaster cast for inadequately developed hip joints, and episodes of near drowning have been overlooked and grossly underestimated by mainstream psychiatrists; this is very surprising in view of their general emphasis on biological factors. For theoreticians and clinicians who see depression as a result of fixation on the oral period of libidinal development, the finding that physical traumas play an important role in the development of this disorder represents a serious conceptual challenge.

It seems perfectly logical, though, in the context of the presented model, which attributes pathogenic significance to COEX systems that include the combined emotional-physical trauma of birth. This fact helps to bridge the gap between academics and clinicians who prefer to emphasize biological factors in the genesis of psychiatric disorders and those who seek psychological explanation. The psychological factors thus do not cause physical symptoms and vice versa; they both have their source in the experience of birth and represent two sides of the same coin.

In contrast to the inhibited depression, the phenomenology of ***agitated depression*** is psychodynamically associated with BPM III. Its basic elements are governed by the third matrix, which can be seen in experiential sessions and post-session intervals. The pent-up energies from birth are not completely blocked, as is the case in inhibited depression, in relation to BPM II. In this situation, the previously jammed energies find a partial outlet and discharge in the form of various destructive and self-destructive tendencies. It is important to emphasize that agitated depression reflects a dynamic compromise between an energetic block and discharge. A full discharge of these energies would terminate this condition and result in healing.

Characteristic features of this type of depression are a high degree of tension, anxiety, psychomotor excitement, and restlessness. People experiencing agitated depression are very active. They tend to roll on the floor, flail around, and beat their heads against the wall. Their emotional pain finds expression in loud crying and screaming, and they might scratch their faces and tear their hair and clothes. Physical symptoms that are often associated with this condition are muscular tensions, tremors, painful cramps, and uterine and intestinal spasms. Intense headaches, nausea, and breathing problems complete the clinical picture.

The COEX systems associated with this matrix deal with aggression and violence, cruelties of various kinds, sexual abuse and assaults, painful medical interventions, and diseases involving choking and a struggle for breath. In contrast with the COEX systems related to BPM II, the subjects involved in these situations are not passive victims; they are actively engaged in attempts to fight back, defend themselves, remove the obstacles, or escape. Memories of violent encounters with parental figures or siblings, fist fights with peers, scenes of sexual abuse and rape, and episodes from military battles are typical examples.

The psychoanalytic interpretation of ***mania*** is even less satisfactory and convincing than that of depression, as many analysts themselves admit (Fenichel 1945). However, most authors seem to agree that mania represents a means of avoiding the awareness of the underlying depression, and that it includes a denial of a painful inner reality and flight into the external world. It reflects the victory of the Ego and the Id over the Superego, with a drastic reduction of inhibitions, an increase of self-esteem, and an abundance of sensual and aggressive impulses.

In spite of all this, mania does not give the impression of genuine freedom. Psychological theories of manic-depressive disorders emphasize the intensive ambivalence of manic patients and the fact that simultaneous feelings of love and hate interfere with their ability to relate to others. The typical manic hunger for objects is usually seen as a manifestation of a strong oral fixation, and the periodicity of mania and depression is considered an indication of its relation to the cycle of satiety and hunger.

Many of the otherwise puzzling features of manic episodes become easily understandable when seen in relation to the dynamics of the perinatal matrices. Mania is psychogenetically linked to the experiential transition from BPM III to BPM IV. It indicates that the individual is partially in touch with the fourth perinatal matrix, but nevertheless still under the influence of the third. To be peaceful, to sleep, and to eat—the typical triad of wishes found in mania—are the natural goals of an organism flooded by the impulses associated with the final stage of birth.

Since the manic person has regressed all the way to the level of biological birth, the oral impulses are progressive and not regressive in nature. They point to the state that the manic individual is craving and aiming for and has not yet consciously achieved, rather than representing regression on the oral level. Relaxation and oral satisfaction are characteristic of the state following biological birth.

In experiential psychotherapy, one can occasionally observe transient manic episodes *in statu nascendi* as phenomena suggesting incomplete rebirth. This usually happens when the individuals involved in the transformation process have reached the final stage of the death-rebirth struggle and have gotten a taste of the feelings of release from the birth agony. However, at the same time, they are afraid, unwilling, and unable to face the remaining unresolved material related to BPM III and experience the ego death. As a result of clinging to this uncertain and tenuous victory, the new positive feelings become accentuated to the point of a caricature. The image of "whistling in the dark" seems to fit this condition particularly well.

The exaggerated and forceful nature of manic emotions and behavior betrays that they are not expressions of genuine joy and freedom, but reaction formations to fear and aggression. I have often observed that LSD subjects whose sessions terminate in a state of incomplete rebirth show all the typical signs of mania. They are hyperactive, move around at a hectic pace, try to socialize and fraternize with everybody in their environment, make inappropriate advances, and talk incessantly about their sense of triumph and well-being, wonderful feelings, and the great experience they have just had.

They might extol the wonders of LSD treatment and spin messianic and grandiose plans to transform the world by making it possible for every human being, and especially politicians, to have the same experience. The breakdown of the superego restraints results in seductiveness, promiscuous tendencies, and obscene gestures, behavior, and talk. Extreme hunger for stimuli and social contact is associated with increased zest, self-love, and inflated self-esteem, as well as indulgence in various aspects of life.

The need for excitement and the search for drama and action that are characteristic of manic patients serve a dual purpose. On the one hand, they provide an outlet for the impulses and tensions that are part of the activated BPM III. On the other hand, engaging in external turbulent situations that match the intensity and quality of the inner turmoil helps to reduce the intolerable "emotional-cognitive dissonance" that threatens manic persons—the terrifying realization that their inner experiences do not correspond to external circumstances. And, naturally, a serious discrepancy between the inner and the outer implies insanity.

Otto Fenichel (1945) pointed out that many important aspects of mania link it to the psychology of carnivals, which provide an opportunity for the socially sanctioned unleashing of otherwise forbidden impulses. This further confirms the deep connection of mania with the dynamic shift from BPM III to BPM IV. In the final stages of the death-rebirth process, many people spontaneously experience visions of colorful carnival scenes. Like in the real life Mardi Gras pageants, this can include images of skulls, skeletons, and other death-related symbols and motifs, which appear in the context of exuberant celebration. In holotropic states, this occurs in the culmination of BPM III, when we start feeling that we might prevail and survive our confrontation with death.

When individuals experiencing this state can be convinced to turn inward to face the difficult emotions that remained unresolved, and complete the (re)birth process, the manic quality disappears from their mood and behavior. In its pure form, the experience of BPM IV is characterized by radiant joy, increased zest, deep relaxation, tranquility, and serenity. In this state of mind, people have a sense of inner peace and total satisfaction. Their joy and euphoria are not exaggerated to the point of grotesque caricature and their behavior does not have the driven and flamboyant quality characteristic of manic states.

The COEX systems psychogenetically related to mania are comprised of memories of situations in which satisfaction was experienced under circumstances of insecurity and uncertainty about the genuineness and continuation of the gratification. Similarly, the expectation of overtly happy behavior in situations that do not justify it seems to feed into the manic pattern. In addition, one frequently finds contrary influences on their self-esteem in the history of manic patients, such as hypercritical and undermining attitudes of one parental figure alternating with overestimation, psychological inflation, and unrealistic expectations coming from the other one. In several of my European patients, I have observed that the alternating experience of total constraint and complete freedom that characterized the custom of swaddling infants seemed to be psychologically related to mania.

It is highly unlikely that the complexity of the clinical image of depression and mania could be explained by specific biochemical changes. It would be hard, for example, to imagine a situation more clearly chemically defined than an LSD session, where we know the chemical structure and exact dose of the substance. And yet, our knowledge of the exact chemical composition of the trigger and of the administered dosage is of little help in explaining the psychological content of the experience.

Depending on circumstances, the LSD subject can experience an ecstatic rapture or a depressive, manic, or paranoid state. Similarly, the symptomatology of depression or mania cannot be accounted for by some simple or even complex chemical processes. If we detect chemical changes in patients with these disorders, there is always the question of whether biological factors play a causal role in the disorder or are its symptomatic concomitants. For example, it is conceivable that the physiological and biochemical changes in manic-depressive disorders represent a replay of the physical conditions of a child who is being born.

During the LSD sessions in our early psychedelic research in Prague, we followed the oxygen saturation of the blood in the nail beds of our patients using colorimetry. We found that the levels of oxygen in their blood dropped when they were reliving their birth. For those who had just relived a forceps birth, we also observed quadrangular bruises on their temples in places where the instrument had been applied, and bluish stripes on the necks of those who had relived birth with the umbilical cord around their neck. This indicates the possibility that the memory of birth extends all the way to the cellular and even biochemical level.

The new understanding of depression that includes the dynamics of basic perinatal matrices offers fascinating new insights into the psychology of ***suicidal tendencies and behaviors***, phenomena which represented a serious theoretical challenge for psychoanalytically oriented interpretations. Any theory that tries to explain the psychology of suicide has to answer two important questions. The first is why a particular individual wants to commit suicide, an act that violates the otherwise mandatory dictate of the self-preservation drive, which is a powerful force that propels the evolution of life in nature. The second equally puzzling question is the choice of the means of suicide. There seems to be a close connection between the state of mind the depressed person is in and the type of suicide he or she contemplates or attempts.

The suicidal drive is not simply an impulse to terminate one's life, but to do it in a particular way. It might seem natural that a person who takes an overdose of tranquilizers or barbiturates would not jump off the cliff or under a train. However, the selectivity of choice also works the other way round: a person who chooses bloody suicide would not use drugs, even if they were easily available. The material from psychedelic research and other forms of deep experiential work with holotropic states throw new light on both the deep motives for suicide and the intriguing question of the chosen method.

At the Psychiatric Research Institute in Prague, we had a colleague, a university professor of psychiatry and toxicology, who had easy access to chemical substances and knew everything about their effects and dosages. And yet, in an episode of severe periodic depression, he decided to commit suicide in his office by three deep razor cuts through his throat. When one of the nurses found him in the morning lying on the floor of his office, she encountered a gory scene, with blood splattered all over his white coat, the carpet, and the papers on his desk. Under the circumstances, an overdose of drugs would seem to be a less drastic and more acceptable solution, but his state of mind seemed to force him to do just what he did.

Suicidal ideation and tendencies can occasionally be observed in any stage of work with holotropic states. However, they are particularly frequent and urgent at the time when subjects are confronting the unconscious material related to the negative perinatal matrices. Observations from psychedelic and holotropic sessions, as well as from episodes of spiritual emergency, reveal that suicidal tendencies fall into two distinct categories that have very specific relations to the perinatal process. We have seen that the experience of inhibited depression is dynamically related to BPM II and that agitated depression is a derivative of BPM III. Various forms of suicidal fantasies, tendencies, and actions can then be understood as unconsciously motivated attempts to escape these unbearable psychological states, using two routes. Each of these alternatives reflects a specific aspect of the individual's early biological history.

Suicide I, or ***nonviolent suicide***, is based on the unconscious memory that the no-exit situation of BPM II was preceded by the experience of intrauterine existence. If an individual suffering from inhibited depression finds the situation intolerable and tries to escape it, the most easily available route in this state seems to be regression into the original undifferentiated unity of the prenatal condition (BPM I). The level of the unconscious involved in this process is usually not accessible, unless the individual has the opportunity for deep experiential self-exploration. Lacking the necessary insight, he or she is attracted to situations in everyday life that seem to share certain elements with the prenatal situation.

The basic unconscious intention underlying this form of suicidal tendencies and behavior is to reduce the intensity of painful stimuli and emotions associated with BPM II and eventually eliminate them. The final goal is to reach the undifferentiated state of "oceanic consciousness" that characterizes embryonic existence. Mild forms of suicidal ideas of this type are manifested as a wish not to exist, or to fall into a deep sleep, forget everything, and not to awaken ever again. People in this condition might go to bed, cover themselves completely with a blanket and stay there for extended periods of time. Actual suicidal plans and attempts in this group involve the use of large doses of hypnotics or tranquilizers, and jumping or walking into water and drowning.

In countries that have cold winters, this unconscious drive to return to the womb can take the form of walking into a deserted plain or forest, lying down, and being covered by a layer of snow. The fantasy behind this situation is that the initial discomfort of freezing disappears and is replaced by feelings of coziness and warmth, like being in a good womb. Suicide by cutting one's wrists in a bathtub full of warm water also belongs to this category. Ending one's life in this way was fashionable in ancient Rome and was used by such illustrious men as Petronius and Seneca. This form of suicide might appear on the surface to be different from others in this category, since it involves blood. However, the psychological focus is on the dissolution of boundaries and merging with the aquatic environment, not on the violation of the body.

Suicide II, or ***violent suicide***, unconsciously follows the pattern once experienced during biological birth. It is closely associated with the agitated form of depression and is related to BPM III. For a person who is under the influence of this matrix, regression into the oceanic state of the womb is not a feasible option, because it would lead through the hellish no-exit stage of BPM II. This would be psychologically far worse than BPM III, since it involves a sense of total despair and hopelessness.

However, what is available as a psychological escape route is the memory that a similar state was once terminated by explosive release and liberation at the moment of biological birth. To understand this form of suicide, it is important to realize that during our biological birth, we were born anatomically, but did not emotionally and physically process and integrate this overwhelming event. The little crying that we see in newborns after birth, episodes of crying in infancy, and "temper tantrums" in childhood, which are usually suppressed and truncated by parents using disciplinary measures, are painfully inadequate means for releasing emotions generated during the many hours of suffering in the passage through the birth canal. The individual contemplating violent suicide is using the memory of his or her biological birth as a recipe for coping with the "second birth," the emergence of the unassimilated emotions and physical sensations into consciousness that are attempting to be processed and released.

As is the case with nonviolent suicide, the individuals involved in this process typically do not have experiential access to the perinatal level of the unconscious. They lack the insight that the ideal strategy in their situation would be to complete the process internally—relive the memory of their birth and connect experientially with the postnatal situation. Unaware of this option, they exteriorize the process and are driven to create a situation in the external world that involves the same elements as biological birth, and that has a similar experiential quality. The basic strategy of violent suicide follows the pattern experienced during delivery—intensification of the tension and emotional suffering to a critical point and then reaching an explosive resolution amidst various forms of biological material.

This description applies equally to biological birth and to violent suicide. Both involve the abrupt termination of excessive emotional and physical tension, an instant discharge of enormous destructive and self-destructive energies, extensive tissue damage, and the presence of organic material, such as blood, feces, and entrails. The juxtaposition of photographs showing biological birth and those depicting victims of violent suicide demonstrate the deep formal parallels between the two situations. It is thus easy for the unconscious to confuse one with the other. The connection between the type of birth trauma and the choice of suicide has been confirmed by clinical research with suicidal adolescents (Jacobson et al. 1987).

The suicidal fantasies and acts that belong to this category involve death under the wheels of a train, in the turbine of a hydroelectric plant, or in suicidal car accidents. Additional examples involve cutting one's throat, blowing one's brains out, stabbing oneself with a knife, or throwing oneself from a window, tower, or cliff. Suicide by hanging seems to belong to an earlier phase of BPM III, characterized by feelings of strangulation, suffocation, and strong sexual arousal. The element of exteriorizing suffocation seems to be involved in suicides by inhalation of carbon monoxide or domestic gas. The category of violent suicide also includes some culture-bound forms of suicide such as harakiri, and running amok.

Running amok was, in the past, seen as an exotic form of suicidal and murderous behavior occurring exclusively in Malaysia. A person afflicted by this disorder ran into a public place, usually a market, and started indiscriminately killing other people with a dagger; he eventually got killed himself or committed suicide. The Malaysians believed that amok was caused by *hantu belian,* an evil tiger spirit that entered one's body and caused the heinous acts. In recent decades, episodes similar to running amok, involving indiscriminate killing that ends with the death of the aggressor, have become increasingly frequent in the United States and other Western countries. A very disturbing aspect of these episodes has been their growing incidence among adolescents and even school children.

As we saw, nonviolent suicide expresses a tendency to reduce the intensity of painful emotional and physical stimuli. The specific choice of means for this type of suicide seems to then be further determined by biographical or transpersonal elements. Violent suicide involves a mechanism of an entirely different kind. As I have already observed, the individuals who were contemplating a particular form of suicide were often already experiencing the physical sensations and emotions that would be involved in its enactment in their everyday life. Experiential work typically intensified these feelings and sensations and brought them into sharp relief.

Thus, those persons whose self-destructive fantasies and tendencies focus on trains or hydroelectric turbines already suffer from intense feelings of being crushed and torn to pieces. Individuals who have a tendency to cut or stab themselves often complain about unbearable pains exactly in those parts of their bodies that they intend to injure, or experience pains in those locations during experiential psychotherapy. Similarly, the tendency to hang oneself is based on deep preexisting feelings of strangulation and choking. Both the pains and choking sensations are easily recognizable as elements of BPM III. If the intensification of symptoms happened in a therapeutic situation with adequate guidance, it could result in a resolution of those uncomfortable sensations and have therapeutic results. The above self-destructive tendencies can thus be seen as expressions of unconscious, misunderstood, and misguided attempts at self-healing.

The mechanism of violent suicide requires a relatively clear memory of the sudden transition from the struggle in the birth canal to the external world and of the ensuing explosive liberation. If this transition was blurred by heavy anesthesia, the individual would be programmed for the future, almost on a cellular level, to escape from severe stress and discomfort into a drugged state. This would create a propensity toward alcoholism and drug abuse or even a tendency to end one's life with an overdose in a person otherwise dominated by BPM III.

Individuals who are under a strong influence of BPM III experience extreme inner pressure and say that they feel like a bomb ready to explode at any moment. These aggressive feelings oscillate between focusing on the destruction of external targets and self-destruction. This is exteriorization of the situation in the birth canal—the former is the fury of the organism that is hurting and struggling for breath and the latter is the introjected force of the uterine contractions. In this situation, murder and suicide are equally possible alternatives or happen simultaneously, such as a mother killing herself and her child.

Linking the mechanism of suicide to BPM III throws an interesting light on the theory of suicide formulated by Karl Menninger. Sigmund Freud concluded that suicidal persons would not have the energy to commit suicide unless they find a person whom they hate and want to kill; the suicide is then actually the killing of this introjected object. Menninger expanded on Freud's idea, suggesting that suicide requires the simultaneous occurrence of three wishes: the wish to be killed, the wish to kill, and the wish to die. All these forces are simultaneously present in the final stage of birth. The wish to die in this context does not relate to physical death, but to symbolic death, the death of the ego.

When suicidal individuals undergo psychedelic or holotropic therapy and complete the death-rebirth process, they see suicide retrospectively as a tragic mistake based on a lack of self-understanding. The average person does not know that one can safely experience liberation from unbearable emotional and physical tension through a symbolic death and rebirth or through reconnecting to the state of prenatal existence. As a result, he or she might be driven by the intensity of discomfort and suffering to seek a situation in the material world that involves similar elements. The extreme outcome is often tragic and irreversible. The drive that these people feel is not really to destroy their body, but to experience psychospiritual death and rebirth.

As we have seen earlier, the experiences of BPM I and BPM IV do not only represent regression to symbiotic biological states, but also have very distinct spiritual dimensions. For BPM I, it is the experience of oceanic ecstasy and cosmic union, for BPM IV, that of psychospiritual rebirth and divine epiphany. From this perspective, suicidal tendencies of both types appear to be distorted and unrecognized cravings for transcendence. They represent a fundamental confusion between suicide and egocide. The best remedy for self-destructive tendencies and the suicidal urge, then, is the experience of ego death and rebirth and the ensuing feelings of cosmic unity.

The fact that the transition between BPM III and BPM IV has an important spiritual component provides a new understanding of a phenomenon that in recent decades has been playing an increasingly important role in the world—the religiously motivated combination of suicide and murder. We have already discussed and explained the combination of suicide and murder as a manifestation of BPM III; the numinosity of BPM IV contributes the religious dimension in the form of a divine reward for this act.

In WWII, Japanese kamikaze pilots had their airplanes specially built or converted from conventional aircrafts and loaded with bombs, torpedoes, and full fuel tanks, which destroyed American ships by colliding with them. They believed that they were doing it for Emperor Hirohito, who was seen in Japan as a representation of God. Muslim suicide bombers believe that killing infidels while sacrificing their own lives will be rewarded by admission to a paradise with beautiful gardens, luscious trees bearing exquisite fruit, exotic birds, and rivers of pure water, honey, and oil. Among the extraordinary delights that will await them will be unlimited hosts of houris, ravishing black-eyed young women waiting to serve the pleasures of the faithful. The sexual potency of the men would be multiplied a hundred times and, having satisfied the sexual desires of their clients, the houris would resume their virginal status.

Alcoholism and Drug Addiction

The observations from holotropic states of consciousness are in general agreement with psychoanalytic theory that sees alcoholism and narcotic drug addiction as being closely related to manic-depressive disorders and suicide. They differ considerably, however, in regard to the nature of the psychological mechanisms involved and the level of the psyche on which they operate. Like suicidal individuals, addicts experience a great amount of emotional pain, such as depression, general tension, anxiety, guilt, and low self-esteem, and they have a strong need to escape these unbearable feelings. We saw earlier that the psychology of depression and suicide cannot be adequately accounted for by oral fixation, which is the interpretation offered by Freudian psychoanalysis. The same is certainly true for alcoholism and drug addiction.

The most basic psychological characteristic of alcoholics and addicts, and their deepest motive for taking intoxicant drugs, is not only the need to regress to the breast, but also a much deeper craving for the experience of the blissful unity of the undisturbed intrauterine life. As we saw earlier, regressive experiences of both of these symbiotic states have intrinsic numinous dimensions. The deepest force behind alcoholism and addiction is thus an unrecognized and misguided craving for transcendence. Like suicide, these disorders involve a tragic error based on an inadequate understanding of one's own unconscious dynamics.

Excessive consumption of alcohol or narcotic drugs seems to be a mitigated analogue of suicidal behavior. Alcoholism and narcotic drug addiction have frequently been described as slow, prolonged forms of suicide. The principal mechanism characteristic for these two groups of patients is the same as for the nonviolent variety of suicide. It reflects an unconscious need to undo the discomfort of the birth process and return to the womb, to the state that existed prior to the onset of delivery. Alcohol and narcotics tend to inhibit various painful emotions and sensations and produce a state of diffused consciousness and indifference toward one's past and present problems. This state bears some superficial similarity to fetal consciousness and the experience of cosmic unity.

However, these resemblances are only superficial, and there are some fundamental differences between alcoholic or narcotic intoxications and transcendental states. Alcohol and narcotics dull the senses, obnubilate consciousness, interfere with intellectual functions, and produce emotional anesthesia. Transcendental states are characterized by a great enhancement of sensory perception, serenity, clarity of thinking, abundance of philosophical and spiritual insights, and an unusual richness of emotions. In spite of some shared features, the intoxication with alcohol and hard drugs represents just a pitiful caricature of the mystical state. Yet the similarity, however tenuous, seems to be sufficient to seduce the addicts into self-destructive abuse.

William James was aware of the fact that what alcoholics were searching for was transcendental experience. He expressed this very succinctly in his book *Varieties of Religious Experience:* "The best treatment for dipsomania (an archaic name for alcoholism) is religiomania" (James 1961). C. G. Jung expressed the same idea in a different way. In his correspondence with Bill Wilson, the founder of AA, he wrote about an alcoholic patient: "His craving for alcohol was the equivalent, on a low level, of the spiritual thirst of our being for wholeness, expressed in medieval language: the union with God."

Jung pointed out that in Latin, the term *spiritus* covers both meanings—alcohol and spirit. He then suggested that the proper formula for treating alcoholism is *"Spiritus contra spiritum."* It expressed his belief that only a deep spiritual experience can save people from the ravages of alcohol (Wilson and Jung 1963). James's and Jung's insights explain the success that the Native American Church has had in helping alcoholic Native Americans by evoking spiritual experiences in peyote ceremonies. Their results have since been confirmed by clinical research with psychedelics (Pahnke et al. 1970, Grof 2001).

The tendency to escape the painful emotions associated with BPM II and related COEX systems through an attempt to recreate the situation in the womb appears to be the most common psychodynamic mechanism underlying alcoholism and drug abuse. However, I have also worked with alcoholics and addicts whose symptoms indicated that they were under the influence of BPM III and yet sought the pharmacological solution for their problems. This clearly involved an alternative mechanism and required a different explanation. As for those clients for whom I could get information about their birth, I found out that they were born under heavy anesthesia.

This explanation certainly makes sense. Birth is typically the first major painful and stressful situation we encounter in our life, unless major crises occurred during embryonic existence. The extraordinary influence of early events in life on subsequent behavior has been repeatedly documented in experiments by ethologists, researchers studying animal instinctual behavior. This is known as "imprinting" (Lorenz 1963, Tinbergen 1965).

The nature of our birth and the way it was handled has a powerful impact on our future life. When our birth is of average duration and severity and we emerge into the world after having successfully negotiated the challenges, it leaves us with a feeling of optimism and confidence toward the difficulties that we encounter in the future. Conversely, an extended and debilitating delivery creates a sense of pessimism and defeatism. It forges an impression of the world as being too difficult to cope with successfully and of ourselves as being helpless and ineffective.

If the pain and discomfort associated with our birth is alleviated or terminated by anesthesia, it leaves a very deep and convincing imprint in our psyche that the way to deal with difficulties in life is to escape into a drug state. It might not be a meaningless coincidence that today's epidemic of drug abuse in the United States involves the generation of people who have been born since American obstetricians started routinely using anesthesia during childbirth, often against the will of the delivering mothers. Since the founding of the Association of Prenatal and Perinatal Psychology, a discipline that applies the findings of experiential therapies and fetal research to birth practices, obstetricians are becoming increasingly aware of the fact that birthing involves more than just body mechanics and that it can have a profound influence on the life of the newborn.

The way delivery and the postnatal period are handled has a profound influence on the emotional and social life of the individual and has important implications for the future of our society. It lays the foundations for either a loving and altruistic relationship with fellow humans, or for a mistrusting and aggressive attitude toward society (Odent 1995). It may also be a critical factor in determining whether the individual will be able to cope with the vicissitudes of life in a constructive way, or will tend to escape the challenges of existence by opting for alcohol or narcotics.

The fact that alcoholism and narcotic drug abuse represent a misguided search for transcendence can also help us understand the healing and transformative effect of profound crises that are usually referred to as "hitting bottom." In many instances, reaching a state of total emotional bankruptcy and annihilation becomes a turning point in the life of the alcoholic or drug addict. In the context of our discussion, this would mean that the individual experienced ego death as part of the transition from BPM III to BPM IV. At this point, alcohol or narcotics are not able to protect him or her anymore from the onslaught of the deep unconscious material. The eruption of the perinatal dynamics then results in a psychosomatic death-rebirth experience that often represents a positive turning point in the life of the alcoholic or addict.

Like all emotional problems, alcoholism and addiction have not only biographical and perinatal, but also transpersonal, roots. Most important among these are influences from the archetypal domain. This aspect of addiction has been particularly explored by therapists with a Jungian orientation. Among archetypes that show important connections with addiction, that of the *puer aeternus,* with its varieties of Icarus and Dionysus, seems to play an important role (Lavin 1987). Many people with whom I have worked also discovered karmic material that seemed to be meaningfully related to their addiction.

Sexual Disorders and Deviations

In classical psychoanalysis, the understanding of sexual problems rests on several fundamental concepts formulated by Freud. The first of these is the notion of *infantile sexuality.* One of the basic cornerstones of the psychoanalytic theory is the discovery that sexuality does not manifest in puberty, but in early infancy. As the libido develops through several evolutionary stages—oral, anal, urethral, and phallic—frustration or overindulgence in any of them can lead to fixation. In mature sexuality, the primary focus is genital, and the pregenital components play a secondary role, mostly as part of the foreplay. Specific psychological stress in later life can cause regression to earlier developmental stages of libidinal development where fixation occurred. Depending on the strength of the defense mechanisms that oppose these impulses, this can result in perversions or psychoneuroses (Freud 1953).

An important concept in the psychoanalytic approach to sexual problems is the *castration complex.* Freud believed that both sexes attribute extreme value to the penis and he considered this to be an issue of paramount importance for psychology. According to him, boys experience excessive fear that they might lose this highly valued organ. Girls believe that they once had a penis and lost it; they wonder why that happened and it makes them more prone to masochism and guilt. Freud's reviewers repeatedly criticized this point of view as a serious distortion and misunderstanding of female sexuality, since it portrays women essentially as castrated males. Leaving out some important aspects of women's life, such as pregnancy, childbirth, and motherhood, and believing that the most important issue for them is having or not having a penis certainly creates a seriously slanted and biased feminine psychology.

Another cornerstone of Freud's sexual theory is the Oedipus complex, the sexual attraction that boys feel toward their mothers and aggression they experience toward their fathers. This is associated with a fear of punishment for these feelings in the form of castration by their fathers. The feminine counterpart of the Oedipus complex, the girls' affection for their fathers and hatred toward their mothers, has been referred to as the Electra complex.

The discussion of Freud's understanding of sexuality would not be complete without mentioning another important concept, his famous *vagina dentata,* the observation that children see the female genitals as a dangerous organ equipped with teeth, which can kill, swallow, or castrate them. Together with the Oedipus and Electra complexes and the castration complex, the fantasy of the ominous female genitals plays a crucial role in the psychoanalytic interpretation of sexual deviations and psychoneurosis.

Freud suggested two reasons for which the sight of female genitals may arouse anxiety in boys. First, the recognition that there are human beings without a penis leads to the conclusion that one might become one of them, which lends power to the castration fears. And second, the perception of the female genitals as a castrating instrument capable of biting is due to an association with old oral anxieties (Fenichel 1945). None of these two reasons is particularly compelling or convincing.

The observations from holotropic states radically expand and deepen the Freudian understanding of sexuality by adding the perinatal domain to the individual unconscious. They suggest that we do not experience our first sexual feelings on the breast, but already in the birth canal. As I have discussed earlier, the suffocation and agony during BPM III seems to generate a sexual arousal of extreme intensity. This means that our first encounter with sexual feelings occurs under very precarious circumstances.

Birth is a situation in which our life is threatened and we experience suffocation, pain, and other forms of extreme physical and emotional discomfort. We inflict pain on another organism and another organism inflicts pain on us. We are also in contact with various forms of biological material: blood, vaginal secretions, amniotic fluid, and, if a catheter and enema are not used, even feces and urine. The typical response to this predicament is a mixture of vital anxiety and rage. These problematic associations form a natural basis for the understanding of the basic sexual dysfunctions, deviations, and perversions.

The recognition of the profound influence of perinatal dynamics on sexuality also clears up some serious theoretical problems associated with Freud's concept of the castration complex. Several important characteristics of this complex, as conceived by Freud, do not make any sense as long as we relate it to the penis. According to Freud, the intensity of the castration fear is so excessive that it equals the fear of death. He also saw castration as psychologically equivalent to the loss of an important human relationship, and suggested that it could actually be activated by such a loss. Among the free associations that often emerge in connection with the castration complex are those dealing with situations involving suffocation and loss of breath. And, as I mentioned earlier, the castration complex is found in both men and women.

None of the above connections would make any sense if the castration complex reflected only concerns about the loss of the penis. Observations from holotropic states show that the experiences, which Freud considered to be the source of the castration complex, actually represent the surface layer of a COEX system superimposed over the traumatic memory of the severing of the umbilical cord. All the inconsistencies that I just mentioned disappear when we realize that many puzzling characteristics of Freud's castration complex actually refer to the separation from the mother at the time when the umbilical cord was cut, and not to the loss of the penis.

Unlike unprovoked spontaneous castration fantasies, facetious verbal threats of castration by adults, and even surgical interventions on the penis such as circumcision or correction of the adhesion of the foreskin *(phimosis)*, the cutting of the umbilical cord is associated with a situation that is potentially or actually life-threatening. Since it severs the vital connection with the maternal organism, it is the prototypical loss of an important relationship. The association of the cutting of the umbilical cord with suffocation also makes eminent sense, since the cord is the source of oxygen for the fetus. And, last but not least, it is an experience that is shared by both sexes.

Similarly, the image of the *vagina dentata* that Freud saw as a naïve infantile fantasy appears in a new light once we accept that the newborn is a conscious being or, at least, that the trauma of birth is recorded in the memory. Rather than being an absurd and silly fabrication of the child's immature psyche, the image of the vagina as a perilous organ reflects the dangers associated with female genitals during childbirth. Far from being a mere fantasy with no basis in reality, it represents a generalization of one's experience in a specific life-threatening situation to other contexts in which it is not appropriate.

The link between sexuality and the potentially life-threatening trauma of birth creates a general disposition to sexual disturbances of various kinds. Specific disorders develop when certain aspects of perinatal memories are then reinforced by postnatal traumas in infancy and childhood. As is the case with emotional and psychosomatic disorders in general, the traumatic experiences that the psychoanalysts see as primary causes of these problems actually serve to reinforce and confirm certain aspects of the

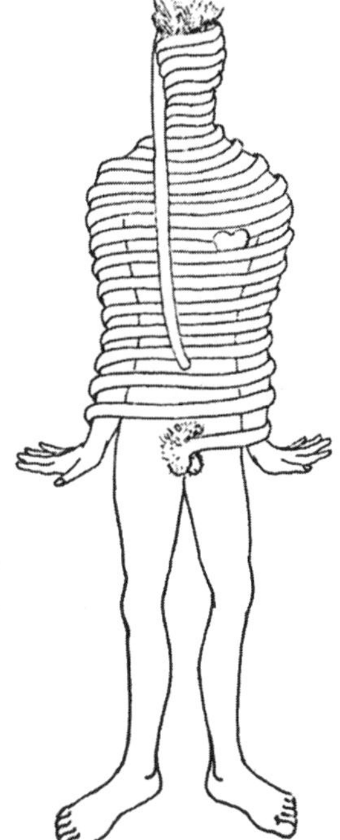

A drawing depicting an experience from a perinatal LSD session, which provided insight into the castration complex and its deep roots in the cutting of the umbilical cord. It combines feelings of constriction of the body with painful umbilical and genital sensations.

birth trauma and facilitate their emergence into consciousness. Like other psychogenic disorders, sexual problems also typically have deeper roots in the transpersonal domain, linking them to various karmic, archetypal, and phylogenetic elements.

Erectile dysfunction *("impotence"),* the inability to develop or maintain an erection, and ***orgastic incompetence*** *("frigidity"),* the inability to attain an orgasm, have a similar psychodynamic basis. The conventional approach to these problems is reflected in their old names *impotence* and *frigidity,* now considered obsolete and politically incorrect. It sees "impotence" as a lack of masculine power and sexual weakness. Orgastic incompetence in women, as the name "frigidity" indicates, is usually interpreted as sexual coldness and a lack of erotic responsiveness. According to my experience, the opposite often seems to be true; it is actually an excess of sexualized perinatal energy that is the problem.

Individuals suffering from these disorders are under the strong influence of the sexual aspect of BPM III. This makes it impossible for them to experience sexual arousal without simultaneously activating all the other elements of this matrix. The intensity of the sexual drive, the aggressive impulses, vital anxiety, and fear of loss of control associated with BPM III then inhibit the sexual act. In both instances, the sexual problems are connected with COEX systems that, besides the perinatal component, also have biographical layers and transpersonal roots—personal and karmic memories of sexual abuse, rape, associations between sex and pain or danger, and similar themes.

The empirical support for the involvement of perinatal dynamics in "impotence" and "frigidity" comes from experiential psychotherapy. When we create a nonsexual situation in which the elements of BPM III can be brought into consciousness and the energy associated with them discharged, impotence can be temporarily replaced by a condition called ***satyriasis***—an excessive sexual drive and appetite. This is due to the fact that a connection has been established between the penis and the sexual energy generated by the trauma of birth. It is now this perinatal energy and not the ordinary libido that is being expressed in the sexual act.

Due to the excessive amount of energy available on the perinatal level, this situation can result in an insatiable appetite and an unusual ability to perform sexually. The men who were not previously able to maintain an erection at all are now capable of having intercourse several times in a single night. The release is usually not fully satisfactory and, as soon as they reach orgasm and ejaculate, the sexual energy starts to build up again. More nonsexual experiential work is necessary to bring this energy to a niveau that can be comfortably handled in a sexual situation. When this condition develops in everyday life, outside of the therapeutic situation, it can persist and manifest as sexual addiction.

In a similar way, when women, who were previously unable to attain an orgasm, discharge the excessive energy associated with BPM III in a therapeutic situation, they can reach a point where they can now allow the orgasm to happen. When this occurs, the initial orgasms tend to be very intense. They are often accompanied by loud, involuntary screams and are followed by several minutes of violent shaking. There might be a tendency to briefly lose control and bruise or scratch the partner's back. Under these circumstances, it is not uncommon for the woman to experience multiple orgasms.

This initial liberation can also lead to an increase of sexual appetite to such a degree that it appears insatiable. We can then see a temporary transformation of "frigidity" into a condition known as ***nymphomania.*** This is characterized by a strong sexual drive and difficulty reaching full release. And again, as in the case of men involved in experiential work for erectile dysfunction, additional inner work in a non-sexual situation is necessary to bring the discharge of perinatal energy to a level where it allows for a more appropriate sexual life.

The amount of sexual energy of perinatal origin seems to be particularly large in individuals whose birth was associated with extended periods of suffocation. Over the years, I have worked with many people who were born with the umbilical cord twisted around the neck. A significant number of them reported that they have experienced unusually strong sexual tension all their life and that they had masturbated excessively in their early childhood. Intense sexual charge generated in situations that involved excessive suffocation might also be an important motivating factor in ischemic sexual practices.

There exists a form of orgastic inability where the fear is not connected with the overwhelming nature of the perinatal energy, which is activated by sexual intercourse and threatening to be unleashed, but with involuntary urination. This seems to be a problem occurring exclusively in women, because of their much shorter urethra and less effective urinary sphincter. Letting go into a sexual orgasm is withheld and blocked because of the fear that it would be associated with embarrassing involuntary urination.

This fear can also present a problem in experiential work with psychedelics or Holotropic Breathwork. Whenever the process brings the woman to the point of letting go, it manifests as an urge to urinate and the session is interrupted by going to the bathroom. In the early work with psychedelics, this sometimes happened ten to fifteen times in a single session and made any therapeutic progress impossible. We found, however, a very easy and unconventional solution for this problem: wearing a diaper or surgical pants and not interrupting the session when the urge occurred. The experience of the contact with warm urine usually brought memories of involuntary urination in childhood, such as episodes of bedwetting or "accidents" at school. This was usually associated with a mixture of feelings—shame and embarrassment, but also sensual pleasure. After a few episodes of this kind, the association between sexual letting go and urination was dissolved and the problem disappeared.

The understanding of the perinatal dimensions of sexuality throws an interesting new light on ***sadomasochism***, a condition that represented a formidable challenge for Freud's theoretical speculations. He struggled with it until the end of his life and never really found a satisfactory solution. The active seeking of pain exhibited by masochistic individuals contradicted one of the cornerstones of Freud's early model, the "pleasure principle." According to this concept, the deepest motivating force in the psyche was the pursuit of pleasure and avoidance of discomfort. Freud was also baffled by the strange fusion of two basic instincts, sexuality and aggression, that is an essential feature of sadomasochism.

It was the existence of sadomasochism and other conditions lying "beyond the pleasure principle" that forced Freud to abandon his early theories and to create an entirely new system of psychoanalysis that included the controversial Thanatos, or death instinct (Freud 1955, 1964). Although Freud never understood the intimate link between death and birth which exists on the perinatal level, these late speculations clearly reflected his intuitive insight that sadomasochism borders on matters of life and death. They also reflected Freud's belief that a viable psychological theory had to include the problem of death.

This was a radical departure from Freud's early work, when he considered death to be irrelevant for psychology because the Id was timeless and did not accept the facts of impermanence and death. Clearly Freud's thinking in this regard was far ahead of his followers, some of whom formulated theories of sadomasochism that tried to derive this condition from relatively trivial biographical situations. An example of this approach is the work of the Czech psychoanalyst Otakar Kučera, who linked sadomasochism to the experience of teething, when aggressive attempts of the child to bite result in self-inflicted pain (Kučera 1959). Explanations of this kind do not even begin to account for the intensity and depth of sadomasochistic impulses.

Sadomasochism and the bondage syndrome can be understood from the connections that exist in the context of BPM III between sexual arousal, physical confinement, aggression, pain, and suffocation. This accounts for the fusion of sexuality with aggression, as well as the link between sexuality and inflicted or experienced pain that characterize these two conditions. The individuals who need to combine sex with such elements as physical restriction, dominance and submission, inflicting and experiencing pain, and strangling or choking are repeating a combination of sensations and emotions that they experienced during their birth. The primary focus of these activities is perinatal, not sexual *per se.* Sadomasochistic experiences and visions are a frequent occurrence in sessions dominated by BPM III.

The need to create a sadomasochistic situation and the unconscious experiential complex mentioned above is not only symptomatic behavior, but also a misguided and truncated attempt of the psyche to expurgate and integrate the original traumatic imprint. The reason why this effort is unsuccessful and does not result in self-healing is the fact that it does not reach deep enough into the unconscious and lacks introspection, insight, and understanding the nature of the process. The experiential complex is acted out without the recognition and awareness of its unconscious sources.

The same is true for ***coprophilia***, ***coprophagia***, and ***urolagnia***, sexual deviations characterized by a strong need to bring feces and urine into the sexual situation. Individuals showing these aberrations seek intimate contact with biological materials that are usually considered repulsive. They become sexually aroused by them and tend to incorporate them into their sexual life. In extreme cases, such activities as being urinated or defecated on, smeared with feces, eating excrement, and drinking urine can be a necessary condition for reaching sexual satisfaction.

A combination of sexual arousal and scatological elements is a rather common experience during the final stages of the death-rebirth process. This seems to reflect the fact that, in the deliveries where no catheterization or enemas are used, many newborns experience intimate contact not only with blood, mucus, and amniotic fluid, but also with feces and urine. In ancient Rome, where this situation was likely more common, it was characterized by the famous saying: *"Inter faeces et urinam nascimur"* (we are born between feces and urine). The natural basis of this seemingly extreme and bizarre deviation is oral contact with feces and urine at the moment when, after many hours of agony and vital threat, the head is released from the firm grip of the birth canal. Intimate contact with such material thus becomes the symbol of a total orgastic release, as well as its necessary prerequisite.

According to psychoanalytic literature, the infant—because of his or her essentially animal nature—is originally attracted to various forms of biological material and only secondarily develops an aversion to them as a result of parental and societal repressive measures. Observations from psychedelic research suggest that this is not necessarily so. The attitude toward biological material is significantly determined by the nature of the encounter with this material during the birth experience. Depending on the specific circumstances, this attitude can be positive or extremely negative.

In some deliveries, the child simply encounters vaginal secretions, urine, or feces as part of the ambience of physical and emotional liberation. In others, this material is inhaled, obstructs the respiratory pathways, and causes terrifying suffocation. In extreme situations of this kind, the life of the newborn has to be saved by intubation and suction that clears the trachea and bronchi and prevents the development of pneumonia. These are two radically different forms of encounter with biological material at birth, one of them positive, the other frightening and traumatic. A situation in which breathing is triggered prematurely and the inhaled biological material threatens the life of the child can generate intense fear and become the basis for a future obsessive-compulsive disorder, as we discussed earlier.

Some extreme forms of criminal sexual pathology, such as ***rape***, ***sadistic murder***, and ***necrophilia***, clearly betray perinatal roots. Individuals experiencing the sexual aspects of BPM III frequently talk about the fact that this stage of the birth process has many characteristics in common with rape. This comparison makes a lot of sense if one considers some of the essential experiential features of rape. For the victim, it involves serious danger, vital anxiety, extreme pain, physical restraint, a struggle to free oneself, choking, and imposed and enforced sexual arousal. The experience of the rapist, in turn, involves the active counterparts of these activities—endangering, threatening, hurting, restricting, strangling, and enforcing sexual arousal. The experience of the victim has many elements in common with that of the child suffering in the clutches of the birth canal, while the rapist exteriorizes and acts out the introjected forces of the uterine contractions, while simultaneously taking revenge on a mother surrogate.

If the memory of BPM III is close to consciousness, it can create a strong psychological pressure on the individual to enact its elements in everyday life—to engage in violent consensual sex or even unconsciously invite dangerous sexual situations. While this mechanism certainly does not apply to all victims of sexual crimes, in some instances it can play an important role. While clearly self-destructive, such behavior contains an unconscious healing impulse. Similar experiences emerging from the subject's own psyche in the context of experiential therapy and with insights into their unconscious sources would lead to healing and psychospiritual transformation.

Due to this similarity between the experience of rape and the birth experience, the rape victim suffers a psychological trauma that reflects not only the painful impact of the rape situation, but also the breakdown of the defenses protecting her or him against the memory of biological birth. The frequent long-term emotional problems following rapes are very probably deepened by the emergence into consciousness of perinatal emotions and psychosomatic symptoms. Therapeutic resolution will then need to include work on the trauma of birth. The influence of the third perinatal matrix is even more obvious in the case of sadistic murders, which are closely related to rapes.

The dynamics of sadistic murder is closely related to that of bloody suicide. The only difference is that, in the former, the individual overtly assumes the role of the aggressor, whereas in the latter, he or she is also the victim. In the last analysis, both roles represent separate aspects of the same personality: the aggressor reflects the introjection of the oppressive and destructive forces of the birth canal, while the victim reflects the memory of the emotions and sensations of the fetus.

Psychosomatic Manifestations of Emotional Disorders

Many emotional disorders, such as psychoneuroses, depressions, and functional psychoses, have distinct physical manifestations. Most common among these are headaches, heart palpitations, excessive sweating, tics and tremors, psychosomatic pains, and various skin afflictions. Equally frequent are gastrointestinal disturbances, such as nausea, loss of appetite, constipation, and diarrhea. Among typical concomitants of emotional problems are also various sexual dysfunctions, such as amenorrhea, irregularities of the cycle, menstrual cramps, or painful vaginal spasms during intercourse. We have already discussed erectile dysfunction and the inability to achieve an orgasm. These conditions can either accompany other neurotic problems or occur as independent primary symptoms.

In some psychoneuroses, such as conversion hysteria, the physical symptoms are very distinct and characteristic, and can represent the predominant feature of the disorder. This is also true for a category of disorders that classical psychoanalysts called *pregenital neuroses;* it includes various tics, stammering, and psychogenic asthma. These conditions represent hybrids between obsessive-compulsive neurosis and conversion hysteria. The personality structure underlying them is obsessive-compulsive, but the main mechanism of defense and symptom formation is conversion, like in hysteria. There also exists a group of medical disorders in which the role of psychological factors is so significant that even traditional medicine refers to them as *psychosomatic diseases.*

This category includes migraine headaches, functional hypertension, colitis and peptic ulcers, psychogenic asthma, psoriasis, various eczemas, and, according to some, even certain forms of arthritis. Mainstream physicians and psychiatrists accept the psychogenic nature of these disorders, but do not offer plausible explanations of the psychogenetic mechanisms involved. Much of the clinical work, theoretical speculations, and research has been based on the ideas of psychoanalyst Franz Alexander, the founder of psychosomatic medicine. Alexander proposed a theoretical model explaining the mechanism of psychosomatic disorders. His key contribution was the recognition that psychosomatic symptoms result from the physiological concomitants of psychological conflict and trauma. According to him, emotional arousal during acute anxiety, grief, or rage gives rise to intense physiological reactions, which lead to the development of psychosomatic symptoms and diseases (Alexander 1950).

Alexander made a distinction between conversion reactions and psychosomatic disorders. In the former, the symptoms have a symbolic significance and serve as a defense against anxiety; this is an important characteristic of psychoneuroses. In psychosomatic disorders, the source of the underlying emotional state can be traced to psychological trauma, neurotic conflicts, and pathological interpersonal relationships, but the symptoms do not serve a useful function. They actually represent a failure of psychological mechanisms to protect the individual against excessive affective arousal. Alexander emphasized that this somatization of emotions occurs only in those individuals who are predisposed and not in healthy ones; however, neither he nor his successors have been able to define the nature of this disposition.

More than six decades later, the situation in the field of psychosomatic medicine is generally very disappointing. It is characterized by a fundamental lack of agreement about the mechanisms involved in the psychogenesis of somatic symptoms and no conceptual framework is considered entirely satisfactory (Kaplan and Kaplan 1967). The lack of clear answers is responsible for the fact that many authors subscribe to the idea of multicausality. According to this view, psychological factors play a significant role in psychosomatic disorders, but one has to also take into consideration a variety of other factors, such as constitution, heredity, organ pathology, nutritional status, environment, and social and cultural determinants. These, of course, cannot be adequately specified, which leaves the question of the etiology of psychosomatic disorders open.

Psychedelic therapy and holotropic breathwork have brought clear evidence that postnatal psychological traumas, in and of themselves, are not sufficient to account for the development of emotional disorders. This is also true, even to a much greater extent, for psychosomatic symptoms and disorders. Psychological conflict, loss of an important relationship, excessive dependency, the child's observation of parental intercourse, and other similar factors, which psychoanalysts see as causal factors, simply cannot account for the nature and intensity of the physiological disturbances involved in psychosomatic disorders.

In light of deep experiential work, any of the psychoanalytically oriented theories of psychosomatic diseases that try to explain them as based solely on psychological traumas in postnatal biography are superficial and unconvincing. The assumption that these disorders can be effectively treated by verbal therapy is equally implausible. Holotropic research has contributed important insights to the theory and therapy of psychosomatic disorders, but possibly the most important of these findings was the discovery of the enormous amount of blocked emotional and physical energy underlying psychosomatic symptoms.

While there can be doubts that psychological biographical traumas

Franz Alexander (1891–1964) was a Hungarian physician and psychoanalyst, one of the founders of psychosomatic medicine and psychoanalytic criminology.

could cause deep functional disturbances or even anatomical damage to the organs, this is a reasonable possibility in the case of the elemental destructive energies from the perinatal layer of the unconscious that manifest in holotropic states. In the most general sense, this observation confirmed the concepts of the brilliant and controversial renegade pioneer of psychoanalysis, Wilhelm Reich. On the basis of his observations from therapeutic sessions, Reich concluded that the main factor underlying emotional and psychosomatic disorders is the jamming and blockage of significant amounts of bioenergy in the muscles and viscera, constituting what he referred to as *character armor* (Reich 1949, 1961).

This, though, is where the parallel between Reichian psychology and the observations from holotropic research ends. According to Reich, this jammed energy is sexual in nature and the reason for its blockage is a fundamental conflict between our biological needs and the repressive influence of society, which interferes with full orgastic release and a satisfactory sexual life. Residual sexual energy that remains unexpressed then jams and finds deviant expression in the form of perversions and neurotic or psychosomatic symptoms. The work with holotropic states offers a radically different explanation. It shows that the pent-up energy we carry in our organism is not accumulated, unexpressed libido, but emotional and physical charge bound in COEX systems.

Part of this energy belongs to biographical layers of these systems that contain memories of psychological and physical traumas from infancy and childhood. A considerable proportion of this energetic charge, though, is perinatal in origin and reflects the fact that the memory of birth has not been adequately processed. It continues to exist in the unconscious as an emotionally and physically incomplete gestalt of major importance. During delivery, extraordinary amounts of energy are generated by the excessive stimulation of the neurons and cannot be discharged because of the confinement of the birth canal. The reason Reich mistook this energy for jammed libido was probably the strong sexual arousal associated with BPM III.

In some instances, prenatal traumas can significantly contribute to the overall negative charge of the COEX systems and participate in the genesis of psychosomatic symptoms. Some people have a very difficult prenatal history that involves such factors as extreme emotional and physical stress of the pregnant mother, impending miscarriage, attempted abortion, toxic womb, or Rh incompatibility. The deepest sources of the energy underlying psychosomatic disorders can typically be traced to the transpersonal domain, particularly to karmic and archetypal elements (see the story of Norbert on pp. 247).

Of particular interest and importance is the observation from deep experiential work that the primary driving forces behind all psychosomatic manifestations are not psychological traumas. What plays the crucial role in their genesis are unassimilated and unintegrated physical traumas, such as memories of the discomfort associated with childhood diseases, operations, injuries, or near drowning. On a deeper level, the symptoms are related to the trauma of birth and even to physical traumas associated with past-life memories. The material underlying psychosomatic pains can include memories of accidents, operations, or diseases from infancy, childhood, and later life, the pain experienced during the birth process, and physical suffering connected with injuries or death in a previous incarnation.

This is in sharp contrast with the views of most psychodynamic schools that tend to attribute the primary role in the genesis of psychosomatic symptoms to psychological conflicts and traumas. According to them, symptoms originate in such a way that these psychological issues are expressed in symbolic body language, or "somatized." For example, holding on and getting rid of certain emotions are seen as psychological factors underlying constipation and diarrhea. Severe pain in the neck and shoulders is a symbolic expression of the client "carrying too much responsibility on his or her shoulders."

Similarly, stomach problems develop in people because they are unable to "swallow" or "stomach" something. Hysterical paralysis reflects a defense against an objectionable infantile sexual action. Breathing difficulties are caused by a mother who is "smothering" the client, asthma is a "cry for the mother," and oppressive feelings on the chest result from "heavy grief." In the same vein, stammering is seen as resulting from a suppression of verbal aggression and an urge to utter obscenities, and severe skin disorders serve as protection against sexual temptation.

The work with holotropic states provides rich opportunities for insights into the dynamics of psychosomatic disorders. It is actually not uncommon to see the transient occurrence of asthmatic attacks, migraine headaches, various eczemas, and even psoriatic skin eruptions *in statu nascendi,* that is, as they emerge into manifestation in psychedelic and Holotropic Breathwork sessions. This is usually associated with insights concerning their psychodynamic roots. On the positive side, dramatic and lasting improvements of various psychosomatic disorders have been reported by therapists and facilitators who use deep experiential techniques in their work. These reports typically describe reliving physical traumas, in particular the birth trauma, and various transpersonal experiences as the most effective therapeutic mechanisms.

Space considerations do not allow me to describe in more detail the new insights into the psychodynamics of the specific psychosomatic disorders and offer illustrative case histories. In this regard, I have to refer the interested readers to my earlier publications (Grof 1985, 2001).

Autistic and Symbiotic Infantile Psychoses, Narcissistic Personality, and Borderline States

Pioneers of ego psychology Margaret Mahler, Otto Kernberg, Heinz Kohut, and others contributed to the classical psychoanalytic classification of several new diagnostic categories that, according to them, have their origin in the early disturbances of object relations. A healthy psychological development proceeds from the autistic and symbiotic stage of primary narcissism through the process of separation and individuation to the attainment of constant object relations. Severe interference with this process and a lack of gratification of basic needs at these early stages can result in serious disorders. According to the degree of these adversities and their timing, these disturbances can lead to autistic and symbiotic infantile psychoses, narcissistic personality disturbance, or borderline personality disorders.

The analysis of the disturbances of object relationships underlying these disorders, found in the literature on ego psychology, is unusually detailed and refined. However, like classical psychoanalysts, ego psychologists fail to recognize that postnatal biographical events cannot adequately account for the symptomatology of emotional disorders. Observations from holotropic states suggest that early traumas in infancy have a profound impact on the psychological life of the individual, not only because they happen to a very immature organism and affect the very foundations of personality, but also because they interfere with the recovery from the birth trauma. They leave a connecting bridge and access to the perinatal unconscious wide open.

The terms used in ego psychology for describing the postnatal dynamics of these disorders betray their underlying prenatal and perinatal dimensions. The symbiotic gratification, to which ego psychologists attribute great significance, applies not only to the quality of breastfeeding and anaclitic satisfaction in infancy, but also to the quality of the prenatal state. The same is true for the detrimental effects of symbiotic deprivation. As an illustration, here is Margaret Mahler's description of the symbiotic phase: "the phase of symbiosis in which the infant behaves and functions as though he and his mother were an omnipotent system (a dual unity) within one common boundary (a symbiotic membrane as it were)" (Mahler 1961). Similarly, the regression to autism and to an objectless state has distinct characteristics of a psychological return to the womb, not just to the early postnatal state.

Other important aspects of the disorders caused by disturbances in the development of object relations clearly point to perinatal dynamics. Splitting the object world into good and bad, which is characteristic of borderline patients, reflects not just the inconsistency of mothering ("good" and "bad mother") emphasized by ego psychologists. On a deeper level, its source is the fundamental ambiguity of the role that the mother plays in the life of the child, even under the best of circumstances. Prenatally and postnatally, she represents a life-giving and life-sustaining being, while during delivery she turns into a pain-inflicting and life-threatening antagonist.

The children suffering from infantile symbiotic psychosis are described in ego-psychological literature as being caught between the fear of separation and the fear of engulfment. This situation clearly has its source in the trauma of birth, rather than in the transition from primary narcissism to object relations. As we saw earlier, the loss of the womb and the onset of delivery is typically experienced as a life-threatening engulfment, and the transition from BPM III to BPM IV is a terrifying experience of separation. These two experiences are incomparably more powerful than the fear of engulfment or separation experienced in the forming of an object relationship. We should also add that the intensity of rage observed in this category of patients is too great to be of postnatal origin and seems to come from perinatal sources.

Psychodynamics of Adult Psychotic States

In spite of an enormous investment of time, energy, and money into psychiatric research, the nature of the psychotic process has remained a mystery. Extensive systematic studies have explored a wide range of constitutional and genetic factors, hormonal and biochemical changes, biological variables, psychological and social determinants, environmental precipitating influences, and many others. None of these have been sufficiently consistent to provide a convincing explanation of the etiology of functional psychoses.

However, even if biological and biochemical research were able to detect processes that show consistent correlation with the occurrence of psychotic states, that would not help us understand the nature and content of psychotic experiences. I have already touched upon this problem in an earlier chapter while discussing laboratory research with LSD. In these experiments, we know the exact composition and dosage of the agent that triggers the experiences and yet that does not bring clarity into the problem of psychoses. Actually, it made the problem more complex; instead of bringing a simple answer to the question about the etiology of psychoses, it initiated a grand new project—searching for answers concerning the mystery of the human psyche, of the universe and existence.

This research only demonstrated the emergence of deep unconscious material into consciousness. It showed that the potential to create these experiences is clearly an inherent property of the human psyche rather than being a product of a pathological process. The phenomenology of functional psychoses combines perinatal and transpersonal experiences in various ways, with the occasional mixture of postnatal biographical elements.

The experiences characteristic of BPM I are represented in the symptomatology of psychotic episodes both in their positive and negative forms. Many patients experience episodes of blissful symbiotic union with the Great Mother Goddess and a sense of being nourished in her womb or on her breast. BPM I can also be experienced as an ecstatic union with other people, with Nature, with the entire universe, or with God *(unio mystica)*. The experiential spectrum of BPM I also includes visions of heavens or paradises from the mythologies of different cultures.

Conversely, there seems to be a deep connection between disturbances of embryonic life and psychotic states that involve paranoid perception and distortion of reality. Many prenatal disturbances involve chemical changes in the mother's body *(toxicosis)*. This seems to explain why so many paranoid patients suspect that somebody is poisoning their food, that some venomous gases are being pumped into their house, or that a wicked scientist is exposing them to dangerous radiation. Experiences of these hostile influences are often accompanied by visions of various evil entities and demonic archetypal beings.

Another source of paranoid feelings is the beginning phase of BPM II. This is not surprising, since the onset of delivery is a major and irreversible disturbance of the prenatal existence. Considering how unpleasant and confusing these situations must be for the fetus, it is not difficult to understand that the emerging memory of the onset of birth or of a serious intrauterine perturbation into the consciousness of an adult can cause feelings of all-pervading anxiety and vital threat. For obvious reasons, the source of this danger cannot be identified and remains unknown. The individual then tends to project these feelings on some threatening situation in the external world—on secret underground organizations, the Nazis, Communists, Freemasons, Ku Klux Klan, or on some other potentially or actually dangerous human group, possibly even on extraterrestrial invaders.

Reliving the onset of delivery often brings experiences of entering into the shamanic or mythological underworld. Fully developed forms of BPM II contribute the motifs of eternal damnation, despair, inhuman tortures and diabolic ordeals to psychotic symptomatology. Many psychotic patients experience what seems like never-ending suffering in hell or tortures that seem to be coming from some ingenious contraptions designed for that purpose.

Psychoanalytic studies showed that the influencing machine, described by many psychotic patients as causing excruciating agony, represents the body of the "bad mother" (Tausk 1933). However, these authors failed to recognize that the dangerous and torturing maternal body belongs to the delivering mother, not to the nursing mother. Other psychotic themes related to BPM II are experiences of a meaningless, bizarre, and absurd world of automata and the atmosphere of grotesque circus sideshows. A brilliant portrayal of these nightmarish experiences can be found in the biomechanoid art of the Swiss genius of fantastic realism, Hansruedi Giger (Grof 2015).

BPM III adds a rich array of experiences that represent various facets of this complex matrix to the clinical picture of psychotic states. The titanic aspect manifests in the form of unbearable tensions, powerful energy flows, clashes, and discharges. The corresponding imagery and ideation is related to violent scenes of wars, revolutions, and bloody massacres. These can often reach archetypal dimensions, and these scenes are portrayed on an enormous scale—a cosmic battle between the forces of Good and Evil, Darkness and Light, angels battling devils, Titans challenging gods, or superheroes fighting mythological monsters. The archetypes of the Witches' Sabbath or Black Mass rituals, combining motifs of death, sex, aggression, and scatology, can also appear in the experiences of psychotic patients.

The transition from BPM III to BPM IV contributes sequences of psychospiritual death and rebirth, apocalyptic visions of destruction and recreation of the world, and the scenes of the Judgment of the Dead or Last Judgment to the spectrum of psychotic experiences. This can be accompanied by identification with Jesus or archetypal figures representing death and resurrection and lead to ego inflation and messianic feelings. This is where fantasies and experiences of Sacred Marriage *(hieros gamos),* fathering a Divine Child or giving birth to it, belong. Experiences of divine epiphany, visions of the Great Mother Goddess or identification with her, encounters with angelic beings and deities appearing in light, and a sense of salvation and redemption also belong to characteristic manifestations of BPM IV.

At the time when I first suggested that much of psychotic symptomatology could be understood in terms of perinatal dynamics (Grof 1975), I was not able to find any clinical studies supporting this hypothesis, or even exploring this possibility. It was astonishing how little attention researchers had given to the possible relationship between psychoses and the trauma of birth. Today, half a century later, there exists important clinical evidence that prenatal disturbances and the trauma of birth play an important role in the genesis of psychoses.

As a matter of fact, inadequate nourishment and viral infections during the mother's pregnancy and obstetric complications during birth, including long labors and oxygen deprivation, are among the few consistently reported risk factors for schizophrenia (Wright et al. 1997, Verdoux and Murray 1998, Dalman et al 1999, Kane 1999, Warner 1999). Due to the strong influence of biological thinking in psychiatry, the interpretations of these data tend to favor the assumption that birth had caused some subtle brain damage undetectable by current diagnostic methods. Mainstream theoreticians and clinicians still fail to acknowledge the paramount role of birth and prenatal disturbances as a major psychotrauma.

While the perinatal experiences described above often represent a combination of biological memories of birth and archetypal motifs with corresponding themes, the phenomenology of psychotic states can also contain various transpersonal experiences in a pure form, without the mixture of biological perinatal elements. The most common of these are experiences of past-life memories, of contact with extraterrestrials, and of encounters with various deities and demonic beings. Occasionally, individuals diagnosed as psychotic can also have very elevated spiritual experiences, such as identification with God, with the Absolute, or with the Metacosmic Void.

Many of these experiences have been reported by mystics, saints, prophets, and spiritual teachers of all ages. It is absurd, as we have seen earlier, to attribute all these experiences to some unknown pathological process in the brain or elsewhere in the body, which is a common practice in modern psychiatry. This naturally raises the question of the relationship between psychosis and mystical experience. I have so far used the terms psychosis and psychotic, as is common in academic psychiatry. As we will see in the next section, the observations and experiences from holotropic states suggest that the concept of psychosis has to be radically redefined.

When we look at these experiences in the context of the large cartography of the psyche that is not limited to postnatal biography, but includes the perinatal and transpersonal domains, it becomes clear that the difference between mysticism and mental disorder is less in the nature and content of the experiences involved than in the attitude toward them, the individual's "experiential style," the mode of interpretation, and the ability to integrate them. Joseph Campbell often used a quote in his lectures that captures this relationship: "The psychotic drowns in the same waters in which the mystic swims with delight." My own reservations toward this otherwise very appropriate quote are related to the fact that the experiences of the mystics are often difficult and taxing, and not necessarily all delightful. But the mystic is capable of seeing these challenges in the larger context of a spiritual journey that has a deeper purpose and a desirable goal.

This approach to psychoses has profound implications not only for theory, but also for therapy and, most importantly, for the course and outcome of these states. The observations from experiential therapy confirm the revolutionary ideas of the pioneers of an alternative understanding of psychosis, C. G. Jung (1960c), Roberto Assagioli (1977), Abraham Maslow (1964), and John W. Perry (1998), in far-reaching ways.

Literature

Abraham, K. 1927. *A Short Study of the Development of the Libido. Selected Papers.* London: Institute of Psychoanalysis and Hogarth Press.

Alexander, F. 1950. *Psychosomatic Medicine.* New York: W. W. Norton.

Assagioli, R. 1977. *Self-Realization and Psychological Disturbances. Synthesis 3-4.* Also in: Grof, S. and Grof, C. (eds). *Spiritual Emergency: When Personal Transformation Becomes a Crisis.* Los Angeles, CA: J. P. Tarcher

Blanck, G. and Blanck, R. 1974. *Ego Psychology I: Theory and Practice.* New York: Columbia University Press.

Blanck, G. and Blanck, R. 1979. *Ego Psychology II: Psychoanalytic Developmental Psychology.* New York: Columbia University Press.

Dalman, C. et al. 1999. Obstetric Complications and the Risk of Schizophrenia: A Longitudinal Study of a National Birth Cohort. *Arch.gen. Psychiat.* 56:234-240.

Fenichel, O. 1945. *The Psychoanalytic Theory of Neurosis.* New York: W. W. Norton.

Freud, S. 1953. *Three Essays on the Theory of Sexuality.* Standard Edition, vol. 7. London: The Hogarth Press & The Institute of Psychoanalysis.

Freud, S. 1955. *Beyond the Pleasure Principle. The Standard Edition of the Complete Works of Sigmund Freud, Vol. 18.* (J.Strachey, ed.), London: The Hogarth Press & The Institute of Psychoanalysis.

Freud, S. 1964. *An Outline of Psychoanalysis.* Standard Edition, vol.23. London: The Hogarth Press & The Institute of Psychoanalysis.

Goodwin, F. K. and Jamison K. R. 1990. *Manic-Depressive Illness.* Oxford, New York: Oxford University Press.

Goodwin, F. K. and Jamison, K.R. 2007. *Manic-Depressive Illness, Bipolar Disorders and Recurrent Depression.* Oxford, New York: Oxford University Press.

Grof, S. 1975. *Realms of the Human Unconscious.* New York: Viking Press.

Grof, S 1985. *Beyond the Brain: Birth, Death, and Transcendence in Psychotherapy.* Albany, NY: State University of New York (SUNY) Press.

Grof, S. 2000. *Psychology of the Future.* Albany, New York: State University of New York (SUNY) Press.

Grof, S. 2001. *LSD Psychotherapy.* Santa Cruz, CA: MAPS Publications.

Grof, S. 2015. *Modern Consciousness Research and the Understanding of Art.* Santa Cruz, CA: MAPS Publications.

Jacobson, B. et al. 1987. Perinatal Origin of Adult Self-Destructive Behavior. *Acta psychiat. Scand.* 76:364-371.

James, W. 1961. *The Varieties of Religious Experience.* New York: Collier.

Jung, C. G. 1960. *The Psychogenesis of Mental Disease. Collected Works, vol. 3. Bollingen Series XX.* Princeton: Princeton University Press.

Kane, J. M. 1999. Schizophrenia: How Far Have We Come? *Current Opinion in Psychiatry* 12:17.

Kaplan, H. S. and Kaplan, H. I. 1967. Current Concepts of Psychosomatic Medicine. In: *Comprehensive Textbook of Psychiatry.* Baltimore: The Williams & Wilkins Co.

Kernberg, O.F. 1976. *Object Relations Theory and Clinical Psychoanalysis.* New York: Jason Aronson.

Kernberg, O.F. 1984. *Severe Personality Disorders: Psychotherapeutic Strategies.* New Haven, CT: Yale University Press.

Kohut, H. 1971. *The Analysis of the Self: A Systematic Approach to the Psychoanalytic Treatment of Narcissistic Personality Disorders.* New York: International Universities Press.

Kučera, O. 1959. On Teething. *Dig. Neurol. Psychiat.* 27:296.

Lavin, T. 1987. Jungian Perspectives on Alcoholism and Addiction. Paper presented at the seminar The Mystical Quest, Attachment, and Addiction. Presentation at a monthlong seminar at the Esalen Institute, Big Sur, CA.

Lorenz, K. 1963. *On Aggression.* New York: Harcourt, Brace and World.

Mahler, M. 1961. On Sadness and Grief in Infancy and Childhood: Loss and Restoration of the Symbiotic Love Object. *The Psychoanalytic Study of the Child.* 16:332-351.

Mahler, M. 2008. *The Psychological Birth of the Human Infant: Symbiosis and Individuation.* New York: Basic Books.

Maslow, A. 1964. *Religions, Values, and Peak Experiences.* Cleveland, OH: Ohio State University.

Moreno, F. et al. 2006. Safety, Tolerability, and Efficacy of Psilocybin in Nine Patients with Obsessive-Compulsive Disorder. *Journal of Clinical Psychiatry* 67(11):1735-40.

Odent, M. 1995. "Prevention of Violence or Genesis of Love? Which Perspective?" Presentation at the Fourteenth International Transpersonal Conference in Santa Clara, California, June.

Pahnke, W. N. Kurland, A. A., Unger, S., Grof, S. 1970. "The Experimental Useof Psychedelic (LSD) Psychotherapy." *Journal of the American Medical Association (JAMA)* 212:856.

Perry, J. W. 1998. *Trials of the Visionary Mind: Spiritual Emergency and the Renewal Process.* Albany, NY: State University of New York (SUNY) Press.

Rank, O. 1929. *The Trauma of Birth.* New York: Harcourt Brace.

Reich, W. 1949. *Character Analysis.* New York: Noonday Press.

Reich, W.1961. *The Function of the Orgasm: Sex-Economic Problems of Biological Energy.* New York: Farrar, Strauss & Giroux.

Spitz, R.,Á. 1965. *The First Year of Life : A Psychoanalytic Study of Normal and Deviant Development of Object Relations.* New York : International Universities Press.

Tausk, V. 1933. On the Origin of the Influencing Machine in Schizophrenia. *Psychoanalyt. Quart.* 11.

Tinbergen, N. 1965. *Animal Behavior.* New York: Time-Life.

Verdoux, H. and Murray, R. M. 1998. What Is the Role of Obstetric Complications in Schizophrenia? *Harv. Ment. Health Lett.*

Warner, R. 1999. New Directions for Environmental Intervention in Schizophrenia: I. The Individual and the Domestic Level. *Mental Health Services* #83, pp. 61-70.

Wilson, W. and Jung, C. G. 1963. Letters republished in: Grof, S. (ed.): Mystical Quest, Attachment, and Addiction. Special edition of the *Re-Vision Journal* 10 (2):1987.

Wright, P. et al. 1997. Maternal Influenza, Obstetric Complications, and Schizophrenia. *Amer. J. Psychiat.* 154: 292.

V

Spiritual Emergency: *Understanding and Treatment of Crises of Transformation*

One of the most important implications of the research into holotropic states of consciousness is the recognition that many spontaneous episodes, which are currently diagnosed as psychoses and indiscriminately treated by suppressive medication, are actually difficult stages of a radical personality transformation and of spiritual opening. If they are correctly understood and supported, these psychospiritual crises can result in emotional and psychosomatic healing, remarkable personality transformation, and consciousness evolution. They also have great heuristic potential (Grof and Grof 1989, 1990).

Episodes of this type can be found in the life stories of shamans, yogis, mystics, and saints. Mystical literature around the world describes these crises as important landmarks on the spiritual path and confirms their healing and transformative potential. Mainstream psychiatrists are unable to see the difference between psychospiritual crises, or even uncomplicated mystical states, and serious mental illness, because of their narrow conceptual framework. Academic psychiatry has a model of the psyche that is limited to postnatal biography and has a strong biological bias. These are serious obstacles in understanding the nature and content of psychotic states.

The term spiritual emergency, which my late wife Christina and I coined for these states, alludes to their positive potential. The Latin word "emergere" means "to emerge," but if a critical situation develops suddenly, it is referred to as an "emergency." This name is thus a play on words suggesting a crisis, but, at the same time, an opportunity to "emerge," to rise to a higher level of psychological functioning and spiritual awareness. In this context, we often refer to the Chinese character for crisis, which illustrates the basic idea of spiritual emergency. This ideogram is composed of two pictograms, one of which represents danger and the other opportunity.

Successful completion and integration of such episodes brings a substantial reduction of aggression, an increase of racial, political, and religious tolerance, ecological awareness, and deep changes in the hierarchy of values and existential priorities. Among the benefits that can result from psychospiritual crises that are allowed to run their natural course are better psychosomatic health, increased zest for life, a more rewarding life strategy, an expanded worldview, and spirituality that is universal, nondenominational, and all-inclusive. It is not an exaggeration to say that a well-integrated psychospiritual crisis can move the individual to a higher level of consciousness evolution.

In recent decades, we have seen a rapidly growing interest in spiritual matters, which leads to extensive experimentation with ancient, aboriginal, and modern "technologies of the sacred," which are mind-expanding techniques that can mediate spiritual opening. Among them are various shamanic methods, Eastern meditative practices, psychedelic substances, powerful experiential psychotherapies, and laboratory methods developed by experimental psychiatry. According to public polls, the number of Americans who have had spiritual experiences has significantly increased in the second half of the twentieth century. It seems that this has been accompanied by a parallel increase of spiritual emergencies.

More and more people seem to realize that genuine spirituality based on profound personal experience is a vitally important dimension of life. In view of the escalating global crisis brought about by the materialistic orientation of Western technological civilization, it has become obvious that we are paying a great price for having denied and rejected spirituality. We have banned a force that nourishes, empowers, and gives meaning to human existence from our lives.

On the individual level, the toll for the loss of spirituality is an impoverished, alienated, and unfulfilling way of life, as well as an increase in emotional and psychosomatic disorders. On the collective level, the absence of spiritual values leads to strategies of existence that threaten the survival of life on our planet, such as the plundering of nonrenewable resources, polluting the natural environment, disturbing the ecological balance, and using violence as a principal means of problem-solving.

It is, therefore, in the interest of all of us to find ways of bringing spirituality back into our individual and collective life. This would have to include not only the theoretical recognition of spirituality as a vital aspect of existence, but also encouragement and the social sanctioning of activities that mediate experiential access to spiritual dimensions of reality. An important part of this effort would have to be the development of an appropriate support system for people undergoing crises of spiritual opening,

Christina Grof (1940–2014), Ph.D.(hc), art and yoga teacher, artist, therapist, and writer. In 1980 she founded the Spiritual Emergence Network (SEN) at the Esalen Institute in Big Sur, California.

which would make it possible to utilize the positive and transformative potential of these states.

In 1980, my wife Christina founded the Spiritual Emergency Network (SEN), an organization that connects individuals undergoing psychospiritual crises with professionals who are able and willing to provide assistance based on the new understanding of these states. Filial branches of SEN now exist in many countries of the world.

Triggers of Spiritual Emergency

In many instances, it is possible to identify the situation that precipitated a psychospiritual crisis. It can be a primarily physical trigger or stress, such as a disease, accident, or operation. Extreme physical exertion or prolonged lack of sleep may also appear to be the most immediate factor. In women, it can be childbirth, miscarriage, or abortion. We have also seen situations where the onset of the process coincided with an exceptionally powerful sexual experience.

In other cases, the psychospiritual crisis begins shortly after a traumatic emotional experience. This can be the loss of an important relationship, such as the death of a child or another close relative, divorce, or the end of a love affair. Similarly, a series of failures or loss of a job or property can immediately precede the onset of spiritual emergency. In predisposed individuals, the "last straw" can be an experience with psychedelic substances or a session of experiential psychotherapy.

One of the most important catalysts of spiritual emergency seems to be deep involvement in various forms of meditation and spiritual practice. This should not come as a surprise, since these methods have been specifically designed to facilitate spiritual experiences. We have been repeatedly contacted by people in whom the ongoing spontaneous occurrence of holotropic states was triggered by the practice of Zen or Vipassana Buddhist meditation, Kundalini yoga, Sufi dhikr, monastic contemplation, or Christian prayer. The possibility of this happening increases if such spiritual practice involves fasting, sleep deprivation, and extended periods of meditation.

The wide range of triggers for spiritual emergency clearly suggests that the individual's readiness for inner transformation plays a far more important role than the external stimuli. When we look for a common denominator or final common pathway of the situations described above, we find that they all involve a radical shift in the balance between the unconscious and conscious processes. Weakening of psychological defenses or, conversely, increase of the energetic charge of the unconscious dynamics, makes it possible for the unconscious (and superconscious) material to emerge into consciousness.

It is well known that psychological defenses can be weakened by a variety of biological stresses, such as physical trauma, exhaustion, sleep deprivation, or intoxication. Psychological traumas can mobilize the unconscious, particularly when they involve elements that are reminiscent of earlier traumas and are part of a significant COEX system. The strong potential of delivery as a trigger of psychospiritual crisis seems to reflect the fact that childbirth combines biological weakening with specific reactivation of the perinatal memories.

Failures and disappointments in the professional and personal life can undermine and thwart the outward-oriented motivations and ambitions of the individual. This makes it more difficult to use external activities as an escape from emotional problems and leads to psychological withdrawal and turning the attention to the inner world. As a result, unconscious content can emerge into consciousness and interfere with the individual's everyday experience or even completely override it.

There seems to be an inverse relationship between outward orientation and pursuit of external material goals, and attention given to inner processes and time spent in introspection. Crises in various sectors of one's life that undermine or destroy positive perspective—the death of close relatives and friends, the breaking up of a marriage or an important relationship, the loss of property or a job, and a series of failures—tend to turn the attention inward and activate the unconscious. The similarity of the current traumas with previous ones, often an entire series of them, then add the emotional power of the corresponding COEXs to the impact of the recent events. The dismal general situation in the world and loss of perspective (e.g. death of the American Dream) can also have a similar effect.

Diagnosis of Spiritual Emergency

When we emphasize the need to recognize the existence of spiritual emergencies, this does not mean an indiscriminate rejection of the theories and practices of mainstream psychiatry. Not all states that are currently diagnosed as psychotic are crises of psychospiritual transformation or have a healing potential. Episodes of non-ordinary states of consciousness cover a very broad spectrum, from purely spiritual experiences to conditions that are clearly biological in nature and require medical treatment. While mainstream psychiatrists generally tend to pathologize mystical states, there also exists the opposite problem of romanticizing and glorifying psychotic states or, even worse, overlooking a serious medical problem.

Many mental health professionals who encounter the concept of spiritual emergency want to know the exact criteria by which one can make the "differential diagnosis" between spiritual emergency and psychosis. Unfortunately, it is impossible in principle to make such a differentiation according to the standards used in somatic medicine. Unlike diseases treated by somatic medicine, psychotic states that are not clearly organic in nature, "functional psychoses," are not medically defined. It is actually highly questionable whether they should be called diseases at all.

Functional psychoses are certainly not diseases in the same sense as diabetes, typhoid fever, or pernicious anemia. They do not yield any specific clinical or laboratory findings that would support the diagnosis and justify the assumption that they are of biological origin. The diagnosis of these states is based entirely on the observation of unusual experiences and behaviors for which contemporary psychiatry, with its painfully superficial model of the human psyche, lacks adequate explanation. Anybody acquainted with the labeling practices in medicine knows that the meaningless attributes "endogenous" or "functional" used for these conditions are tantamount to admission of this ignorance. At present, there is no reason to refer to these conditions as "mental diseases" and to assume that the experiences involved are products of a pathological process in the brain that have yet to be discovered.

If we give it some thought, we realize it is highly unlikely that a pathological process afflicting the brain could, in and of itself, generate the incredibly rich experiential spectrum of the states currently diagnosed as psychotic. How could abnormal processes in the brain possibly generate such experiences as culturally specific sequences of psychospiritual death and rebirth, convincing identification with Jesus on the cross or with the dancing Shiva, an episode involving death on the barricades in Paris during the French revolution, or complex scenes of alien abduction?

Chemical changes can catalyze such experiences, but cannot, in and of themselves, create the intricate imagery and the rich philosophical and spiritual insights that spiritual emergencies often provide. And they certainly could not mediate access to accurate new information about various aspects of the universe. This becomes obvious when we look at the effects of psychoactive substances with known chemical structures and the doses in which they are used. The administration of LSD and other psychedelics and entheogens can account for the emergence of deep unconscious material into consciousness, but cannot explain its nature and contents.

To understand the phenomenology of psychedelic experiences requires a much more sophisticated approach than a simple reference to abnormal biochemical or biological processes in the body. This requires a comprehensive approach that has to include transpersonal psychology, parapsychology, mythology, philosophy, and comparative religion. The same is true in regard to psychospiritual crises.

The experiences that manifest in spiritual emergencies are clearly not artificial products of aberrant pathophysiological processes in the brain, but belong to the psyche. Naturally, to be able to see it this way, we have to transcend the narrow understanding of the psyche that is offered by mainstream psychiatry and use a vastly expanded conceptual framework. Examples of such enlarged models of the psyche are the cartography described earlier in this book, Roberto Assagioli's psychosynthesis (Assagioli 1976), Ken Wilber's spectrum psychology (Wilber 1977), and C. G. Jung's concept of the psyche as *anima mundi,* or the world soul, which includes the historical and archetypal collective unconscious (Jung 1959). Such a large and comprehensive understanding of the psyche is also characteristic of the great Eastern philosophies and the mystical traditions of the world.

Since functional psychoses are not defined medically but psychologically, it is impossible to provide a rigorous differential diagnosis between spiritual emergency and psychosis the same way it is done in medical practice, as with different forms of encephalitis, brain tumors, or dementias.

Considering this fact, is it possible to make any diagnostic conclusions at all? How can we approach this problem and what can we offer in lieu of a clear and unambiguous differential diagnosis between spiritual emergency and psychiatric disease?

A viable alternative is to define the criteria that would make it possible to determine which individual, experiencing an intense spontaneous holotropic state of consciousness, is likely to be a good candidate for a therapeutic strategy that validates and supports the process. We can also attempt to determine under what circumstances using an alternative approach would not be appropriate, and when the current practice of routine psychopharmacological suppression of symptoms would be preferable.

A necessary prerequisite for such an evaluation is a good medical examination that eliminates the possibility of conditions which are organic in nature and require biological treatment. Once this is accomplished, the next important guideline is the phenomenology of the non-ordinary state of consciousness in question. Spiritual emergencies involve a combination of biographical, perinatal, and transpersonal experiences, which were described earlier. Experiences of this kind can be elicited in a group of randomly selected "normal" people not only by psychedelic substances, but also by such simple means as meditation, shamanic drumming, faster breathing, evocative music, bodywork, and a variety of other non-drug techniques.

Those of us who work with Holotropic Breathwork see such experiences daily in our workshops and seminars and have the opportunity to appreciate their healing and transformative potential. In view of this, it is difficult to attribute similar experiences to some exotic and yet unknown pathology when they occur spontaneously in the middle of everyday life. It makes eminent sense to approach these experiences in the same way that they are approached in holotropic sessions—to encourage people to surrender to the process and to support the emergence and full expression of the unconscious material that becomes available.

Another important prognostic indicator is the person's attitude to the process and his or her experiential style. It is generally very encouraging when people who have holotropic experiences recognize that what is happening to them is an inner process, are open to experiential work, and interested to try it. Transpersonal strategies are not appropriate for individuals who lack this elementary insight, predominantly use the mechanism of projection, or suffer from persecutory delusions. The capacity to form a good working relationship with an adequate amount of trust is an absolutely essential prerequisite for psychotherapeutic work with people in crisis.

It is also very important to pay attention to the way clients talk about their experiences. The communication style often distinguishes, in and of itself, promising candidates from inappropriate or questionable ones. It is a very good prognostic indicator when the person describes the experiences in a coherent and articulate way, however extraordinary and strange their content might be. In a sense, this would be similar to hearing an account of a person who has just had a high dose psychedelic session and intelligently describes what might appear to be strange and extravagant experiences to an uninformed person.

The following two cases illustrate the attitude, both toward the inner process and in the communication style, which would make a client either a good or problematic candidate for treatment of a spiritual emergency.

The first client comes to a psychiatrist with these complaints: "Since the delivery of my daughter about two weeks ago, I have been having strange experiences. Powerful streams of energy that feel like electric discharges are running up my spine and making my body shake in a way that is difficult to control. I experience waves of strong emotions—anxiety, sadness, anger, or joy—that come unexpectedly and for no reason. Sometimes I see lights that take the shape of deities or demons. I don't believe in reincarnation, but sometimes I see flashes of what seem to be memories from other times and countries that I seem to recognize as if I had lived there before. What is happening to me? Am I going crazy?" This person is clearly bewildered and confused by strange experiences, but sees this situation as an internal process and is willing to accept advice and help. This would qualify this situation as a spiritual emergency and promise a good therapeutic outcome.

The second client presents a very different picture. He is not describing his symptoms and asking for psychiatric advice. He tells, instead, a story about his enemies: "My neighbor is out to get me; he is trying to destroy me. He pumps toxic gases into my bedroom and gets into my house at night through a tunnel in the cellar and poisons the food in my refrigerator. I have no privacy in my own home; he's placed bugging devices and hidden microcameras everywhere. All the information goes to the Mafia. My neighbor is on their payroll; they are paying him large amounts of money to get rid of me, because I have such high moral principles that it is getting in the way of their plans. And the money for this whole thing is coming from the Middle East, mostly petrodollars." This client clearly lacks the fundamental insight that this situation has anything to do with his own psyche. It is unlikely that he would agree to a joint journey of self-exploration and healing and form a good therapeutic relationship.

Varieties of Spiritual Emergency

The issue of classifying psychospiritual crises is closely related to the problem of their differential diagnosis. Is it possible to distinguish and define certain specific types or categories among them in the way that the Diagnostic and Statistical Manual of Mental Disorders (DSM V-revised), used by traditional psychiatrists, does? Before we address this question, it is necessary to emphasize that the attempts to classify psychiatric disorders, with the exception of those that are clearly organic in nature, have been painfully unsuccessful.

There is no general agreement about diagnostic categories among American psychiatrists or psychiatric societies in other countries. Although the DSM has been revised and changed a number of times—usually after heated debates and with much dissent—clinicians keep complaining that they have difficulties matching the symptoms of their clients with the official diagnostic categories. It has become clear that the attempts to create a satisfactory and useful DSM have failed; the American National Institute of Mental Health (NIMH) currently rejects any research projects using this instrument.

Spiritual emergencies present a similar problem; if anything, assigning people in psychospiritual crises to well-defined diagnostic pigeonholes is particularly problematic because of the fact that their phenomenology is unusually rich and can draw on all the levels of the psyche. The symptoms of psychospiritual crises represent a manifestation and exteriorization of the deep dynamics of the psyche. The individual human psyche is a multidimensional and multilevel system with no internal partitions and boundaries. Memories from postnatal life and contents of the Freudian individual unconscious form a seamless continuum with perinatal and transpersonal experiences. We cannot, therefore, expect to find clearly defined and demarcated types of spiritual emergency.

However, our work with individuals in psychospiritual crises, exchanges with colleagues doing similar work, and a study of literature have convinced us that it is possible and useful to outline certain major forms of psychospiritual crises which have sufficiently characteristic features to be differentiated from each other. Naturally, their boundaries are not clear and, in practice, we will see some significant overlaps. The following list includes the most important varieties of psychospiritual crises that we have observed:

1. *Shamanic initiatory crisis*
2. *Awakening of Kundalini*
3. *Episodes of unitive consciousness (Maslow's "peak experiences")*
4. *Psychological renewal through return to the center (John Weir Perry)*
5. *Crisis of psychic opening*
6. *Past life experiences*
7. *Communication with spirit guides and "channeling"*
8. *Near-death experiences (NDEs)*
9. *Close encounters with UFOs and alien abduction experiences*
10. *Possession states*
11. *Alcoholism and drug addiction*

Shamanic Initiatory Crisis

The career of many shamans—witch doctors or medicine men and women in different cultures—begins with a dramatic involuntary visionary state that anthropologists call "shamanic illness." During such episodes, future shamans usually withdraw psychologically or even physically from their everyday environment and have powerful holotropic experiences. They typically undergo a visionary journey into the underworld, the realm of the dead, where they are attacked by demons and exposed to horrendous tortures and ordeals.

This painful initiation culminates in experiences of death and dismemberment, followed by rebirth and ascent to celestial regions. This might involve transformation into a bird, such as an eagle, falcon, thunderbird, or condor, and a flight to the realm of the cosmic sun. The novice shaman can also have the experience of being carried by these birds to the solar realm. In some cultures, the motif of magic flight is replaced by reaching the celestial region by climbing the world tree, a rainbow, a pole with many notches, or a ladder made of bows and arrows.

In the course of these arduous visionary journeys, novice shamans develop deep connections with the forces of nature and with animals, both in their natural form and their archetypal versions—"animal spirits" or "power animals." When these visionary journeys are successfully completed, they can be profoundly healing. In the process, novice shamans often free themselves from emotional, psychosomatic, and sometimes even physical diseases. For this reason, anthropologists refer to shamans as "wounded healers."

In many instances, the involuntary initiates attain deep insights into the energetic and metaphysical causes of diseases and learn how to heal themselves, as well as others. Following the successful completion of the initiatory crisis, the individual becomes a shaman and returns to his or her people as a fully functioning and honored member of the community. He or she assumes the combined role of a healer, priest, and visionary artist.

In our workshops and professional training, modern Americans, Europeans, Australians, and Asians have often experienced episodes that bore a close resemblance to shamanic crises during their Holotropic Breathwork sessions. Besides the elements of physical and emotional torture, death, and rebirth, such states involved experiences of connection with animals, plants, and elemental forces of nature. The individuals experiencing such crises also often showed spontaneous tendencies to invent chants and rituals that were similar to those created by shamans of various cultures. On occasion, mental health professionals with this experience have been able to use the lessons from their journeys and create modern versions of shamanic procedures.

The attitude of native cultures toward shamanic crises has often been explained by the lack of elementary psychiatric knowledge and the resulting tendency to attribute every experience and behavior that these people do not understand to supernatural forces. However, nothing could be farther from the truth. Cultures that recognize shamans and show them great respect have no difficulty in differentiating them from individuals who are crazy or sick.

To be considered a shaman, the individual has to successfully complete the transformational journey and ground and integrate the episodes of challenging holotropic states of consciousness. He or she has to be able to function at least as well as other members of the tribe. The way shamanic crises are approached and treated in these societies is an extremely useful and illustrative model of dealing with psychospiritual crises in general.

The Awakening of Kundalini

The manifestations of this form of psychospiritual crisis resemble the descriptions of the awakening of *Kundalini,* or the *Serpent Power,* found in ancient Indian literature. According to the yogis, Kundalini is the generative cosmic energy, feminine in nature, which is responsible for the creation of the cosmos. In its latent form, it resides at the base of the human spine in the subtle or energetic body, which is a field that permeates, as well as surrounds, the physical body. This latent energy can become activated by meditation, by the intervention of an accomplished spiritual teacher *(guru),* by specific exercises, childbirth, or for unknown reasons.

The activated Kundalini, called *shakti,* rises through the *nadis,* energy channels or conduits in the subtle body. As it ascends, it clears old traumatic imprints and opens the centers of psychic energy, called *chakras;* these are located at the crossings of the three main nadis—*sushumna, ida*, and *pingala.* This process, although highly valued and considered benevolent in the yogic tradition, is not without dangers and requires expert guidance by a guru whose Kundalini is fully awakened and stabilized. The most dramatic signs of Kundalini awakening are physical and psychological manifestations called *kriyas.*

The kriyas are intense sensations of energy and heat streaming up the spine, which are associated with violent shaking, spasms, and twisting movements. Powerful waves of seemingly unmotivated emotions, such as anxiety, anger, sadness, or joy and ecstatic rapture, can surface and temporarily dominate the psyche. This can be accompanied by visions of brilliant light or various archetypal beings and a variety of internally perceived sounds. Many people involved in this process also have powerful experiences with what seem to be memories from past lives. Involuntary and often uncontrollable behaviors complete the picture: speaking in tongues, chanting unknown songs or sacred invocations *(mantras),* assuming yogic postures *(asanas)* and gestures *(mudras),* and making a variety of animal sounds and movements.

C. G. Jung and his colleagues dedicated a series of special seminars to this phenomenon (Jung 1996). Jung's perspective on Kundalini proved to be probably the most remarkable error of his entire career. He concluded that the awakening of Kundalini was an exclusively Eastern phenomenon and predicted that, as a result of depth psychology, it would take at least one thousand years before this energy would be set into motion in the

Lee Sannella, M.D. (1916–2003), author, psychiatrist, ophthalmologist and eye surgeon. Sannella brought to the attention of Western professional circles the phenomenon of awakening the Kundalini (Serpent Power), previously known only from Indian yogic literature.

West. In the last several decades, however, unmistakable signs of Kundalini awakening have been observed in thousands of Westerners. The credit for drawing attention to this phenomenon belongs to California psychiatrist and ophthalmologist Lee Sannella, who single-handedly studied hundreds of these cases and summarized his findings in his book *The Kundalini Experience: Psychosis or Transcendence* (Sannella 1987).

Episodes of Unitive Consciousness ("Peak Experiences")

American psychologist Abraham Maslow studied hundreds of people who had had unitive mystical experiences, and coined the term *peak experiences* for them (Maslow 1964). He expressed sharp criticism of Western psychiatry's tendency to confuse such mystical states with mental diseases. According to him, they should be considered supernormal, rather than abnormal, phenomena. If they are not interfered with and are allowed to run their natural course, these states typically lead to better functioning in the world and to "self-actualization" or "self-realization"—the capacity to express one's creative potential more fully and to live a more rewarding and satisfying life.

Psychiatrist and consciousness researcher Walter Pahnke developed a list of basic characteristics of a typical peak experience, based on the work of Abraham Maslow and W. T. Stace. He used the following criteria to describe this state of mind (Pahnke and Richards 1966):

Unity (inner and outer)
Strong positive emotion
Transcendence of time and space
Sense of sacredness (numinosity)
Paradoxical nature
Objectivity and reality of the insights
Ineffability
Positive aftereffects

As this list indicates, when we have a peak experience, we have a sense of overcoming the usual fragmentation of the mind and body, and feel that we have reached a state of unity and wholeness. We also transcend the ordinary distinction between subject and object, and experience ecstatic union with humanity, nature, the cosmos, and God. This is associated with intense feelings of joy, bliss, serenity, and inner peace. In a mystical experience of this type, we have a sense of leaving ordinary reality, where space has three dimensions and time is linear. We enter a metaphysical, transcendent realm, where these categories no longer apply. In this state, infinity and eternity become experiential realities. The numinous quality of this state has nothing to do with previous religious beliefs; it reflects a direct apprehension of the divine nature of reality.

Descriptions of peak experiences are usually full of paradoxes. The experience can be described as "contentless, yet all-containing;" it has no specific content, but seems to contain everything in a potential form. We can have a sense of being simultaneously everything and nothing. While our personal identity and the limited ego have disappeared, we feel that we have expanded to such an extent that our being encompasses the entire universe. Similarly, it is possible to perceive all forms as empty, or emptiness as being pregnant with forms. We can even reach a state in which we see that the world exists and does not exist at the same time.

The peak experience can convey what seems to be ultimate wisdom and knowledge in matters of cosmic relevance, which the Upanishads describe as "knowing That, the knowledge of which gives the knowledge of everything." This revelation does not involve knowledge of various aspects of

Abraham Maslow, Ph.D. (1908–1970), American psychologist, best known for creating Maslow's hierarchy of needs, researching spontaneous mystical experiences ("peak experiences"), and cofounding humanistic and transpersonal psychology.

the world as studied by materialistic science, but the deepest nature of reality, as well as our own nature. In Buddhism, a similar type of knowledge is called transcendental wisdom *(prajñāpāramitā);* it dispels our ignorance about the most fundamental aspects of existence *(avidyā).*

What we have learned during this experience is ineffable; it cannot be described by words. The vocabulary of our language, which is designed to communicate about objects and events in the material world, seems to be inadequate for this purpose. Yet, the experience can profoundly influence our system of values and strategy of existence. People familiar with Eastern spiritual philosophies often resort to specific terminology developed in countries with many centuries of experience in the exploration of holotropic states of consciousness—India, Tibet, China, and Japan.

Due to the generally benign nature, great healing, and transformative potential of the peak experiences, this is a category of spiritual emergency that should be least problematic. Peak experiences are by their nature transient and self-limited; there is absolutely no reason why they should be seen and treated as manifestations of mental disease. And yet, due to the ignorance of our culture and misconceptions of the psychiatric profession concerning spiritual matters, many people who experience them receive pathological labels, end up hospitalized, and their process is truncated by suppressive medication.

Psychological Renewal Through Return to the Center

Another important type of transpersonal crisis was described by California psychiatrist and Jungian analyst John Weir Perry, who called it the "renewal process" (Perry 1974, 1976, 1998). Due to its depth and intensity, this is the type of psychospiritual crisis that is most likely diagnosed as a serious mental disease. The experiences of people involved in the renewal process are so strange, extravagant, and far from everyday reality, that it seems obvious that some serious pathological process must be affecting the functioning of their brains. But, as we will see, it is this type of psychospiritual crisis that provides the most convincing evidence against the proposition that holotropic states are products of a pathological process afflicting the brain.

Individuals involved in this kind of crisis experience their psyche as a colossal battlefield where a cosmic fight is being played out between the forces of Good and Evil, or forces of Light and Darkness. They are preoccupied with the theme of death—ritual killing, sacrifice, martyrdom, and afterlife. The problem of opposites fascinates them, particularly issues related to the differences between sexes. They experience themselves as the center of fantastic events that have cosmic relevance and are important for the future of the world. Their visionary states tend to take them farther and farther back—through their own history and the history of humanity, all the way to the creation of the world and the original ideal state of paradise. In this process, they seem to strive for perfection, trying to correct things that went wrong in the past.

After a period of turmoil and confusion, the experiences become more and more pleasant and start moving toward a resolution. The process often culminates in the experience of *hieros gamos,* or "sacred marriage," in which the individual is elevated to an illustrious or even divine status and experiences union with an equally distinguished partner. This indicates that the masculine and feminine aspects of the personality are reaching a new balance. The sacred union can be experienced either with an imaginary archetypal figure, or is projected onto an idealized person from one's life, who then appears to be a karmic partner or a soulmate.

At this time, one can also have experiences portraying what Jungian psychology interprets as symbols representing the Self, the transpersonal

John Weir Perry, M.D. (1914–1988) was a Jungian psychiatrist, pioneer in alternative understanding of psychosis, and founder of two experimental residential facilities: Diabasis, in San Francisco; and Chrysalis in San Diego, California.

center that reflects our deepest and true nature. It is related to, but not totally identical with, the Hindu concept of Atman-Brahman, the Divine Within. In visionary states, it can appear in the form of a source of light of supernatural beauty, radiant spheres, precious stones, exquisite jewels, pearls, and other similar symbolic representations. Examples of this development from painful and challenging experiences to the discovery of one's divinity can be found in John Perry's books (Perry 1953, 1974, 1976, 1998) and in *The Stormy Search for the Self,* our book on spiritual emergencies (Grof and Grof 1990).

At this stage of the process, these glorious experiences are interpreted as a personal apotheosis, a ritual celebration that raises one's experience of oneself to a highly exalted human status or to a state above the human condition altogether: a great leader, a world savior, or even the Lord of the Universe. This is often associated with a profound sense of spiritual rebirth that replaces the earlier preoccupation with death. As the process approaches completion and integration, it usually brings visions of an ideal future—a new world governed by love and justice, where all ills and evils have been overcome. As the intensity of the process subsides, the person realizes that the entire drama was an inner psychological transformation and did not involve external reality.

According to John Perry, the renewal process moves the individual in the direction of what Jung called "individuation"—a full realization and expression of one's deep potential. One aspect of Perry's research deserves special notice, since it produced what is probably the most convincing evidence against a simplistic biological understanding of psychoses. Perry was able to show that the experiences involved in the renewal process exactly match the main themes of royal dramas that were enacted in many ancient cultures on New Year's Day.

In all these cultures, such ritual dramas celebrating the advent of the New Year were performed during what Perry called "the archaic era of incarnated myth." This was the period in the history of these cultures when the rulers were considered to be incarnated gods and not ordinary human beings. Examples of such god-kings were the Egyptian pharaohs, the Peruvian Incas, the Hebrew and Hittite kings, and the Chinese and Japanese emperors (Perry 1966). The positive potential of the renewal process and its deep connection with archetypal symbolism, evolution of consciousness, and specific periods of human history represents a very compelling argument against the theory that these experiences are chaotic pathological products of diseased brains.

The Crisis of Psychic Opening

An increase of intuitive abilities and the occurrence of psychic or paranormal phenomena are very common during spiritual emergencies of all kinds. However, in some instances, the influx of information from nonordinary sources, such as precognition, telepathy, or clairvoyance, becomes so overwhelming and confusing that it dominates the picture and constitutes a major problem in and of itself.

Among the most dramatic manifestations of psychic opening are out-of-body experiences. In the middle of everyday life, and often without any noticeable trigger, one's consciousness seems to detach from the body and witness what is happening in the surroundings or in various remote locations. The information obtained during these episodes by extrasensory perception often corresponds to actual reality and can be verified. Out-of-body experiences occur with extraordinary frequency in near-death situations, where the accuracy of this "remote viewing" has been established by systematic studies (Ring 1982, 1985, Ring and Valarino 1998).

People experiencing intense psychic openings might be so much in touch with the inner processes of others that they exhibit remarkable telepathic abilities. They might verbalize accurate incisive insights into other people's minds concerning various issues that these individuals are trying to hide. This can frighten, irritate, and alienate others so severely that it often becomes a significant factor contributing to unnecessary hospitalization or drastic treatment procedures. Similarly, the accurate precognition of future situations and clairvoyant perception, particularly occurring repeatedly in impressive clusters, can seriously disturb the person in crisis, as well as those around them, since it undermines their notion of reality.

In experiences that can be called "mediumistic," one has a sense of losing one's own identity and taking on the identity of another person. This can involve assuming the other person's body image, posture, gestures, facial expression, feelings, and even thought processes. Accomplished shamans, psychics, and spiritual healers can use such experiences in a controlled and productive way. Unlike the persons in spiritual emergency, they are capable of taking on the identity of others at will and then resuming their own separate identity after they accomplish the task of the session. During the crises of psychic opening, the sudden, unpredictable, and uncontrollable loss of one's ordinary identity can be very frightening.

People in spiritual crisis often experience uncanny coincidences that link the world of inner realities, such as dreams and visionary states, to happenings in everyday life. This phenomenon was first recognized and described by C. G. Jung, who gave it the name *synchronicity* and explored it in a special essay (Jung 1960). The study of synchronistic events helped Jung realize that archetypes were not principles limited to the intrapsychic domain. It became clear to him that they have what he called a "psychoid" quality, which means they govern not only the psyche, but also happenings in the world of consensus reality. I have explored this fascinating topic in my other writings (Grof 2000, 2006) and will return to it in a later chapter of this work.

Jungian synchronicities represent authentic phenomena and cannot be ignored and discounted as accidental coincidences. They also should not be indiscriminately dismissed as pathological distortions of reality, the perception of meaningful relations where, in actuality, there are none. This is a common practice in contemporary psychiatry where any allusion to meaningful coincidences is automatically diagnosed as a "delusion of reference." In the case of true synchronicities, any open-minded witnesses who have access to all the relevant information recognize that the coincidences involved are beyond any reasonable statistical probability. Extraordinary synchronicities accompany many forms of spiritual emergency, but in crises of psychic opening, they are particularly common.

Past Life Experiences

Among the most dramatic and colorful transpersonal experiences occurring in holotropic states are what appear to be memories from previous incarnations. These are sequences that take place in other historical periods and in other countries, and are usually associated with powerful emotions and physical sensations. They often portray the people, circumstances, and historical settings involved in great detail. Their most remarkable aspect is a convincing sense of remembering and reliving something that one has already seen *(déjà vu)* or experienced *(déjà vecu)* at some time in the past. These experiences provide fascinating insights into the belief in karma and reincarnation, which has been independently developed and held by many religious and cultural groups in different parts of the world.

The concept of karma and reincarnation represents the cornerstone of Hinduism, Buddhism, Jainism, Sikhism, Zoroastrianism, the Tibetan Vajrayana Buddhism, and Taoism. Similar ideas occurred in such geographically, historically, and culturally diverse groups as various African tribes, native Americans, pre-Columbian cultures, the Hawaiian kahunas, practitioners of the Brazilian umbanda, the Gauls, and the Druids. In ancient Greece, several major schools of thought subscribed to this concept, including the Pythagoreans, the Orphics, and the Platonists. The Essenes, the Pharisees, the Karaites, and other Jewish and semi-Jewish groups also adopted the concept of karma and reincarnation, and it formed an important part of the kabbalistic theology of medieval Judaism. Other groups also adhered to this belief, including the Neo-Platonists and Gnostics.

The rich and accurate information that these "past-life memories" provide, as well as their healing potential, impels us to take them seriously. When the content of a karmic experience fully emerges into consciousness, it can suddenly provide an explanation for many otherwise incomprehensible aspects of one's daily life. Strange difficulties in relationships with certain people, unsubstantiated fears, and peculiar idiosyncrasies and attractions, as well as otherwise baffling emotional and psychosomatic symptoms, suddenly seem to make sense as karmic carryovers from a previous lifetime. These problems typically disappear when the karmic pattern in question is fully and consciously experienced.

Past-life experiences can complicate life in several different ways. Before their content emerges fully into consciousness and reveals itself, one can be haunted in everyday life by strange emotions, physical sensations, and visions without knowing where they come from or what they mean. Experienced out of context, these experiences naturally appear incomprehensible and irrational. Another kind of complication occurs when a particularly strong karmic experience starts emerging into consciousness in the middle of everyday activities and interferes with normal functioning.

One might also feel compelled to act out some of the elements of a karmic pattern before it is fully experienced and understood or completed. For instance, it might suddenly seem that a certain person in one's present life played an important role in a previous incarnation, the memory of which is emerging into consciousness. When this happens, one may seek emotional contact with a person who now appears to be a "soulmate" from one's karmic past or, conversely, seek a confrontation with an adversary from another lifetime. This kind of activity can lead to unpleasant complications, since the alleged karmic partners usually have no basis in their own experiences for understanding this behavior.

Even if one manages to avoid the danger of acting out, the problems are not necessarily over. After a past-life memory has fully emerged into consciousness and its content and implications have been revealed to the person, there remains one more challenge. One has to reconcile this experience with the traditional beliefs and values of the Western civilization. Denial of the possibility of reincarnation represents a rare instance of complete agreement between the Christian Church and materialistic science. Therefore, in Western culture, acceptance and intellectual integration of a past-life memory is a difficult task for either an atheist or a traditionally raised Christian.

Assimilation of past-life experiences into one's belief system can be a relatively easy task for someone who does not have a strong commitment to Christianity or to the materialistic worldview. The experiences are usually so convincing that one simply accepts their message and might even feel excited about this new discovery. However, fundamentalist Christians and those who have a strong investment in rationality and the traditional scientific perspective can be catapulted into a period of confusion when they are confronted with convincing personal experiences that seem to challenge their belief system.

Communication with Spirit Guides and "Channeling"

Occasionally, in a holotropic experience, one can encounter a being who assumes the position of a teacher, guide, protector, or simply a relevant source of information. Such beings are usually perceived as discarnate humans, superhuman entities, or deities existing on higher planes of consciousness and endowed with extraordinary wisdom. Occasionally, they introduce themselves as extraterrestrials from distant stars, such as Sirius or the Pleiades. Sometimes they take on the form of a person; at other times, they appear as radiant sources of light, or simply let their presence be sensed. Their messages are usually received in the form of direct thought transfer or through other extrasensory means. In some instances, communication can take the form of verbal messages.

A particularly interesting phenomenon in this category is *channeling*, which has received much attention from the public and mass media in recent decades. A "channeling" person transmits messages to other people, which were received from a source that appears to be external to his or her consciousness. It occurs through speaking in a trance, using automatic writing, or recording telepathically received thoughts. Channeling has played an important role in the history of humanity. Among the channeled spiritual teachings are many scriptures of enormous cultural influence, such as the ancient Indian Vedas, the Qur'an, and the Book of Mormon. A remarkable modern example of a channeled text is *A Course in Miracles,* recorded by psychologist Helen Schucman and William Thetford

Helen Schucman, Ph.D. (1909–1981), clinical and research psychologist at Columbia University in New York City, who channeled the book *A Course in Miracles.*

(Anonymous 1975).

Experiences of channeling can precipitate a serious psychological and spiritual crisis. One possibility is that the individual involved can interpret the experience as an indication of beginning insanity. This is particularly likely if the channeling involves hearing voices, a well-known symptom of paranoid schizophrenia. The quality of the channeled material varies from trivial and questionable chatter to extraordinary information. On occasion, channeling can provide consistently accurate data about subjects to which the recipient was never exposed. This can then appear to be a particularly convincing proof of the involvement of supernatural influences, and can lead to serious philosophical confusion for an atheistic person or a scientist with a materialistic worldview.

Spirit guides are usually perceived as advanced spiritual beings on a high level of consciousness evolution, who are endowed with superior intelligence and extraordinary moral integrity. This can lead to highly problematic ego inflation in the channeler, who might feel chosen for a special mission and see it as a proof of his or her own superiority.

Near-Death Experiences (NDEs)

World mythology, folklore, and spiritual literature abound in vivid accounts of the experiences associated with death and dying. Special sacred texts have been dedicated exclusively to descriptions and discussions of the posthumous journey of the soul, such as the *Tibetan Book of the Dead (Bardo Thödol),* the *Egyptian Book of the Dead (Pert em hru),* and their European counterpart, *Ars Moriendi, (The Art of Dying).* Pre-hispanic examples of eschatological texts include the Nahuatl (Aztec) Codex Borgia, describing the death and rebirth of Quetzalcoatl (Plumed Serpent), and the epic story of the death and rebirth of the Hero Twins Hunahpú and Xbalanqué, included in the Mayan Popol Vuh (Grof 1994).

In the past, the eschatological mythology was discounted by Western scholars as a product of fantasy and the wishful thinking of primitive people who were unable to face the fact of impermanence and their own mortality. This situation changed dramatically after the publication of Raymond Moody's international bestseller *Life After Life,* which brought scientific confirmation of these accounts and showed that an encounter with death can be a fantastic adventure in consciousness. Moody's book was based on reports of 150 people who had experienced a close confrontation with death, or were actually pronounced clinically dead, but regained consciousness and lived to tell their stories (Moody 1975).

Moody reported that people who had near-death experiences (NDEs) frequently witnessed a review of their entire lives in the form of a colorful, incredibly condensed replay, which occurred over the course of only a few seconds. Consciousness often detached from the body and floated freely above the scene, observing it with curiosity and detached amusement, or traveled to distant locations. Many people described passing through a dark tunnel or funnel toward a divine light of supernatural brilliance and beauty.

This light was not physical in nature, but had distinctly personal characteristics. It was a Being of Light, radiating infinite, all-embracing love, forgiveness, and acceptance. In a personal exchange, often perceived as an audience with God, these individuals received lessons regarding existence and universal laws and had the opportunity to evaluate their past by these new standards. Then they chose to return to ordinary reality and live their lives in a new way, congruent with the principles they had learned. Since Moody's publication, his findings have been repeatedly confirmed by other researchers.

Most survivors emerge from their near-death experiences profoundly changed. They have a universal and all-encompassing spiritual vision of reality, a new system of values, and a radically different general strategy of life. They have a deep appreciation for being alive and feel kinship with all living beings, as well as a concern for the future of humanity and the planet. However, the fact that the encounter with death has a great positive potential does not mean that this transformation is easy.

Near-death experiences very frequently lead to spiritual emergencies. A powerful NDE can radically undermine the worldview of the people involved, because it catapults them abruptly and without warning into a reality that is diametrically different from their everyday life. A car accident in the middle of rush-hour traffic or a heart attack while jogging can launch someone within a few seconds into a fantastic visionary adventure that tears his or her ordinary reality asunder. Following an NDE, people might need special counseling and support to be able to integrate these extraordinary experiences into their everyday life.

Close Encounters with UFOs and Alien Abduction Experiences

The experience of encountering extraterrestrial spacecrafts and their crews, and of abduction by alien beings, can often precipitate serious emotional and intellectual crises that have much in common with spiritual emergencies. This requires an explanation, since most people consider UFOs in terms of four alternatives: actual visitation by alien spacecraft, hoaxes, the misperception of natural events and devices of terrestrial origin, and psychotic hallucinations. Alvin Lawson made an attempt to explain UFO abduction experiences as misinterpretations of the trauma of birth, using my own concept of Basic Perinatal Matrices (Lawson 1984). His conclusions were not convincing and fell short of doing justice to this complex and intriguing phenomenon.

Descriptions of UFO sightings typically refer to lights that have an uncanny, supernatural quality. These lights resemble those mentioned in many reports of visionary states. C. G. Jung, who dedicated a special study to the problem of "flying saucers," or "things seen in the skies," suggested that these phenomena might be archetypal visions originating in the collective unconscious of humanity, rather than psychotic hallucinations or actual visits by extraterrestrials (Jung 1964). He supported his thesis through careful analysis of stories about flying discs that had been told throughout centuries and of reports about mysterious apparitions that had occasionally caused crises and mass panic.

It has also been pointed out that the extraterrestrial beings involved in these encounters have important parallels in world mythology and religion, systems that have their roots in the collective unconscious. The alien spacecrafts and cosmic flights depicted by those who were allegedly abducted or invited for a ride resemble the descriptions of the chariot of the Vedic god Indra, Ezekiel's flaming machine depicted in the Bible, or the glorious fiery vehicle of the Greek sun god Helios. The fabulous landscapes and cities visited during these journeys resemble the visionary experiences of paradises, celestial realms, and cities of light.

The abductees often report that the aliens had taken them into a laboratory and subjected them to physical examinations and strange experiments using various exotic instruments. This often involved probing the cavities of their bodies, with a special emphasis on the genital organs. The abductees also frequently describe what seem to be genetic experiments aimed at creating hybrid offspring. These interventions are usually very painful and occasionally border on torture. This brings the experiences of the abductees close to the initiatory crises of the shamans and to the ordeals of the neophytes in the aboriginal rites of passage.

There is also another reason why a UFO experience can precipitate a spiritual emergency. It is similar to the problem mentioned earlier in relation to spirit guides and channeling. The alien visitors are often seen as representatives of civilizations that are incomparably more advanced than ours, not only technologically but also intellectually, morally, and spiritually. Such contact often has very powerful mystical undertones and is associated with insights of cosmic relevance. It is thus easy for the recipients of such special attention to interpret it as an indication of their own uniqueness.

Abductees might feel that they have attracted the interest of superior beings from an advanced civilization because they themselves are in some way exceptional and particularly suited for a special purpose. In Jungian psychology, a situation in which the individual claims the luster of the archetypal world for his or her own person is referred to as "ego inflation." For these reasons, experiences of "close encounters" can lead to serious transpersonal crises.

People who have experienced the strange world of UFO encounters and alien abduction need professional help from someone who has a general knowledge of archetypal psychology and who is also familiar with the specific characteristics of the UFO phenomenon. Experienced researchers, such as Harvard psychiatrist John Mack, have brought ample evidence that the alien abduction experiences represent a serious conceptual challenge for Western psychiatry, and materialistic science in general, and that it is naive and indefensible to see them as manifestations of mental disease or discard them altogether. He concluded that these experiences qualify as "anomalous phenomena," observations that seriously challenge our current scientific worldview (Mack 1994, 1999). His experiences with this research inspired him to start the Program for Extraordinary Experience Research (PEER) in 1993.

Over the years, I have worked with many individuals who had experiences of alien abduction in psychedelic sessions, Holotropic Breathwork, and in spiritual emergencies. Almost without exception, these episodes were extremely intense and experientially convincing; on occasion, they also had definite psychoid features. In view of my observations, I am convinced that these experiences represent phenomena *sui generis* and deserve to be seriously studied. The position of mainstream psychiatrists who see them as products of an unknown pathological process in the brain is clearly oversimplistic and highly implausible.

The alternative, considering the UFOs to be actual visits of aliens from other celestial bodies, is equally implausible. An extraterrestrial civilization capable of sending spaceships to our planet would have to have technical means that we can hardly imagine. We have enough information about the planets of the solar system to know that they are unlikely sources of such an expedition. The distance between the solar system and the nearest stars amounts to several light years. Negotiating such distances would require velocities approaching the speed of light or interdimensional travel through hyperspace. A civilization capable of such achievements would very likely have technology that would make it impossible for us to differentiate between hallucinations and reality. Until more reliable information

John Mack, M.D., (1929–2004), psychoanalyst, parapsychologist, Pulitzer Prize-winning author, and leading researcher of alien abduction and UFO phenomena.

is available, it seems most plausible to see the UFO experiences as manifestations of archetypal material from the collective unconscious.

Possession States

People in this type of transpersonal crisis have a distinct feeling that their psyche and body have been invaded and that they are being controlled by an evil entity or energy with personal characteristics. They perceive it as coming from outside their own personality and as being hostile and disturbing. It might appear to be a confused discarnate entity, a demonic archetypal being, or the consciousness of a wicked person invading them by means of black magic and hexing procedures.

There are many different types and degrees of such conditions. In some instances, the true nature of this disorder remains hidden. The problem manifests as serious psychopathology, such as antisocial or even criminal behavior, suicidal depression, murderous aggression or self-destructive behavior, promiscuous and deviant sexual impulses and acting out, or excessive use of alcohol and drugs. It is often not until such a person starts experiential psychotherapy that "possession" is identified as a condition underlying these problems.

In the middle of an experiential session, the face of a possessed person can become cramped and take the form of a "mask of evil," and the eyes can assume a wild expression. The hands and body might develop strange contortions, and the voice may become altered and take on an otherworldly quality. When this situation is allowed to develop, the session can bear a striking resemblance to exorcisms in the Catholic Church, or exorcist rituals in various aboriginal cultures. The resolution often comes after dramatic episodes of choking, projectile vomiting, and frantic physical activity, or even temporary loss of control. If sequences of this kind are properly treated, they can be unusually healing and transformative, and often result in a deep spiritual conversion of the person involved. A detailed description of the most dramatic episode of this kind that I have observed during my entire professional career can be found in my book *When the Impossible Happens* ("Interview with the Devil: The Case of Flora")(Grof 2006).

Other times, the possessed person is aware of the presence of the "evil entity" and spends a lot of effort trying to fight it and control its influence. In the extreme version of the possession state, the problematic energy can spontaneously manifest and take over the person in the middle of everyday life. This situation resembles the one described earlier for experiential sessions, but the individual here lacks the support and protection provided by the therapeutic context. Under such circumstances, he or she can feel extremely frightened and desperately alone. Relatives, friends, and often even therapists tend to withdraw from the "possessed" individual and respond with a strange mixture of metaphysical fear and moral rejection. They often label the person as evil and refuse further contact.

This condition clearly belongs in the category of "spiritual emergency," in spite of the fact that it involves negative energies and is associated with many objectionable forms of behavior. The demonic archetype is by its very nature transpersonal, since it represents the negative mirror image of the divine. It also often appears to be a "gateway phenomenon," comparable to the terrifying guardians flanking the doors of Eastern temples. It hides access to a profound spiritual experience, which often follows after a possession state has been successfully resolved. With the help of somebody who is not afraid of its uncanny nature and is able to encourage its full conscious manifestation, this energy can be dissipated and remarkable healing occurs.

Alcoholism and Drug Addiction as Spiritual Emergency

It makes sense to describe addiction as a form of spiritual emergency, in spite of the fact that it differs in its external manifestations from more obvious types of psychospiritual crises. As with the possession states, the spiritual dimension is obscured by the destructive and self-destructive nature of the disorder. While in other forms of spiritual emergency people encounter problems because of their difficulty in coping with mystical experiences, in addiction, the source of the problem is a strong spiritual longing and the fact that the contact with the mystical dimension has not been made.

There exists ample evidence that behind the craving for drugs or alcohol is the unrecognized craving for transcendence or wholeness. Many recovering people talk about their restless search for some unknown missing element or dimension in their lives and describe their unfulfilling and frustrating pursuit of substances, food, relationships, possessions, or power, which reflects an unrelenting effort to satiate this craving (Grof 1993). We already discussed a certain superficial similarity that exists between mystical states and intoxication by alcohol or hard drugs. Both of these conditions share the sense of dissolution of individual boundaries, the disappearance of disturbing emotions, and the transcendence of mundane problems. Although the intoxication with alcohol or drugs lacks many important characteristics of the mystical state, such as serenity, numinosity, and richness of philosophical insights, the experiential overlap is sufficient to seduce alcoholics and addicts into abuse.

William James wrote about this connection in *Varieties of Religious Experience:* "The sway of alcohol over mankind is unquestionably due to its power to stimulate the mystical faculties of human nature, usually crushed to earth by the cold facts and dry criticisms of the sober hour. Sobriety diminishes, discriminates, and says no; drunkenness expands, unites, and says yes" (James 1961). He also saw the important implications of genuine transcendental experiences for successful therapy.

C. G. Jung's independent insight in this regard was instrumental in the development of the worldwide network of Twelve Step Programs. It is not generally known that Jung played a very important role in the history of Alcoholics Anonymous (AA). The information about this little-known aspect of Jung's work can be found in a letter that Bill Wilson, the co-founder of AA, wrote to Jung in 1961 (Wilson and Jung 1963).

Jung had a patient, Roland H., who came to him after having exhausted other means of recovery from alcoholism. Following a temporary improvement after a year's treatment with Jung, he suffered a relapse. Jung told him that his case was hopeless and suggested that his only chance was to join a religious community and hope for a profound spiritual experience. Roland H. joined the Oxford Group, an evangelical movement emphasizing self-survey, confession, and service. There he experienced a religious conversion that freed him from alcoholism. He then returned to New York City and became very active in the Oxford Group there. He was able to help Bill Wilson's friend, Edwin T., who in turn helped Bill Wilson in his personal crisis. In his powerful spiritual experience, Bill Wilson had a vision of a worldwide fellowship chain of alcoholics helping each other.

Years later, Wilson wrote Jung a letter, in which he brought the important role that Jung played in the history of AA to his attention. Jung understood the basic strategy for treating alcoholism and expressed it in his response to Wilson as "Spiritus contra spiritum": deep spiritual experiences are the antidote to alcoholism. James's and Jung's insights have since been confirmed by clinical research programs using psychedelic therapy with alcoholics and narcotic drug addicts (Pahnke et al. 1970, Grof 2001).

Treatment of Spiritual Emergencies

The psychotherapeutic strategy for individuals undergoing spiritual crises reflects the principles that we have discussed earlier in this book. It is based on the realization that these states are not manifestations of an unknown pathological process, but results of a spontaneous movement in the psyche that has healing and transformative potential. The understanding and appropriate treatment of spiritual emergencies requires a vastly extended model of the psyche that includes the perinatal and transpersonal dimensions.

The nature and degree of the therapeutic assistance that is necessary depends on the intensity of the psychospiritual process involved. In mild forms of spiritual emergency, the person in crisis is usually able to cope with the holotropic experiences in the course of everyday life. All that he or she needs is the opportunity to discuss the process with a transpersonally oriented therapist, who provides constructive feedback and helps the client to integrate the experiences into everyday life.

If the process is more active, it might require regular sessions of experiential therapy to facilitate the emergence of the unconscious material and the full expression of emotions and blocked physical energies. The general strategy of this approach is identical with that used in Holotropic Breathwork sessions. When the experiences are very intense, we just have to encourage the client to surrender to the process. If we encounter strong psychological resistance, we might occasionally use faster breathing and releasing bodywork, like in the termination periods of breathwork sessions. Holotropic Breathwork as such is indicated only if the natural unfolding of the process reaches an impasse.

These intense experiential sessions can be complemented with Gestalt practice, Dora Kalff's Jungian sandplay, or bodywork with a psychologically experienced practitioner. A variety of auxiliary techniques can also prove extremely useful under these circumstances. Among them are writing in a journal, painting mandalas, expressive dancing, and jogging, swimming, or other sport activities. If the client is able to concentrate on reading transpersonally oriented books, particularly those specifically focusing on the problem of psychospiritual crises or some specific aspect of his or her inner experiences, it can be extremely helpful.

People whose experiences are so intense and dramatic that they cannot be handled on an outpatient basis represent a special problem. There are practically no facilities that offer twenty-four-hour supervision without the use of routine, suppressive psychopharmacological intervention. Creating such alternative centers is a necessary prerequisite for the effective therapy of spiritual emergencies in the future.

Several of these kinds of experimental facilities used to exist in California, such as John Perry's Diabasis in San Francisco and Chrysalis in San Diego, or Barbara Findeisen's Pocket Ranch in Geyserville, California, but they were short-lived. Although the cost of these programs was about one-third of traditional psychiatric treatment, these experimental facilities were not financially sustainable. Since the insurance companies refused to pay for alternative forms of therapy, the costs had to be covered by the patients or their relatives. This occasional support was not sufficient or reliable enough to offset the situation.

In some places, helpers have tried to overcome this deficiency by creating teams of trained facilitators who took shifts in the client's home for the duration of the episode. Managing intense acute forms of spiritual emergency requires some extraordinary measures, though, whether it occurs in a special facility or in a private home. Extended episodes of this kind can last for days or weeks and can be associated with a lot of physical activity, intense emotions, loss of appetite, and insomnia. This brings a danger of dehydration, vitamin and mineral deficiency, and exhaustion. An insufficient food supply can lead to hypoglycemia, which is known to weaken psychological defenses and bring additional material from the unconscious. This can lead to a vicious cycle that perpetuates the acute condition. Tea with honey, bananas, or other foods that contain glucose can be of great help in breaking this circle and grounding the process.

A person in intense psychospiritual crisis is usually so deeply involved in his or her experience that they forget about food, drink, and basic hygiene. It is thus up to the helpers to take care of the client's basic needs. Since the care for people undergoing the most acute forms of spiritual emergency is unusually demanding, the helpers have to take shifts to protect their own mental and physical health. To guarantee comprehensive and integrated care under these circumstances, it is necessary to keep a log and carefully record the intake of food, liquids, and vitamins.

Sleep deprivation, like fasting, tends to weaken the defenses and facilitate the influx of unconscious material into consciousness. This can also lead to a vicious cycle that needs to be interrupted. It might, therefore, be necessary to occasionally give the client a minor tranquilizer or a hypnotic to secure sleep. In this context, medication is seen as a purely palliative measure and is not considered therapy, which is the way tranquilizing medication is often presented in mainstream psychiatry. The administration of minor tranquilizers or hypnotics interrupts the vicious cycle and gives the client the rest and energy necessary to continue with the uncovering process the following day.

In later stages of spiritual emergency, when the intensity of the process subsides, the person no longer requires constant supervision. He or she resumes the responsibility of their own basic personal care and gradually returns to everyday activities and duties. The overall duration of the stay in a protected environment depends on the rate of stabilization and integration of the process. If necessary, we might schedule occasional experiential sessions and recommend the use of selected complementary and auxiliary approaches. Regular discussions about the experiences and insights from the time of the episode can be of great help in integrating it.

The treatment of alcoholism and drug addiction presents some specific problems and has to be discussed separately from that of other spiritual emergencies. More specifically, it is the element of physiological addiction and the progressive nature of the disorder that require special measures. Before dealing with the psychological problems underlying addiction, it is imperative to break the chemical cycle that perpetuates the use of substances. The individual has to go through a period of withdrawal and detoxification in a special residential facility.

Once this is accomplished, the focus can turn to the psychospiritual roots of the disorder. As we have seen, alcoholism and drug addiction represent a misguided search for transcendence. For this reason, to be successful, the therapeutic program has to include a strong emphasis on the spiritual dimension of the problem as an integral part. Historically, the programs of Alcoholics Anonymous (AA) and Narcotics Anonymous (NA), fellowships offering a comprehensive approach based on the Twelve Step philosophy outlined by Bill Wilson, have been the most successful in combating addiction.

Following the program step by step, the alcoholic or addict recognizes and admits that they have lost control over their lives and have become powerless. They are encouraged to surrender and let a higher power of their own definition take over. A painful review of their personal history produces an inventory of their wrongdoings. This provides the basis for making amends to all the people whom they have hurt with their addiction. Those who have reached sobriety and are in recovery are then urged to carry the message to other addicts and to help them overcome their own habit.

The Twelve Step Programs are invaluable in providing support and guidance for alcoholics and addicts from the beginning of treatment and throughout the years of sobriety and recovery. Since the focus of this book is the healing potential of holotropic states, we will now explore whether and in what way these states can be useful in the treatment of addiction. This question is closely related to the Eleventh Step, which emphasizes the need "to improve through prayer and meditation our conscious contact with God as we understand God." Since holotropic states can facilitate mystical experiences, they clearly fit into this category.

Over the years, I have had extensive experience with the use of holotropic states in the treatment of alcoholics and addicts, as well as in the work with recovering people who used them to improve the quality of their sobriety. I participated in a team at the Maryland Psychiatric Research Center in Baltimore that conducted large, controlled studies of psychedelic therapy with alcoholics and hard drug addicts (Grof 2001). I have also had the opportunity to witness the effect of serial Holotropic Breathwork sessions on many recovering people in the context of our training.

In my experience, it is highly unlikely that either Holotropic Breathwork or psychedelic therapy can help alcoholics and addicts when they are actively using. Even deep and meaningful experiences do not seem to have the power to break the chemical cycle involved. Therapeutic work with holotropic states should be introduced only after alcoholics and addicts have undergone detoxification, overcome the withdrawal symptoms, and reached sobriety. Only then can they benefit from holotropic experiences and do some deep work on the psychological problems underlying their addiction. At this point, holotropic states can be extremely useful in helping them to confront traumatic memories, process the difficult emotions associated with them, and obtain valuable insights into the psychological roots of their abuse.

Holotropic experiences can mediate the process of psychospiritual death and rebirth that is known as "hitting bottom," and is a critical turning point in the life of many alcoholics and addicts. The experience of ego death happens in a protected situation where it does not have the dangerous physical, interpersonal, and social consequences that it would have if it happened spontaneously in the client's natural surroundings, especially with the risk of confusion between "egocide" and suicide. Holotropic states can also mediate experiential access to profound spiritual experiences, the true object of the alcoholic's or addict's craving, and thus make it less likely that they will seek unfortunate surrogates in alcohol or narcotics.

The programs of psychedelic therapy for alcoholics and addicts conducted at the Maryland Psychiatric Research Center were very successful, in spite of the fact that the protocol limited the number of psychedelic sessions to a maximum of three. At a six-month follow-up, more than fifty percent of chronic alcoholics and one-third of narcotic drug addicts participating in these programs were still sober and were considered "essentially rehabilitated" by an independent evaluation team (Pahnke et al. 1970, Savage and McCabe 1971, Grof 2001). Recovering people in our training and workshops, almost without exception, see Holotropic Breathwork as a way of improving the quality of their sobriety and facilitating their psychospiritual growth.

In spite of the evidence of their beneficial effects, the use of holotropic states in recovering people found strong opposition among some conservative members of the Twelve Step movement. These people assert that alcoholics and addicts seeking any form of a "high" are experiencing a "relapse." They pass this judgment not only when the holotropic state involves the use of psychedelic substances, but also extend it to experiential forms of psychotherapy and even to meditation, an approach explicitly recommended in the original description of the Eleventh Step.

It is likely that this extremist attitude goes back to Bill Wilson, the co-founder of AA, and his experiences with LSD (Lattin 2012). After twenty years of sobriety, Bill Wilson became interested in LSD and had a series of sessions with Aldous Huxley and Gerald Heard under the supervision of Los Angeles psychedelic pioneers Sidney Cohen and Betty Eisner. Bill Wilson became very enthusiastic about the effects of this substance; he felt that the sessions helped him significantly with his chronic depression and opened him up to a spiritual perception of the world. As he approached his 70th birthday, he developed a plan to have LSD distributed at all AA meetings nationwide.

Bill Wilson's use of LSD and his proposal caused considerable controversy within AA. Many of his close associates, including Dr. Jack Norris, then Chairman of the AA Board of Trustees, were very concerned about his use of psychedelics and his controversial idea for the future of AA. The plan was eventually quashed by more rational voices and Bill Wilson was asked to discontinue his experiments with LSD. In 1958, he defended his drug use in a long letter, but soon afterwards, he removed himself from the AA governing body to be free to do his experiments.

We are confronted with two conflicting perspectives on the relationship between holotropic states of consciousness and addiction. One of them sees any effort to depart from the ordinary state of consciousness to be unacceptable for an addicted person and qualifies as a relapse. This attitude demands sobriety at any cost, even if it means "white-knuckling it." The AA members who represent this attitude do not seem to see any problem in the enormous amount of coffee that is typically served and consumed in the AA meetings and the number of cigarettes that are usually smoked there. The opposing view is based on the idea that seeking a spiritual state is a legitimate and natural tendency of human nature, and that striving for transcendence is the most powerful motivating force in the psyche (Weil 1972). Addiction is then seen as a misguided and distorted form of this effort and the most effective remedy for it is facilitating access to a genuine spiritual experience.

The future will decide which of these two approaches will be adopted by professionals and by the recovering community. In my opinion, the most promising development in the treatment of alcoholism and drug abuse would be a marriage of the Twelve Step Programs, the most effective method for treating alcoholism and addiction, with transpersonal psychology, which can provide a solid theoretical basis for spiritually grounded therapy. Responsible work with holotropic states of consciousness would be a very logical and integral part of such a comprehensive approach.

In the 1990s, my wife Christina and I organized two conferences of the International Transpersonal Association (ITA) in Eugene, Oregon, and in Atlanta, Georgia, called Mystical Quest, Attachment, and Addiction. These meetings demonstrated the feasibility and usefulness of bringing together the Twelve Step Programs and transpersonal psychology. The empirical and theoretical justification for such merging was discussed in several publications (Grof 1987, Grof 1993).

The concept of "spiritual emergency" is new, though, and will undoubt-

R. D. Laing, M.D. (1927–1989), Scottish psychiatrist, pioneer of alternative understanding and treatment of psychoses, with his wife Jutta.

edly be complemented and refined in the future. However, we have repeatedly seen that even in its present form, as defined by Christina and myself, it has been of great help to many individuals in crises of transformation. We have observed that when these conditions are treated with respect and receive appropriate support, they can result in remarkable healing, deep positive transformation, and a higher level of functioning in everyday life. This has often happened in spite of the fact that, in the present situation, the conditions for treating people in psychospiritual crises are far from ideal.

In the future, the success of this endeavor could increase considerably, if people capable of assisting individuals in spiritual emergencies could have a network of twenty-four-hour centers for those whose experiences are so intense that they cannot be treated on an outpatient basis. At present, the absence of such facilities and lack of support from the insurance companies for unconventional approaches represent the most serious obstacles in the effective application of the new therapeutic strategies.

Literature

Anonymous. 1975. *A Course in Miracles.* New York: Foundation for Inner Peace.

Assagioli, R. 1976. *Psychosynthesis.* New York: Penguin Books.

Grof, C. 1993. *The Thirst For Wholeness: Attachment, Addiction, and the Spiritual Path.* San Francisco, CA: Harper.

Grof, C. and Grof, S.1990. *The Stormy Search for the Self: A Guide to Personal Growth through Transformational Crisis.* Los Angeles, CA: J. P. Tarcher.

Grof, S. 1987. Spirituality, Addiction, and Western Science. *Re-Vision Journal* 10:5-18.

Grof, S. and Grof, C. (eds.) 1989. *Spiritual Emergency: When Personal Transformation Becomes a Crisis.* Los Angeles, CA: J. P. Tarcher.

Grof, S. 1994. *Books of the Dead: Manuals for Living and Dying.* London: Thames and Hudson.

Grof, S. 2000. *Psychology of the Future: Lessons from Modern Consciousness Research.* Albany, NY: State University of New York (SUNY) Press.

Grof, S. 2001. *LSD Psychotherapy.* Santa Cruz, CA: MAPS Publications.

Grof, S. 2006. *When the Impossible Happens: Adventures in Non-Ordinary Realities.* Louisville, CO: Sounds True.

James, W. 1961. *The Varieties of Religious Experience.* New York: Collier.

Jung, C. G. 1959. *The Archetypes and the Collective Unconscious.* Collected Works, vol. 9,1. Bollingen Series XX, Princeton, N.J.: Princeton University Press.

Jung, C. G. 1960. *Synchronicity: An Acausal Connecting Principle.* Collected Works, vol. 8, Bollingen Series XX. Princeton: Princeton University Press.

Jung, C. G. 1964. *Flying Saucers: A Modern Myth of Things Seen in the Skies.* In: Collected Works, vol. 10. Bollingen Series XX. Princeton: Princeton University Press.

Jung, C. G. 1996. *The Psychology of Kundalini Yoga: Notes on the seminars given in 1932 by C. G. Jung* (Soma Shamdasani, ed.). Bollingen Series XCIX. Princeton: Princeton University Press.

Lattin, D. 2012. *Distilled Spirits.* Oakland, CA: University of California Press.

Lawson, A. 1984. Perinatal Imagery In UFO Abduction Reports. *Journal of Psychohistory* 12:211.

Mack, J. 1994. *Abductions: Human Encounters with Aliens.* New York: Charles Scribner Sons.

Mack, J. 1999. *Passport to the Cosmos: Human Transformation and Alien Encounters.* New York: Crown Publishers.

Maslow, A. 1964. *Religions, Values, and Peak Experiences.* Cleveland, OH: Ohio State University.

Moody, R.A. 1975. *Life After Life.* New York: Bantam.

Pahnke, W. N. and Richards, W. E. 1966. Implications of LSD and Experimental Mysticism. *Journal of Religion and Health.* 5:175.

Pahnke, W. N., Kurland, A. A., Unger, S., Savage, C. and Grof, S. 1970. The Experimental Use of Psychedelic (LSD) Psychotherapy. *J. Amer. Med. Assoc.* 212:1856.

Perry, J. W. 1953. *The Self in the Psychotic Process.* Dallas, TX: Spring Publications.

Perry, J. W. 1966. *Lord of the Four Quarters.* New York: Braziller.

Perry, J. W. 1974. *The Far Side of Madness.* Englewood Cliffs, NJ: Prentice

Hall.
Perry, J. W. 1976. *Roots of Renewal in Myth and Madness.* San Francisco, CA: Jossey-Bass Publications.
Perry, J. W. 1998. *Trials of the Visionary Mind: Spiritual Emergency and the Renewal Process.* Albany, NY: State University of New York (SUNY) Press.
Ring, K. 1982. *Life at Death: A Scientific Investigation of the Near-Death Experience.* New York: Quill.
Ring, K. 1985. *Heading Toward Omega: In Search of the Meaning of the Near-Death Experience.* New York: Quill.
Ring, K. and Valarino, E. E. 1998. *Lessons from the Light: What We Can Learn from the Near-Death Experience.* New York: Plenum Press.
Sannella, L. 1987. *The Kundalini Experience: Psychosis or Transcendence?* Lower Lake, CA: Integral Publishing.
Savage, C. and McCabe, O. L. 1971. Psychedelic (LSD) Therapy of Drug Addiction. In: *The Drug Abuse Controversy* (Brown, C. C. and Savage, C., eds.) Baltimore, MD.: Friends of Medical Science Research Center.
Weil, A. 1972. *The Natural Mind.* Boston: Houghton Mifflin.
Wilber, K. 1977. *The Spectrum of Consciousness.* Wheaton, IL: Theosophical Publishing House.
Wilson, W. and Jung, C. G. 1963. Letters republished in: Grof, S. (ed.): Mystical Quest, Attachment, and Addiction. *Special edition of the Re-Vision Journal* 10 (2):1987.

VI

Holotropic Breathwork:
A New Approach to Psychotherapy and Self-Exploration

Holotropic Breathwork is an experiential method of self-exploration and psychotherapy that my late wife Christina and I developed in the mid-1970s at the Esalen Institute in Big Sur, California. This approach induces deep holotropic states of consciousness through a combination of very simple means: accelerated breathing, evocative music, and a bodywork technique that helps to release residual bioenergetic and emotional blocks.

The sessions are usually conducted in groups; participants work in pairs and alternate in the roles of "breathers" and "sitters." The process is supervised by trained facilitators who assist participants whenever special intervention is necessary. Following the breathing sessions, participants express their experiences by painting mandalas and sharing accounts of their inner journeys in small groups. Follow-up interviews and various complementary methods are used, if necessary, to facilitate the completion and integration of the breathwork experience.

In both theory and practice, Holotropic Breathwork combines and integrates various elements from modern consciousness research, depth psychology, transpersonal psychology, Eastern spiritual philosophies, and native healing practices. It differs significantly from traditional forms of psychotherapy, such as psychoanalysis and various other schools of depth psychology, which primarily use verbal means. It shares certain common characteristics with the experiential therapies of humanistic psychology, such as Gestalt practice and the neo-Reichian approaches, which emphasize direct emotional expression and work with the body. However, the unique feature of Holotropic Breathwork is that it utilizes the therapeutic potential of holotropic states of consciousness.

Ancient and native cultures used holotropic states for centuries or even millennia in their ritual, spiritual, and healing practices. The extraordinary healing power of these states was confirmed by modern consciousness research conducted in the second half of the twentieth century. This research has also shown that the phenomena occurring during these states represent a critical challenge for the current conceptual frameworks used by academic psychiatry and psychology, as well as for their basic metaphysical assumptions. The work with Holotropic Breathwork requires a new understanding of consciousness and of the human psyche, both healthy and diseased. The basic principles of this new psychology were discussed in the second chapter of this encyclopedia, as well as my other writings (Grof 2000, Grof and 2012).

Essential Components of Holotropic Breathwork

Holotropic Breathwork combines faster breathing, evocative music, and releasing bodywork to induce intense holotropic states of consciousness, which have a remarkable healing and transformative power. This method provides access to biographical, perinatal, and transpersonal domains of the unconscious and thus to deep psychospiritual roots of emotional and psychosomatic disorders. It also makes it possible to utilize the mechanisms of healing and personality transformation that operate on these levels of the psyche. The process of self-exploration and therapy in Holotropic Breathwork is spontaneous and autonomous; it is governed by clients' own inner healing intelligence rather than by following the instructions and guidelines of a particular school of psychotherapy.

Most of the recent revolutionary discoveries concerning consciousness and the human psyche on which Holotropic Breathwork is based are only new for modern psychiatry and psychology. They have a long history as integral parts of the ritual and spiritual life of many ancient and native cultures, as well as their healing practices. The basic principles of Holotropic Breathwork represent rediscovery, validation, and the modern reformulation of ancient wisdom and procedures, some of which can be traced back to the dawn of human history. The same is also true for the principal constituents used in the practice of Holotropic Breathwork: breathing, instrumental music and chanting, bodywork, and mandala drawing or other forms of artistic expression. They have been used for centuries or even millennia in the healing ceremonies and ritual practices of all preindustrial human groups.

The Healing Power of Breath

In ancient and preindustrial societies, the breath has played a very important role in cosmology, mythology, and philosophy, as well as in ritual and spiritual practices. Various breathing techniques have been used since time immemorial for religious and healing purposes. Since the earliest times, virtually every major psychospiritual system seeking to comprehend human nature has viewed breath as a crucial link between nature, the human body, the psyche, and the spirit.

In ancient Indian literature, the term *prāna* meant not only physical breath and air, but also the sacred essence of life. Similarly, in traditional Chinese medicine, the word *chi* refers to the cosmic essence and the energy of life, as well as to the air we breathe into our lungs. In Japan, the corresponding word is *ki*. Ki plays an extremely important role in Japanese spiritual practices and martial arts. In ancient Greece, the word *pneuma* meant air or breath as well as spirit, or the essence of life. The Greeks also saw breath as being closely related to the psyche. The term *phren* was used both for the diaphragm, the largest muscle involved in breathing, and the mind (as we see in the term schizophrenia, which literally means split mind).

In the old Hebrew tradition, the same word, *ruach,* denoted both breath and creative spirit, which were seen as identical. The following quote from Genesis shows the close relationship between God, breath, and life: "Then the Lord God formed a man [Hebrew "Adam"] from the dust of the ground, and breathed into his nostrils the breath of life, and the man became a living being." In Latin, the same name was used for breath and spirit—*spiritus.* Similarly, in Slavic languages, spirit and breath have the same linguistic root.

In native Hawaiian tradition and medicine (kanaka maoli lapa'au), the word *ha* means the divine spirit, wind, air, and breath. It is contained in the popular Hawaiian *aloha,* an expression that is used in many different contexts. It is usually translated as presence *(alo)* of the Divine Breath *(ha).* Its opposite, *ha'ole,* meaning without breath or without life, is a term that native Hawaiians have applied to white-skinned foreigners since the arrival of the infamous British sea captain James Cook in 1778. The kahunas, "Keepers of Secret Knowledge," have used breathing exercises to generate spiritual energy *(mana).*

It has been known for centuries that it is possible to influence consciousness through techniques that involve breathing. The procedures that have been used for this purpose by various ancient and preindustrial cultures cover a wide range, from drastic interference with breathing to subtle and sophisticated exercises of various spiritual traditions. The original form of baptism practiced by the Essenes, for example, involved forced submersion of the initiate under water for an extended period of time. This resulted in a powerful experience of death and rebirth. In some other groups, the neophytes were half-choked by smoke, strangulation, or compression of the carotid arteries.

Profound changes of consciousness can be induced by both extremes in the breathing rate, hyperventilation and prolonged withholding of breath, as well as by using these two extremes in an alternating fashion. Very sophisticated and advanced methods of this kind can be found in the ancient Indian science of breath, or *prānāyāma.* William Walker Atkinson, an American writer who was influential during the turn-of-the-century (1890s–1900s) spiritual-philosophical movement, wrote a comprehensive treatise on the Hindu science of breath under the pseudonym Yogi Ramacharaka (Ramacharaka 1903).

Specific techniques involving intense breathing or withholding of breath are also part of various exercises in Kundalini Yoga, Siddha Yoga, the Tibetan Vajrayana, Sufi practice, Burmese Buddhist and Taoist meditation, among many other spiritual systems. Indirectly, the depth and rhythm of breathing can be profoundly influenced by ritual artistic performances, such as the the Balinese monkey chant or Ketjak, the Inuit Eskimo throat music, the Tibetan and Mongolian multivocal chanting, and the singing of kirtans, bhajans, or Sufi chants.

More subtle techniques, which emphasize special awareness in relation to breathing rather than changes of the respiratory dynamics, have a prominent place in Buddhism. *Anāpānasati* is a basic form of meditation taught by the Buddha; it literally means "mindfulness of breathing" (from the Pali *anāpāna,* meaning inhalation and exhalation and *sati,* meaning mindfulness). Buddha's teaching of anāpāna was based on his experience using it as a means of achieving his own enlightenment. He emphasized the importance of being mindful not only of one's breath, but using the breath to become aware of one's entire body and of all of one's experience. According to the Anāpānasati Sutta *(sutra),* practicing this form of meditation leads to the removal of all defilements *(kilesa).* The Buddha taught that systematic practice of anāpānasati would lead to the final release *(nirvāna* or *nibbāna).*

Anāpānasati is practiced in connection with Vipassana *(insight meditation)* and Zen meditation *(shikantaza,* which means "just sitting"). The essence of anāpānasati as the core meditation practice in Buddhism, especially the Theravada school, is to be a passive observer of the natural involuntary breathing process. This is in sharp contrast with the yogic prānāyāma practices, which employ breathing techniques that aim for rigorous control of the breath. Anāpānasati is not, however, the only Buddhist form of breathing meditation. In the Buddhist spiritual practices used in Tibet, Mongolia, and Japan, breath control plays an important role. The cultivation of special attention to breathing also represents an essential part of certain Taoist and Christian practices.

In the development of materialistic science, breathing lost its sacred meaning and was stripped of its connection to the psyche and spirit. Western medicine reduced it to an important physiological function. The physical and psychological manifestations that accompany various respiratory maneuvers have all been pathologized. The psychosomatic response to faster breathing, the so-called *hyperventilation syndrome,* is considered a pathological condition, rather than what it really is: a process that has an enormous healing potential. When hyperventilation occurs spontaneously, it is routinely suppressed by the administration of tranquilizers, injections of intravenous calcium, and the application of a paper bag over the face to increase the concentration of carbon dioxide and combat the alkalosis caused by faster breathing.

In the second half of the twentieth century, Western therapists rediscovered the healing potential of breath and developed techniques that utilize it. We have experimented with various approaches involving breathing in the context of our month-long seminars at the Esalen Institute in Big Sur, California. These included both breathing exercises from ancient spiritual traditions under the guidance of Indian and Tibetan teachers, as well as techniques developed by Western therapists. Each of these approaches has a specific emphasis and uses breath in a different way. In our own search for an effective method, we tried to simplify this process as much as possible.

We came to the conclusion that it is sufficient to breathe faster and more effectively than usual, with full concentration on the inner process. Instead of emphasizing a specific technique of breathing, we follow the general strategy of holotropic work: to trust the intrinsic wisdom of the body and follow the inner clues. In Holotropic Breathwork, we encourage people to begin the session with faster and somewhat deeper breathing, tying inhalation and exhalation into a continuous circle of breath. Once in the process, they find their own rhythm and way of breathing.

We have been able to repeatedly confirm Wilhelm Reich's observation that psychological resistances and defenses are associated with restricted breathing (Reich 1949, 1961). Respiration is an autonomous function, but it can also be influenced by volition. The deliberate increase of breathing typically loosens psychological defenses and leads to a release and emergence of unconscious (and superconscious) material. Unless one has witnessed or experienced this process personally, it is difficult to believe, on theoretical grounds alone, in the power and efficacy of this technique.

The Therapeutic Potential of Music

In Holotropic Breathwork, the consciousness-expanding effect of breath is combined with evocative music. Like breathing, music and other forms of sound technology have been used for millennia as powerful tools in ritual and spiritual practice. Monotonous drumming, rattling, chanting, instrumental music, and other forms of sound-producing techniques have always been some of the principal tools of shamans in different parts of the world. Many preindustrial cultures have quite independently developed drumming rhythms that have remarkable effects on the electric activity of the brain in laboratory experiments (Goldman 1952; Jilek 1974, 1982; Kamiya 1969; Neher 1961, 1962).

The archives of cultural anthropologists contain countless examples of powerful trance-inducing methods that combine instrumental music, chanting, and dancing. In many cultures, sound technology has been used specifically for healing purposes in the context of intricate ceremonies. The Navajo healing rituals conducted by trained singers have astounding complexity that has been compared to the scores of Wagnerian operas. The trance dance and extended drumming of the !Kung Bushmen of the African Kalahari Desert have enormous healing power, as has been documented in many anthropological studies and movies (Lee and DeVore 1976; Katz 1976).

The healing potential of the syncretistic religious rituals of the Caribbean islands and South America, such as the Cuban Santeria or Brazilian umbanda, is recognized by many professionals in these countries who have traditional Western medical training. Remarkable instances of emotional and psychosomatic healing occur in the meetings of Christian groups using music, singing, and dance, such as the Snake Handlers (Holy Ghost People), and the revivalists, or members of the Pentecostal Church.

Some spiritual traditions have developed sound technologies that do not just induce a general trance state, but have a specific effect on consciousness and the human psyche and body. The Indian teachings postulate a specific connection between certain acoustic frequencies and the individual chakras or subtle energy centers of the human body. With systematic use of this knowledge, it is possible to influence the state of consciousness in a predictable and desirable way. The ancient Indian tradition called *nada yoga,* or the way to union through sound, is known to maintain, improve, and restore emotional, psychosomatic, and physical health and well-being.

Extraordinary vocal performances used for ritual, spiritual, and healing purposes include the multivocal chanting of the Tibetan Gyotso monks as well as the Mongolian and Tuva shamans, the Hindu bhajans and kirtans, the Santo Daime chants *(icaros)* used in ayahuasca ceremonies, the throat music of the Inuit Eskimo people, and the sacred chants *(dhikrs)* of various Sufi orders. These are just a few examples of the extensive use of instrumental music and chanting for healing, ritual, and spiritual purposes.

We used music systematically in the program of psychedelic therapy at the Maryland Psychiatric Research Center in Baltimore, Maryland, and have learned much about its extraordinary potential for psychotherapy. Carefully selected music seems to be of particular value in holotropic states of consciousness, where it has several important functions. It mobilizes emotions associated with repressed memories, brings them to the surface, and facilitates their expression. It helps to open the door into the unconscious, intensifies and deepens the therapeutic process, and provides a meaningful context for the experience. The continuous flow of music creates a carrier wave that helps the subject move through difficult experiences and impasses, overcome psychological defenses, surrender, and let go. In Holotropic Breathwork sessions, which are usually conducted in groups, music has an additional function: it masks the noises made by the participants and weaves them into a dynamic aesthetic gestalt.

In order to use music as a catalyst for deep self-exploration and experiential work, it is necessary to learn a new way of listening and relating to music in a manner that is alien to our culture. In the West, we frequently employ music as an acoustic background that has little emotional relevance. Typical examples would be the use of popular music at cocktail parties, or piped music *(muzak)* in shopping areas and workspaces. A different approach used by sophisticated audiences is the disciplined and attentive listening to music in theaters and concert halls. The dynamic and elemental way that music is used in rock concerts comes closer to the use of music in Holotropic Breathwork. However, the attention of participants in such events is usually extroverted and the experience lacks an element that is essential in holotropic therapy or self-exploration: sustained, focused introspection.

In holotropic therapy, it is essential to surrender completely to the flow of music, let it resonate in one's entire body, and to respond to it in a spontaneous and elemental fashion. This includes manifestations that would be unthinkable in a concert hall, where crying or even coughing is seen as a disturbance and causes annoyance and embarrassment. In holotropic work, one should give full expression to whatever the music is bringing out, whether it is loud screaming or laughing, baby talk, animal noises, shamanic chanting, or talking in tongues. It is also important not to control any physical impulses, such as bizarre grimacing, sensual movements of the pelvis, violent shaking, or intense contortions of the entire body. Naturally, there are exceptions to this rule: destructive behavior directed toward oneself, others, and the physical environment is not permissible.

We also encourage participants to suspend any intellectual activity, such as trying to guess the composer or the culture from which the music comes. Other ways of avoiding the emotional impact of the music involve engaging one's professional expertise—judging the performance of the orchestra, guessing which instruments are playing, and criticizing the technical quality of the recording or of the music equipment in the room. When we avoid these pitfalls, music can become a very powerful tool for inducing and supporting holotropic states of consciousness. For this purpose, the music has to be of superior technical quality and be played at a sufficient volume to drive the experience. The combination of music with faster breathing has a remarkable mind-manifesting and consciousness-expanding power.

As far as the specific choice of music is concerned, I will only mention the general principles and give a few suggestions based on our experience. After a certain time, each therapist or therapeutic team develops a list of their favorite pieces for various stages of the sessions. The basic rule is to respond sensitively to the phase, intensity, and content of the participants' experience, rather than trying to program it. This is in congruence with the general philosophy of holotropic therapy, particularly the deep respect for the wisdom of the self-healing intelligence, for the collective unconscious, and for the autonomy and spontaneity of the healing process. In general, it is important to use music that is intense, evocative, and conducive to a positive experience. We try to avoid selections that are jarring, dissonant, and anxiety-provoking. Preference should be given to music of high artistic quality that is not well known and has little concrete content.

One should avoid playing songs and other vocal pieces in languages known to the participants, which would convey a specific message or suggest a specific theme. When vocal compositions are used, they should be in foreign languages so that the human voice is perceived as just another musical instrument. For the same reason, it is preferable to avoid pieces which evoke specific intellectual associations and tend to program the content of the session, such as Richard Wagner's or Mendelssohn-Bartholdy's wedding marches and overtures to Bizet's Carmen or Verdi's Aida.

The session typically begins with activating music that is dynamic, flowing, and emotionally uplifting and reassuring. As the session continues, the music gradually increases in intensity and moves to powerful rhythmic pieces, preferably drawn from ritual and spiritual traditions of various native cultures. Although many of these performances can be aesthetically pleasing, the main purpose for the people that developed them is not entertainment, but the induction of holotropic experiences. An example here could be the dance of the whirling dervishes, accompanied by beautiful music and chants. It is not designed to be admired as a superb ballet performance, but to take people to the experience of God.

About an hour and a half into the session of Holotropic Breathwork, when the experience typically culminates, we introduce what we call *breakthrough music*. The selections used at this time range from sacred music—masses, oratoria, requiems, and other strong orchestral pieces—to excerpts from dramatic movie soundtracks. In the second half of the session, the intensity of the music gradually decreases and we bring in loving and emotionally moving pieces *(heart music)*. Finally, in the termination period of the session, the music has a soothing, flowing, timeless, and meditative quality.

Most practitioners of Holotropic Breathwork collect musical recordings and tend to create their own favorite sequences for the five consecutive phases of the session: ***(1) opening music, (2) trance-inducing music, (3) breakthrough music, (4) heart music,*** and ***(5) meditative music.*** Some of them use music programs that are pre-recorded for the entire session; this allows the facilitators to be more available for the group, but makes it impossible to adjust the selection of the music to the energy of the group. On special occasions, we might have the luxury of using live music. This is the common practice in rituals of native cultures; it makes it possible for the musicians and the participants to interact with each other and creatively feed off each other's energy.

The Use of Releasing Bodywork

The physical and emotional response to Holotropic Breathwork varies considerably from one person to another and also from session to session. Most commonly, faster breathing brings, at first, more or less dramatic psychosomatic manifestations. The textbooks on respiratory physiology refer to this response to accelerated breathing as the "hyperventilation syndrome." They describe it as a stereotypical pattern of physiological responses that consists primarily of tensions in the hands and feet *("tetany"* or *"carpopedal spasms")*. We have conducted more than 40,000 Holotropic Breathwork sessions and have found the current medical understanding of the effects of faster breathing to be incorrect.

There are many individuals for whom fast breathing carried over a period of several hours does not lead to a classical hyperventilation syndrome, but to progressive relaxation, intense sexual feelings, or even mystical experiences. Others develop tensions in various parts of the body but do not show signs of the carpopedal spasms. Moreover, in those who develop tensions, continued faster breathing does not lead to progressive increase of the tensions, but tends to be self-limited. It typically reaches a climactic culmination, followed by profound relaxation. The pattern of this sequence has a certain resemblance to a sexual orgasm.

In repeated holotropic sessions, this process of increasing tensions and subsequent relaxation tends to move from one part of the body to another in a way that varies from person to person. The overall amount of muscular tensions and of intense emotions tends to decrease with the number of sessions. What happens in this process is that faster breathing, extended for a long period of time, changes the person's chemistry so that blocked physical and emotional energies, which are associated with various traumatic memories, are released and become available for peripheral discharge and processing. This makes it possible for the previously repressed content of these memories to emerge into consciousness and be integrated.

It is a healing process that should be encouraged and supported, and not a pathological process that needs to be suppressed, as is common in medical practice. Physical manifestations that develop during the breathing in various areas of the body are not simple physiological reactions. They show a complex psychosomatic structure and usually have specific psychological meaning for the individuals involved. Sometimes they represent an intensified version of tensions and pains from everyday life, such as chronic symptoms that appear at times of emotional or physical stress, fatigue, weakening from an illness, or the effects of using alcohol or marijuana. Other times, they can be recognized as the reactivation of old latent symptoms that the individual suffered from in infancy, childhood, puberty, or some other time in life.

The tensions that we carry in our body can be released in two different ways. The first of them involves abreaction and catharsis—the discharge of pent-up physical energies through tremors, twitches, intense body movements, coughing, and vomiting. Both abreaction and catharsis also typically include the release of blocked emotions through crying, screaming, or other types of vocal expression. We talk about abreaction when the emotional and physical discharges are connected with the emergence of a specific traumatic memory. Aristotle's term, catharsis, is used to describe a general cleansing discharge of emotions and physical energies without a specifiable source and content. These are mechanisms that have been well known in traditional psychiatry since Sigmund Freud and Joseph Breuer published their studies on hysteria (Freud and Breuer 1936).

Various abreactive techniques have been used in traditional psychiatry for the treatment of traumatic emotional neuroses. Abreaction also represents an integral part of the new experiential psychotherapies, such as the neo-Reichian work, Gestalt practice, and primal therapy. The second mechanism that can mediate the release of pent-up physical and emotional tensions plays an important role in Holotropic Breathwork, rebirthing, and other forms of therapy using breathing techniques. It represents a new development in psychiatry and psychotherapy and can, at times, be even more effective than abreaction.

Deep tensions surface in the form of unrelenting muscular contractions of various duration *(tetany)*. By sustaining these muscular tensions for extended periods of time, the body consumes enormous amounts of previously pent-up energy and simplifies its functioning by disposing of them. The deep relaxation that typically follows the temporary intensification of old tensions or the appearance of previously latent ones bears witness to the healing nature of this process.

These mechanisms have their parallels in sport physiology, where it is well known that it is possible to do work and train the muscles in two different ways, through *isotonic* and *isometric* exercises. As the names suggest, during isotonic exercises, the tension of the muscles remains constant while their length oscillates. During isometric exercises, the tension of the muscles changes, but their length remains the same the whole time. A good example of isotonic activity is boxing, while weightlifting or bench-pressing are distinctly isometric exercises.

Both of these mechanisms are extremely effective in releasing and resolving deep-seated chronic muscular tension. In spite of their superficial differences, they have much in common, and in Holotropic Breathwork, they complement each other very effectively. In many instances, the difficult memories, emotions, and physical sensations that emerge from the unconscious during Holotropic Breathwork sessions are spontaneously resolved, and the breathers end up in a deeply relaxed meditative state. In this case, no external interventions are necessary and the breathers remain in this state until they return to the ordinary state of consciousness.

If the breathing in and of itself does not lead to a good completion and there are residual tensions or unresolved emotions, facilitators should offer participants a specific form of bodywork, which helps them to reach a better closure for the session. The general strategy of this work is to ask the breather to focus his or her attention on the area where there is unreleased tension and to do whatever is necessary to intensify the existing physical sensations. The facilitators then help to intensify these feelings even further by appropriate external intervention. While the attention of the breather is focused on the energetically charged problem area, he or she is encouraged to find a spontaneous reaction to this situation.

This response should not reflect a conscious choice of the breather, but be fully determined by the unconscious process. It often takes an entirely unexpected and surprising form—animal-like vocalizations, talking in tongues or an unknown foreign language, a shamanic chant from a particular culture, gibberish, or baby talk. Equally frequent are completely unexpected physical reactions, such as violent tremors, jolts, coughing, and vomiting, as well as various characteristic animal movements—climbing, flying, digging, crawling, slithering, and others. It is essential that the facilitators encourage and support what is spontaneously emerging, rather than apply some technique offered by a particular school of therapy.

This work should be continued until the facilitator and the breather reach an agreement that the session has been adequately concluded. The breather should end the session in a comfortable and relaxed state. We have repeatedly heard from breathers at this stage: "I have never been this relaxed in my whole life!" or "I feel for the first time in my life that I am really in my body." After getting clearance from the facilitators, the breathers who have completed the session move to the art room to draw their mandalas.

Supportive and Nourishing Physical Contact

In Holotropic Breathwork, we also use a different form of physical intervention which is designed to provide support on a deep preverbal level. This is based on the observation that two fundamentally different forms of traumas exist, which require diametrically different approaches. This distinction is currently not recognized by mainstream psychotherapists. Borrowing the terminology from British law, the first of these traumas can be referred to as *trauma by commission.* This form of trauma results from external intrusions that damaged the future development of the individual, such as physical, emotional, or sexual abuse, frightening situations, destructive criticism, humiliation, or ridicule. These traumas represent foreign elements in the unconscious that can be brought into consciousness, energetically discharged, and resolved.

Although this distinction is not recognized in conventional psychotherapy, the second form of trauma, *trauma by omission* is radically different in nature and requires a different approach. It actually involves the opposite problem: a lack of positive experiences that are essential for a healthy emotional development. An infant, as well as an older child, has strong primitive needs for instinctual satisfaction and security that pediatricians and child psychiatrists call *anaclitic* (from the Greek *anaklinein,* meaning to lean upon). These involve the need to be held and experience skin contact, be caressed, comforted, played with, and be the center of human attention. When these needs are not met, it has serious negative consequences for the future of the individual.

Many people have a history of emotional deprivation, abandonment, and neglect in infancy and childhood that resulted in serious frustration of the anaclitic needs. Others were born premature and spent their first months of life in an incubator without intimate human contact. The only way to heal this type of trauma is to offer a corrective experience in the form of supportive physical contact in a holotropic state of consciousness. For this approach to be effective, the individual has to be deeply regressed to the infantile stage of development, otherwise the corrective measure does not reach the developmental level on which the trauma occurred.

Depending on the circumstances and on previous agreement, this physical support can range from simple hand-holding or touching the forehead to full body contact. The use of nourishing physical contact is a very effective way of healing early emotional trauma, but using it requires following strict ethical rules. We have to explain the rationale of this technique to the breathers and sitters before the session and get their approval to use it. Under no circumstances can this approach be practiced without previous consent and no pressure can be used to obtain this permission. For many people with a history of sexual abuse, physical contact is a very sensitive and charged issue.

Very often, those who most need such healing touch have the strongest resistance to it. It can sometimes take time and several sessions before a person develops enough trust toward the facilitators and the group to be able to accept this approach and benefit from it. Supportive physical contact has to be used exclusively to satisfy the needs of the breathers and not those of the sitters or facilitators. By this, I do not only mean sexual needs or needs for intimacy which, of course, are the most obvious issues. Equally problematic can be the sitter's strong need to be needed, loved, or appreciated, unfulfilled maternal needs, and other less extreme forms of emotional wants and desires.

An incident from one of our workshops at the Esalen Institute in Big Sur, California, can serve as a good example. At the beginning of our five-day seminar, one of the participants, a postmenopausal woman, shared with the group how much she had always wanted to have children and how much she suffered because this had not happened. In the middle of the Holotropic Breathwork session, in which she was the sitter for a young man, she suddenly pulled the upper part of her partner's body into her lap and started to rock and comfort him. Her timing could not have been worse; as we found out later in the group sharing, he was at that time in the middle of a past-life experience that featured him as a powerful Viking warrior on a military expedition. He described, with a great sense of humor, how he initially tried to experience her rocking as the movement of the boat on the ocean. However, when she added comforting baby talk, that made it impossible for him to continue and brought him back to ordinary reality. The maternal needs of the woman in the workshop were so strong that they took over and she was unable to objectively assess the situation and act appropriately.

It is usually quite easy to recognize when a breather has regressed to early infancy. In a deep age regression, the wrinkles on the face tend to disappear and the individual actually looks and behaves like an infant. This can involve various infantile postures and gestures, as well as copious salivation and thumb sucking. At other times, the appropriateness of offering physical contact is obvious from the context; for example, when the breather has just finished reliving biological birth and looks lost and forlorn.

We have never had any problems with this method, as long as it was used in a group setting. We had explained the rationale of this approach to the participants, and they all understood it. Everything was done in the open and everybody saw what was happening. Bringing this therapeutic strategy into private practice and using it in a one-on-one situation behind closed doors requires special caution concerning boundaries. There have been cases when therapists using this method in the privacy of their office ran into serious ethical problems.

The use of nourishing physical contact in holotropic states in order to heal traumas caused by abandonment, rejection, and emotional deprivation was developed by two London psychoanalysts, Pauline McCririck and Joyce Martin. They used this method, which they called fusion therapy, with their LSD patients. During their sessions, their clients spent several hours in deep age regression, lying on a couch covered with a blanket, while Joyce or Pauline lay by their side, holding them in a close embrace like a good mother would do to comfort her child (Martin 1965).

Their revolutionary method effectively divided and polarized the community of LSD therapists. Some of the practitioners realized that this was a very powerful and logical way to heal "traumas by omission"—emotional problems caused by emotional deprivation and lack of good mothering. Others were horrified by this radical "anaclitic therapy." They warned that close physical contact between therapist and client in a non-ordinary state of consciousness would cause irreversible damage to the transference/countertransference relationship.

At the Second International Conference on the use of LSD in psychotherapy, held in May 1965 in Amityville, New York, Joyce and Pauline showed their fascinating film on the use of the fusion technique in psychedelic therapy. In a heated discussion that followed, most of the questions revolved around the transference/countertransference issues. Pauline provided a very interesting and convincing explanation on why this approach presented fewer problems in this regard than an orthodox Freudian approach. She pointed out that most patients who come to therapy experienced a lack of affection from their parents in their infancy and childhood. The cold attitude of the Freudian analyst tends to reactivate the resulting emotional wounds and triggers desperate attempts on the part of the patients to get the attention and satisfaction that had been denied to them (Martin 1965).

By contrast, according to Pauline, fusion therapy provided a corrective experience by satisfying the old anaclitic cravings. Having their emotional wounds healed, the patients recognized that the therapist was not an appropriate sexual object and were able to find suitable partners outside of the therapeutic relationship. Pauline explained that this paralleled the situation in the early development of object relationships. Individuals who receive adequate mothering in infancy and childhood are able to emotionally detach from their mothers and fathers and find mature relationships. By contrast, those who experienced emotional deprivation remain pathologically attached and go through life craving and seeking the satisfaction of primitive infantile needs. We occasionally used fusion therapy in the psychedelic research program at the Maryland Psychiatric Research Center, particularly in the work with terminal cancer patients (Grof 2006).

In the mid-1970s, when we developed Holotropic Breathwork, anaclitic support became an integral part of our workshops and training. Before closing this section on bodywork, I would like to address one question that often comes up in the context of holotropic workshops or lectures on experiential work: "Why should reliving traumatic memories be therapeutic rather than represent a retraumatization?" The best answer can be found in the article "Unexperienced Experience" by Irish psychiatrist Ivor

Browne (Browne 1990). He suggested that in therapy we are not facing an exact replay or repetition of the original traumatic situation, but rather the first full experience of the appropriate emotional and physical reactions to it. This means that the traumatic events are recorded in the person at the time when they happen but are not fully consciously experienced, processed, and integrated.

In addition, the person who is confronted with the previously repressed traumatic memory is no longer the helpless and vitally dependent child or infant that he or she was in the original situation, but a grown adult. The holotropic state induced in powerful experiential forms of psychotherapy thus allows the individual to be present and operate simultaneously in two different sets of space-time coordinates. Full age regression makes it possible to experience all the emotions and physical sensations of the original traumatic situation from the perspective of the child, but at the same time analyze and evaluate the memory in the therapeutic situation from a mature adult perspective.

This understanding is supported by the reports of breathers who relived challenging traumatic memories. From the viewpoint of an outside observer, they appeared to be in a lot of pain and suffering immensely. However, after the session, they said that they actually had a positive subjective feeling about the process. They felt that they were purging pain from their bodies and experienced relief rather than suffering.

Mandala Drawing: The Expressive Power of Art

Mandala is a Sanskrit word that means "circle" or "completion." In the most general sense, this term can be used for any design showing complex geometrical symmetry, such as a spiderweb, arrangement of petals in a flower or blossom, seashell (e.g. a sand dollar), image in a kaleidoscope, stained glass window in a Gothic cathedral, or labyrinthine design. The mandala is a visual construct that can be easily grasped by the eye, since it corresponds to the structure of the organ of visual perception. The pupil of the eye itself has a simple mandala form.

In ritual and spiritual practice, the term 'mandala' refers to images which can be drawn, painted, modeled, or danced. In the Tantric branches of Hinduism, Buddhism, Vajrayana, and Jainism, this word refers to elaborate cosmograms composed of elementary geometrical forms (points, lines, triangles, squares, and circles), lotus blossoms, and complex archetypal figures and scenes. They are used as important meditation aids which help practitioners to focus attention inside and lead them to specific states of consciousness.

Although the use of mandalas in the Tantric branches of Hinduism, Buddhism, and Jainism has been particularly refined and sophisticated, the art of mandala drawing as a part of spiritual practice can be found in many other cultures. Examples of particularly beautiful mandalas are the *nierikas,* which are yarn paintings of the Huichol Indians from Central Mexico that portray visions induced by the ritual ingestion of peyote. Elaborate sand paintings used by the Navajo people in healing and other rituals, and the bark paintings of the Australian Aborigines, also include many intricate mandala patterns.

The use of mandalas in the spiritual and religious practice of various cultures, as well as in alchemy, attracted the attention of C. G. Jung, who noticed that similar patterns appeared in the paintings of his patients at a certain stage of their psychospiritual development. According to him, the mandala is a "psychological expression of the totality of the self." In his own words: "The severe pattern imposed by a circular image of this kind compensates the disorder and confusion of the psychic state—namely, through the construction of a central point to which everything is related" (Jung 1959).

Our own use of mandala drawing was inspired by the work of art therapist Joan Kellogg, who was a member of our team at the Maryland Psychiatric Research Center in Baltimore, Maryland, conducting psychedelic therapy. In her work as art therapist in psychiatric hospitals in Wyckoff and Paterson, New Jersey, Joan had given hundreds of patients a piece of paper with an outline of a circle and painting supplies and asked them to paint whatever came into their mind. She was able to find significant correlations between the psychological problems and clinical diagnoses of these patients and specific aspects of their paintings, such as choice of colors, preference for sharp or round shapes, use of concentric circles, dividing the mandala into sections, and whether or not they respected the boundaries of the circle.

At the Maryland Psychiatric Research Center, Joan compared the mandalas that the experimental subjects were painting before and after their psychedelic sessions, looking for significant correlations between the basic features of the mandalas, the content of the psychedelic experiences, and the outcome of their therapy. We have found her method to be extremely useful in our work with Holotropic Breathwork. Joan herself saw the mandala drawing as a psychological test and described the criteria for interpretations of their various features in several papers (Kellogg 1977, 1978). In our work, we do not interpret the mandalas, but use them in the sharing groups as a source of information about the breathers' experiences.

An interesting alternative to mandala drawing is the method of "SoulCollage," developed by Seena B. Frost (Frost 2001). Many participants in holotropic workshops, training, and therapy experience psychological blocks when they are confronted with the task of drawing or painting. This usually has its roots in some traumatic experiences that they had as children with their teachers and/or peers in art classes, or in their generally low self-esteem that makes them doubt their abilities and paralyzes their performance.

SoulCollage helps these people overcome their emotional blocks and resistances; it is a creative process which almost anyone can do since it uses already existing paintings or photographs. Instead of drawing and painting supplies, participants receive a rich selection of illustrated magazines, catalogs, calendars, greeting cards, and postcards. They can also bring their personal photos from a family album or pictures of people, animals, and landscapes they have themselves taken. Using scissors, they cut out pictures or fragments that seem appropriate to portray their experience; they fit them together and glue them on pre-cut mat board cards. If they participate in ongoing groups, they eventually end up with a deck of cards, which have deep personal meaning for them. They can take these cards to a friend's house, to sessions of individual therapy or support groups, or use them as decorations in their home.

The Course of Holotropic Sessions

The nature and course of holotropic sessions varies considerably from person to person, as well as from session to session. Some individuals remain entirely quiet and almost motionless. They may be having very profound experiences but give the impression that nothing is happening or that they are sleeping. Others are activated and show rich motor activity, to the point that they are agitated and frantic. They experience intense tremors and complex twisting movements, roll and flail around, assume fetal positions, behave like infants struggling in the birth canal, or look and act like newborns. Crawling, slithering, swimming, digging, or climbing movements are also quite common.

Occasionally, the movements and gestures can be extremely refined, complex, quite specific, and differentiated. They can take the form of strange animal movements, emulating snakes, birds, or feline predators, and be associated with corresponding sounds. Sometimes breathers spontaneously assume various yogic postures and ritual gestures *(asanas* and *mudras)* with which they are not intellectually familiar. In rare instances, the automatic movements and/or sounds resemble ritual or theatrical performances from different cultures—shamanic chanting, Javanese dances, Balinese monkey chants *(ketjak),* Japanese Kabuki, or talking in tongues, which is reminiscent of Pentecostal meetings.

The emotional qualities observed in holotropic sessions cover a very wide range. On one side of the spectrum, participants can encounter feelings of extraordinary well-being, profound peace, tranquility, serenity, bliss, cosmic unity, or ecstatic rapture. On the other side are episodes of indescribable terror, all-consuming guilt, murderous aggression, or eternal doom. The intensity of these emotions can transcend anything that can be experienced or even imagined in the everyday state of consciousness. These extreme emotional states are usually associated with experiences that are perinatal or transpersonal in nature.

In the middle of the experiential spectrum that is observed in Holotropic Breathwork sessions are less extreme emotional qualities that are closer to what we know from our daily existence: episodes of anger, anxiety, sadness, hopelessness, and feelings of failure, inferiority, shame, guilt or disgust. These are typically linked to biographical memories; their sources are traumatic experiences from infancy, childhood, and later periods of life. Their positive counterparts are feelings of happiness, emotional fulfillment, joy, sexual satisfaction, and a general increase in zest and vitality.

Sometimes faster breathing does not induce any physical tensions or difficult emotions, but leads directly to increasing relaxation, a sense of expansion and well-being, and visions of light. The breather can feel flooded with feelings of love and experiences of mystical connection to other people, nature, the entire cosmos, and God. These positive emotional states arise most often at the end of the holotropic sessions after the challenging and turbulent parts of the experience have been worked through. Occasionally, positive or even ecstatic feelings extend over the course of the entire session.

It is surprising how many people in our culture, because of either strong Protestant ethics or other reasons, have great difficulty accepting ecstatic experiences unless they follow suffering and hard work, if then. They often respond to them with a sense of guilt or with a feeling that they do not deserve them. It is also common, particularly in mental health professionals, to react to positive experiences with mistrust and suspicion that they are "reaction formations," which hide and mask some particularly painful, unpalatable, and unacceptable material. When that is the case, it is very important to assure the breathers that positive experiences are extremely healing and encourage them to accept them without reservation as unexpected grace.

Properly integrated Holotropic Breathwork sessions result in profound emotional release, physical relaxation, and a sense of well-being. Serial breathwork sessions present an extremely powerful and effective method of stress reduction and can bring remarkable emotional and psychosomatic healing. Another frequent result of this work is a connection with the numinous dimensions of one's own psyche and of existence in general. Some trained facilitators have used the deep relaxing effects of Holotropic Breathwork and offered it to various companies under the label of "stress reduction"; others have utilized the bonding effect of Holotropic Breathwork workshops and described it as a method for "team building."

The healing potential of breath is strongly emphasized in Kundalini yoga, in which episodes of faster breathing are used in the course of meditative practice *(bhastrika)* or occur spontaneously as part of the emotional and physical manifestations, known as kriyas. This is consistent with my own experience that similar spontaneous episodes of faster breathing occurring in psychiatric patients, which are diagnosed as the *hyperventilation syndrome,* are attempts at self-healing. They should be encouraged and supported rather than routinely suppressed, which is the common medical practice.

The duration of Holotropic Breathwork sessions vary from individual to individual and from session to session. It is essential, for the best possible integration of the experience, that the facilitators and sitters stay with the breather as long as he or she is in the process. In the terminal stage of the session, good bodywork can significantly facilitate emotional and physical resolution. Intimate contact with nature can also have a very calming and grounding effect and help the integration of the session. Particularly effective in this regard is exposure to water, such as soaking in a hot tub or swimming in a pool, a lake, or in the ocean.

Mandala Drawing and the Sharing Groups

When the session is completed and the breather returns to the ordinary state of consciousness, the sitter accompanies him or her to the mandala room. This room is equipped with a variety of art supplies such as pastels, magic markers, and watercolors, as well as large drawing pads. On the sheets of these pads are pencil drawings of circles about the size of dinner plates. The breathers are asked to sit down, meditate on their experience, and then find a way of expressing what happened during the session with the use of these tools.

There are no specific guidelines for the mandala drawing. Some people simply produce color combinations, others construct geometric mandalas or figurative drawings and paintings. The latter might represent a vision that occurred during the session or a pictorial travelogue with several distinct sequences. On occasion, the breather decides to document a single session with several mandalas reflecting different aspects or stages of the session. In rare instances, the breather has no idea what he or she is going to draw and produces an automatic drawing.

We have also seen instances when the mandala did not illustrate the immediately preceding session, but actually anticipated the session that followed. This is in congruence with C. G. Jung's idea that the products of the psyche cannot be fully explained from preceding historical events. In many instances, they have not just a retrospective, but also a prospective (teleological or finalistic) aspect. Some mandalas thus reflect a movement in the psyche that Jung called the individuation process and reveal its forthcoming stage. A possible alternative to mandala drawing is sculpting with clay. We introduced this method when we had blind participants in the group who could not draw a mandala. It was interesting to see that some of the other, sighted participants preferred to use this medium, when it was available, or opted for a combination of a mandala and a three-dimensional figure.

Later during the day, breathers bring their mandalas to a sharing session where they talk about their experiences. The strategy of the facilitators who lead the group is to encourage maximum openness and honesty in sharing the experience. The willingness of participants to reveal the content of their sessions, including various intimate details, is conducive to the bonding and development of trust in the group. It encourages others to share with equal honesty, which deepens, intensifies, and accelerates the therapeutic process.

In contrast to the practice of most psychotherapeutic schools, facilitators abstain from interpreting the experiences of the participants. The reason for this is the lack of agreement among the existing schools concerning the functioning of the psyche, its principal motivating forces, and the cause and meaning of the symptoms. Under these circumstances, any interpretations are questionable and arbitrary. Another reason for abstaining from interpretations is the fact that psychological contents are typically overdetermined and can be meaningfully related to several levels of the psyche (Grof 2010, Grof 1975). Giving a supposedly definitive explanation or interpretation also carries the danger of freezing the process and interfering with the therapeutic progress.

A more productive alternative is to ask questions that help to elicit additional information from the perspective of the client who, being the experiencer, is the ultimate expert as far as his or her experience is concerned. When we are patient and resist the temptation to share our own impressions, participants very often find their own explanations that best fit their experiences. On occasion, it can be very helpful to share our observations from the past concerning similar experiences or point out connections with experiences of other members of the group. When the experiences contain archetypal material, it can be helpful to use C. G. Jung's method of *amplification*—pointing out parallels between a particular experience and similar mythological motifs from various cultures—or to consult a good dictionary of symbols.

Follow-Up and Use of Complementary Techniques

On the days following intense sessions that involved a major emotional breakthrough or opening, a wide variety of complementary approaches can facilitate good integration. Among these are discussions about the session with an experienced facilitator, writing down the content of the experience, drawing additional mandalas, meditation, and movement meditation, such as Hatha yoga, tai-chi, or qi-gong. Good bodywork with a practitioner who allows emotional expression, jogging, swimming, and other forms of physical exercise, or expressive dancing can be very useful if the holotropic experience freed access to large amounts of previously pent-up physical energy.

A session of Dora Kalff's Jungian sandplay (Kalff and Kalff 2004), Fritz Perls' Gestalt therapy (Perls 1976), Jacob Moreno's psychodrama (Moreno 1948), or Francine Shapiro's eye movement desensitization and reprocessing (EMDR) (Shapiro 2001) can be of great help in refining insights into the holotropic experience and understanding its content. Many Holotropic Breathwork facilitators have found it interesting and useful to include Bert Hellinger's family constellation work in their workshops, which is his adaptation of a process that he learned in Africa when he served as Catholic priest and missionary with the Zulu people (Hellinger 2003).

Therapeutic Potential of Holotropic Breathwork

Christina and I developed and practiced Holotropic Breathwork outside of a clinical setting in our month-long seminars and shorter workshops at the Esalen Institute in Big Sur, California, in various breathwork workshops in many other parts of the world, and in our training program for facilitators. I have not had the opportunity to test the therapeutic efficacy of this method in the same rigorous way I was able to when I conducted psychedelic therapy. The psychedelic research at the Maryland Psychiatric

Research Center (MPRC) involved controlled clinical studies with psychological testing and a systematic, professionally conducted follow-up.

However, the therapeutic results of Holotropic Breathwork have often been so dramatic and meaningfully connected with specific experiences in the sessions that I have no doubt Holotropic Breathwork is a viable form of therapy and self-exploration. We have seen numerous instances over the years when participants in the workshops and the training were able to break out of depression that had lasted several years, overcome various phobias, free themselves from consuming irrational feelings, and radically improve their self-confidence and self-esteem. We have also witnessed the disappearance of severe psychosomatic pains on many occasions, including migraine headaches, and radical and lasting improvements for, or even complete clearing of, psychogenic asthma.

On many occasions, participants in the training or workshops favorably compared their progress in several holotropic sessions to years of verbal therapy. When we talk about evaluating the efficacy of powerful forms of experiential psychotherapy, such as work with psychedelics or Holotropic Breathwork, it is important to emphasize certain fundamental differences between these approaches and verbal forms of therapy. Verbal psychotherapy often extends over a period of years and major exciting breakthroughs are rare exceptions, rather than commonplace events.

When changes of symptoms occur in verbal psychotherapy, it happens on a broad time scale and it is difficult to prove their causal connection with specific events in therapy or the therapeutic process in general. By comparison, in a psychedelic or Holotropic Breathwork session, powerful changes can occur in the course of a few hours and they can be convincingly linked to specific experiences. The changes observed in Holotropic Breathwork are not limited to conditions traditionally considered emotional or psychosomatic. In many cases, breathwork sessions led to the dramatic improvement of physical conditions that in medical handbooks are described as organic diseases.

Some of the dramatic improvements included the clearing of chronic infections (sinusitis, pharyngitis, bronchitis, and cystitis) after bioenergetic unblocking opened blood circulation in the corresponding areas. Another example is a woman with osteoporosis, who found that her bones solidified during the course of holotropic training, which has remained unexplained to this day. We have also seen the restitution of full peripheral circulation in fifteen people suffering from Raynaud's disease, a disorder that involves coldness of hands and feet, accompanied by dystrophic changes of the skin.

In several instances, Holotropic Breathwork led to a striking improvement of arthritis. In all these cases, the critical factor conducive to healing seemed to be the release of excessive bioenergetic blockage in the afflicted parts of the body, followed by vasodilation. The most astonishing observation in this category was a dramatic remission of advanced symptoms of *Takayasu arteritis,* a disease of unknown etiology, which is characterized by the progressive occlusion of arteries in the upper part of the body. It is a condition that is usually considered progressive, incurable, and potentially lethal.

In many cases, the therapeutic potential of Holotropic Breathwork was confirmed in clinical studies, conducted by practitioners who we had trained, and who independently use this method in their work. A significant number of clinical studies was also conducted by psychiatrists and psychologists in Russia, who have not participated in our training for facilitators. A list of studies involving or related to Holotropic Breathwork is included in a special section of the bibliography in our book on Holotropic Breathwork (Grof and Grof 2010).

On many occasions, we have also had the opportunity to receive informal feedback from people years after their emotional, psychosomatic, and physical symptoms had improved or disappeared, following holotropic sessions in our training or in our workshops. This has shown us that the improvements achieved in holotropic sessions are often lasting. I hope that the efficacy of this interesting and promising method of self-exploration and therapy will be confirmed in the future by well-designed extensive clinical research.

Biological Mechanisms Involved in Holotropic Breathwork

In view of the powerful effect Holotropic Breathwork has on consciousness, it is interesting to consider the physiological and biochemical mechanisms that might be involved. Many people believe that when we breathe faster, we simply bring more oxygen into the body and the brain. But the situation is actually much more complicated. It is true that faster breathing brings more air and thus oxygen into the lungs, but it also eliminates carbon dioxide (CO_2) and causes vasoconstriction in certain parts of the body. Since CO_2 is acidic, reducing its content in the blood increases the alkalinity of the blood (pH) and in an alkaline setting, relatively less oxygen is being transferred to the tissues. This in turn triggers a homeostatic mechanism that works in the opposite direction: the kidneys excrete urine that is more alkaline to compensate for this change.

The brain is also one of the areas in the body that can respond to faster breathing by vasoconstriction, which reduces the amount of oxygen coming in. In addition, the degree of gas exchange does not depend only on the rate of breathing, but also on its depth, which determines the volume of the "dead space" in which the exchange between CO_2 and oxygen does not occur. The situation is therefore quite complex and it is not easy to assess the overall situation in an individual case without a battery of specific laboratory examinations.

However, if we take into consideration all the above physiological mechanisms, the situation during Holotropic Breathwork very likely resembles that of being high in the mountains, where there is less oxygen and the CO_2 level is decreased by compensatory faster breathing. The cerebral neocortex, being the youngest part of the brain from an evolutionary point of view, is generally more sensitive to a variety of influences (such as alcohol and anoxia) than the older parts of the brain. This situation would thus cause inhibition of the cortical functions and intensified activity in the archaic parts of the brain, making the unconscious processes more available.

It is interesting that many individuals, as well as entire cultures that lived in extreme altitudes, were known for their advanced spirituality. We can think in this context of the yogis in the Himalayas, the Tibetan Buddhists in the Qingzang high plateau, and the ancient Incas and Q'eros in the Peruvian Andes. It is tempting to attribute it to the fact that, in an atmosphere with a lower content of oxygen, they had easy access to transpersonal experiences. However, an extended stay in high elevations leads to physiological adaptations, including compensatory hyperproduction of red blood cells in the spleen. The acute situation during Holotropic Breathwork might, therefore, not be directly comparable to an extended stay in high mountains.

In any case, there is a long way from the description of the physiological changes in the brain to the extremely rich array of phenomena induced by Holotropic Breathwork, such as authentic experiential identification with animals, archetypal visions, or past life memories. This situation is similar to the problem of the psychological effects of LSD. This is a substance with a known chemical structure that we can administer in exact dosages. However, this knowledge does not provide any clues for understanding the experiences that it triggers. The fact that both of these methods can induce transpersonal experiences, in which there is access to accurate new information about the universe through extrasensory channels, makes it difficult to accept that such experiences are stored in the brain.

Aldous Huxley, after having had sessions with mescaline and LSD, came to the conclusion that our brain cannot possibly be the source of the rich and fantastic array of phenomena that he had experienced. He suggested that the brain more likely functions like a reducing valve that shields us from an infinitely larger cosmic input. Concepts such as "memory without a material substrate" (Foerster 1965), Sheldrake's "morphogenetic fields" (Sheldrake 1981), and Laszlo's "psi field" or "Akashic holofield" (Laszlo 2004) bring important support for Huxley's idea and make it increasingly plausible.

In conclusion, I would like to compare psychotherapy using holotropic states of consciousness, in general, and Holotropic Breathwork, in particular, with talking therapies. Verbal methods of psychotherapy attempt to get to the roots of emotional and psychosomatic problems indirectly by helping the clients to remember relevant forgotten and repressed events from their life or reconstruct them indirectly through the analysis of dreams, neurotic symptoms, or distortions of the therapeutic relationship (transference).

Most verbal psychotherapies use a model of the psyche which is limited to postnatal biography and to the Freudian individual unconscious. They also employ techniques that cannot reach the perinatal and transpersonal domains of the psyche and thus the deeper roots of the disorders they are trying to heal. The limitations of verbal therapies are particularly obvious in relation to memories of traumatic events that have a strong physical component, such as difficult birth, episodes of near-drowning, choking caused by the inhalation of foreign objects, injuries, or diseases. Traumas of this kind cannot be worked through and resolved by talking about them; they have to be relived and the emotions and blocked physical energies attached to them fully expressed.

Other advantages of Holotropic Breathwork are of an economic nature; they are related to the ratio between the number of participants in breathwork groups and the number of trained facilitators needed. In the 1960s, when I was in training analysis, it was estimated that a classical psychoanalyst was able to treat about eighty patients in his or her entire lifetime. In spite of all the changes psychotherapy has undergone since Freud's times, the ratio between the number of clients needing treatment and the number of professional therapists available for this task continues to be very unfavorable.

A typical Holotropic Breathwork group requires one trained facilitator per eight to ten group participants. Although it might be objected that traditional group psychotherapy has a similar or even better therapist/client ratio, it is important to take into consideration that in breathwork groups, each participant has a personal experience focused specifically on his or her problems. Holotropic Breathwork offers much more powerful therapeutic mechanisms and it utilizes the healing potential of the other group members, who do not need to have special training to be good sitters.

Sitters also repeatedly report what a profound experience it was for them to assist others, what a privilege it was to witness such a personal and intimate process of another human being, and how much they learned from it. A significant number of people who have attended Holotropic Breathwork workshops became very interested in the process and decided to enroll in the training for facilitators. The number of people from different countries who have completed our training and have become certified as facilitators has recently exceeded 2,000. Although not all of them actually offer workshops, this "chain reaction" effect of Holotropic Breathwork is a very hopeful sign for future controlled clinical studies.

I would also like to mention an exciting trend: the theoretical knowledge and practical skills that participants acquire in Holotropic Breathwork training are useful for and applicable to the entire spectrum of holotropic states of consciousness. This includes those induced by psychedelic substances and various non-drug means, such as spiritual practices and shamanic methods, or occurring spontaneously ("spiritual emergencies").

In view of the current worldwide renaissance of interest in psychedelic research and, particularly, the success of MDMA therapy with PTSD patients and of psilocybin- and LSD-assisted psychotherapy in the treatment of patients with life-threatening illnesses who suffer from deep anxiety, it is conceivable that in the near future, a significant number of sitters might be needed if some of these treatments go mainstream. The California Institute of Integral Studies (CIIS), anticipating this possibility, recently launched an accredited course for sitters in psychedelic sessions and has decided to use Holotropic Breathwork for training the candidates in this program until it becomes possible to legally offer them psychedelic training sessions.

Literature

Browne, I. 1990. "Psychological Trauma, or Unexperienced Experience." *Re-Vision Journal* 12(4):21-34.

Foerster, H. von. 1965. *Memory without a Record. In: The Anatomy of Memory* (D. P. Kimble, ed.). Palo Alto: Science and Behavior Books.

Freud, S. and Breuer, J. 1936. *Studies in Hysteria.* New York, NY: Penguin Books.

Freud, S, 2010. *The Interpretation of Dreams.* Strachey, James. New York: Basic Books A Member of the Perseus Books Group.

Frost, S. B. 2001. *SoulCollage.* Santa Cruz, CA: Hanford Mead Publications.

Goldman, D. 1952. "The Effect of Rhythmic Auditory Stimulation on the Human Electroencephalogram." *EEG and Clinical Neurophysiology* 4: 370.

Grof, S. 1975. *Realms of the Human Unconscious: Observations from LSD Research.* New York. Viking Press. Republished as *LSD: Gateway to the Numinous.* Rochester, VT: Inner Traditions.

Grof, S. 2000. *Psychology of the Future: Lessons from Modern Consciousness Research.* Albany, NY: State University of New York (SUNY) Press.

Grof, S. 2006. *The Ultimate Journey: Consciousness and the Mystery of Death.*

Santa Cruz, CA: MAPS Publications.

Grof, S. and Grof, C. 2010. *Holotropic Breathwork: A New Approach to Self-Exploration and Therapy.* Albany, NY: State University of New York (SUNY) Press.

Hellinger, B. 2003. *Farewell Family Constellations with Descendants of Victims and Perpetrators* (C. Beaumont, translator). Heidelberg, Germany: Carl-Auer-Systeme Verlag.

Jilek, W. J. 1974. *Salish Indian Mental Health and Culture Change: Psychohygienic and Therapeutic Aspects of the Guardian Spirit Ceremonial.* Toronto and Montreal: Holt, Rinehart, and Winston of Canada.

Jilek, W. 1982. "Altered States of Consciousness in North American Indian Ceremonials." *Ethos* 10:326-343.

Jung, C. G. 1959. *Mandala Symbolism.* Translated by R. F. C. Hull. Bollingen Series. Princeton, NJ: Princeton University Press.

Kalff, D. and Kalff, M. 2004. *Sandplay: A Psychotherapeutic Approach to the Psyche.* Cloverdale, CA: Temenos Press.

Katz, R. 1976. The Painful Ecstasy of Healing. *Psychology Today,* December.

Kellogg, J. 1977. The Use of the Mandala in Psychological Evaluation and Treatment. *Amer. Journal of Art Therapy* 16:123.

Kellogg, J. 1978. *Mandala: The Path of Beauty.* Baltimore, MD: Mandala Assessment and Research Institute.

Laszlo, E. 2004. *Science and the Akashic Field: An Integral Theory of Everything.* Rochester, VT: Inner Traditions.

Lee, R. B. and DeVore, I. (eds.) 1976. *Kalahari Hunter-Gatherers: Studies of the !Kung San and Their Neighbors.* Cambridge, MA: Harvard University Press.

Martin, J. 1965. LSD Analysis. Lecture and film presented at the Second International Conference on the Use of LSD in Psychotherapy held at South Oaks Hospital, May 8-12, Amityville, NY. Paper published in: H. A. Abramson (ed.) *The Use of LSD in Psychotherapy and Alcoholism.* Indianapolis, IN: Bobbs-Merrill. Pp. 223-238.

Moreno, J. L. 1948. "Psychodrama and Group Psychotherapy." *Annals of the New York Academy of Sciences* 49 (6):902-903.

Neher, A, 1961. "Auditory Driving Observed with Scalp Electrodes in

Normal Subjects." *Electroencephalography and Clinical Neurophysiology* 13:449-451.

Neher, A. 1962. "A Physiological Explanation of Unusual Behavior Involving Drums." *Human Biology* 14:151-160

Perls, F. 1976. *The Gestalt Approach and Eye-Witness to Therapy.* New York, NY: Bantam Books.

Ramacharaka (William Walker Atkinson). 1903. *The Science of Breath.* London: Fowler and Company, Ltd.

Reich, W. 1949. *Character Analysis.* New York, NY: Noonday Press.

Reich, W. 1961. *The Function of the Orgasm: Sex-Economic Problems of Biological Energy.* New York, NY: Farrar, Strauss, and Giroux.

Shapiro, F. 2001. *Eye Movement Desensitization and Reprocessing: Basic Principles, Protocols, and Procedures.* New York, NY: Guilford Press.

Sheldrake, R. 1981. *A New Science of Life: The Hypothesis of Formative Causation.* Los Angeles, CA: J.P. Tarcher.

Index

C

F

T

About the Publisher

Founded in 1986, the Multidisciplinary Association for Psychedelic Studies (MAPS) is a 501(c)(3) non-profit research and educational organization that develops medical, legal, and cultural contexts for people to benefit from the careful uses of psychedelics and marijuana. **Learn more about our work at maps.org.**

MAPS furthers its mission by:

- Developing psychedelics and marijuana into prescription medicines
- Training therapists and establishing a network of treatment centers
- Supporting scientific research into spirituality, creativity, and neuroscience
- Educating the public honestly about the risks and benefits of psychedelics and marijuana.

Why Give?
maps.org/donate

Your donation will help create a world where psychedelics and marijuana are available by prescription for medical uses, and where they can safely and legally be used for personal growth, creativity, and spirituality. Donations are tax-deductible as allowed by law, and may be made by credit card, or by personal check made out to MAPS. Gifts of stock are also welcome, and we encourage supporters to include MAPS in their will or estate plans (**maps.org/bequests**).

MAPS takes your privacy seriously. The MAPS email list is strictly confidential and will not be shared with other organizations. The *MAPS Bulletin* is mailed in a plain white envelope.

Sign up for our monthly email newsletter at **maps.org**.

MAPS
PO Box 8423, Santa Cruz CA 95061 USA
Phone: 831-429-MDMA (6362) • Fax: 831-429-6370
E-mail: **askmaps@maps.org**
Web: **maps.org** | **psychedelicscience.org**

MAPS-Published Books
maps.org/store

Ayahuasca Religions: A Comprehensive Bibliography & Critical Essays by Beatriz Caiuby Labate, Isabel Santana de Rose, and Rafael Guimarães dos Santos, translated by Matthew Meyer
ISBN: 978-0-9798622-1-2 $11.95

Drawing it Out by Sherana Harriet Francis
ISBN: 0-9669919-5-8 $19.95

Healing with Entactogens: Therapist and Patient Perspectives on MDMA-Assisted Group Psychotherapy by Torsten Passie, M.D.; foreword by Ralph Metzner, Ph.D.
ISBN: 0-9798622-7-2 $12.95

Honor Thy Daughter by Marilyn Howell, Ed.D.
ISBN: 0-9798622-6-4 $16.95

LSD: My Problem Child by Albert Hofmann, Ph.D. (4th English edition, paperback)
ISBN: 978-0-9798622-2-9 $15.95

LSD Psychotherapy by Stanislav Grof, M.D. (4th Edition, Paperback)
ISBN: 0-9798622-0-5 $19.95

Modern Consciousness Research and the Understanding of Art; including the Visionary World of H.R. Giger by Stanislav Grof, M.D.
ISBN: 0-9798622-9-9 $29.95

The Ketamine Papers: Science, Therapy, and Transformation edited by Phil Wolfson, M.D., and Glenn Hartelius, Ph.D.
ISBN: 0-9982765-0-2 $24.95

The Manual of Psychedelic Support: A Practical Guide to Establishing and Facilitating Care Services at Music Festivals and Other Events edited by Annie Oak, Jon Hanna, Kaya, Svea Nielsen, Twilight, and Zevic Mishor, Ph.D.
ISBN: 978-0998276519 $19.95

The Secret Chief Revealed by Myron Stolaroff
ISBN: 0-9660019-6-6 $12.95

The Ultimate Journey: Consciousness and the Mystery of Death by Stanislav Grof, M.D., Ph.D. (2nd edition)
ISBN: 0-9660019-9-0 $19.95

Shipping and Handling

Shipping varies by weight of books.
Bulk orders are welcome. Please contact MAPS for details.
Books can be purchased online by visiting **maps.org** (credit card or Paypal), over the phone by calling +1 831-429-MDMA (6362), or through your favorite local bookstore.

You may also send orders by mail to:
MAPS
P.O. Box 8423
Santa Cruz, CA, 95061
Phone: +1 831-429-MDMA (6362)
Fax: +1 831-429-6370
E-mail: **orders@maps.org**
Web: **maps.org**

About the Author

Stanislav Grof, M.D., Ph.D., is a psychiatrist with over sixty years of experience researching non-ordinary states of consciousness, and one of the founders and chief theoreticians of transpersonal psychology. He was born in Prague, Czechoslovakia, where he also received his scientific training, including his M.D. from the Charles University School of Medicine and his Ph.D. (Doctor of Philosophy in Medicine) from the Czechoslovakian Academy of Sciences. He was also granted honorary doctoral degrees from the University of Vermont in Burlington, Vermont, the Institute of Transpersonal Psychology in Palo Alto, California, the California Institute of Integral Studies (CIIS) in San Francisco, and the World Buddhist University in Bangkok, Thailand.

He conducted his early research at the Psychiatric Research Institute in Prague, where he was principal investigator of a program exploring the heuristic and therapeutic potential of LSD and other psychedelic substances. In 1967, he received a scholarship from the Foundations Fund for Research in Psychiatry in New Haven, Connecticut, and was invited to serve as Clinical and Research Fellow at Johns Hopkins University and the research unit of Spring Grove Hospital in Baltimore, Maryland.

In 1969, he became Assistant Professor of Psychiatry at Johns Hopkins University, and continued his research as Chief of Psychiatric Research at the Maryland Psychiatric Research Center in Catonsville, Maryland. In 1973, he was invited as Scholar-in-Residence to the Esalen Institute in Big Sur, California, where he developed, with his late wife Christina, Holotropic Breathwork, an innovative form of experiential psychotherapy that is now being used worldwide.

Dr. Grof was the founder of the International Transpersonal Association (ITA) and for several decades served as its president. In 1993, he received an Honorary Award from the Association for Transpersonal Psychology (ATP) for major contributions to and development of the field of transpersonal psychology, given at the occasion of the 25th Anniversary Convocation held in Asilomar, California. In 2007, he received the prestigious Vison 97 lifetime achievement award from the Foundation of Dagmar and Václav Havel in Prague, Czechoslovakia. In 2010, he received the Thomas R. Verny Award from the Association for Pre- and Perinatal Psychology and Health (APPPAH) for his pivotal contributions to the field. He was also invited as consultant for special effects in the science fiction films *Brainstorm* (MGM) and *Millenium* (20th Century Fox).

Among Dr. Grof's publications are over 160 articles in professional journals and many books, including *Realms of the Human Unconscious,* republished as *LSD: Gateway to the Numinous* (2009); *Beyond the Brain* (1985); *LSD Psychotherapy* (1978); *The Cosmic Game* (1990); *Psychology of the Future* (2000); *The Ultimate Journey* (2006); *When the Impossible Happens* (2006); *Books of the Dead* (1994); *Healing Our Deepest Wounds* (2012); *Modern Consciousness Research and the Understanding of Art* (2015); *The Call of the Jaguar* (2002); *Beyond Death* (1980); *The Stormy Search for the Self* (1990); *Spiritual Emergency* (1989); and *Holotropic Breathwork* (2010) (the last four with Christina Grof).

These books have been translated into twenty-two languages, including German, French, Italian, Spanish, Portuguese, Dutch, Swedish, Danish, Russian, Ukrainian, Slovenian, Romanian, Czech, Polish, Bulgarian, Hungarian, Latvian, Greek, Turkish, Korean, Japanese, and Chinese.

Since April 2016, he has been happily married to Brigitte Grof. They live together in Germany and California and travel the inner and outer worlds in tandem, conducting seminars and Holotropic Breathwork workshops worldwide.

His website is **stanislavgrof.com**.

Stanislav Grof, M.D., Ph.D.

Stanislav Grof's research on psychedelic therapies, Holotropic Breathwork, and transpersonal states of consciousness is unparalleled in psychology and psychiatry. This two-volume work is a unique encyclopedic summary of six decades of extraordinary explorations; essential reading for anyone interested in an integrative approach to the many-leveled realms of the human unconscious.

—**Fritjof Capra,** author of *The Tao of Physics* and *The Web of Life,* coauthor of *The Systems View of Life*

Stanislav Grof's decades of ground-breaking exploration of consciousness and the healing potential of non-ordinary states has touched thousands of lives and inspired healing practitioners around the world. The growing acceptance of psychedelic research and treatment in mainstream medicine stems in large part from Stan's work, and the treatment methods used in modern clinical trials draw directly from what he has learned about the wise and skillful use of psychedelics. *The Way of the Psychonaut* is a valuable resource that will continue to teach and inspire psychedelic therapists into the future.

—**Michael Mithoefer, M.D.,** and **Annie Mithoefer, B.S.N.,** MDMA-assisted psychotherapy researchers

The Way of the Psychonaut is an overview of the human journey inward by someone who has led the way and discovered a new path or two. Stanislav Grof has spent his life exploring consciousness, especially non-ordinary states, and in this book he shares his maps and revolutionary findings. This book is a perfect dose of wisdom, opening us all to the nature of mind.

—**Wes Nisker,** meditation teacher, author of *Essential Crazy Wisdom*

If you have ever wondered what it would have been like to sit down and talk with Freud, Jung, or William James, you now have the opportunity to read the current, living works of one of the leading psychological theorists in modern history. Stanislav Grof serves as our guide through the territory of our own consciousness—from our core essence to the furthest, most extraordinary frontiers. Scholarly, radical, historic, and original, this book is written in a completely accessible way—each page holds the potential to stretch your mind just that little bit more.

—**Cassandra Vieten, Ph.D.,** President, Institute of Noetic Sciences, author of *Living Deeply: The Art and Science of Transformation in Everyday Life* and *Spiritual and Religious Competencies in Clinical Practice: Guidelines for Mental Health Professionals.*